Personal Adjustment

AN APPROACH
THROUGH THE STUDY OF
HEALTHY PERSONALITY

THE MACMILLAN COMPANY
NEW YORK · CHICAGO
DALLAS · ATLANTA · SAN FRANCISCO
LONDON · MANILA
BRETT-MACMILLAN LTD.
TORONTO

SIDNEY M. JOURARD, Ph.D.
UNIVERSITY OF FLORIDA

Personal Adjustment

AN APPROACH

THROUGH THE STUDY OF

HEALTHY PERSONALITY

THE MACMILLAN COMPANY • **NEW YORK**

TO MY MOTHER, ANNA JOURARD, AND
MY LATE FATHER, ALBERT LOUIS JOURARD,
IN ACKNOWLEDGMENT . . .

Preface

The present work is an attempt to provide the reader with an explicit concept of healthy personality. Professional students of personality have succeeded in describing the diverse forms of unhealthy personality, but they have barely touched upon the problem of describing health. In most works which deal with abnormal psychology, psychiatry, or mental health, a person is adjudged healthy, or "normal," if he has no clinical symptoms of pathology. Yet we know now that personality health is more than mere freedom from symptoms. Just as there is a difference in medicine between freedom from medical symptoms of disease and optimum physical health, so is there a difference between a personality which is "not sick" and one which is healthy.

This book is an outgrowth of a course in Mental Hygiene which the author taught at Emory University during his tenure there, from 1951 to 1956. The course was presented in various ways during this time, ranging from extended discussion of defense mechanisms, to a "diluted" survey of abnormal behavior. Many times, the students asked the instructor the very specific questions: "We are getting a good idea of what maladjustment looks like, but what does good adjustment look like? What is mental health? What is healthy personality?" These were embarrassing questions, and they were answered evasively: "We can't really answer; people differ very much from each other; what is good adjustment for one person may be bad adjustment for another."

But then an idea became implanted in the author's mind. Perhaps one could regard healthy personality as an expression of *values*. Unhealthy personality—mental illness—refers to behavior which is negatively valued by society, and usually by the patient. If this were so, then the obverse should also be true: healthy personality should reflect the best values for man which prevail in society. When the problem was stated in this fashion, it became possible to survey relevant literature in which students of personality attempted to spell out their concepts of man's potential for growth. The writings of Freud, Fromm, Horney, Maslow, Riesman, Rank, Mowrer—to name but a few—provided a virtually untapped mine for this purpose.

The author's course then went through drastic revisions from quarter to quarter, until finally a sequence of topics was selected for discussion and study with this orientation: "What is the range within which this aspect of personality varies? What versions of this trait are regarded as unhealthy? What versions are common, or 'normal'? What versions are held to be healthy?"

Although the concept of healthy personality was formulated as an organizing principle for a college course, it soon became apparent that many other functions could be served by such a concept. It is a commonplace that psychiatrists have not devoted much attention to the problem of measuring "clinical improvement." A concept of healthy personality might serve as the basis for devising measuring tools which could be employed to assess the effects of therapy.

It was discovered that in many introductory psychiatry courses in medical schools, little attention was paid to the definition of personality health. Instead, students were introduced to psychopathology and told that the decision as to what is healthy or normal is best left to their judgment. A book which attempts an explicit definition of health can help lay down a frame of reference for the medical specialty of psychiatry.

The lay reader is often puzzled by his readings of popular psychology and psychiatry, for in these sources the sick and the pathological are lovingly expounded, in meticulous detail. Health is either bypassed or presented in vague terms, much after the fashion of an inspirational sermon. A detailed exposition of personality health could serve as a basis for making intelligent comparisons between what is observed in the self and other people, and what students of personality are discovering to be man's potential for growth and happiness.

The research scientist who studies mental health has long been handicapped in his work by the lack of a criterion. The present book will not solve this problem, but it may serve as a first step toward developing a variety of criteria for assessing present mental health and for measuring improvement following some mental-health program.

This book, then, is an attempt to describe the "symptoms" of healthy personality. In addition to description, an attempt is made wherever possible to explain how personality health is achieved, by pointing out the independent variables of which it is a function.

The professional reader may observe that certain traditional concepts have been redefined at various places throughout the text, and certain new concepts have been introduced. The principle which guided both the redefinition of old terms and the introduction of new ones may be stated as follows: "Is the concept so defined that it permits observation, measurement, and evaluation of behavior and experience?" It is hoped that such changes in terminology as have been introduced will serve these purposes. Most technical terms that are employed are defined when introduced. The book will have failed in one of its aims if research and measurement have not been stimulated by at least some of the themes expounded.

As noted above, the book was written primarily for use in college courses entitled "Mental Hygiene," "Psychology of Adjustment," etc. However, it may possibly find good use as a text for introductory courses in psychiatry at medical colleges. It is further hoped that advanced students of personality and of clinical psychology will read the volume, if for no reason other than the stimulation they may find to further research into the problem of mental health. Finally, it is hoped professional psychotherapists—psychiatrists, psychologists, and social workers—will examine the book to challenge themselves to work through the problem of explicit criteria for the effectiveness of their therapeutic work.

It seems a certainty to the author that one day personality hygiene will become a full-fledged, positive applied science, with laws of its own. This means we shall be able to state with confidence that certain variables or conditions are *known* (from research) to promote the development of healthy personality. But this laudable goal can never be achieved unless we first have a concept in mind of what healthy personality looks like. Every applied science must have a valued goal set up in explicit terms before research can be undertaken to select the best means of achieving this goal. Healthy personality is such a valued goal. Personality-research scientists will be able to find the ways of reaching this goal after a positive and explicit concept of health has been arrived at. It is hoped this volume may serve as a first step in the direction of defining health for applied-research purposes.

A few comments about the organization of the book may help orient the reader in advance of his study of the text. The first chapter introduces the problem of making health-evaluations about personality and describes some of the attempts which have already been made to provide health-criteria. The second chapter may be viewed as a partial theory of motivation (need-theory), and some criteria are introduced for making judgments about the "health" of a person's needs and motives.

The third chapter seeks to specify what healthy cognition is, in contrast with normal and unhealthy cognition, and attempts to indicate the conditions under which reality-contact is achieved and maintained.

The fourth chapter is concerned with emotions; healthy patterns of emotional behavior and responsiveness are described in contrast with normal and unhealthy emotionality.

The problem of sexuality is raised in the next chapter, and criteria are provided for the specification of healthy sexuality.

In succession, interpersonal behavior, interpersonal relationships, and love are all discussed around a similar framework of definitions, descriptions of healthy, normal, and unhealthy patterns, and specifications of the conditions which promote the healthy pattern.

Next, the "structure" of personality is given consideration. First, a partly revised formulation of the theory of the self-structure is introduced, along with criteria for judging the health of a given self-structure. The problem of growth versus defense of the self-structure is next analyzed, and detailed consideration is given to the various growth-evasion tactics (defense mechanisms). In the following chapters, the body-image, and the conscience are examined from the standpoint of health-criteria.

The last chapter introduces the problem of personality therapy. Personality therapy is there regarded as one means by which knowledge of the conditions of personality health can lead to control of those conditions.

A section at the end of each chapter combines notes and references. The student is encouraged to read those references which are marked with an asterisk (*), in order to broaden his perspective on the topics with which they are concerned.

To publicly acknowledge the assistance and encouragement of certain persons in the preparation of this book is a special privilege for the author. Dr. Paul Secord provided much helpful criticism and encouragement when the book was little more than a conversation piece at coffee sessions. Dr. A. H. Maslow gave a highly detailed critique of the first-draft manuscript which proved invaluable to the author as a guide for revising and polishing all sections. The author's students in Psychology 205 (Mental Hygiene) at Emory University, between 1951 and 1956 were more helpful than they perhaps realize, for their questions and interested participation in class got the book started. The psychology department at Emory University, under Dr. M. C. Langhorne's chairmanship, afforded a stimulating milieu for research and writing. Miss Elizabeth Rivers merits much thanks for her tireless work in typing the finished manuscript. To all these persons the author is grateful. Special thanks are due the people (who must be nameless) who undertook personality therapy with the author. In striving to help them grow, he hopes that he grew with them; certainly he learned much from them. Finally, Toni Jourard and the children—Jeff, Marty, and Leonard—are thanked for the gift of time to write much of this book during family hours.

SIDNEY M. JOURARD

Contents

Personal Adjustment

AN APPROACH
THROUGH THE STUDY OF
HEALTHY PERSONALITY

CHAPTER 1

The Definition of Healthy Personality

WHAT IS HEALTH?

Most of us think we know what we mean when we speak of health. Yet a little critical thinking will reveal that the meaning of the term is very elusive. We assume we are healthy when we are not sick. Everyone knows what it means to be sick. It means that our body hurts; we have a fever, we lack energy, and we lose interest in everything except getting well. But what is this condition of health that we lose when we become sick? Doctors describe the state of health in terms of physiological indices of one kind or another, "normal" body temperature, "normal" white-cell count, "normal" heart-rate and blood pressure, etc. These are all signs that our body is functioning "well." [1]

It becomes apparent that health refers to a mode of bodily functioning which is *valued*. [2] Everybody *wants* to be healthy, to have a body which is free from pain, has lots of energy, and which will last a long time. Perhaps here we have a very general definition of health: that mode of organ-functioning which insures that the body will be pain-free, energetic, and long-lived.

But to-day, when we speak of health, we draw a distinction between physical health and mental health. What is referred to by the term mental health? Does it mean the same thing as physical health? Can we say that a healthy mind is one which is free of pain, has lots of energy, and lives a long time? Not likely, for we cannot find the mind anywhere. The body can be seen, dissected, felt, weighed, and measured. The mind cannot be dealt with in this fashion. Since this is the case, how can we speak of mental health, or of a healthy mind? [3]

As an alternative to the term mental health, we shall speak of *healthy personality*. But personality is not an object or thing which can be studied like the body. Personality is an abstract term which refers to the stable and characteristic ways in which a person reacts to life situations. The observer can see how a person behaves in a given situation. On the basis of prolonged observation, he can note consistencies in the ways in which an individual reacts. These consistencies in reaction patterns are called *traits*.[4] The student is doubtless familiar with the traits of his mother, father, roommate, or friends. He has observed the way these people behave in a variety of situations, and he can probably predict with some accuracy how they will react to some future situations. When we say that he knows the personality of his father, we mean he knows how his father is most likely to respond to typical life situations, for example, a request for the loan of the family car, or an invitation to play golf.

But if personality refers to the more or less stable reaction patterns of an individual, what is healthy personality? Obviously, it refers to a way of behaving that is valued. By whom is it valued? In a very strict sense we might say healthy personality refers to ways of behaving that are valued by the "mental hygienist," or personality hygienist, as he will be called in this book. It is also possible that these ways of behaving are valued by the person himself, and by society as a whole.

We may well ask at this point, "Why should the personality hygienist be specially qualified to pass judgment on how people ought to behave in order to become happy and healthy?" The reason is to be found in the fact that personality hygienists, especially the practising therapists of personality, have studied man more minutely than he has ever been studied throughout history. On the basis of their intimate knowledge of the subjective side of man, they have gradually evolved a conception of man's potentials for growth and happiness as well as for misery and regression. Further, they have begun to crystallize knowledge as to the conditions which will help man attain happiness and growth, and to fill in the outlines of a rough picture of what healthy personality and healthy behavior look like.

Since healthy personality refers to valued ways of behaving in life situations, let us examine the problem of the evaluation of behavior in more detail.

THE EVALUATION OF BEHAVIOR

The task of describing and explaining behavior belongs to the research psychologist; he is concerned with observing, experimenting, and manipulating behavior in order to determine its "laws." The evaluation of behavior is another problem. It involves comparing the behavior which is observed with some standard, value, or ideal. An illustration will clarify the distinction between explaining behavior, and evaluating it. But it should be emphasized first, that explanation and evaluation both are dependent upon accurate observation and recording of the behavior in question. Before the scientist can undertake his investigation of the conditions that have been responsible for the behavior in which he is interested, he must first have secured an accurate set of observations of this behavior. The evaluator requires not only an accurate description of the behavior at hand, he requires also a very precise and detailed specification of the standards with which he will make his comparisons. Let us now present our illustration:

A man becomes anxious whenever he is in the presence of his boss. Each time his boss enters his workroom, the employee's efficiency drops markedly.

The research psychologist would be interested in answering questions of this sort: What factors are responsible for the employee responding with anxiety to the appearance and behavior of his boss? Upon what factors is work efficiency dependent?

The applied psychologist, or evaluating psychologist would formulate questions of this kind: How *should* an employee respond to the presence of his boss in order that we should call him a "healthy" employee? How *does* he respond in fact? If the evaluating psychol-

ogist was an applied personality hygienist, he would seek ways and
means of transforming the employee's reaction from its present form
into one which was more in line with the concept of personality
health.

THE DIAGNOSIS OF HEALTHY PERSONALITY

Let us examine in this section the way in which personality health
has been diagnosed by the layman, by the psychiatrist and clinical
psychologist of to-day, and by the personality hygienist of the future.

THE LAYMAN. The man in the street generally arrives at a diagnosis of personality health in an indirect manner. He assumes that
someone is healthy until he observes some emotional reactions, or
some decisions which do not make sense to him. When these deviant
reactions occur, he will assume that the person in question is insane,
or "crazy." What he is actually doing is asserting that if he were
in that situation, he would not react that way; he cannot understand
why the person responds as he does. It is entirely possible that the
"crazy" person comes from a different culture or social class, and if
he were being judged by a person from his own country or group
he would be adjudged quite normal, or healthy.

THE PSYCHIATRIST AND CLINICAL PSYCHOLOGIST. As a general rule
psychiatrists and clinical psychologists deal primarily with unhealthy
personalities. They are consulted by individuals who are unhappy,
ineffectual in their work and interpersonal relationships, and who
want professional assistance in getting well. The psychiatrist or
clinical psychologist is faced with the problem of making a diagnosis
of the patient which will facilitate effective therapy. Thus the task
which he faces combines both explanation, or understanding of the
patient's personality structure, and evaluation of his personality.

In order to promote understanding the therapist will investigate
the life history of the patient, perhaps interview some members of
the patient's family, examine the results of clinical tests of personality, viz.: the Rorschach, TAT, Minnesota Multiphasic Personality
Inventory, etc. On the basis of all of this information he will strive
to formulate a picture of his patient's personality, with the aim of
facilitating or directing the task of restoring the patient to normality
or health.

But the concept of health, in clearly stated terms, has not been used by the average psychiatrist and clinical psychologist as a base line for evaluating a patient's personality. What has more commonly been done is to compare the individual with the assorted concepts of mental disease, for instance, schizophrenia, obsessive-compulsive neurosis, and hysteria. If his present traits resemble those of the mentally ill person, as these are listed in psychological test-manuals and in textbooks of psychiatry and abnormal psychology, then he is generally labelled a victim of that disease. The normal or healthy personality seems, in much contemporary literature, to be the individual who does not have recognizable symptoms of mental illness. When therapy has been completed, the symptoms of neurosis or psychosis have been banished and the patient is said to be improved or cured. Yet his personality structure may still include traits a personality hygienist would regard as unhealthy, despite the fact that these traits do not qualify as psychiatric symptoms.

THE PERSONALITY HYGIENIST. A personality hygienist will be defined in a special way in this section: he is a person who has formulated an explicit and detailed concept of healthy personality. When he makes a diagnosis of personality health, he will make relevant observations and measurements of every aspect of personality for which he has constructed standards of health. Then he will make a careful comparison of each of these observations with his personality-health standards. It might theoretically be possible for him to construct a special evaluation chart similar to the one on page 6.

The solid lines and shaded area indicate the degree or limits within which each trait of personality must fall in order to be adjudged healthy. The dotted line indicates the degree or nature of each trait observed in the person under consideration. Inspection of the chart would then tell the observer *in which specific traits* the person deviates from personality health. This procedure might make possible *differential* personality therapy [5]—the changing of selected unhealthy aspects of personality so they conform with the concept of healthy personality.

It is even possible such a graphic procedure would permit development of a newer, more functional classification scheme for unhealthy personalities; [6] in one group would be placed all those persons who, for example, had "unhealthy emotionality," while in another group

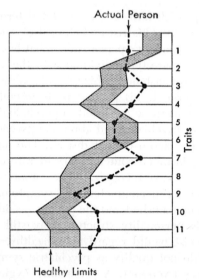

Actual Person

Traits
1
2
3
4
5
6
7
8
9
10
11

Healthy Limits

would be placed those whose predominant deviation from person-ality health was "impaired reality-contact." Such a graphic pro-cedure would facilitate the research task of the personality hygienist enormously. If ways and means could be discovered for measuring each of the traits of healthy personality, then a variety of valuable research questions could be raised and answered; for example, the question (to be resolved by means of factor analysis) of whether or not all the traits of healthy personality were determined by a lesser number of "factors" or "source traits." [7] Further, specific research could be undertaken in order to ascertain just which factors or vari-ables are responsible for each of the traits that have been listed. Might we find, for example, that all the deviations from personality health could be explained as a function of impaired reality-contact? If this were found, then an investigation could be made of the factors determining reality-contact in order to ascertain which of these factors are responsible for the present array of "symptoms," i.e., deviations from health.

WHAT ARE THE VALUES OF PERSONALITY HYGIENISTS?

Since healthy personality is the name given to behavior patterns which are positively valued by a personality hygienist, what are the standards in terms of which he makes his value-judgments? How does an individual have to behave in order to elicit the judgment "He is healthy" from a personality hygienist? Another way of asking this question is: "What does a healthy personality look like? How does the person act in various life situations?"

Actually, it is impossible to describe a healthy personality *in toto*, for we cannot describe any personality as a whole. The best we can do is describe a sampling of the person's traits. We do not know any person completely, for we have never observed everything the person has done. We can, however, describe and evaluate as much of the person's behavior as we do observe. If we try to describe a hypothetical healthy personality, we must be content with some very general statements about traits that are valued. Some general descriptions of healthy personality have been published, and before we proceed in later chapters to describe healthy traits, we shall present a few of these portraits or thumbnail sketches of healthy personality. These portraits represent attempts at defining the stimulus which elicits the judgment "healthy" from a professional personality hygienist.

MASLOW'S "SELF-ACTUALIZING PERSON." Maslow [8] has listed a number of general traits of the *"self-actualizing" person*, who constitutes his version of healthy personality. Self-actualization refers to the process of fulfilling the potential inherent in the person. According to Maslow, a person cannot actualize himself until he has a background rich in the gratification of certain basic needs: physical satisfactions, safety, love, and esteem. With these needs fully gratified, he can then direct his energies to the task of self-actualization—productive scientific or artistic work, organizational work, or whatever other talents he may have. The self-actualizer, as Maslow describes him (from a sample of real people whom he adjudged self-actualizing), has the following characteristics, in contrast with average people and sick people:

1. More efficient perception of reality and more comfortable relations with it.
2. Acceptance of self, others, and nature.
3. Spontaneity: in inner life, thoughts, impulses, etc.
4. Problem centering: interest in problems outside himself, having some mission in life, some task to fulfill.

5. The quality of detachment: need for privacy.
6. Autonomy: independence of culture and environment.
7. Continued freshness of appreciation.
8. The mystic feeling, oceanic experience: ". . . feelings of limitless horizons opening up to the vision, the feeling of being simultaneously more powerful and also more helpless than one ever was before. . . ."
9. *Gemeinschaftsgefühl:* deep feeling of identification, sympathy and affection for mankind as a whole.
10. Deep and profound interpersonal relations.
11. Democratic character structure.
12. Discrimination between means and ends.
13. Philosophical, unhostile sense of humor.
14. Creativeness.
15. Resistance to enculturation: a sort of inner resistance to complete conformity with cultural standards.
16. Certain "imperfections."

This is an impressive list of traits. The student is strongly advised to read Maslow's description of the self-actualizing person in the original in order to obtain a fuller understanding of them.

THE PSYCHOANALYSTS' "GENITAL CHARACTER." Sigmund Freud, the founder of psychoanalysis, formulated a rather complex theory of the development of sexual behavior in the human. He recognized certain stages of development through which each person was thought to pass: the oral, anal, phallic, latency, and finally, the genital stage of sexual development. The *genital character* was the fully matured and developed healthy personality.

Freud did not spell out his conception of the genital character in any detail, although he did indicate in some places in his writings a conception of normality or health. As goals for therapy, he spoke of promoting the capacity for love and for work, *genital primacy*, the strengthening of the ego, and making the unconscious conscious. It is to the writings of Abraham, Reich, and Jones,[9] that we must turn for an explicit statement of the traits of the healthy (genital) character. From the relevant writings of these men, we abstract the following traits, stated in technical terms, but with nontechnical explanations.

1. ESTABLISHMENT OF GENITAL PRIMACY. The person, in his sexual strivings, does not limit himself to "forepleasure" and pregenital activities, such as looking, stroking, aggressing, or being passive. In-

stead, he seeks and is capable of achieving a full genital orgasm. His sexuality is not blocked by guilt, anxiety, or other factors; he has an "orderly libido economy." He alternates between sexual tension and adequate sexual release.

2. PREGENITAL STRIVINGS ARE SUBLIMATED AND/OR GRATIFIED IN FOREPLEASURE ACTS. Infantile sexual strivings, anal, oral, and phallic, are not repressed, but rather "sublimated." That is, they provide the energy for socially valued activities. In addition, they can be directly gratified in adult sexual activities as part of sexual play which is not an end in itself, but rather a means toward genital orgastic satisfaction.

3. THE OEDIPUS COMPLEX IS OUTGROWN. The person has given up incestuous claims on the mother (or father), and the wish for the destruction of the father (or mother). Instead, he is seeking a love-partner on her (his) own merits, and not because she (he) resembles the mother (father). The person has overcome his mixed feelings toward both parents and feels friendly affection for them, and for people in general.

4. THE EGO IS FREE FROM A BATTLE WITH THE ID, and hence can engage in rational thinking and rational action unencumbered by anxiety and thwarted sexuality. Stated another way, the ego is so strengthened as to be relatively stronger than other agencies of personality (id, superego) and in relation to the demands of others and the stresses of external reality.

5. THE PERSON CAN FEEL PLEASURE AND PAIN MORE FULLY, since he is not obliged to repress his feelings and impulses.

To this sketchy outline of the genital character, we may add a few more characteristics which are coming to be viewed as evidence of the successful attainment of the genital stage. These additional characteristics may be regarded as indications that a person has genuinely grown out of the conflicts of his childhood. They include the *capacity to do productive work*, unencumbered by needs to compensate for inferiority feelings; freedom from irrational guilt stemming from an overly severe, infantile superego; and the ability to "regress" without fear—to throw off dignity and pretense and to act spontaneously under appropriate social circumstances.

Probably the main determiner of all these traits which characterize the genital character is a strong ego, one sign of which is profound contact with reality. In the average person, many fears and anxieties persist from childhood, and interfere with the person's capacity to function fully in the immediate present. When a person has attained genitality, most of these fears have been subjected to "reality-testing," and found to be unwarranted. Hence, the genital character is really a much freer person than the average, or normal individual.

ROGERS' "FULLY FUNCTIONING PERSON," Carl Rogers,[10] the founder of "nondirective" or "client-centered" counseling, has recently attempted to spell out "the general characteristics of the person who has completed psychotherapy" (p. 1). The *fully functioning person* may be viewed as his concept of healthy personality. The three cardinal traits of the fully functioning person are listed as follows:

1. THE PERSON IS OPEN TO HIS EXPERIENCE. By this phrase, Rogers means that the individual does not deny, blot out, or distort any perception, memory, fantasy, etc., in order to avoid the experience of threat to his self-structure. Rather, he strives to apprehend fully all of his inner experience, no matter how unpleasant or unpalatable it may be.

2. THE PERSON LIVES IN AN EXISTENTIAL FASHION. The term "existential" in this sentence refers to the subjective conviction that "each moment in experience is new." It implies that the person has the inner feeling he is moving, or growing, and that he has no preconceived notion what he will eventually become, as a person. This is in contrast with nonexistential living, wherein the person strives to avoid new experiences, and strives to remain what he now is forever more.

3. THE PERSON WOULD FIND HIS ORGANISM A TRUSTWORTHY MEANS OF ARRIVING AT THE MOST SATISFYING BEHAVIOR IN EACH EXISTENTIAL SITUATION. He would do what he felt to be right in this immediate moment, and would find this in general a competent and trustworthy guide to his behavior (p. 9). This implies that the individual would not rely on advice, or on a sense of duty as a guide to conduct, but rather on his total and fully experienced self-structure.

THESE DESCRIPTIONS OF PERSONALITY HEALTH ARE EMPIRICAL. Let it be asserted here that these conceptions and descriptions of a healthy personality are not simply wishful or utopian pictures. The authors of the descriptions of the *self-actualizing person*, the *genital character*, and the *fully functioning person* were in a peculiarly advantageous position to draw these portraits, which represent abstractions and generalizations from direct experience with people. They observed unhappy and miserable persons; they applied means of treatment designed to help these persons; and they observed directly what the people could become if the conditions were right.

BEHAVIORAL INDICES OF HEALTHY PERSONALITY

We spoke above of the way in which physicians utilized certain physiological signs as indices of the health of the total body, e.g., a body temperature of 98.6 degrees, a certain optimum white-cell count, etc. From the writings of a number of psychologists and psychiatrists we can present some behavioral indices of healthy personality. The authors in question appear to select some trait as a sort of index of the health of the total personality; that is, if the person "has" this trait to the valued extent, he is adjudged healthy.

WILHELM REICH: "ORGASTIC POTENCY." [11] Reich believed the capacity to experience a full sexual climax, or orgasm, was the most important single sign of personality health. He believed, with Freud, that the neurotic individual was one who had been obliged to give up sexual satisfactions because of anxiety and guilt, and hence was unable to relax, and to experience the full gratification of his sexual needs. One of the many aims of the treatment process was to restore *orgastic potency* to the neurotic man or woman.

WILLIAM BLATZ: "INDEPENDENT SECURITY." [12] Blatz is a prominent child psychologist in Canada. He believes that self-reliance is the trait which reveals the health or lack of health of a personality. Self-reliance is manifested by a person who has attained some measure of *independent security*. By independent security, Blatz means "the state of consciousness which accompanies a willingness to accept the consequences of one's own decisions and actions" (p. 165). He distinguishes between dependent security and independent security. In the former, "an agent (some other person) accepts the responsibility for the consequences of an individual's actions. The individual then feels free to act in accordance with his own desires and wishes because he does not have to accept the consequences of his behavior" (p. 165). Independent security "can be attained in only one way—by the acquisition of a skill through learning. Whenever an individual

is presented with a situation for which he is inadequately prepared
. . . he must make one of two choices—he must either retreat or
attack. . . . The individual must, if he is to attack, emerge from the
state of dependent security and accept the state of *insecurity* (my
italics). This attack will, of course, result in learning. . . . The individual . . . learns that satisfaction results from overcoming the
apprehension and anxiety experienced when insecure, and that he
may thus reach a state of independent security through learning."

Just as Reich might appraise the health of a given personality in
terms of the degree of orgastic potency that might be present, so
might Blatz assess personality health in terms of the extent to which
independent security had been attained in various realms of life, e.g.
work, interpersonal relationships, etc.

HARRY STACK SULLIVAN: "NON-PARATAXIC INTERPERSONAL RELA-
TIONS." [13] Sullivan was a highly influential American psychiatrist.
He developed what is called the "interpersonal school" in psychiatry.
He believed the proper study of psychiatry was not the person as
such, but rather his relationships with people. A neurotic or psychotic
individual was seen as a person who established predominantly
"parataxic" relationships with other people; that is, he behaved
toward people "as if" they had traits, feelings or attitudes which in
reality they did not possess. Patients seem to assume the people
whom they deal with now have attitudes and opinions once held by
people in their past. By implication then, healthy personality would
be manifested by a person who establishes *non-parataxic relationships* with others; that is, his concepts about other people are
realistic, not confused by his past experiences. In Sullivan's own
words: "One achieves mental health [that is, manifests healthy per-
sonality] to the extent that one becomes aware of one's interpersonal
relations" (p. 102). This epigrammatic statement implies that a person achieves and maintains healthy personality only if his beliefs
about himself and other people are *accurate*. It is only through
accurate beliefs and knowledge that a person can achieve lasting
"satisfactions and security," which Sullivan sees as the major goals
or aims of behavior. Satisfactions refer to the gratification of bodily
needs, such as the need for food, rest, sexual gratification; "security,"
in his writings, refers to the acquisition of objects, and responses from
others, carrying the meanings of affection, status, esteem, etc. (p. 6).

ALFRED ADLER: [14] "SOCIAL FEELING" (GEMEINSCHAFTSGEFÜHL). Adler was the former psychoanalyst who broke away from Freud and established the school of thought known as "Individual Psychology." He regarded *social feeling*—its presence or absence—as the indicator of personality health. Social feeling, as the lengthy German word has been translated, refers to a sense of identification or one-ness with all of mankind. John Donne's poem, which contains the line, "I am involved in all mankind," expresses the meaning of *gemeinschaftsgefühl*. The unhealthy personality, to Adler, was one who devoted all of his energies to the acquisition of power, in order to reassure himself against feelings of inferiority. This "compensation" for inferiority feelings impelled a person to compete with others rather than allowing him to love them.

ERICH FROMM: "PRODUCTIVE ORIENTATION." [15] Erich Fromm is a contemporary psychoanalyst who is often classified as a "neo-Freudian." He has attempted to revise many of the theories promulgated by Freud, so that these theories will be better reconciled with contemporary knowledge in sociology and anthropology, and with the tradition of "humanistic ethics." According to Fromm, personality health has been achieved to the extent that the person displays a *productive orientation*. The term orientation refers to the ways in which a person relates to the world and the people in it. A productive orientation is that way of relating to the world which transforms it so as to satisfy better the needs of a person. Stated another way, productivity consists in producing the objects and conditions necessary to growth and happiness. The productive character is able, through the use of his own skills and knowledge, to produce whatever is necessary to make him happy and healthy.

KAREN HORNEY: "SELF-REALIZATION." [16] Karen Horney, another neo-Freudian, singled out the relation of a person to his "real self" as the index of health. The individual who is "alienated from his self" is not healthy. The person who *realizes his self*—who experiences his own feelings and will, who acknowledges and assumes responsibility for his own actions—is displaying healthy personality.

OTTO RANK: "CREATIVITY." [17] Otto Rank, an early psychoanalyst who deviated from the orthodox teachings of Freud, called attention to *creativity* as an index of personality health. The person who displays creativity is the individual who accepts and affirms his own will, and his own individuality. He is not afraid to make innovations, to be different from other persons. It should be noted that Rank's writings on the subject of creativity and will-affirmation have influenced the views of Rogers and Fromm to a considerable extent.

DISCUSSION OF BEHAVIORAL INDICES OF HEALTHY PERSONALITY. The small list of single indices of personality health could be extended considerably. We shall limit ourselves to the few that have been mentioned. It becomes apparent that the authors who use these traits as indicators of personality health are revealing their values, which is as it should be. They are stating that the traits mentioned are both means for the attainment of healthy personality and signs that it has been attained. It is probably true, however, that the traits mentioned above are correlated with each other. That is, the authors in question probably share many values and would probably agree that all the traits are highly desirable for an individual to possess. If we could pick out, for example, a person who displayed orgastic potency, and presented him to Blatz, Blatz would undoubtedly find that he manifested independent security. Sullivan would find non-parataxic interpersonal relations, and Adler would see social feeling, etc. Actually, this is a problem which could readily be resolved through empirical research—measurements could be developed for the several traits; these tests could be administered to a group of subjects, and correlation coefficients could be calculated to ascertain if changes in one trait are associated with changes in others. One suspects this would be the case.

So far, we have presented three thumbnail sketches of overall healthy personality: Maslow's, the psychoanalysts', and Rogers'. We have also presented some single indicators of the health of the total personality. We might now raise the question, what is the point in attempting to describe in detail a concept of healthy personality? There are many very practical uses to which an explicit description of the personality valued by the mental hygienist could be put.

USES OF A CONCEPT OF HEALTHY PERSONALITY

A clearly stated definition of healthy personality can be useful for (a) research into personality health, (b) evaluating the results of personality therapy, (c) evaluating the effects of personality-hygiene measures on a given population, and (d) for self-evaluation purposes.

PERSONALITY-HEALTH RESEARCH. Millions of dollars annually are spent on research into ways and means of improving the personality health of the nation, and of curing the mentally ill. A detailed description of the healthy personality would be invaluable to the researcher, for it would enable him to solve such problems as: How many unhealthy personalities are there? What are the varying degrees of personality illness prevalent in a given group? How to promote healthy personality?

EVALUATION OF PERSONALITY THERAPY.[18] A neurotic or psychotic person undergoing psychotherapy wants to know when he has become healthy, and of course, so does his therapist. A clear concept of personality health would make it possible to devise objective means of rating the overall health of the personality, and disclose which traits have become healthy through treatment, and which traits are as yet in need of improvement.

EVALUATION OF PERSONALITY-HYGIENE WORK. Personality-hygiene workers are a very industrious group who make speeches, show films, offer courses, conduct discussion groups, etc., all with the aim of promoting personality health. The problem of evaluating the effects, if any, of these well-intended measures, is a staggering one. Clearly formulated concepts of healthy personality would make it possible for the worker to make before and after tests of his population in order to determine what effects he has produced.

SELF-EVALUATION. Every student certainly has asked himself the question, "Am I crazy, or am I all right?" Unfortunately, the criteria against which they compare themselves are often unclear. A specific formulation of the traits of healthy personality would permit the individual to study himself, and compare his present traits with the traits valued by the personality hygienist.

NORMAL OR MODAL PERSONALITY, HEALTHY PERSONALITY, AND IDEAL PERSONALITY

Personality, as we have seen, refers to the totality of the reaction-patterns, or traits, of an individual. We have often equated normal with healthy in reference to physical health, and also with reference to personality health. For purposes of clarity in thinking, we shall draw distinctions among normal, healthy and ideal.

NORMAL OR MODAL PERSONALITY. There are few words that have been used with so many meanings as "normal." In physical medicine, the term is used as synonymous with health. In statistics, normal means, literally, characteristic of the norm; that is, common, average, or representative of a group. In earlier works on mental hygiene, to be normal meant that a person was free from the symptoms of mental disease. In the present work, normal will be used in the statistical sense, referring to traits that are typical, representative, or "modal." In fact, we shall prefer the word *modal* to normal, since in the statistical sense it means roughly the same thing, and yet it is free of the additional connotations of normal. *Normal* or *modal personality*, then, refers to the traits which characterize an individual who is representative of, or similar to a larger class of persons.[19] We could speak of a modal, middle-class American or a modal college professor, or a modal Okinawan. It is the modal personality which sociologists and anthropologists describe in their field studies of societies. They ignore individual differences among members of a group, and strive to depict the reaction patterns which are shared by the group members. Naturally, there are many practical uses to which knowledge of modal personality can be put. If we know what reaction patterns to expect from people in general, we can influence and control their behavior to a marked degree. Thus, if we know that people like an individual who smiles and passes compliments, and that if people like you they will buy what you sell, it follows that salesmen should be trained to smile and pass compliments. The politician directs his speeches toward the modal personality. He tries to determine what most people in his audience want to hear and then speaks accordingly, hoping they will all respond favorably to his remarks.

Obviously, the modal personality is not necessarily a healthy personality. There may be many traits quite common within the general population, which a personality hygienist would deplore. For example, it might be normal for people to repress certain feelings, but the hygienist would regard this as an unhealthy trait.

HEALTHY PERSONALITY.[20] This term refers to an individual who reacts to life situations in ways that are valued by the personality hygienist. We have already noted some of the traits regarded as signs of personality health. It would be appropriate here to provide a highly general definition of healthy personality—one which goes beyond the present opinions of hygienists. We shall state, then, that **an individual displays healthy personality when he is able to gratify his needs through behavior that conforms with both the norms of his society and the requirements of his conscience.**

Actually, this definition implies that there can be no specific description of healthy personality which applies to all societies at all times. But it does specify what the person must do in order to warrant the judgment that he is a healthy personality. It specifies:

1. He experiences satisfaction. Satisfaction produces the emotional state known as happiness, or contentment. Most authorities would agree that without satisfaction, there can be no healthy personality. A person who is chronically dissatisfied can hardly be called a healthy personality. We have not, as yet, specified what satisfaction consists of. In a later chapter, we shall attend to this problem.

2. The person must find satisfaction in a special way. He cannot behave in just any way in order to secure satisfaction. He must act in ways that are within the framework of law, custom, and morality that prevails in his society. Further, healthy personality implies that conscience—the morals and values acquired by a person during the process of socialization—must be considered during the quest for satisfaction.

Since needs and values vary from person to person, and society to society, and since law, custom and morality vary from society to society, it follows that the present work deals with the healthy personality *for our culture*. We shall describe the traits that are valued in Western society by Western personality hygienists.

There are some authors, notably Fromm and Maslow, who hold the view that some needs are universal, or independent of the culture, and that humans, because they *are* human and not functioning at the level of reflex and instinct, must have certain gratifications or else they become less than human, or sick. Thus, Fromm [21] asserts that man needs a sense of *relatedness* to his fellow man; a sense of *transcendence*, the capacity to create and to be the master of nature rather than nature's passive victim; a sense of *rootedness*, the feeling of belonging to a group, preferably a feeling of brotherliness with all mankind; a sense of *identity*, the feeling of being separate from others, of being oneself; and finally, man needs a *frame of orientation and devotion*, some philosophy of life, or religion, which gives meaning and direction to his life. The implication of this view is that unless man achieves some form of satisfaction of these needs—no matter what culture or society he lives in—he will fall short of the full status of a human being, and by our standards, he will be "sick" or insane.

Maslow [22] has been equally explicit. He asserts that man must experience a succession of basic-need gratifications before he can develop to full health. Unless physical satisfactions, security, love and recognition are accorded to a person, irrespective of time or place, he will fail to develop fully.

At the present time, we may regard these two authors' views as highly plausible hypotheses about human needs.

IDEAL PERSONALITY. The healthy personality may actually be described as the personality which mental hygienists regard as ideal. But in any society there are many value-systems, and many ideals in terms of which behavior is evaluated. Ideal personality refers to the cluster of traits which are regarded as ideal, or valuable, by persons who share certain values. Thus, we could speak of an ideal physician—he would behave in ways that most physicians envy, admire, and strive to emulate. An ideal mother, husband, father, spouse —these can all be described with some accuracy by almost anyone. The method of formulating a portrait of an ideal person (that is, ideal for the person being interviewed) is simply to ask him how doctors, mothers, spouses, etc., *should be;* how they should behave.[23] The author once asked his class what traits they wished they possessed, or felt they should possess. The group characterized the ideal person as: honest, intelligent, aggressive, sympathetic, understanding, devout in religion, obedient to parents, self-reliant, willing to take initiative, able to take orders, a success with the opposite sex, sexually abstinent until marriage, well-rounded, highly skilled in some area, possessing a good sense of humor, willing to fight for what was near and dear, avoiding hurting people, etc. It becomes apparent that many of these traits are logically contradictory one with the other. It would be difficult to be an ideal personality. Whenever we speak of ideal personality, or for that matter, of normal and healthy personality, it will be necessary to specify ideal—to whom? Or normal—to what group? Or healthy—in whose opinion?

Ideals play a decisive role in human behavior and are very important factors in attaining, or failing to attain, a healthy personality. In a later chapter, we shall attend in considerable detail to the role that values and ideals play in personality hygiene.

THE ANALYSIS OF HEALTHY PERSONALITY

Although there has been disagreement among the various attempts to describe healthy personality, there is a growing consensus of informed opinion concerning the traits of healthy personality. In the chapters which follow, this rather vague image of healthy personality will be analyzed into some of its component traits and an attempt will be made to describe the range of reactions to certain situations, the determiners of those reactions, and finally the version of the reactions which is considered healthy.

In the chapter which follows immediately, the concept of needs is analyzed and redefined. We have stated that a healthy personality is one who is able to satisfy his needs in certain special ways. Needs obviously are very important in our discussion, so it will be necessary to go into considerable detail in order to spell out the role that needs play in behavior in general. When once we have secured an understanding of the influence of needs on behavior, we can tackle the more limited problem of the role of needs in healthy personality.

SUMMARY

Physical health refers to a mode of bodily functioning which is *valued* by physicians, whose opinions as "experts" are accepted by laymen in our culture. Mental health, or *personality health*, as it will be called throughout this volume, refers to ways of behaving that are valued, for good reasons, by personality hygienists in our culture.

Evaluation of behavior involves (a) accurate observation and description of behavior, and (b) comparison of behavior with explicit standards of various kinds. The layman evaluates behavior, usually, from the standpoint of whether or not other people's behavior is

similar to his own, and vice versa. Where a difference between self
and others is noted, the conclusion is often drawn that the different
person is "crazy." The psychiatrist compares the behavior of people
with his concepts of "mental illness." If a person's behavior resembles
the behavior expected in mental disease, then the person is so
labelled. If his behavior does not resemble that of the "mentally ill,"
then he is adjudged "normal." The clinical psychologist uses various
tests as a means of refining and making more objective the impressions of the psychiatrist. The personality hygienist makes explicit a
concept of personality health, and compares the behavior which he
observes in a given person with this concept of health. If there
is overlap, then the person is adjudged healthy. If not, a detailed list
of deviations from health is prepared. These deviations are called
"symptoms."

Some examples of attempts to describe healthy personality were
provided. Maslow's *self-actualizing person*, the psychoanalysts'
genital character, and Rogers' *fully functioning person* were described, and some single-trait indices of personality health were
listed.

Some of the uses to which a concept of personality health could
be put were described. Finally, distinctions were drawn among
normal or *modal* personality, *healthy* personality, and *ideal* personality.

NOTES AND REFERENCES

RECOMMENDED READINGS ARE MARKED WITH AN ASTERISK (°)

1. See Sunderman, F. W. and Boerner, F., *Normal values in clinical
      medicine*, Philadelphia, Saunders, 1949, for a differentiated,
      quantitative conception of physical health.
2. Parsons has described physical illness as a variety of "deviant be-
      havior," while the therapeutic efforts of physicians is regarded as
      a variety of "social control." This is a brilliant and provocative
      parallel. See Parsons, T., "Illness and the role of the physician: a
      sociological perspective," *Amer. J. Orthopsychiat.*, 1951, 21,
      452–460.
°3. The distinction between mind and body, and the resolution of the

psychosomatic dualism has been a problem which has plagued psychologists and philosophers for centuries. See Brown, J. F., *Psychodynamics of abnormal behavior*, New York, McGraw-Hill, 1940, Ch. 3. Brown outlines the problem with clarity and elegance, and presents the modern attempt to resolve the dualism by the adoption of the "organismic point of view."

*4. This is a highly simplified account of traits. The serious student is referred to Allport, G. W., *Personality: a psychological interpretation*, New York, Holt, 1937, Ch. 11, 12. Students of personality regard Allport as the most influential exponent of trait-theory.

5. In modern medicine, differential diagnosis of illness leads to differential therapy or treatment. In modern psychiatry, although there is a highly developed classification of "mental diseases," treatment is relatively unspecific. Shock therapy, surgery, "psychotherapy," or administration of assorted drugs constitute the major treatment methods, and there are no generally accepted clear-cut indications of when to use what, and no valid evidence to assure the therapist that he is attempting the right kind of therapy. An excellent beginning at a concept of differential *psychotherapy* is Wolberg, B., *The technique of psychotherapy*. New York: Grune and Stratton, 1954.

6. The contemporary "disease-classification" system that is adopted by psychiatrists is not proving to be a very useful one. "Mental diseases" are grouped into categories on the basis of "symptoms"; yet the same symptoms may be produced by different causal factors, thus requiring widely different treatment. Further, similar causal factors may produce widely different symptoms in different people. The student is referred to Brown, J. F., *op. cit.*, Ch. 4, for a more detailed development of this comment. Ideally, a classification of unhealthy personalities would place in one category all those individuals whose deviations from personality health were caused by similar factors, and for whom, by implication, similar treatment would be indicated.

*7. Cattell, R. B., *Personality: a systematic theoretical and factual study*, New York, McGraw-Hill, 1950. In Ch. 1, 2, Cattell reviews the different ways of describing personality. In Ch. 2 especially, he draws a distinction between surface traits and source traits.

*8. Maslow, A. H., *Motivation and personality*, New York, Harper, 1954. See Ch. 12, and read in full for a highly articulate concept of healthy personality. We shall be referring constantly to Maslow's highly provocative writings.

9. Abraham, K., *Selected papers on psychoanalysis,* London, Hogarth, 1949, Ch. 25. Reich, W., *Character analysis,* New York, Orgone Institute Press, 1949, pp. 164–170. Jones, E., "The concept of a normal mind," *Int. J. Psychoanal.,* 1942, 23, pp. 1–8. See also Erikson's contribution to Senn, M. J. E. (ed.), *Symposium on the healthy personality,* New York, Josiah Macy Foundation, 1950, pp. 91–146. Erikson provides criteria for evaluating personality health at different stages of development. Hartmann, H., "Psychoanalysis and the concept of health," *Int. J. Psychoanal.,* 1939, **20,** Parts 3 and 4, gives a superb analysis of the concept of health.

10. Rogers, C. R., *The concept of the fully functioning person.* (Mimeographed manuscript, privately circulated, 1954.)

11. Reich, W., *op. cit.,* Check index for page references to orgastic potency.

°12. Blatz, W., *Understanding the young child,* Toronto, Clarke, Irwin, 1944, Ch. 9. Blatz's discussion of "security" is a very articulate and explicit statement of some ideas which can be found stated in other ways by such authors as Rank, Mower, Horney, etc. Blatz has been a vigorous opponent of many of the theoretical views held by psychoanalysts.

13. Sullivan, H. S., *Conceptions of modern psychiatry,* Washington, William Alanson White Psychiatric Foundation, 1947, pp. 102–106.

14. Adler, A., *Understanding human nature,* New York, Permabooks, 1949, pp. 30–32.

°15. Fromm, E., *Man for himself,* New York, Rinehart, 1947, pp. 82–106.

°16. Horney, Karen, *Neurosis and human growth,* New York, Norton, 1950, Ch. 1.

°17. See the discussion of Rank in Thompson, Clara, *Psychoanalysis: evolution and development,* New York, Hermitage, 1950, pp. 174–182. Rank's writings are rather difficult for the beginning student to understand, and so the reader is advised to consult a secondary source first.

18. This problem has vexed therapists for many years. Eysenck presents a strong argument to the effect that personality therapy is no more effective at "curing" mentally ill people than simply leaving them alone or hospitalizing them. See Eysenck, H. J., "The effects of psychotherapy: an evaluation," *J. consult. Psychol.,* 1952, **16,** 319–324. A promising approach to the problem of evaluating therapy may be seen in Miles, H. W., Barrabee, E. L., and Fine-

singer, J. E., "Evaluation of psychotherapy," *Psychosom. Med.*, 1951, 13, 83.

*19. See Inkeles, A. and Levinson, D. J., "National character: the study of modal personality and sociocultural systems," Ch. 26 in Lindzey, G. (ed.), *Handbook of social psychology*, Cambridge, Addison-Wesley, 1954. This chapter is a fine review of the literature in this area, with a discussion of methods of investigation.

20. There is room for a very detailed scholarly work which will review the concepts of healthy personality as these have been expounded through the ages by various psychologists, philosophers, theological writers, etc. The student can become sensitized to the values of anybody who writes about people—whether novelist, poet, moralist, or scientist—by looking for signs of value, e.g., "Whom does the novelist portray as the hero?" The hero's traits will reflect the values of the author, or perhaps of the audience for whom the author is writing. It should be pointed out, however, that "healthy personality" is actually a special case of the more general class "ideal personality," or "valued personality." And we can always ask, "What traits are valued by whom? And for what ends?"

*21. Fromm, E., *The sane society*, New York, Rinehart, 1955, pp. 30–66.

22. Maslow, A. H., *op. cit.*

*23. The student "should" read Horney's chapter on the "Tyranny of the should" at this point. See Horney, K., *op. cit.*, Ch. 3. "Shoulds" refer to ways in which a person believes he must act, if he is to maintain self-esteem, or parental approval, or if he is to obtain any other valued ends. A more sophisticated method for ascertaining the characteristics of an ideal personality is provided by *the critical incident technique*. This method consists in asking persons, not to list abstract traits which they value, but rather to describe in full detail some behavior in a concrete situation which they had actually observed, and which exemplifies the ideal. See Flanagan, J. C., "The critical incident technique," *Psychol. Bull.*, 1953, 51, 327–358. This author reviews the research work which has been accomplished to date with this method.

QUESTIONS FOR REVIEW AND EXAMINATION

1. Before you have read any further, what is your present concept of a healthy personality?

2. Distinguish among description, evaluation, and explanation of behavior. Give illustrations for each.

3. What is the formal difference among *normal* (modal) personality, *ideal* personality, *healthy* personality, and *sick* personality?

4. What useful functions, if any, can be served by explicit descriptions of normal personality and healthy personality?

5. What do the various descriptions of healthy personality which are given in this chapter have in common with each other?

6. Use the concepts employed in this chapter as a guide to describing and evaluating the personality of someone you know.

CHAPTER 2

Needs and Healthy Behavior

We described a healthy personality as one which comprises traits that enable an individual to *gratify his needs* with behavior that is personally and socially acceptable. What is a need? What does a person need? What does he need it for? What consequences follow when a person obtains what he needs? When he fails to obtain what he needs? Are some needs more important than others? Important to whom, and for what? Are some needs common, and others rare? Are some needs socially acceptable, and others not? Are some needs conscious, and others not? These are fundamental questions, and adequate answers to them will facilitate an understanding of both behavior and personality health.

We shall introduce our discussion with some technical considerations. Let us first recognize that behavior is a continuous process, changing in direction, content, and meaning from time to time. The author awoke this morning, ate his breakfast, drove with his son to the garage to have his automobile serviced, then walked home with the boy, went to a neighbor's house to use the typewriter, and proceeded to work on this chapter. No sooner had one behavior sequence ended, than another was commenced. Let us analyze this continuous "flow" of behavior into components. We will call each

25

component a *need-satisfaction sequence*.[1] Thus, eating breakfast is one sequence, driving the car to the garage is another, walking home still another, and working on the manuscript still another. These need-satisfaction sequences cease only with death.

WHAT IS A NEED?

Psychologists speak of people, and organisms, as having needs of all kinds. Arguments occur among psychologists as to the nature of needs: are they psychological or physiological? There are controversies as to the origins of needs: innate or acquired? There are controversies as to the number of needs: one need, two needs, or dozens, even hundreds? What is a need? Murphy [2] defines a need as "the lack of something which if present would give satisfaction." Krech and Crutchfield [3] refer to needs as a special case of the more general concept "psychological tensions." Murray [4] speaks of needs as ". . . force[s] . . . in the brain region . . . which organize perception, apperception, intellection, conation, and action in such a way as to transform in a certain direction an existing, unsatisfying situation."

Are these authorities talking about the same thing, or is each referring to something different? Is one correct and the others wrong? Murray enumerates well over thirty needs as part of the "make-up" of man, while Snygg and Combs [5] list only two. Learning theorists distinguish between primary and secondary, or acquired needs. Who is correct? Does it make any difference? Certainly it makes a difference if we value accurate knowledge. Yet, in our present work we can bypass much of this controversy without being unduly handicapped in our exposition. We shall modify Murphy's succinct definition and call a need a judgment which a person makes concerning what is required in order to attain some valued end. The attainment of this end produces an inner experience called satisfaction. We do not know much about the physiology of satisfaction, but each person knows what satisfaction feels like.

It should be asserted that needs are always experienced (at least by adults) as a need *for* something. They always include a cognitive component. Nobody has a need without its being a need for something. Let us call the something a *need-object*.

NEED-OBJECTS. The object which the person discovers or believes will produce satisfaction is called the *need-object*. Need-objects can be almost anything: thoughts, beliefs, perceptions, memories, and fantasies. They can be things: food, clothing, money, houses, cars, typewriters. They can be the reactions of others: affection-responses, approval-responses, jealousy-responses, etc. At one time or another, everyone needs or wants any and all of these objects.

A person must act in various ways in order to obtain need-objects. This behavior is called *instrumental behavior*. It has an aim or purpose, namely to secure the need-objects, and produce satisfaction. We can regard almost everything that a person does as instrumental action; it is always need-determined and pointed toward the attainment of the need-object. We can evaluate instrumental action from a number of viewpoints. These include the achievement viewpoint—is the behavior efficient in obtaining the need-object? They include also a moral viewpoint—is the behavior good? A health viewpoint—does the behavior promote happiness, and growth of personality?

INSTRUMENTAL BEHAVIOR

Let us inquire further into instrumental behavior, or "coping behavior," as Maslow calls it.[6] What is instrumental behavior? Does it differ from some other kinds of behavior? What are its properties? Under what conditions can it occur, and under what conditions is it disrupted, or disorganized?

Instrumental behavior refers to all the behavior which is actually or potentially subject to the voluntary control of the person. In neurological terms, we could say that instrumental behavior is mediated by, or under the control of, the higher portions of the nervous system, especially the motor portions of the cerebral cortex. Since instrumental behavior is under voluntary control, it is flexible and capable of being highly differentiated. This flexibility makes learning possible.

We draw a distinction between instrumental behavior and *disorganized behavior*.[7] Disorganized behavior is less subject to voluntary control than instrumental behavior. It occurs when physiological tension becomes too strong. The tension-level that disorganizes instrumental behavior, and causes it to be replaced by disorganized behavior is called the *disorganized-behavior-threshold*. Sometimes it will be called the *frustration-threshold*. In other words, a person is capable of precise instrumental action only when tension is kept below this threshold. The reader is asked to try to solve a mathematics problem, or repair a watch, or play a sonata when he is very hungry, or very angry. His skill will be markedly impaired. An important area for future research is the systematic exploration of the conditions under which a person can engage in instrumental behavior with optimum efficiency. Industrial psychologists have approached this problem with studies of the effects of fatigue and distraction on worker-efficiency, but more research needs to be done.

Instrumental action is impossible until the body has matured to a certain point. An infant has a very limited instrumental behavior repertoire. What little he can do is handled by automatic reflexes. His overt behavior expresses his need-tensions, and can hardly be called instrumental. We couldn't call his behavior "instrumental" until he has achieved voluntary control over it.

At this point, let us make a rather startling and yet obvious observation. In all societies, instrumental behavior is valued more than disorganized behavior. In fact, if it were not, the society would not survive. (It should be pointed out that expressive behavior under appropriate circumstances is also valued.) It is only because instrumental behavior is valued that the control of emotional tension becomes a problem. Strong emotional tension disorganizes instrumental behavior and so it is largely condemned. Suppose for some reason instrumental behavior was condemned. Then, the person who displayed the greatest amount of emotional expressiveness would be granted the highest status in society. The problem in socializing children would then change. People would no longer seek ways and means of reducing the frequency and explosiveness of emotional outbursts. Rather, they would seek ways and means of minimizing instrumental action. The man with most prestige would be the most ineffective, least skilled, the most emotional man. Some English gentlemen, as portrayed in the plays of G. B. Shaw and Oscar Wilde, almost fulfill the above requirements.

Instrumental action is valued, however, and a broad repertoire of **learned** instrumental behavior-patterns (skills) is an important means of obtaining satisfactions and maintaining personality health. Let us briefly indicate the role of skills in maintaining personality health.

SKILLS AND PERSONALITY HEALTH. The guiding definition of the healthy personality states that the *ability* to achieve gratifications is an important aspect of personality health. Our attention is focused on such factors as intelligence, learning capacity, competence, and know-how, and on such personality traits as autonomy and perseverance.

Broadly speaking, a person has four paths open to him when he is in a condition of need-tension. He can satisfy the need directly, with appropriate instrumental behavior or skill; he can solicit the help of some other person to solve the problem or obtain the need-objects for him; he can pursue some substitute need-object; or he can do without, and just live with his privation.

The personality hygienist would regard the first of these paths as ideal with respect to health in most instances, for a number of reasons. Autonomy—the ability to achieve gratifications by one's own efforts—is a valued trait, and a broad skill-repertoire contributes to autonomy. The more skills a person has already acquired, and the more capacity he has to learn new ones when the need for them arises, the more he moves in the direction of autonomy. This is not to say that dependency upon others is an unhealthy state of affairs per se. Dependency is inescapable for the human being. But undue dependency has consequences of an unhealthy sort, as we shall see in later chapters. In anticipation, we can state that overdependency upon others to provide gratifications may force a person to suppress and repress much of his real self, so as not to offend the person upon whom he is dependent. Autonomy can prevent the development of many varieties of unhealthy personality, especially those which follow from repression of the real self.

NEED-TENSION

A person acts in instrumental fashion in order to obtain need-objects. What factors determine the emergence of now this, then that, instrumental behavior pattern? Why will a person, in succession, walk, talk, read, knit, eat, swim, caress, paint, etc.? The most important and immediate determiner is *need-tension*.

Psychologists adopted the concept of tension from physics. One now speaks of psychological tension. What is it? The human being experiences tension and goes through a process of diagnosis and judgment. He *feels* something, an alteration in his usual, felt tension-level and -quality, and he labels it: I feel hungry, or bored, etc. When his felt-tension-level and -quality deviate from the feeling-state he likes best (which he might call "feeling right") he tries to diagnose the cause of this deviation from optimum. He then makes a judgment of what he needs in order to feel good. Finally, he experiences a wish or a longing for the need-objects in question. Need-tension may thus be defined as the subjective experience of wanting something. In order to get this something (the need-object), the person engages in appropriate instrumental behavior.

The experience of wanting something is almost certainly accompanied by some complex pattern of underlying neurophysiological events.[8] Our knowledge in this area, however, is incomplete. We shall limit ourselves to the psychology of need-tension, and leave the neurology and physiology of need to researchers in those respective disciplines.

So far, we have asserted that needs are important determiners of behavior and that need-satisfaction is an integral component of the definition of healthy personality. Let us now inquire into some general characteristics of need-tension and, later, we shall examine in greater detail the role that needs play in behavior.

NEED-TENSIONS SUCCEED ONE ANOTHER. Behavior is a never-ending stream, terminating only with death. It can be broken down into components which we have called need-satisfaction sequences. A need-tension arises, the person strives to obtain the appropriate need-object, he experiences satisfaction, and then another need-tension arises. The attainment of the need-object produces satisfaction or happiness, but this state of affairs doesn't last. No sooner is it achieved, than some other felt-deficit arises, and the person is off again in pursuit of other need-objects.

NEED-TENSIONS HAVE DURATION. There is always some interval between the first awareness of a need-tension (wish) and its quiescence through attainment of the need-object. As the delay increases in length, the intensity of the tension increases. Up to a certain level of tension, it remains possible for the person to behave effectively in instrumental fashion. Beyond that level, behavior ceases to be instrumental and becomes disorganized with respect to the attainment of the goal. When this tension-level has been reached, we speak of *frustration*. The only time that frustration cannot occur is during the nine-month gestation period *in utero*. At that time, the tissue-needs of the fetus are met immediately by the blood stream of the mother. With birth comes delay and frustration. Frustration is an important factor in personality health and illness, and so we will return to a more detailed account of frustration in a later section.

NEED-TENSIONS CONFLICT WITH ONE ANOTHER. The person never has the experience of wanting one and only one thing at a given time. Rather, the person has many needs which may all be in various degrees of arousal at the same time. Consequently, he faces the problem of choice. What need-objects will he pursue first? In securing one need-object, will he be obliged to forego other need-objects? The experience of conflict among needs is an inevitable aspect of being human. To be human is to have conflict. As with frustration, conflict is such an important factor in personality health that we shall devote a separate section to an exposition of healthy and unhealthy reactions to conflict.

NEED-TENSIONS MAY BE CONSCIOUS AND UNCONSCIOUS. A need is said to be conscious when the person is fully aware of the associated tension, and labels it accurately. It is possible, however, for an individual to have need-tensions which he is aware of but does not identify accurately; or he may refuse to think about the relevant need-objects. Where this is the case, we have a situation in which an important behavior determinant—the need-tension—is present and operative, influencing the person's behavior, but where appropriate instrumental action is not possible. One can act with accuracy and efficiency only when the nature of the "lack" is identified and the appropriate need-object is known. Thus, if the need is not clearly recognized, behavior will be influenced in uncontrollable ways, and the need will not be gratified.

Again, in a later section we will devote more time to an investigation of the role of unconscious needs in behavior and to the factors responsible for their being unconscious.

We will say here that the personality hygienist values the ability to identify needs with precision and regards an individual as unhealthy when he does not know what he needs. Indeed, the person who does not know what he needs will almost certainly remain frustrated and unhappy because his satisfactions will only occur by chance. He will not be able to go directly in quest of satisfaction.

Let us now inquire into the role that need-tensions play in influencing the nature and direction of behavior. For the present, we shall ignore the difference between conscious and unconscious needs.

NEED-TENSIONS AND BEHAVIOR

Behavior is a very complex process which can be analyzed into many components. We shall not make an exhaustive analysis; rather, we shall select some aspects of behavior which have been studied in their relation to need-tensions, and which have some relevance to our theme of healthy personality. We shall discuss the influence of need-tensions on cognition, valences, and instrumental action. Then we shall inquire into the problems of need-frustration, need-conflict, and the problem of unconscious need-tensions. Finally, we shall discuss the role that need-gratification plays in personality development and health.

NEED-TENSIONS AND COGNITION

Murphy [9] defines cognition as "any process by means of which one arrives at knowledge." Knowledge is comprised fundamentally of beliefs.[10] How do we acquire knowledge, that is, beliefs? Perception is an important source of knowledge; so are reasoning, imagination, fantasy, and remembering. We shall examine the role needs play in each of these cognitive processes. Let us begin our discussion with an examination of the role played by need-tensions in perception.

NEED-TENSIONS AND PERCEPTION. Perception is the process of observing. We speak of the *perceptual field,* which refers to the totality of information provided to a person by his various sense organs at any given moment. The perceptual field can be analyzed into component parts: the visual field, auditory field, olfactory and gustatory fields, the organic and kinesthetic fields, etc. In other words, there is a field corresponding to each of our receptor systems.

The total perceptual field is always organized into "figure" and "ground." Figure refers to the focus of attention—that which the individual is observing most closely. Ground refers to everything else the sense organs yield, but which is not being closely observed. Right now, this page and these words are probably the figure in the reader's perceptual field, while all other sights, sounds, smells, feelings, etc., are blurrily merged into the ground (background).

Need-tensions influence the process of perception in three major ways. They determine perceptual selection (attention), perceptual thresholds, and the interpretation of sensory information (apperception).

1. NEED-TENSIONS AND PERCEPTUAL SELECTION (ATTENDING). The total perceptual field at any given moment comprises a great many things: sights, sounds, smells, etc. Need-tensions help to determine which sensory field and which content within it will be figure. Interests, attitudes, values, expectancy, emotions may all be viewed as special types of need-tension. Thus, the student reading this section will find that his visual field is predominant over other fields, and the words on this page are figure in contrast with the furniture in the room, the surface of the table on which the book rests, etc.

An individual can attend to anything which is available to his senses or which is "inside his head." Figure can be the perception of external or internal sensory changes, and it can also be the content of fantasy, or memory, or thinking. Thus, a person may be quite out of contact with things going on about him, because, at the moment, he is paying attention to his daydreams, or he is solving a mathematics problem, or thinking about the events which occurred on last night's date with a pretty girl.

The figure in an individual's *cognitive* field (which includes both the total perceptual field and the contents of fantasy, thinking, and remembering) can be regarded as a need-object, or related to need-objects. The figure in the total cognitive field is thus a need-determined *selection* from everything available to a person's awareness—sights and sounds, memories, daydreams, etc.

We learn a lot about a person's needs by studying what he attends to. A fashion-designer, sitting on a streetcar will notice all the clothing worn by the passengers, while the hungry man will notice only the aroma of fresh bread coming from a package held by the person next to him. The subjects in some starvation experiments at Minnesota [11] paid minute attention to food-advertisements in the magazines they read, and they thought about food almost unremittingly. Advertisers are well aware of the influence of needs on attending. They face the technical problem of making sure their advertisements are competing successfully with myriads of other stimuli for customers' attention. They strive to insure that their ads will contain attention-grabbing stimuli—stimuli that have relevance as objects for the needs of the observer. Advertising layouts in magazines thus utilize half-clad women, pictures of high-status people, etc., on the premise that these will pertain to the readers' needs.

2. NEED-TENSIONS AND PERCEPTUAL THRESHOLDS. To recognize something means to classify or label it accurately. Accurate recognition of some object—i.e., labelling it in a way that other observers would confirm—is referred to as *veridical* perception. The *recognition-threshold* refers to the intensity of the stimulus, or the amount of information provided to the observer, which enables accurate recognition. The problem of scaling and measuring the intensity of the stimulus is one which has been solved for various experimental purposes. If we were interested in visual recognition-thresholds, we could vary the illumination under which a stimulus was presented; or we could vary the length of time it was exposed to the observer. A high recognition-threshold means the stimulus must be presented at high degrees of intensity, while a low threshold means the stimulus can be recognized at low intensities.

A number of ingenious experiments have demonstrated that needs influence recognition-thresholds in two ways: by increasing them and by lowering them. An increased recognition threshold is referred to as *perceptual defense*. It is as if the individual has a need *not* to recognize, or to see some given object. This increase in threshold is very closely allied in meaning to the psychoanalytic concept of *denial*, which is defined as a defense mechanism a person engages in so he may be protected from painful perceptions.[12]

Eriksen [13] flashed pictures containing aggressive scenes, succorant scenes (scenes depicting passive, dependent care), and homosexual scenes at varying exposure-times to a group of psychiatric patients. It was known from the patients' life histories and from certain test scores that some had problems relating to hostility and aggression, others had intense dependency-needs, and others problems relating to homosexuality. Eriksen found significant positive relationships between "disturbance scores" on the tests which measured these need-areas and the degree of perceptual-threshold elevation for the corresponding need scenes. The more disturbed a person was with respect to hostility, passivity, and homosexuality, the higher was his recognition-threshold for scenes depicting those needs.

Perceptual defense is illustrated in everyday living by some homely examples. We are all familiar with the hero worshipper who cannot see blemishes in his paragon's appearance or conduct, even though these are quite obvious to his friends, who are not emotionally involved with the hero. Further, the worshipper needs much more evidence than an indifferent person before he will believe his hero *has* imperfections. We all need *not* to see certain things in order to feel right, and so we don't see them.

A reduction of recognition-thresholds is referred to as *perceptual sensitization,* or *vigilance.* In this instance, the individual is likely to recognize need-objects at very reduced intensities of exposure. The mother, anxious over her child's welfare, hears his call when no one else hears a sound. The doctor can hear his telephone when he is in the garden, but his guests do not. The prospector seeking gold can see the minute variations in rock color which signify the presence of the mineral, while a disinterested party sees nothing of the sort.

Stein [14] used a procedure similar to Eriksen's in testing thresholds for the recognition of aggressive pictures. He found that some of his subjects consistently showed *lower* recognition-thresholds (sensitization, or vigilance) for aggressive pictures than they did for neutral pictures, and other subjects consistently showed *higher* recognition thresholds for aggressive pictures than they did for neutral pictures. He concluded perceptual defense and perceptual sensitization are consistent modes of defense against unacceptable stimuli for different persons.

3. AUTISM AND PERCEPTION. Murphy defines autism as the "movement of cognitive processes in the direction of need-satisfaction." [15] Autistic perceptions are interpretations determined more by needs than by sensory data. When ambiguous stimuli are presented to a person, his interpretation of the stimuli will give more information about his needs than about the structure of the stimulus.

Autistic perceptions are referred to in psychiatry as *illusions* and as *hallucinations.*[16] An illusion is best described as a need-determined misinterpretation of some stimulus which is actually present. Autistic illusions must be distinguished from illusions which derive from peculiarities of the structure of the sensory apparatus, as for example, the well-known optical illusions. Autistic illusions always refer to interpretations of ambiguous stimuli or, if the needs are intense, autistic interpretations may be made even of highly structured and definite stimuli.

Illusions are common in the realm of "social perception," the interpretation of the motives and feelings of another person. The anxious person sees hostility in the behavior of people when they are not hostile. The lover sees love in the facial expression of his sweetheart, even when she despises him.

Hallucinations are perceptual experiences in the absence of any adequate stimulus. They are most often to be found among persons whom a psychiatrist would call psychotic. But this statement is not very helpful, because one of the reasons for calling a person psychotic is the presence of hallucinations. Hallucinations result from a loss of the ability to discriminate between subjective and objective, inner and outer, or between perception and imagination. A person may believe he hears voices, or sees visions, or feels touches—yet there is no objective stimulus present. Presumably, he has vividly imagined, or "imaged" these experiences, and is unaware he has created them. Night dreams are hallucinations; they comprise vivid perceptual experiences without benefit of environmental stimuli. The dreamer is not aware he is dreaming until he has awakened. The conscious hallucinator is like a person who cannot "wake up" (to empirical reality).

The content of autistic interpretations of reality will tell a trained investigator a lot about a person's hopes, wishes, fears or suspicions.

4. NEEDS AND PERCEPTUAL INTERPRETATION (APPERCEPTION). Perception is immediate in the normal course of events. A person sees or hears something which has a definite meaning to him. It is possible to slow down this rapid process experimentally so there is some delay between the awareness that something (a stimulus) is there and correct identification of the object.

The interpretation a person makes of any stimulus is quite subject to autistic influences when the stimulus is ambiguous, or when the needs are intense. Under these conditions, a person will assign a meaning to the stimulus that is more determined by his needs than by evidence or logic.

The behavior of another person is highly ambiguous with respect to its motivation [17] If we dislike someone, we are likely to interpret their motives in an unsavory light. If we love a person, we cannot conceive of them having a nasty or unpalatable motive for their actions, no matter how nasty the behavior may be.

The well-known projective tests of personality capitalize on this influence of needs on apperception. The Thematic Apperception Test, a collection of pictures of people, is presented to a subject, and he is asked to tell what the people are thinking, feeling, doing, etc. On the basis of his stories, the skilled interpreter infers a good deal of information about the needs of the subject. Many experimental investigations have been conducted utilizing stories which subjects make up to pictures from the TAT, incomplete sentences, etc., as indices of the strength of certain needs, viz., the "need for achievement" and the "need for affiliation." [18] The investigators analyze the stories which subjects make up about the test-stimuli and rate them for signs of need-strength. The stronger the need, the more powerful is its influence on behavior. Clinical psychologists use the TAT and other projective devices as a basis for making inferences about dominant needs, or defenses against needs, thus helping a therapist gain an understanding of his patient's symptoms.

NEEDS AND BELIEF. We behave in the world, not as it "is," but as we believe it to be. Psychologists speak in this connection of the "assumptive world," [19] or the phenomenal world. It should be apparent that we will behave differently with a person when we believe he hates us than if we believe he likes us. Yet it is possible for the beliefs to be wrong. Let us distinguish between veridical, or accurate beliefs and autistic beliefs, which are beliefs more determined by needs than by evidence or logic. It is not always easy to acquire accurate beliefs, but without them, our instrumental action can never be effective. Accurate beliefs steer our instrumental behavior to our goals.

Beliefs are likely to be autistic unless active steps are taken by the person to insure that they are veridical. In general, we tend to believe what we want or need to believe. To paraphrase Freud, the reality-principle always has to fight the pleasure-principle in cognition. We want to believe someone likes us, and so we do even though the evidence, if carefully sifted, would refute the belief. We need to believe we are honest, in order to maintain self-esteem. Yet, a careful survey of our own behavior would lead compellingly to the evaluation of ourself as dishonest. So we refrain from such a survey and continue to believe in our own virtue.

The scientist is so aware of the influence of wishes, hopes, or needs on belief that he takes elaborate precautions against believing anything about his subject-matter until these beliefs have been adequately checked. The author is well aware of the sneaky influence of autism on beliefs in research work. It has often happened when he has been running statistical computations that the results have supported his cherished hypotheses beyond his wildest dreams. A sober re-checking often has had the consequence of making the proof evaporate as a computation error.

A convenient name for autistic beliefs is already available for us in the field of psychiatry—the concept of *delusion*. A person will hang on to a delusion despite all efforts to dispel it. Thus, the paranoid individual cannot be convinced he is not Napoleon, and that people are not trying to kill him. But hospitalized psychotics are not the only persons with delusions. Every reader of this book has his repertoire of beliefs which are maintained because they "feel good," or because it would hurt to doubt these beliefs. An especially potent source of delusions is to be found in the collection of beliefs about one's own personality called the self-concept. In a later chapter we shall return to this theme, but we can anticipate our remarks by asserting that many of our cherished beliefs about our personality are autistic rather than veridical. Indeed, one of the aims in psychotherapy is to transform delusions about oneself into veridical beliefs.

NEED-TENSIONS AND FANTASY. The content of our daydreams and night dreams is wholly autistic. We dream about various need-satisfactions, our emotions are expressed in dreams, our wildest fears and hopes are materialized in our day and night dreams. The reader is asked to examine the content of his fantasies prior to falling asleep, or when he is relaxing after a meal. He will find they include murders of disliked people, fulfillment of ambitions, etc. The well-known story of Walter Mitty [20] illustrates nicely the autistic quality of fantasy. Sleeping dreams are usually very distorted and senseless as they are recalled. Yet Freud was able to show that the content of night dreams was primarily determined by unfulfilled wishes, or needs. He developed an elaborate theory [21] to account for the bizarre, often symbolical, content of dreams.

NEEDS, REMEMBERING, AND FORGETTING. The process of remembering past events is strongly influenced by need-tensions. The very activity of remembering is determined by one's momentary needs. We search our past experiences for solutions to present problems, for story-telling purposes, for the answers to examination questions, etc.

But we cannot blithely assume that everything we recall is veridical. Bartlett showed that recall from the past is distorted, highly selective, with some details added and other details dropped out, because of the effect of needs, cultural bias, interests, and attitudes.[22]

The experience of forgetting—an inability to recall events which one is certain one knows—is common to everyone. Freud was the first to suggest that forgetting is an active, need-determined process. He termed it *repression.* There is a diversity of clinical, anecdotal, and experimental evidence [23] to support the conclusion that much forgetting is a function of a need to forget in order to maintain self-esteem.

One can often infer many of the needs or feelings of an individual from observations of what is remembered, and what is forgotten. As a general principle, we might assert that people have a tendency to remember clearly only those past events which reflect favorably on their present concept of self.

Needs, Psychological Valences, and Canalization

Valence is a term Kurt Lewin borrowed from the physical sciences. He used it to describe the psychological experiences of "attractiveness" and "repulsion" induced by the things around us. We may speak of things as having positive, negative, and neutral valences for a person. Thus, when one is hungry, a well-spread table has positive valence. When one is gorged, the same table may repel the individual; it has negative valence. Things of no relevance as objects for a person's needs are said to have neutral valence.

Persons are not indifferent to the characteristics of possible need-objects. Every human establishes preferences for certain *kinds* of need-objects. There are millions of edible foodstuffs in the world, but a person will like, or prefer, only a narrow selection within this broader range. Hardly any middle-class Americans would eat grass-hoppers, crickets, wichety grubs, mule meat, cat, dog, or rat meat. Yet all these are edible, and there are societies in which they are preferred. The establishment of preferences in need-objects is referred to as *canalization*. One speaks of needs being canalized to various need-objects. Once canalizations are established, they seem to have marked stability. Murphy [24] asserts that they never change. Individuals develop a taste or preference in food, friends, music, art, even in scenery. Their needs never feel adequately satisfied except with the canalized objects. The author can readily eat hors d'oeuvres before a meal, and consume enough calories to constitute a meal. But to him, a meal, to be satisfying, must include meat, vegetables, salad, dessert, and coffee.

Need-canalizations help to define the individuality of a person, as well as his social group and class membership. The upper-class individual deplores the newly rich because they have such deplorable taste. In order to change one's social class, one must also change one's tastes. This is often difficult to do. The comic strip "Bringing up Father" illustrates the difficulty that Jiggs has in changing his lower-class tastes in food, fun, music, etc., so that they conform with those of the upper class.

Needs and Learning

Need-tensions provide the impetus for learning. When an individual wants or needs something, he must usually learn appropriate ways of behaving in order to obtain the need-object.

An individual's needs will impel a person to learn, and they help determine the content of learning: what is learned. An individual learns to speak in order to communicate with others. He learns to swim in order to stay afloat and move in water. He learns politeness in order to elicit favorable responses toward him from others. He learns cleanliness and obedience in order to avoid punishment and to obtain affection and acceptance. All of the learned traits of personality (in distinction to constitutional attributes) can be regarded as a record of past needs; so for that matter can all skills and habitual behavior-patterns which involve nonpersonal objects.

Needs also play a role in determining *how* we learn. There is an entire body of theory and research which explores the role of *reinforcement* in learning. Reinforcement is generally thought to consist in a reduction of need-tensions, and hence the subjective experience of satisfaction.

THE SATISFACTION OF NEEDS

Maslow aptly pointed out that psychologists devote too little attention to the phenomenon of need-satisfaction.[25] Yet many important consequences follow from need-satisfaction.

A need is said to be satisfied when the appropriate need-object has been obtained and related to in a way that removes, changes, or reduces the level and quality of felt tension. Eating a preferred food produces hunger gratification. Being told by some admired person that you are a fine man will gratify your need for affection or status.

Our guiding definition of healthy personality places a marked emphasis on need-satisfaction. There can be no healthy personality without satisfaction of the individual's basic needs. Later, we will draw a more precise distinction between basic, or healthy needs, and unhealthy needs.

What are the major consequences of need-satisfaction? The most obvious of these is the experience of "feeling good." This feeling is, of course, valued.

Another important consequence of need-satisfaction is the fact that when one need has been gratified, it becomes possible for new and "higher" needs to direct behavior. The more needs a person has gratified, the greater will be the diversity of new needs he will experience. With the arousal of new needs will come the necessity for learning new instrumental habits. The final consequence of need-diversity will be the enrichment and diversification of personality.

NEEDS AND FRUSTRATION

It is rare that a need-tension will be immediately reduced. There is always delay, an interval between the first awareness of a lack or want and the attainment of the appropriate need-objects. With delay, there is usually associated an increase in the level of tension experienced by the person. If the tension increases beyond a certain point (a level which varies from person to person on any given need, and which varies in the same person for different needs), the individual's behavior will become disorganized, inefficient, and irrational.

We shall reserve the word frustration to refer to the level of tension which produces *irrational, disorganized* conduct. This meaning of the word corresponds roughly to the usage adopted by Maier.[26] Maier distinguishes between motivated behavior and frustration-instigated behavior. The former refers to instrumental responses aimed at the attainment of a need-object. Frustration-produced behavior has as its sole aim the reduction of frustration tension. Consequently, it may not be very well adapted to the requirements of the environment. A frustrated person is one who cannot reason, whose behavior is no longer instrumental toward the attainment of usually valued ends and need-objects. All he can do is "blow off steam."

Frustration is undesirable from a personality-hygiene point of view. When it can be avoided, it is desirable that it should be. Delay in gratification is not a bad thing for personality hygiene, however. As long as the level of tension permits effective instrumental action, delay can actually promote personality health, for it makes sure a person will feel his tensions acutely enough to get into action. In addition, experience with delay helps to build up "frustration resistance," or *ego strength*—a desirable consequence for personality health.

The desirable reaction to tension-increase brought on by gratification delay or interference is one which involves: (a) increased persistence in efforts to attain the need-objects; (b) increased flexibility, or variability in the methods adopted to reach the goal; (c) if the need-objects cannot be obtained by these procedures, the healthy thing to do is seek a substitute need-object.

An example will illustrate the healthy reactions to gratification delay. A person may want very badly to obtain a date with a given girl. She refuses him. Her refusal may spur him to greater effort. He then modifies his approach; he changes his behavior so that it is more pleasing to her, he showers her with attention, etc. If she accedes, fine. If she does not, the man is wise to give her up and pursue some other girl. Naturally, this is not always easy to do—yet it must be done if we are to regard the individual as healthy.

If the young man's need-tensions increase beyond his frustration threshold, then we may expect to find any of a wide variety of frustration-produced behavior-patterns, none of which will attain the objective: a date with the girl. He may explode into anger; he may cry; he may withdraw from the situation before he has really tried; he may retreat into fantasies about conquest, etc,

FRUSTRATION-THRESHOLDS. (THRESHOLDS OF BEHAVIOR DISORGANIZA-TION.) We pointed out there is a level of tension below which the person can think rationally, and behave effectively. When the tension increases above this point, efficiency breaks down, and irrational thinking and expressive behavior take the place of rational thinking and instrumental action. This hypothetical point on the tension continuum is called the *frustration-threshold*. If we had some way of quantifying tension of all kinds—need-tensions and emotional tensions, irrespective of quality and source—it could be demonstrated that the frustration-threshold varies from person to person on a given need, and within the person for the same need at different times, or for different needs.

A housewife "needs" her house to be very neat, orderly and clean. In the forenoon, her three-year-old son might spill a glass of milk, leave his toys in disarray and scatter magazines all over the newly-cleaned living room. Her reaction at the time is one of mild anger, followed by efficient attempts to set things straight. At five-thirty in the afternoon, the child repeats his efforts at messing up the house. This time the mother "explodes"—she spanks the child, hurls some chinaware herself, and is unable to begin preparations for supper until she has vented all the tension the mess has provoked.

We do not know why frustration-thresholds vary within the person, or between persons. We can agree that frustration-produced behavior is unhealthy, since it prevents a person from keeping his wits in order to find satisfactions. There is personality-hygiene value in high frustration-thresholds. A good deal of basic psychological research is required in order to discover: (a) a means of quantifying tension independent of the need in question; (b) the amount of tension which produces disorganization; and (c) the correlates of frustration-thresholds as these vary between persons and within the person. When this research has been successfully accomplished, it will be possible to discover means for increasing frustration-thresholds in the general population, as a project in public personality hygiene.

Even without benefit of the fruits of systematic research, we can make a few observations about correlates of frustration-thresholds. It can easily be demonstrated that *optimum physical health* produces high frustration-thresholds. When a person is run-down, weak, fatigued, he is less able to carry out instrumental action in the face of interference and even minor stress. He frustrates easily.

A broad repertoire of skills will decrease the frequency of frustrating experiences, even if it doesn't affect the frustration-thresholds. The more skills a person has acquired, the less frequently he will be blocked in his quest for satisfying need-objects. The unskilled person is more likely to experience frustration than the competent person. The young child has many wants and few skills, and will generally experience frequent frustration unless adults intervene to make sure he enjoys a reasonable number of satisfactions.

FRUSTRATION AND DISORGANIZED BEHAVIOR. Instrumental behavior is generally quite flexible and variable; if one way of acting fails to secure the need-object, then the person tries behaving another way.

When delay or interference becomes great, or when the need-tensions are unduly high, the efficiency of the person's behavior breaks down.[27] He can no longer control his behavior and select the response patterns most likely to attain the need-objects. He is now frustrated, and he will manifest some form of disorganized behavior. If the disorganized behavior is allowed to run its course, it will reduce the tension-level to a point where rational, instrumental behavior again becomes possible. Frustration-produced behavior is not correlated with the demands of the environment, and as a consequence, the frustrated person behaves irrationally, he is "not himself," he has "lost control of himself." Now we shall ask, what are the common forms of disorganized behavior that are induced by frustration? They include aggressive behavior, regressive behavior, withdrawal and inactivity (depression), stereotypy, and the manifestation of various defense mechanisms, which include repression, projection, and rationalization. It should be pointed out that the behavior occurring during frustration is not subject to voluntary control—the frustrated person does not have choice. The frustration-produced behavior "just happens." Maier has shown with animal and human subjects, that behavior under frustration is generally *consistent*. Some people aggress, others cry, others withdraw—and they generally do this consistently. Some of Maier's frustrated rats made the same incorrect response hundreds of times, when forced to perform in the frustrated state—an excellent illustration of the way in which frustration can produce stereotyped and highly fixated behavior.[28]

CONFLICTING NEEDS

It is common for a person to experience conflict between wants, or need-tensions. He may want to study, and also to go out to the movies. He may want to marry one girl, and at the same time he loves another. He may want to have fun, but also be good.

We shall assert that the healthy thing to do with conflict is to admit its existence, study all the alternatives as rationally as one can in the light of one's value-system, make a decision, act on it, and accept all the consequences which follow. Among the consequences to be accepted are the regrets over what one has lost in connection with the abandoned alternatives. No decision can ever be made without some fear that it is the wrong decision. There is nothing inconsistent with personality health in the idea that a decision, once made, will still leave the person uncertain that it is the best or "rightest" one.

UNCONSCIOUS NEED-TENSIONS AND BEHAVIOR

Ordinarily a person behaves in ways that produce consequences he wants to produce. We are justified in assuming the consequences of an individual's responses are consciously intended. We can check this assumption readily by asking the individual why he did what he did. If he has no reason to lie, he will agree he behaved that way to produce the consequences he did.

But we may observe a person acting in ways that produce consequences he definitely did not want to produce. If he is asked, he will assert vigorously that he had no intention of producing those consequences. In these situations, the observer is justified in assuming that the behavior was influenced by unconscious motives. These include feelings, emotions, or, in more general terms, need-tensions.

What is an *unconscious need-tension*? As a rule, need-tensions are experienced by the person as a desire for something, a wish to do something, etc. Is it possible for a person to have need-tensions which he does not recognize? Does it make sense to speak of unconscious wishes, wants, feelings or emotions?

There is a lot of clinical and anecdotal evidence, supported by a little experimental verification, to support the assumption that unconscious motives exist and influence behavior. Freud was the first psychologist to devote systematic attention to the role of unconscious need-tensions in behavior, and since his first writings a good deal of attention has been devoted to the subject by other psychologists. A convincing experimental demonstration of unconscious motivation was published by Erickson.[29] He showed how persons could carry out post-hypnotic suggestions without knowing the real reasons. The real reasons were the hypnotist's commands. The experimental subject would make up reasons or rationalizations for his actions.

We may assume that need-tensions will influence behavior whether or not they are recognized and accurately labelled by the person who has them.

Why would any need-tensions become unconscious? Perhaps Freud was correct in assuming that the more appropriate question was rather, why will any needs become conscious?

We shall assert that a need-tension will be conscious, and accurately labelled by the person unless: (a) the individual's conscience comprises values which strongly condemn the very fact of having such needs, much less acting upon them; (b) the person has had experiences in the past where behavior instigated by the need-tensions resulted in extreme pain, loss of parental love, or punishment; in this case, the need-tension becomes a cue which triggers off anxiety; or (c) in the past, the longings for need-objects have met with frustration.

In these circumstances, the need-tensions will not be recognized, or acted on with appropriate instrumental responses. In the past, when they were recognized they led to guilt, anxiety, or the anticipation of frustration. In order to reduce these painful tensions, the person stopped thinking about the longings in question, and occupied his thoughts and awareness with other, less painful need-tensions. Repression is the name given to the response of "stopping thinking," [30] of not allowing oneself to think, remember, evaluate, or fantasy, about painful subject-matter.

But the need-tensions, or at least their physiological substratum, will persist in spite of repression, and continue to influence the behavior of the individual. The difference between conscious and unconscious needs lies in the fact that a person cannot control behavior provoked by unconscious determiners.

THE INFERENCE OF MOTIVES—CONSCIOUS AND UNCONSCIOUS. We continuously read, or try to read the motives of the other person. The most common bases that are employed for inferring the intentions, feelings, and needs of the other person are: (a) Observations of his facial expression, tone of voice, and gestures, which generally disclose what the person is feeling; and (b) Observations of the instrumental action and its consequences; from the actions and consequences, the observer formulates hypotheses as to the need-tensions of the behaver—his aims, intentions, wishes, etc.

Ordinarily, we are able to check our inferences about the motives of the other person by asking him. His verbal report is generally used to validate our hypotheses. He will correct us, agree with us, or disagree with our formulations of his motives.

When are we justified in assuming that the motives of the other person are unconscious? We can never be absolutely certain, but we can entertain the hypothesis of unconscious motivation (a) when the person acts in ways that produce consequences he *denies* intending to produce; (b) when he manifests many expressive signs of emotional tensions, feelings, etc., without acknowledging to the observer he feels any of these things; and (c) when there are obvious *inconsistencies* in behavior at different times, e.g., kindness and brutality, intelligent and stupid behavior.

In addition to these general "signs" of unconscious motivation, there are many other more subtle indicators that unconscious need-tensions may be present and operative. These include:

1. Dream-content which seems bizarre and incomprehensible to the dreamer.
2. Fantasy-content which surprises and shocks the day-dreamer.
3. Errors and slips in speech, writing, and gestures.
4. Body posturing and evidence of bodily tensions.
5. The forgetting of intentions, names, etc.
6. Accidents of all kinds.
7. Performance on certain projective tests.

ILLUSTRATIONS OF LIKELY INSTANCES OF UNCONSCIOUS MOTIVATION. The author, influenced by Freud's monumental books, the *Psychopathology of Everyday Life,* and the *Interpretation of Dreams* [31] has collected some examples from his experience that seem to disclose unconscious motivation.

1. AN EXAMPLE FROM DREAMS. A nine-year-old child was judged by all who knew him to be very "good." He was extremely obedient to his parents and affirmed his love for his father in almost every conversation with anybody. He related this dream to the author:

"I dreamed that I was a soldier, and we had a very mean and cruel officer. One day, when nobody was around, he was beating up a very nice lady. I took my machine gun and shot him a million times. He fell into a lot of little pieces when I was finished."

One does not have to be a professional interpreter of dreams to suspect that the officer was a symbolic version of his father, toward whom the boy had strong, but repressed hostility, while the "nice lady" was his mother, to whom he was very attached in oedipal fashion.

2. AN EXAMPLE FROM FANTASY. A student preparing for the ministry related with embarrassment and guilt that he was afraid to be alone, or without some busy-work to perform. When asked why, he said that as soon as he was idle, his mind filled with the most "sinful and voluptuous images of sex." He couldn't understand why this should be, as he was ordinarily a very upright and "clean-thinking" young man.

3. SLIPS OF THE TONGUE AND PEN. The following item came from a local newspaper: A minister had spent some time in Hollywood, and was interviewed by a local reporter with respect to his impressions. The article related how the minister deplored the moral turpitude of many of Hollywood's citizens. The article ended with this sentence (the italics are mine): "It is a shame the way our nation's best entertainers, in their lives offstage, are forever making *pubic* spectacles of themselves." The author does not know who was responsible for omitting the crucial *l* in the italicized word—the minister, the reporter, the copy-reader, or the linotypist.

4. EXAMPLES FROM BODY POSTURING AND TENSIONS. Fromm,[32] Reich,[33] and other psychoanalysts have suggested that variations in the muscle-tonus of parts of a person's body may reflect repressed

emotions and need-tensions. Fromm mentions that the person with a "receptive" character-orientation may have a very soft, almost suckling, mouth. Everyone has had the experience of a flaccid handshake from a person who denies that he is insincere. A female student complained that men were forever "making passes" at her, yet she denied having any erotic interest in males. Observation revealed she was extremely coquettish in her bodily movements. She wiggled her hips when walking, pushed her chest high; when talking with a man, she glued her eyes, alternately opened and narrowed, to his. Repressed hostility may be manifested by excessive muscular tension in the forehead, neck, or shoulders, often resulting in headaches, a "pain in the neck," and back pain.[34]

5. FORGETTING OF INTENTIONS, NAMES. The author "forgot" to write a letter of recommendation for a graduate student whom he disliked for a number of irrational reasons, and discovered this fact shortly after the deadline. Fortunately the student, who was competent, received the position without benefit of the letter.

6. ACCIDENTS. Accidents may result in disadvantage either to the person himself, or to others, depending upon the unconscious motivation—guilt in the former, hostility in the latter. A woman spilled ink on the manuscript her husband was working on (neglecting her as he did the work), as she cleaned his study. A man made a mistake which cost him his position, a position he had obtained in competition with a friend about whom he had secretly conveyed damaging information to the prospective employer.

7. EXAMPLES FROM PROJECTIVE TESTS. A 22-year-old undergraduate student consulted with the author for help with vague guilt feelings; an inability to study; and fierce headaches which occurred whenever he went home, or was obliged to spend any time with the Dean, one of two of his professors, or with the boss at a job where he worked regularly during the summer. He appeared to be extremely polite and deferential to authority. (He used the word sir in almost every sentence when talking to the author.) In the Thematic Apperception Test, many of his stories included some expression of violence and hatred toward the authority figures which were seen or imagined. About TAT Card 12M, which shows an old man stretching his hand toward the reclining figure of a younger man, the student told this story:

"This boy is having a nap. The old man, his father, is coming in to get him out of bed so he'll get back to his studies. His father has been nagging him for ages about how lazy he is. The boy has been putting up with this for a long time. This is the last straw. When he wakes up, he'll be so mad he'll start beating on his father. He'll grab a chair and start mashing in his head. When he finishes, his old man will be a bloody pulp. The boy will get the electric chair, but he won't care, it was worth it."

It is not too far-fetched to infer there is at least some unconscious hostility toward authority-figures in this young man.

There is no discovered way, as yet, to prove that an inference of unconscious motivation is warranted. Nevertheless, it can be shown that the motives a person will consider as possible determiners of his behavior will change under special circumstances. A patient entering psychotherapy may behave in ways that hurt or humiliate his wife; yet at the outset, he may vigorously deny having any hostile feelings toward her. As the therapy proceeds, he may gradually entertain the hypothesis he has hostile feelings toward her. Finally he can admit having hostile feelings, without any guilt or anxiety whatsoever. In addition, his hostility, if rational and warranted, may come to be expressed much more openly than was the case before. And it very often happens that recognition and understanding of irrational hostility will reduce or eliminate it.

UNCONSCIOUS MOTIVES AND HEALTHY PERSONALITY. The personality hygienist regards repression, generally, as an unhealthy mechanism and unconscious motives as unhealthy motives. The reason for this condemnation lies in the fact that it is only when one's own needs are accurately diagnosed that one can effectively find ways of gratifying them. Repressed needs must remain chronically unfulfilled needs. Their influence on behavior is chronic and interferes with the emergence into consciousness of other, higher needs.

In addition to the above reason the personality hygienist condemns unconscious needs as unhealthy because the mechanism of repression is regarded as an undesirable or unhealthy way of solving problems. Repression is undertaken because of an overly strict conscience or self-ideal—it is regarded as healthier to attempt to change the conscience and self-ideal or to accept the fact that one is not as "good" as one would like to believe. Repression is undertaken as a means of warding off anxiety. There are more effective and healthier ways of handling anxiety. Repression is undertaken to ward off the possibility of painful frustration. There are healthier ways of avoiding frustration, including learning more effective skills. It is only in instances where repression forestalls serious psychosis that a personality hygienist would regard repression as desirable. There are some persons with latent personality illnesses who are able to ward off an acute onset of manifest symptoms only by *sustained* repression. In these cases, repression may be said to serve a useful function—repression is the lesser of two evils.

Healthy and Unhealthy Needs

Can we evaluate needs from a personality-hygiene point of view? Can we speak of healthy needs? Unhealthy needs? If so, what are our criteria for determining whether or not a need is healthy?

healthy needs. Healthy needs contribute to a person's continued growth toward self-actualization. Whatever a person wants or needs in order more fully to develop his potential individuality must be regarded as a healthy need. People differ widely in what they need in order to grow, just as plant and animal forms differ in what they need to develop fully. Yet humans also share many needs, simply because they are human.

Maslow's [35] well-known hierarchy of human needs serves as an excellent illustration of a hypothesis concerning shared requisites to personality growth toward self-actualization. Maslow asserts that people have physical needs, safety needs, love needs, and esteem needs. If all of these are successively gratified; that is, if the person can get enough food, rest, water; reassurance as to freedom from danger to his physical life; love and esteem from others, then it will be possible for him to grow toward self-actualization. There is basic validity in Maslow's need-hierarchy hypothesis. When a person is starving, he will ignore everything else in his quest for food. When he is in danger of death, he will drop all else in order to save himself. If he is well fed and safe, the affection and love of others may become important; but it will not be important if he is starving or in danger. He will probably ignore the demands and opinions of people whose affection is important to him if he is starving. But if he is loved, he may then pursue recognition for achievements. Yet he may forego these efforts if his love-life is in jeopardy. Many ambitious people are unable to produce good work when their affectional life is unsatisfactory. The acme of personality development in Maslow's scheme is the self-actualizing person. The most important value for the self-actualizer is dedication to some art, science, or cause. Maslow regards self-actualization as improbable except under conditions of prior gratification of the needs lower in the hierarchy. It is obvious that a distinction must be drawn between an artist, or scientist, who performs his craft in order to obtain recognition, and the true self-actualizer, who follows his craft where it leads him, despite unpopularity, or persecution. Freud may be viewed as a self-actualizer; he pursued his psychoanalytic work in spite of poverty, ostracism, and active professional opposition.

A useful question to ask is: "What does person X need in order to grow?" Because of marked individual differences in gratification history, it is apparent that each person will have an idiosyncratic set of requirements that must be fulfilled before he can grow closer toward self-actualization. One person might need more unconditional love; another might need more recognition; another might need to move to a safer environment. Still another might need to be nursed at the breast at age 50, in order to gratify infantile need-tensions so that higher needs can emerge.

A personality therapist is trained to diagnose what a patient needs in order to move closer to healthy personality. He then provides what is needed, or steers the patient in ways which will lead him to the needed satisfactions.

For example, a person with an unhealthy personality may seek professional help. After a period of observation, the therapist may begin to suspect the person is uncertain about his basic lovability; his "symptoms" consist in behavior which indicates a lack of adequate love and, at the same time, an attempt to secure love which fails. The therapist conveys by his attitude toward the patient that he accepts him, or likes him. Over a period of time, the patient may come to feel accepted or loved by his therapist. He changes his behavior toward him and simultaneously toward other people. New needs emerge, and he learns new behavior-patterns in order to gratify them. His personality has thus changed, and he is moving again in the direction of self-actualization, rather than stultifying in his previous impasses.

UNHEALTHY NEEDS. A need is unhealthy when its gratification does not contribute to the further growth of the person, when it actually prevents further growth. A person may pursue certain need-objects for the satisfactions they afford. As long as he pursues just those goals, he may be perpetuating his present status as an unhealthy personality.

The long range consequences of gratifying some need are the clearest indications of whether or not it is a healthy need. It has long been recognized by professional moralists, laymen, and psychologists, that the pleasure-principle will get a person in trouble. Children have been advised by Aesop to "look before they leap"; most parents' efforts are aimed at inculcating a sense of foresight in the children. One of the early recognized criteria of maturity, i.e., valued behavior, was the ability to substitute the reality-principle for the pleasure principle. This means the ability to postpone "impulse-discharge" until reality-testing is carried out. From these considerations we can conclude that a given need is unhealthy, not per se but rather when the consequences which follow from its gratification jeopardize other values, especially growth toward self-actualization.

Let us give some examples of unhealthy needs. In order to feel calm, and free from anxiety or guilt, a person might need to drink enough whisky to become mildly intoxicated. Since there are other, healthier, ways to get rid of painful tensions, we should have to regard his need for alcohol as an unhealthy need. Why? Because the alcohol may indeed relieve tensions, in the short run, but nothing is being done by the person to alter the conditions responsible for the guilt or anxiety in the first place.

In order to maintain self-esteem, it may be important for a person (i.e., he needs) continuously to enhance his power or prestige. If he pursues his job activities exclusively, other interests or values will suffer. For example, his marriage, or relations with his children, may deteriorate measurably. In order to improve them, it might be necessary to spend less time, effort and thought on his job. He may find it difficult to drop his job long enough to straighten up the home front, since time off the job signifies to him that he is falling behind, or losing in the race for top position. Many marriages have been ruined because a person's self-esteem was wholly dependent upon his job, so that he could not attend to other needs and interests.

Maslow has pointed out that unhealthy needs, such as the compulsive need for safety, sexuality, job-success, approval by others, cruelty, etc., are derived from an insufficiency of gratification of healthy needs. That is, these goals for instrumental behavior—reassurance, frequent sex experiences, promotions in rank and salary, indiscriminate approval from others, the destruction of other people —all stem from insufficiencies of gratification of health-promoting needs. The implication is clear that if a person is fed and physically tended, if he is raised in physical safety, if he is loved enough and reassured as to his worth and value as a person—he will then be less likely to pursue these substitute goals in life in a compulsive fashion, and will have more chances of "actualizing" himself.

A SUGGESTED CATALOGUE OF VALUED ENDS

Maslow's theory of human motivation speaks of a "hierarchy of needs." In the light of the foregoing discussions, we would assert that satisfaction, safety, love, esteem, and self-actualization are not needs, but rather values, or valued ends. The abstract term "need" actually implies valued ends. Need always implies needing something (the object) *for* the attainment or preservation of a valued end.

Now, let us present a fairly systematic way of thinking about values and needs. We shall present a brief list of some common valued ends, a list of the kinds of instrumental action necessary to attain these, the kinds of need-objects which are required as means to these ends, and some of the consequences of failure to attain the valued ends. Later, we shall comment on some of the consequences which follow when a person does not have these values (and hence the needs), and when he does not arrange them into a hierarchy which society defines as the "right" hierarchy.

The following table probably includes most of the values which determine needs and direct the behavior of people in our society.

Now we can assert that each society has its characteristic system of values, and more than that, we can assert that there is a more or less rigidly defined hierarchy into which these values of a society are

Valued End	Instrumental Action	Need-Objects	Common Deprivation Symptoms
Physical health.	A diet and daily regime which maintains health, and forestalls infection, trauma, debilitation.	Food, clean surroundings, absence of chronic environmental stresses.	Any and all symptoms of physical illness, including pain, weakness.
Physical gratification.	Eating, drinking, sexual intercourse, elimination of urine and feces, body massage, relaxation.	Food, fluids, a mate, etc.	Frustration, fantasy and preoccupation about need-objects, inability to undertake other pursuits.
Good appearance.	Grooming, diet, exercise, cosmetics, plastic surgery.	Nice clothes, good food, cosmetics.	Inferiority feelings.
Security of life, health, and present sources of gratification.	Taking precautions against dangers; anticipating danger and neutralizing it, or escaping from it.	A special arrangement of the physical and social environment which signifies safety and security.	Anxiety, worry, inability to pursue other ends while danger is at hand.
Affection from desired sources.	The behavior which is necessary to "win" affection from other people.	Responses from other persons which signify affection, e.g., kisses, hugs, the words "I like you."	Anxiety, low self-esteem, depression. Inability to pursue other ends, or a compensatory quest for other ends to make up for lack of affection; or a compulsive quest for affection at any cost to other values.

55

Valued End	Instrumental Action	Need-Objects	Common Deprivation Symptoms
Understanding of self by valued others.	Honest communication of one's "real self."	A person who shares one's values, and who is permissive and accepting.	Loneliness, hostility to others, anxiety.
Passive care.	Behavior which promotes love from others.	A parent, spouse, or very close friend.	Anxiety, compulsive quest for independence.
Recognition for achievements.	Actual achievements that are valued.	Appreciative people.	Resentment, hostility, boastfulness.
Self-esteem.	Behavior which accords with conscience and self-ideal. Actual achievements.	Actual success; symbols of achievement and respectability.	Guilt, inferiority feelings, anxiety over loss of status, envy of people with higher status, self-hate, depression.
Release of emotional tensions.	Expressive behavior: laughing, crying, release of hostility.	A permissive social environment—persons who will not punish or penalize for expressing feelings.	Chronic emotional tensions, inability to work or to concentrate, muscular pain, headaches, psychosomatic symptoms.
Similarity to valued others.	Identification, conforming behavior.	Valued models available; acceptance by a valued group.	Anxiety, fear that other values are in jeopardy because one is different.

Valued End	Instrumental Action	Need-Objects	Common Deprivation Symptoms
Sense of identity.	Expression of real self.	Permissive social environment which values some individuality. Acceptance of person *as he is* by others.	Feelings of powerlessness, of "self-alienation," of being a "nobody."
Contemplation of beauty.	Looking, listening.	Nature, art, music, literature.	Boredom, feeling of emptiness.
Life-philosophy.	Study, thinking, worship.	Wisdom from people, experience and books; a place of worship.	Anxiety, aimlessness, feeling that life has no point or purpose.
Personality growth.	Challenging work, meeting new people, loving others.	Work, opportunity to travel, study; new people.	Boredom, impasses in relationships with people, unhappiness.
Autonomy.	Learning new skills.	Money, challenge.	Feeling dependent and insecure.
Happy and growing dependents.	Love.	Spouse, children, close friends.	Feeling selfish, useless, "unfulfilled."

arranged. The successfully socialized member of a society is one who has adopted, or "internalized" the values and their hierarchical arrangement. He is what might be meaningfully called well-adjusted to his culture. The *happy* member of a society is one who has been able to implement these values, to attain them in ways which are approved by the society. It is only when all members of a society share similar values, and arrange them in a similar hierarchy that we can then say they have similar needs. It is only when physical satisfaction is valued, or long life, that food and shelter can be viewed as needs. As values change, or as their hierarchical order changes, so will change the needs of a person. He who does not value status, for example, does not need to act in ways which would be instrumental in attaining it. The abstainer doesn't need liquor, and the celibate doesn't need women.

Needs, then, must not be viewed as fixed things, or as "givens"; rather, the word need always refers to a judgment of what is required as a means toward any specific valued end. A healthy personality is able to get what he needs in order to arrive at his valued ends. These valued ends are not at odds with his society's values (although at times the healthy personality may be a rebel),[36] and the instrumental behavior which he engages in is consistent with social mores and with his own conscience.

THE HEALTHY PERSONALITY AND HIS NEEDS

In this section we will switch our focus away from a technical discussion of needs and look at needs as they appear in a hypothetical healthy personality.

Maslow already has written extensively on this subject,[37] and we will refer the reader to his contributions, limiting ourselves to a more general overview.

The healthy personality is fully cognizant of his needs whenever they arise. He does not repress or distort them but strives to identify and label them with accuracy. He may suppress any action with reference to needs which his value-system does not affirm, but he at least knows what he is foregoing and why. Even feelings and needs of which he is ashamed, because of their infantile or antisocial nature, he will admit as his own, though he will not act on their promptings.

Thus, a healthy adult personality may be able to admit longings to be cared for like an infant, or to engage in socially unacceptable sexual activities, but he would be unlikely to act on these promptings. He simply admits that they exist.

The healthy personality, because of a rich gratification history, is not pursuing physical gratifications, security, or fame in a compulsive fashion; rather, he is motivated by the desire to grow, to become more himself, to find and to make actual the potentialities which are inherent in his make-up.

SUMMARY

Behavior may be analyzed into need-satisfaction sequences. A *need* is defined as a *judgment* which a person makes concerning what he requires in order to attain some valued end. A *need-object* is that which the person believes will produce satisfaction. In order to obtain need-objects the person engages in *instrumental behavior.* Instrumental behavior is under voluntary control, it is flexible, and it is organized, or selected, for its instrumental value as a means of attaining desired need-objects. Instrumental behavior is possible only when tensions of all kinds are kept below some critical level. When tensions rise beyond this level, called the *disorganized-behavior-threshold,* instrumental behavior breaks down, and disorganized behavior takes its place.

Need-tension is the word used to describe the subjective experience of *wanting something.* Need-tensions are important determiners of instrumental action. Need-tensions succeed one another, they always involve some delay, they may conflict one with the other, and they may be conscious or unconscious.

Need-tensions impose an influence on perception by helping to determine perceptual selection, perceptual thresholds, and apperception. *Autism* is the term used to describe the fact that perception will be unrealistic unless active steps are taken by the person to counteract the influence of need-tensions on cognition. Need-tensions will impose a strong influence on *beliefs, fantasy, remembering,* as well as on perception. Need-tensions help to determine psychological *valences,* and preferences from among need-objects (*canalizations*) are established as a consequence of satisfaction. Needs impose a strong influence both on what is learned, as well as on the process of learning itself.

Need-satisfaction enables new need-tensions to arise and influence behavior.

When needs are not gratified, need-tensions may increase to the point where instrumental behavior is no longer possible, and disorganized behavior replaces it. When need-tensions increase beyond the critical point where instrumental action is no longer possible, we speak of *frustration*. The frustration-*threshold* is the tension-level at which disorganized behavior emerges. Disorganized behavior may also be referred to as *frustrated* behavior.

When need-tensions are in conflict, the valued activity for the person to engage in is *decision*.

Need-tensions may be *unconscious*, and yet influence behavior. The observer may infer the presence and nature of unconscious need-tensions, or motives, by studying the dreams and fantasies, errors and accidents, body-posture, and incidents of forgetting, which a person may manifest.

Needs are referred to as healthy when their satisfaction produces consequences that a personality hygienist would call healthy.

Since needs refer to judgments about what will be effective in attaining various *valued ends*, a suggested list of common valued ends is presented. These include physical health, physical satisfaction, good appearance, security, affection, being understood, passive care, recognition, self-esteem, release of emotional tensions, similarity to others, a sense of identity, contemplation of beauty, a life-philosophy, personality growth, autonomy, and happy dependents.

NOTES AND REFERENCES

RECOMMENDED READINGS ARE MARKED WITH AN ASTERISK (*)

*1. Cameron, N. and Magaret, A., *Behavior pathology*, New York, Houghton Mifflin, 1951. See pp. 32–43 for an excellent discussion of need-satisfaction sequences.

*2. Murphy, G., *Personality: a biosocial approach to origins and structure*, New York, Harper, 1947, p. 992. See also, Maslow, A. H., "Deficiency motivation and growth motivation," in M. R. Jones (ed.), *Nebraska Symposium on Motivation,* Lincoln, University of Nebraska Press, 1955.

3. Krech, D. and Crutchfield, R. S., *Theory and problems of social psychology,* New York, McGraw-Hill, 1948, pp. 40–42.
4. Murray, H., *et al.,* *Explorations in personality,* New York, Oxford University Press, 1938, p. 124.
5. Snygg, D. and Combs, A., *Individual behavior,* New York, Harper, 1949.
°6. Maslow, A. H., *Motivation and personality,* New York, Harper, 1954, pp. 179–186, 296.
°7. See the excellent discussion of disorganized behavior in Cameron and Magaret, *op. cit.,* Ch. 15. In this connection, see also the extensive bibliography put out by the Army: *A bibliography for the development of stress-sensitive tests,* PRB Technical Research Note 22, Dept. of the Army, the Adjutant General's Office, 1953.
8. Kempf, E., *The autonomic functions and personality,* Washington, Nerv. & Ment. Dis. Pub., 1918. Kempf expounded the very plausible view that the source of tensions giving rise to instrumental behavior was imbalance, or "segmental cravings" associated with the autonomic nervous system. The central nervous system was ascribed the function of ascertaining what stimuli were needed in order to restore autonomic balance, and to steer behavior toward the appropriate need-objects. There is also reason to believe that a person engages in instrumental action—motor, intellectual, and perceptive, for its own sake—*for the sheer pleasure of performing.* See Murphy, G., *op. cit.,* on "activity drives" and "sensory drives," pp. 107–116. Also Hendrick, I., "Work and the pleasure principle," *Psychoanalyst. Quart.,* 1943, **12,** 311–329.
9. Murphy, G. *op. cit.,* p. 982.
10. Krech, D. and Crutchfield, R. S., *op. cit.,* Ch. 5, 6.
11. Franklin, J. C., Schiele, B. C., Brozek, J. and Keys, A., "Observations on human behavior in experimental semistarvation and rehabilitation," *J. clin. Psychol.,* 1948, **4,** 28–44.
12. Fenichel, O., *The psychoanalytic theory of neurosis,* New York, Norton, 1945, pp. 144–146.
13. Eriksen, C. W., "Perceptual defense as a function of unacceptable needs," *J. abn. soc. Psychol.,* 1951, **47,** 302–308.
14. Stein, K. B., "Perceptual defense and perceptual sensitization under neutral and involved conditions," *J. Pers.,* 1953, **21,** 467-478.
15. Murphy, G., *op. cit.,* p. 980.

16. See Cameron, N. and Magaret, A., *op. cit.*, pp. 392–405, for a discussion of delusions, and pp. 426–477 for a discussion of hallucinations.

17. Cameron, N. and Magaret, A., *op. cit.*, pp. 374–375, for a fuller discussion of this point.

18. McClelland, D., *et al.*, *The achievement motive*, New York, Appleton-Century-Crofts, 1953, gives a report of the work on the achievement-need. See French, Elizabeth, and Chadwick, Irene, "Some characteristics of affiliation motivation," *J. abn. soc. Psychol.*, 1956, **52**, 296–300 for a report of an experiment dealing with the affiliation-motive.

19. A convenient summary for the interested student of this point of view is given in Ittelson, W. H. and Cantril, H., *Perception: a transactional approach*, Garden City, New York, Doubleday, 1954.

20. Thurber, James, "The secret life of Walter Mitty" in Thurber, J., *My world and welcome to it*, New York, Harcourt, Brace, 1937.

°21. Freud, S., *The interpretation of dreams*, in Brill, A. A. (ed.), *The basic writings of Sigmund Freud*, New York, Modern Library, 1938.

°22. Bartlett, F. C., *Remembering*, London, Cambridge University Press, 1932.

23. See the series of articles concerned with this area of research, viz.: Rosenzweig, S., "An experimental study of 'repression' with special reference to need-persistive and ego-defensive reactions to frustration," *J. exp. Psychol.*, 1943, **32**, 64–74. Alper, Thelma G., "Memory for completed and incompleted tasks as a function of personality: an analysis of group data," *J. abn. soc. Psychol.*, 1946, **41**, 403–420. Eriksen, C. W., "Psychological defenses and 'ego strength' in the recall of completed and incompleted tasks," *J. abn. soc. Psychol.*, 1954, **49**, 45–50. Jourard, S. M., "Ego strength and the recall of tasks," *J. abn. soc. Psychol.*, 1954, **49**, 51–58. The present author's study did not confirm the findings of the other workers.

24. Murphy, G., *op. cit.*, Ch. 8.

25. Maslow, A. H., *op. cit.*, Ch. 6.

26. See Maier's book for a detailed description of his researches and his theory of frustration. Maier, N. R. F., *Frustration. The study of behavior without a goal*, New York, McGraw-Hill, 1949.

27. See note 7 for a bibliography of research which documents this assertion.

28. Maier, N. R. F., *op. cit.*

29. Erickson, M. G., "Experimental demonstrations of the psychopathology of everyday life," *Psychoanal. Quart.*, 1939, **8**, 338–353.

30. *Cf.* Dollard, J. and Miller, N. E., *Personality and psychotherapy*, New York, McGraw-Hill, 1950, p. 220.

31. In Brill, A. A., *op. cit.*

32. Fromm, E., *Man for himself*, New York, Rinehart, 1947.

33. Roich, W., *Character analysis*, New York, Orgone Institute Press, 1949.

*34. See Moloney, J. C., *The magic cloak: A contribution to the psychology of authoritarianism*, Wakefield, Mass., Montrose Press, 1949, pp. 99–101. See also Ch. 13 for a discussion of diverse psychosomatic symptoms which Moloney found to be associated with repressed hostility in persons who lived in authoritarian social settings. The entire book is an excellent treatise on authoritarianism. For experimental demonstrations of muscular tension, see Malmo, R. B., Shagass, C. and Davis, J. F., "Electromyographic studies of muscular tension in psychiatric patients under stress," *J. clin. exper. Psychopath.*, 1951, **12**, 45–66.

35. Maslow, A. H., *op. cit.*

*36. See Lindner, R., *Prescription for rebellion*, New York, Rinehart, 1952. Also Riesman, D., *Individualism reconsidered*, Glencoe, Illinois, The Free Press, 1954, especially Ch. 6, "The saving remnant." These authors and others, including Fromm and Maslow, point out the dangers of *over*conformity to society, and the importance of the ability to affirm one's own individuality when this is opposed by society. Rank and Neitzsche also held these views. We would assert that rebellion per se is not healthy.

37. See especially Maslow, A. H., *op. cit.*, note 2.

QUESTIONS FOR REVIEW AND EXAMINATION

1. What is a human "need"? What is meant by need-objects?

2. What is instrumental behavior? How does it differ from disorganized behavior?

3. How do skills contribute to personality health?

4. What are the major general characteristics of need-tensions?

5. In what major ways do need-tensions help to determine cognition? Valences and canalization? Learning?

6. Define and illustrate what is meant by autism in perception, memory, and thinking.

7. What consequences follow from need-satisfaction? From need-deprivation?

8. Why are many motives unconscious? How do unconscious motives betray themselves to the observer? Why are unconscious needs thought to be unhealthy?

9. What is the difference between a healthy need and an unhealthy need?

10. What is the connection between needs and values? List some common valued ends, and the needs which they give rise to.

11. Use the concepts employed in this chapter as the basis for describing and evaluating the needs and behavior of someone you know, and of yourself.

CHAPTER 3

Reality-Contact and Healthy Personality

A person's beliefs and tacit assumptions about the world play a fundamental role in the determination of his behavior. For instance, if he assumes the ground on which he is standing will support his weight, he will walk over that ground without giving the matter another thought. If he believes that another person is hostile toward him, he may become anxious or angry, and he may avoid or even strike the other person.

We have seen (in Chapter 2) that beliefs about the world may not always be accurate. Needs and emotions, wishes, and lack of sufficient information, may all promote the acquisition and affirmation of beliefs which are false. False beliefs about the world interfere with the effectiveness of instrumental behavior; they are responsible for interpersonal relationships which are marked by misunderstandings and impasses; they cause a person to make inappropriate emotional responses—in short, personality health would appear to be impossible of achievement in the absence of accurate beliefs.

The person suffering from a personality illness such as hysteria or schizophrenia can be shown to have beliefs about himself and about other people, animals, etc., which simply are not true. Consequently, his behavior will appear strange to an observer. His

65

reactions will make sense only when the observer learns how the patient perceives the world and what he believes about it.[1] The individual with a personality illness is often described as a sufferer from inefficient *reality-contact.*

When a person has efficient reality-contact, he formulates accurate beliefs about the world. Since reality-contact plays such a crucial role in personality health—indeed it is a sine qua non—it will repay us to inquire in more detail into the means by which we acquire beliefs and test them for accuracy and truth.[2]

SOURCES OF BELIEF

A person's major sources of belief are *perception, authority, intuition, memory,* and *imagination.*

PERCEPTION AND BELIEF. An old saying states that "seeing is believing." For centuries, the assumption has been that one's senses do not lie, that perception is the final test of a proposition or belief. Yet students of perception have been able to show with many demonstrations [3] that the senses will tell the truth only under special conditions. Unless these conditions are met, the senses will lie.[4]

The more appropriate question to ask concerning perception would seem to be, "Under what conditions will a person identify some object before him as a tree rather than something else?" not, "Why, when a person is confronted with a tree, will he see that tree?" When the question is stated the first way, it shows clearly that it is possible to vary a stimulus in many ways; and it is possible to leave the stimulus constant, vary some aspect of the person, and yet have the person believe there is a tree before him.

We can do most justice to the facts gathered about the process of perception if we assert that *accurate perception is not a "given," but rather it is an achievement.*

The upshot of this proposition is that, though we may believe what we see (or hear, smell, or feel), yet our belief may be unwarranted. The belief only becomes warranted when it has been tested. In fact, the personality hygienist can state with almost dogmatic emphasis the following rule of thumb: since accurate beliefs about the world are essential to healthy behavior, the person is advised to view all of his perceptions as *hypotheses,* postponing action

on the basis of them until after these hypotheses have been checked.
The wanderer in the desert "sees" an oasis, and believes that it is
there; when he arrives at the approximate location, he finds nothing.
He has "seen" a mirage. The psychotic sees visions, hears voices,
and feels things crawling over him; he believes that some stimuli
are responsible for these experiences. Yet, no other observer can see
these things when he reports their presence. He is "hallucinating."
Recently, pharmacologists have been experimenting with the drugs
lysergic acid and mescaline, which induce visual hallucinations.
These drugs illustrate how a visual perception which the observer
fully "believes," can be induced experimentally.

By means of hypnosis, a person can be induced to see things which
are not there, and he can be induced not to see things which are
there. These kinds of evidence should suffice to show that seeing is
not grounds for believing. The more appropriate way to put it would
be, "Seeing is grounds for suspecting." When a person reports some
extraordinary perception, for example, a flying saucer, it can be assumed some factor has been responsible for the perceptual experience. But in view of the more profound knowledge which students
of perception have acquired concerning perceptual processes, it is
naive to assume that an external stimulus is the only possible factor
which could have induced the conviction a flying saucer was actually there. Subjective factors, such as wishes, fears, expectancies,
coupled with an ambiguous stimulus field, could readily account for
the experiences which underlie reports of such observations.

The interests of personality health are best served when an individual regards the evidence of his senses as hypotheses which will
not be regarded as warranted beliefs until after they have been
subjected to critical reasoning and further observations.

AUTHORITY AND BELIEF. A person may act on beliefs which were
acquired from some authority: a person, a book, or public opinion.
Such beliefs would facilitate effective instrumental action only if
the authority had tested them and found them valid. It is a good
thing from a personality-hygiene standpoint, to have authoritative
sources of authentic, tested beliefs about all manner of things. But
this proposition must be qualified. The person who would attain or
preserve personality health is advised to regard the pronouncements
of authority-figures as *hypotheses* just as he regards his own per-

ceptions and inferences. They should not be believed as fixed truths to be acted upon until critical appraisal has been attempted. Naturally, there are occasions when it is urgent that a person act on the basis of authoritative beliefs, but as a rule, corroborative attempts should be undertaken by the person to insure maximally successful action. Authorities can be wrong.

There is a healthy way in which authorities may be used,[5] as the following paragraph will show. When a person wants to know something with certainty, and his personal experience is too limited for him to know the answers, he can consult any authoritative source who seems likely to possess the desired facts. But when the questions have been answered, or the rules for action laid down by the authority, the individual should then seek to test, criticize, or otherwise appraise the validity of the beliefs he has acquired. If it is a matter of fact about which he is concerned, he might cross-examine his authority to determine the nature and quality of the evidence upon which the facts have been grounded; or he might check the pronouncements of his authority against some other sources, e.g., the library, or other experts. If the questions which the person brought to an authority-figure were concerned with ways and means of doing things, then the individual can try out the suggested ways and means along with others, to determine which ways are the most efficacious. If rules for action are not periodically tested and compared, a person may follow an authority's advice for years, overlooking the possibility that there are better ways of doing things.

A highly dependent person has little faith in his own ability and is usually "alienated from his real self."[6] He would likely be unable to trust his own judgments and observations, and would therefore seek out authoritative sources for knowledge and for rules of action. Such a person would be secure only so long as his authority-figures were accessible. If anything separated him from them, he would feel lost and anxious. There is obvious personality hygiene value in being able to arrive at knowledge autonomously.

INTUITION AS A SOURCE OF BELIEF. Some people believe things on the basis of intuition. The dictionary definition of intuition is as follows (Webster): "Immediate apprehension or cognition." It implies that something is known to be true on self-evident grounds, or on the basis of a very strong feeling of truth. Evidence and critical reasoning are not involved in intuitive beliefs—they are just felt to be true. Examples of intuitive beliefs are the conviction someone loves you or hates you, the belief in God, etc.

Beliefs arrived at through intuition must be assessed by the student of personality hygiene in the same way as beliefs obtained through perception and from authority: they must be regarded as hypotheses of doubtful validity until they have been subjected to critical scrutiny and test.

Another word that is more often used by the layman for intuitive beliefs is *hunch*. A person seldom can tell what cues or signs were responsible for his hunches; he only knows that from time to time he experiences a hunch—about the prospective winner of a horse race, about another person, about the impending death of someone near and dear—and this hunch carries a very powerful feeling of truth with it. In consequence, the person may act on his hunches, in spite of logical evidence and common sense. Concerning hunches and first impressions, the following may be said. When they are formulated by competent experts in some field, they may indeed be very accurate and valid. Many physicians can make diagnoses of diseases on the basis of intuition, or hunch, and they cannot specify to an intern exactly why they arrive at just that diagnosis, which turns out later to be quite correct. But since there is no magic in the world, it is possible in principle to ascertain the empirical cues which produce hunches. Oddly enough, there are unhealthy personalities who make a sort of fetish out of hunches and intuitions. They distrust conventional scientific modes of inquiry and the beliefs which they yield, and prefer to base their action on hunches, intuition, and inspiration. Whenever there is a choice between a rationally arrived-at belief, and one predicated on intuition, they habitually choose the latter. There is evidence to show that the late Adolf Hitler directed his battles on the basis of intuition, often against the reasoned advice of his military experts. The fact that he was right from time to time doesn't prove the superiority of his intuition over military science. Hitler won battles and lost a war.

Hunches and intuition might better be called *wishes*. Very often the belief which has been arrived at through intuition coincides nicely with a person's wishes. The fact that from time to time hunches turn out true may be attributed to chance rather than to any other explanation. If an impersonal statistical count were made of the relative correctness of hunches and reasoned, tested beliefs, it would inevitably be found that hunches lose out in the comparison. Maybe people become addicted to acting on hunches in accordance with this learning-theory precept: aperiodic reinforcement produces stronger habits than regular reinforcement. Hunches "work" with just enough unpredictable success to encourage action in accordance with them. The hunch-addict often forgets, or represses his recall of the times when his hunches misled him.

The healthy thing to do with hunches or intuitions is to acknowledge them, even be glad they occur, but to postpone action on or belief in them until they have been tested. There is no inherent superiority of beliefs which stem from the unconscious over beliefs arrived at in more mundane ways—romantics and anti-intellectuals to the contrary.

MEMORY AS A SOURCE OF BELIEF. "My memory says that I did it, my pride says that I could not have done it, and in the end, my memory yields." This quotation expresses an empirical fact—that one's recall of past events is not always faithful and accurate. Just as perception is "functionally selective"—we do not pay attention to and observe everything which is present in the perceptual field—so is recalling the past a functionally selective activity. We do not remember everything we observed, everything we did, and everything which happened to us. At any given moment, we recall what we need or want to recall as means to assorted valued ends. If our immediate valued end is the solution of a familiar problem, we recall how we solved it in the past and repeat the performance. If we need to bolster flagging self-esteem by recalling some praiseworthy past event, then this is what we will recall. If we need to deprecate ourselves, because of momentary guilt-feelings, we will recall only those past events which will show what sorry specimens we are.

But recall is not only a selective process. It is also a *creative* process. We do not recall the past with photographic accuracy, except under special conditions. Rather, we *create the past*, each time that we attempt to recall. Bartlett [7] showed that the process of remembering is more similar to the creative process of writing fiction than it is to the activity of a newspaper reporter. The version of the past which we construct at any given moment is a function of our valued ends of the moment. If we need to see ourselves as a knight in armor, a Don Juan, or Paul Bunyan, then the "facts" of our past somehow become very plastic and changeable; in the telling they come out as we would have wanted them to occur, and not as they actually did occur. Many an old-timer, in the process of "recalling" (i.e., constructing a glorified version of) his early days, has been deflated before his audience by a wife or friend who then "tells the facts as they really happened." Many students have enjoyed the classroom demonstrations of the unreliability of eye-witness testimony, as this is recorded after the instructor has arranged some dramatic event to occur in the class; or the experiments in serial reproduction, which illustrate how a message gets recreated in the process of word-of-mouth transmission from person to person.

In view of all of these facts, we can assert that memory is useful as a source of hypotheses, just as are perception, authority, and intuition; but if valid beliefs are of importance, as they often are, then the person is advised to regard his memories as hypotheses, hypotheses to be checked by means of historical research. This involves seeking the testimony of contemporary witnesses, consulting written documents, cross-checking, etc. The person who trusts his memory without checking must be viewed as a conceited fellow indeed, when we become aware of the many factors which conspire to make recall inaccurate.

IMAGINATION AND BELIEF. A person can imagine almost anything under the sun, as well as many things which simply do not exist. The activity of imagining may be regarded as a special variety of thinking. It is known that people can think in words, or language, and that they can also think in *images*.[8] Individuals differ in their ability to think in images. There is evidence to show that people think in images before they learn to think in words and abstract symbols, that vivid imagery is more characteristic of children than it is of adults. The reader can test his own imagery right now by attempting to picture in his mind the face of his mother, or the sound of someone's voice, the taste of yesterday's main course at supper, or the feel of cold water trickling down his back. Some readers may find they can image these things vividly, almost like perceiving them. Others will only be able to think about them, without being able to experience them clearly.

A small child has a difficult time telling the difference between a perceptual experience which has been produced by some stimulus and an image which he has simply been thinking about. Eventually, however, he will learn that thinking about a meal—though it may have been a vivid experience—does not fill his stomach. Yet, under certain conditions, even an adult will sometimes confuse imaged experiences with actual perceptions. In other words, he may imagine he sees something, or hears something (no sensory stimulus is responsible for the experience) and then believe that something is there. This confusion of imagination for reality is most likely to occur when the objective conditions for accurate perception are less than optimum, and when inner factors, such as wishes, emotions, and the like are very strong. Thus, a person waiting impatiently for a friend at a street corner late at night may imagine that every passer-by is his friend. A timid person sitting alone in the house "hears" footsteps of prowlers all through the house, or "sees" faces peering into each window. The function of reality-testing is to separate what is real from what is wished, feared, and imagined.

REALITY-TESTING: CHANGING INACCURATE BELIEFS INTO ACCURATE BELIEFS

We have given the reasons why accurate beliefs are important for personality hygiene, and we have pointed out the common sources of beliefs and the factors which can and do make beliefs inaccurate. Now, let us inquire into the means by which inaccurate beliefs are changed into accurate beliefs; in other words, let us explain how reality-testing is carried out.

Reality-testing is simply scientific inquiry adapted to every day living. It is the systematic application of doubt to our own beliefs. In the last analysis, reality-testing involves the comparison of beliefs with evidence, in accordance with the customary rules of logic.

Let us begin our discussion of reality-testing with some rather extreme examples taken from the realm of unhealthy behavior, or psychopathology.

A person believes he has a number of enemies who are systematically trying to kill him. As observers of this person, we might assign him to a psychiatric disease-category—in this instance, paranoia. But this classification of the person helps us to understand nothing, really, about him. We can, however, ask a number of very relevant questions: How did he arrive at this persecutory belief? What evidence does he adduce to support his belief? Is there any other way of interpreting the evidence which he interprets as proof of a plot against his life?

We might find there were very subtle reasons for the person acquiring the belief a plot exists against his life but that the belief, when first acquired, had very little to do with evidence. We might find that for reasons of incompetence the person is failing in his profession, but his pride will not allow him to admit his failure is a consequence of incompetence. The belief in a plot may have arisen like an inspiration—it helps him to make sense of his failure in a way which does not cause him to lose self-esteem. The reason he is failing is that he cannot devote his undivided attention to his work —he must always be on guard for his life. Once he believes this, that his life is in jeopardy, it is easy to (mis)interpret everything that anyone does as part of the plot.

But let us ignore for the time being the over-all function which the belief in a plot serves for the person's pride, and study the belief just as we would study an assertion a scientist makes about some body of data. When a scientist asserts something about the field of his specialty, all of his colleagues leap upon his assertion like a group of hungry vultures lighting on their prey. They demand to see the evidence on which he rests his claim. They consider a number of other possible interpretations of his evidence, and require the scientist to show cause why they should not believe these alternate explanations of the data, rather than the explanation he is proffering. Thus, in psychological research, a psychologist might assert that rats have convulsions because of a conflict into which they have been thrust. The conflict explanation need be believed only after other possible convulsion-provoking factors have been shown *not* to be operative. In one case, it has been shown that it was not conflict alone, but rather intense auditory stimulation which induced convulsions in rats.

The paranoid person interprets other people's behavior as evidence in support of his belief that a plot is in progress against his life. If we examine this evidence, we may find something like the

following. He sees two people across the room talking to one another. All that he observes, really, is two people conversing. He assumes they are talking about him and his prospective death. In
reality, they may be talking about the weather, politics, or women.
Then the paranoid man may act on the basis of his belief, without
checking the validity of the belief. He may shoot these men "in self-
defense."

It was once commonly believed that "night air" caused malaria,
and so people kept their windows shut at night. One wonders how
many respiratory ailments followed as a consequence of insufficient
ventilation during sleep. It was only when mosquitoes were found
to carry the infecting agents for malaria that the previous belief
came to be generally rejected. Many semiliterate people carry with
them an entire collection of unfounded beliefs about dietetics,
health, climate, etc., and regulate their lives in accordance with these
beliefs.[9]

Let us provide the reader with a concrete series of instructions for
carrying out reality-testing. It should then be possible for him to
examine and test any belief about anything by the application of
these rules.

RULES FOR REALITY-TESTING

1. State the belief very clearly.
2. Ask, "What evidence is there to support this belief?"
3. Ask, "Is there any other way, or ways, of interpreting this evidence?"
4. How consistent is the belief with other beliefs which are known to
be valid?

Now, we shall illustrate. A student believes his teacher dislikes
him. Let us put words in his mouth, and arrange an imaginary mono-
logue.

"My teacher hates me. What evidence do I have for this belief?
Why, the fact that he gave me a very low grade, plus the fact that
yesterday when I greeted him in the hall, he didn't turn my way
to acknowledge the greeting. But let me see, is there any other way
of interpreting this evidence? Well, what factors can produce low
grades? One of them is insufficient study, and faulty understanding
of the course. As it happens, I haven't cracked a book all quarter,
and I cut half my lectures to play billiards and go to the burlesque.

Maybe that's why I flunked. But what about the fact that I greeted the professor, and he didn't even nod? Well, maybe he didn't hear me. I must admit I spoke very low, and the hall was noisy. Finally, this professor is widely believed to be extremely fair and impartial in his dealings with students, and so my belief about his hating me isn't consistent with his reputation."

Systematic application of this set of rules will help the reader to make sure his beliefs come closer to accuracy than would be the case if he ignored the activity of reality-testing.

We have shown, so far, the common sources of our beliefs, the importance to effective instrumental action of accurate beliefs, and the means by which beliefs may be tested for their accuracy. Let us now inquire into some of the factors which promote the formulation of *inaccurate beliefs*. These factors may broadly be classified into two categories—*objective* and *subjective*.

OBJECTIVE PROMOTERS OF INACCURATE BELIEFS. Inaccurate beliefs are most likely to be formulated about some aspect of the world when there is insufficient information available. People find it difficult to suspend judgment and to tolerate prolonged doubt and uncertainty.[10] Consequently, when only partial information is available, because of faulty conditions for observation, the person is likely to misinterpret the evidence and act on it, even though later facts may reveal he has been wrong.

SUBJECTIVE PROMOTERS OF INACCURATE BELIEFS. The subjective factors which promote the formulation of inaccurate beliefs include strong emotions, wishes, values, expectancies, etc. These factors are most likely to promote inaccurate beliefs when the evidence which confronts a person is ambiguous (see Chapter 2, autism).

Orson Welles' famous broadcast about the "invasion" from Mars illustrates the operation of both sets of factors.[11] He presented a drama over the radio, in which one of the characters was a very convincing news announcer. He made a speech, just as would a newscaster, that an invasion from Mars was in progress. Many people who heard this panicked. The sober reality tester would have figured: "What do I believe? That there is an invasion from Mars? On what evidence? A radio report? Let's check the local station and find out if it was an authentic report, or part of some drama or other." In doing this, he would have discovered the truth. But with only fragmentary evidence, and with strong fear latent in large numbers of people, it was possible for Welles to induce them to believe something very terrifying.

SOME AREAS WHERE INACCURATE BELIEFS ARE COMMON. In our earlier discussion of autism, it was pointed out that inaccurate cognition was most likely to occur when the stimulus field was ambiguous, and when need-tensions and emotions were at a relatively high level. There are a number of areas in life where both conditions are met and where, in consequence, inaccurate beliefs are most likely to be found.

THE SELF-CONCEPT: BELIEFS ABOUT ONE'S OWN PERSONALITY. A person stands so close to his own behavior and feelings he cannot obtain the detachment and dispassion necessary for clear self-observation. In addition, he has powerful self-esteem motives operating to impel him to ignore and misinterpret much of his own conduct and motivation. Consequently a person is very likely to acquire a self-concept—a repertoire of beliefs concerning what and who he is—which departs considerably from the conclusions that might be drawn by a more detached observer. We shall treat this subject in greater detail in a later section.[12]

OTHER-CONCEPTS: BELIEFS ABOUT THE PERSONALITIES OF OTHERS. The motives and behavior of another person are almost intrinsically ambiguous. This ambiguity, plus the fact we acquire very strong emotional reactions to other persons, increase the probability our beliefs about their personalities will be inaccurate. The prevalence of prejudice and misunderstanding is ample testimony to this fact. In a later chapter, we shall develop this point in greater detail.[13]

BELIEFS ABOUT DEPRESSIONS, PLAGUES, AND OTHER CATASTROPHES. These complex phenomena are beyond the understanding of most people except experts because they affect people so profoundly; they are powerful instigators of emotion, and hence deterrents to reality-contact. People have devised all kinds of beliefs and ideologies to explain why these phenomena occur, including witchcraft, voodoo-ism, the will of the gods, fate, etc. Few of these animistic beliefs stand up under scientific scrutiny.

SOCIALLY TABOOED SUBJECT MATTER. Every society has taboos directed against certain kinds of behavior, including even looking at certain classes of phenomena. Thus, in some primitive tribes, it is forbidden for a commoner to look on the person of the king. In our society, it is forbidden that young children shall observe sexual intimacies of their parents; or for that matter, in some families, it is forbidden even to ask questions relating to sexuality. Under such conditions, since there is little opportunity for "feed-back" of correct data, persons will construct beliefs about forbidden phenomena and objects which can never be subjected to reality-testing. The author recalls an 18-year-old female college student who believed that menstruation was a punishment imposed only on those girls who practised excessive masturbation. In her family, sex was a taboo subject even for discussion and she evidently managed to conduct her life so that she learned none of the facts of life from her peers. A teacher and a personality therapist can collect numerous examples of the kinds of bizarre beliefs which arise concerning subject matter and topics that have been taboo for the students and patients.

BARRIERS TO REALITY-TESTING

Reality-testing is a variety of instrumental behavior. The valued end, or goal of reality-testing, is the attainment of accurate beliefs. When we regard reality-testing as instrumental behavior, we immediately see that it has the general properties of such behavior (see Chapter 2)—it is motivated by relevant need-tensions; it is subject to voluntary control; it is flexible and modifiable through learning and experience. In addition, it can be blocked by barriers similar to those which block other kinds of instrumental behavior such as the barriers which prevent effective sexual behavior, emotional behavior, interpersonal behavior, or loving behavior.

One of the most common barriers to instrumental action (including reality-testing) is fear of the anticipated consequences.

FEAR. Certain beliefs may be crucial to the security of an individual, i.e., to his freedom from fear and anxiety. For example, a person may need to believe that his parents love him; if he should begin to doubt their love for him, he might become overwhelmed with anxiety. Therefore he refrains from testing the validity of his belief in their love. In fact, they may hate him.

PRIDE. Pride may deter a person from engaging in reality-testing. His self-esteem may rest on certain beliefs which, if proven unfounded, would plunge the individual into the depths of despair, guilt, and depression. Thus, a person may believe that he is competent in some area. The proof of competence is often to be found in successful competition. The person may avoid competition like the plague, lest he lose the contest. So long as he never tests his belief in his own superiority, the person can blithely maintain his self-esteem on the basis of his untested belief.

AFFECTION. Laymen have long recognized that a favorable attitude, or a feeling of affection toward a person or object, will "blind" his perceptions. When one likes another person, for example, the affection is often grounded implicitly on certain beliefs about the personality of the other person. These beliefs may never be tested because of the affection, despite the fact that much evidence may be readily available to refute the beliefs. The person does not want to test his beliefs about the object of his affections.

WISHES. Everyone has wishful concepts of himself, other people, and reality in general. We *want* the world to be a certain way, and so we *believe* it is the way we wished it to be. Wishful beliefs are most common among children, whose cognition is guided by the pleasure principle. According to the psychoanalysts,[14] maturity is characterized by replacement of the pleasure-principle by the reality-principle, by which it is meant that behavior is coordinated with accurate perception and belief rather than wishful thinking and perception. Yet we never entirely lose this powerful influence of wishes on our beliefs, and everyone who seeks reality-contact must fight unremittingly against the influences of his wishes on his beliefs. The scientist is the one who most recognizes this, and he has established rigorous patterns of observation and stern criteria for proof in order to neutralize the influence of wishes on belief. Anyone who has undertaken scientific research, and who wants a certain hypothesis to be true, will recall occasions when he was reluctant to study his results lest his wishes be blasted by the data, and his fears upheld.

HOSTILITY. When we hate another person, we justify our hatred with strong beliefs concerning the vile traits of the object of our hatred. So strong may be the hate that we will never take the pains to check, periodically, the validity of these beliefs. It is almost as if we need our hatred, and we are reluctant to find any cause to abandon it—which might be necessary if we discover that our beliefs about the hateful traits of the other person are unwarranted.

PREJUDICE. Prejudice for or against entire groups of persons, e.g., Negroes, Jews, orientals, or more generally, "foreigners," may rest on false beliefs about members of those groups. The prejudiced individual avoids evidence which would refute his beliefs in the desirable or undesirable characteristics of these persons. He may even refuse to read or listen to the results of reality-testing measures carried out by disinterested investigators. Allport [15] has documented the tenacity with which prejudiced beliefs are held in spite of evidence provided by social scientists.

PROMOTING THE REALITY-TESTING HABIT

Since reality-testing appears to be such a valuable sort of instrumental behavior, we may well ask, "How can it be encouraged?"

This question is basically one which could be solved through the methods of applied psychology. Education and personality therapy are two means by which a respect for reality and a desire for truth can be inculcated into persons.

EDUCATION AND REALITY-CONTACT. Public education is believed to be the most important means by which a person arrives at a broad grasp of basic truths, accurate beliefs, about the world. Education is thought to consist of the dispensing of facts, in the teaching of skills basic to the acquisition of new facts, and the critical testing of old ones. Any teacher knows that students at all levels do not come into the classroom in a state of cognitive emptiness. Every student from kindergarten up to graduate school has his repertoire of beliefs—some accurate, and many inaccurate—which serve as a barrier to the acquisition of newer, more tested ones. Part of the skill in teaching consists in drawing out a student's present beliefs and encouraging him to test these against more reliable information.

PERSONALITY THERAPY AND REALITY-CONTACT. One of the most widely held aims of personality therapists, irrespective of theoretical orientation, is to increase reality-contact and promote the reality-testing habit. In taking measures designed to "strengthen the ego" of the patient, the psychoanalyst is hoping to help the patient gain enough courage and strength to test present erroneous beliefs and to face painful aspects of reality, including the realities of the patient's own past behavior.

MEASURING REALITY-CONTACT

The most basic means for measuring reality-contact is to compare what a person believes with "the facts." This involves getting some explicit statement of what a person believes and having at hand some criterion against which to compare it. The criterion may be observable facts, or, it may be the opinion of qualified experts.

Thus, we can ask a person what he believes about engines, the causes of rain, how babies are born, or why people contract colds. The more that a person's beliefs depart from reality, the more deviant, ineffective, and unhealthy we might expect his behavior to be.

Psychologists have devised some sophisticated but still crude means for the actual measurement of reality-contact. One of these is an adaptation of the Rorschach Test. Norms have been assembled, based on the responses of thousands of unhospitalized (i.e., normal) people to the ink-blots. These responses serve as a crude standard of what is accurate, or realistic.[16] When a person interprets some aspect of a blot in a way that differs from these norms, and does this repeatedly, he is deemed to suffer from some impairment in reality-contact. It is assumed that if he perceives ink-blots in a deviant manner from most other people, he will also perceive and believe other things in a deviant manner.

There is a great advantage to objective means of measuring the extent to which a person is in contact with reality, but almost anyone can approximate an objective test by simply asserting his beliefs clearly and comparing them with some criterion. The criteria against which beliefs might be compared include facts, the opinions of others deemed to be competent, and, in some instances, logic. Often, a person might believe something against the opinion of the majority, and yet be right in his belief. Many scientific discoveries which threatened man's pride met with considerable opposition from laymen and scientific colleagues alike, though later, the unpopular beliefs come to be affirmed more widely. Thus, the work of Copernicus,

Galileo, Freud, and Darwin all met both learned and ignorant opposition. All those workers were undoubtedly viewed by many of their contemporaries as being "crazy" and "unrealistic."

In a personality hygiene program, the measurement of reality-contact will come to be a very urgent problem, as will the problem of improving the reality-contact of the broad mass of people. One might say that all measures aimed at increasing education, knowledge, and the habit of reality-testing among large numbers of people are personality-hygiene measures. The facts about life and the world may not be pleasant for some people, but since we seem to live in a world of facts there is considerable advantage to be gained from knowing them.

LIVING IN THE "RAW" WORLD

It is probably the lot of the human being that once he has learned speech, his perception of reality is always filtered through, and guided by, his *concepts* of reality. For example, if you learn the concept gun, and then look at a gun, you probably see something entirely different from what a primitive savage might; guns have no place, nor even a word to describe them, in his culture.[17]

Words, concepts, or symbols may be said to *limit* what a person will actually observe in a concrete situation. Once a concept has been learned, a person will look at a given object only long enough to place it in its proper category or to assign an appropriate name to it. He may then ignore, or fail to observe much of what is actually there before him. We are all familiar with the bigoted person who, once he has determined that a person is a Jew or a Negro, never looks further at the person. He "knows" the properties of "all" members who fall into those classes. In reality, the bigot fails to observe the enormous amount of variation among members of a class of any sort.[18]

The ability to break down broad categories and classes and to discern the individual, the particular, the unique, is a valuable one from the personality hygiene point of view. This is not to say that "rubricizing" is a bad thing.[19] On the contrary it appears to be inescapable. But the ability to see what is there, to transcend labels and classes and apprehend the thing before one's view, is a means of enriching one's knowledge of the world and of deepening one's contact with reality.[20] To be able to see the "raw world" involves the ability to abandon presently held concepts and categories. Something of this ability is possessed by the productive scientist who deliberately ignores the orthodoxies and looks ever afresh at the raw data which prompted the formation of present-day concepts and categories.

The artist probably possesses the ability to apprehend the unique, the individual object, to a marked degree.

The ability to set conventional categories and concepts aside and to look fully at the world with minimal preconceptions seems to be a trait which facilitates scientific discovery, art, human relations, and more generally, an enrichment of the sensory experiences of living. From these points of view, then, we could agree with Maslow that the capacity to discern the particular is a valuable thing.

It is only valuable, however, for a person who already has been exposed to his society's ways of classifying objects and people. The person who is not capable of forming concepts and categories along lines similar to those of his society is judged to be insane. Indeed, one of the most sensitive indicators of latent schizophrenia is bizarre ways of making abstractions and forming concepts or generalizations from experience. It would appear that the capacity to abandon conventional concepts at will and to classify the world in a deviant, or experimental, manner is valuable *only* when the person can then show that his new conceptualization fits into the present scheme of things, or at least it can prove to be useful for human and social purposes.

SUMMARY

Accurate perceptions and accurate beliefs about the world are necessary conditions for effective instrumental behavior. When a person has such accurate perceptions and beliefs, he is said to be in contact with reality. *Reality-contact* is generally considered to be both a sign of personality health and a means by which personality health is achieved and maintained.

Beliefs about the world are acquired through perception, from authority, from intuition, memory, and imagination. The point is

made that all of these sources are fallible and that the beliefs derivative from these sources will be inaccurate unless they have been subjected to *reality-testing.*

Reality-testing is a process of checking the validity of presently
hold beliefs. It involves the comparison of these beliefs with evidence and a study of their compatibility with other beliefs.

Inaccurate beliefs are promoted by stimulus ambiguity and by
emotions, needs, feelings, etc. Inaccurate beliefs are commonly found
pertaining to the self-concept, concepts of others, catastrophic occurrences such as depressions, floods, etc., and socially taboo subject-matter.

Some barriers to reality-testing include fear, pride, affection,
wishes, hostility, and prejudice.

Education and personality therapy are factors which have, as part
of their function, the promotion and strengthening of the reality-
testing habit.

Reality-contact may roughly be measured by comparing a person's
beliefs with evidence and by the use of certain adaptations of the
Rorschach Test.

The ability voluntarily to perceive the world in ways which differ
from the conventional is discussed as a valuable buffer against too
rigid reality-contact.

NOTES AND REFERENCES

RECOMMENDED READINGS ARE MARKED WITH AN ASTERISK (*)

*1. See Cantril, H., *The "why" of man's experience,* New York, Macmillan, 1950, pp. 87–104, for an elaboration of the concept of "the
assumptive world." See also Snygg, D. and Combs, A., *Individual
behavior,* New York, Harper, 1949, Ch. 2, for a discussion of the
"phenomenal field."

*2. This discussion of beliefs may be richly supplemented by reference
to the well-documented exposition in Krech, D. and Crutchfield,
R. S., *Theory and problems of social psychology,* New York,
McGraw-Hill, 1948, Ch. 5, 6.

3. Ittelson, W. H., *The Ames demonstrations in perception,* Princeton,
Princeton University Press, 1952.

°4. See Murphy, G., *Personality: a biosocial approach to origins and structure*, New York, Harper, 1947, especially Ch. 14, 15. The student is further advised to refresh his memory for basic researches in perception with reference to a standard text in introductory psychology. See for example, Ruch, F. L., *Psychology and life*, 4th ed., New York, Scott, Foresman, 1953, Ch. 10.

°5. This "healthy way" is probably possible only with the kind of authority-figure which Fromm described as "rational authority." See Fromm, E., *Escape from freedom*, New York, Rinehart, pp. 164–165.

6. Horney, K., *Neurosis and human growth*, New York, Norton, 1950, Ch. 6.

7. Bartlett, F. C., *Remembering*, London, Cambridge University Press, 1932.

°8. Werner, H., *The comparative psychology of mental development*, rev. ed., Chicago, Follett, 1948, Ch. 4 gives a discussion of imagery, well-documented with research data.

°9. Whiting, J. W. M. and Child, I. L., *Child training and personality*, New Haven, Yale University Press, 1953, Ch. 6.

10. Frenkel-Brunswik, Else, "Intolerance of ambiguity as an emotional and perceptual personality variable," *J. Pers.*, 1949, **18**, 108–143.

°11. See Cantril, H., *The psychology of social movements*, New York, Wiley, 1941, for an analysis of the "invasion."

12. Chapter 10.

13. Chapter 7.

14. See Freud, S., "Formulations regarding the two principles in mental functioning," in Freud, S., *Collected papers*, Vol. IV, London, Hogarth, 1953, Ch. 1.

15. Allport, G., *The nature of prejudice*, Cambridge, Addison-Wesley, 1954.

16. Cf. Hertz, Marguerite, *Frequency tables to be used in scoring responses to the Rorschach Ink-Blot Test*, 3rd ed., Cleveland, Western Reserve University, 1946. An application of this approach has been developed as a kind of short-form test of reality-contact. See McReynolds, P., "Perception of Rorschach concepts as related to personality deviations," *J. abn. soc. Psychol.*, 1951, **46**, 131–141.

°17. The field of semantics is devoted to a study of how concepts both facilitate and inhibit accurate cognition. See Hayakawa, S. I., *Language in action*, New York, Harcourt, Brace, 1941, for a readable introduction to this area of inquiry.

18. Allport, G., *op. cit.*, Ch. 2. Allport gives an excellent analysis of the process of categorization as it applies to prejudice.

*19. Maslow, A. H., *Motivation and personality*, New York, Harper, 1954. Ch. 14 is an excellent elaboration of the points being made here.

*20. Maslow, A. H., "Deficiency motivation and growth motivation," in M. R. Jones (ed.), *Nebraska Symposium on Motivation*, Lincoln University of Nebraska Press, 1955. In this contribution, Maslow distinguishes between deficiency-motivated and growth-motivated perception. The latter variety is of the kind discussed in this section.

QUESTIONS FOR REVIEW AND EXAMINATION

1. Why are accurate beliefs about the world important to a person, if he is to achieve healthy personality?

2. What are the major sources of belief that are available to a person?

3. What is meant by "reality-testing," and how is it carried out?

4. What are the major determiners of inaccurate beliefs about the world?

5. What are some very common areas in which widespread inaccuracy of knowledge and belief may be found?

6. List the major barriers to reality-testing, and explain how they interfere with this activity.

7. How do our concepts about things in the world sometimes "blind" us to what is actually there before us? What is meant by "living in the 'raw' world"?

8. Use the concepts employed in this chapter as a guide for describing and evaluating your relationship with reality or that of some other person whom you know.

CHAPTER 4

Healthy Emotional Behavior

Emotion plays a very important role in personality health and in physical health. The psychiatrist looks for signs of "irrational affects" and for signs of "blunted affect" when he is trying to decide whether a patient is suffering from a neurosis or psychosis. The psychosomatic physician is interested in whether or not a patient chronically represses and suppresses certain feelings, on the premise that unreleased emotional tension can produce physical illness. The psychologist knows that excessive emotional tension interferes with the capacity to work efficiently, think and reason clearly, and perceive accurately. And the layman knows that if he is "too emotional," people think he is childish, while if he is "too unemotional," no one will like him on the grounds that he doesn't "have a heart," or that he's "too cold."

There are two aspects of emotion which are relevant to the present context: emotional *arousal*, and emotional *release*. We are interested in the conditions under which a person will or will not become emotionally aroused, and we are interested in what he does when emotional tension has been aroused. Healthy emotionality in the broadest sense means that (a) the conditions for emotional arousal in a person meet certain standards, and (b) the way in which a person behaves following arousal will produce certain valued consequences. These consequences include the riddance of undesired tensions, or the attainment of desired ones, and the maintenance and enhancement of other values. These other values include such things as self-respect, one's job, friendships, etc. A person is said to display unhealthy emotionality when he does not respond emotionally as he is supposed or expected to, and when his emotionally-provoked behavior endangers his health, safety, his position, or anything else which he or society deems important.

WHAT IS AN EMOTION?

This is a question which has vexed students of human nature for centuries.[1] Is emotion simply a quality of feeling or tension? Is it a pattern of distinct neurophysiological responses which a physiologist might detect and record with his specialized instruments? Is it a pattern of facial expression, bodily posture, muscular tonus and tone of voice which a layman can observe with his unaided senses? Actually emotion is all these things occurring simultaneously in some given situation. But we are not interested in all aspects of emotion in this volume. What follows is a highly selective discussion of emotion along lines relevant to personality hygiene. Let us begin with the concept of *emotional tension* or *affect*, as it is often called. The layman's word for emotional tension is "feelings."

EMOTIONAL TENSION (*affects*). Most of the time, a person experiences a quality of inner feeling which he might call "calm," "ordinary," and "collected." Let us call this quality his *modal tension-level* and *-quality*. Suppose that the person is walking along, feeling nothing in particular, and a complete stranger comes up to him and spits squarely in his face. The person will experience more than warm fragrant moisture dripping down his cheek. He will experience an alteration in his modal tension-state—a distinct change which he has no difficulty in identifying as anger. Something about the fact of having been spat upon has produced a radical change in his modal tension-state. He feels he has been insulted, and he always gets angry when insulted. The tension which he has labelled "anger" is one of the many which people are capable of experiencing. Emotional tension is the general term which we shall use to refer to these specific affects, which include fear, anxiety, affection, hostility, depression, excitement, and others.[2]

It should be stated that when a person is conscious of angry tension within himself (through introspection), the outside observer can notice certain facial expressions, gestures, signs of autonomic nervous system activity, such as blushing or blanching, changes in the rate and depth of breathing, and muscular tremor.[3] In addition, if the person were to report further on his inner state he might report, not only the presence of angry affect, but also a lot of thinking along lines of this sort: "Why that dirty so-and-so. He insulted me. I'm going to let him have it square on the jaw."

It becomes apparent that emotional tension is only a small part of a much more complex phenomenon which we shall call the *emotional response*. In addition to affect, the emotional response includes cognitive aspects (what the person thinks, perceives), conative aspects (what he intends to do), and complex responses of the voluntary and involuntary nervous and muscular systems. For purposes of simplicity and clarity, and because our interest in this chapter is primarily on emotional tensions, we shall use the term emotional response to refer specifically to the emotional tension component of the total response. The reader must not forget, however, that all of the other phenomena are occurring at the same time as the affects.

EMOTIONAL TENSION AND EMOTIONAL BEHAVIOR. Emotional tension may be welcomed by the person and sought out as a goal in itself, or it may be unwanted, so that the person will strive to get rid of the tension once it has arisen. Thus, a person may become bored with the sameness of his tension-state and seek thrills and fights, just because he enjoys the experience of mild fear, or hot rage. Or, he may have come to detest certain emotional tensions and even to fear them; when emotional tensions arise, he strives to get rid of them as quickly as he possibly can. Behavior which is directed toward the change or reduction of emotional tensions in the self we shall call *emotional behavior*.

THE ORIGIN OF EMOTIONAL RESPONSES

The question may be raised, "How does it come about that some stimulus will provoke an emotional response in a person?" Anyone can observe that the same stimulus will provoke emotional tension in one person but not in another; that the stimulus may provoke entirely different emotional responses in two different persons, or in the same person at different times. Thus, a stern look and a loud bellow from the boss may evoke fear in the employee, anger from the boss's wife, laughter from the boss's colleague, and intellectual curiosity in the boss's psychoanalyst. If the employee should obtain a much better job, and is no longer dependent upon his boss, he may respond to the stern look and the bellow on that happy day with indifference or with a triumphant counter-blast of hostility—he'll tell the boss exactly how he feels about him.

In view of the fact of wide individual differences in emotional responsiveness to a stimulus, and wide intra-individual variability in response to the same stimulus, we may well ask how we come to acquire our emotional habits. By *emotional habit* we are referring to a stable association between some class of stimuli or objects, and some emotional tension, such as anxiety and hostility.

On the basis of present-day knowledge about emotion, it may be said that emotional habits are learned (not inborn), and further, they are learned through the mechanisms of *conditioning, identification,* and *socialization.*

CONDITIONING AND EMOTIONAL RESPONSES. The reader is no doubt familiar with the experimental procedure discovered by Pavlov, and named conditioning. In brief, the laboratory procedure of conditioning involves:

1. Discovering some response, or reflex which can regularly be elicited by some stimulus, called the *unconditioned stimulus.* Examples of such reflexes and the unconditioned stimuli which stably will evoke them are: eye-blink, a puff of air; knee-jerk, a blow on the patellar tendon; salivation, the presence of food or acid in the mouth. The response itself, when considered together with its relevant unconditioned stimulus, is described as an *unconditioned response.*

2. Presenting a neutral stimulus along with the unconditioned stimulus for a number of trials. After a suitable number of pairings of the neutral stimulus with the unconditioned stimulus, the former will come to elicit the response ordinarily evoked by the unconditioned stimulus. When this has occurred, the previously neu-

tral stimulus is given the name *conditioned stimulus,* and the response is now called a *conditioned response.*

As a laboratory procedure, conditioning has been used by scientists to study brain functions,[4] and to discover some of the "laws of
learning."[5] Animal trainers use conditioning principles in order to
train animals to perform all manner of tasks. But aside from being
the name for a laboratory procedure, conditioning has come to be
given a much more generalized meaning; it refers now to any occasion that a neutral stimulus is presented along with an effective
stimulus, such that the former comes to elicit the response regularly
evoked by the latter.

It has come to be recognized that the manner in which affective
responses to stimuli are acquired is analogous with (if not identical
to) the laboratory procedure for establishing a conditioned response.
The affect, fear, for example, appears to be a by-product of experience with painful stimulation. The painful unconditioned stimulus
produces activity of the autonomic nervous system. Other stimuli,
such as the sight, sound, or smell of the painful stimulus become
conditioned stimuli for these autonomic responses. Thus, the person
comes to respond with emotional tension to conditioned stimuli that
were associated with the pain-producing, unconditioned stimulus.[6]
In a sense, the conditioned stimuli become signals that the unconditioned stimulus is close by. This signal-function of a conditioned
stimulus is what we call the cognitive component of an emotional
response. The technical name for this "cognitive component" is
expectancy.[7]

A person perceives some stimulus. Past experience has led him to
expect, or predict that some other stimulus will be forthcoming—
one which will affect him in a pleasurable or painful way. He sees his
father frown, and he becomes anxious—he expects a spanking. He
sees his father smile, and he feels good—he expects to get a present.
Emotional responses thus are strongly determined by the *interpretation of the stimulus*—by the expectancy which past experience has
built up in the person.

EXPECTANCIES AND EMOTIONAL RESPONSES. An expectancy may
technically be defined as a prediction that *B* will follow *A,* where
A is a conditioned stimulus, and *B* an unconditioned stimulus. Expectancies are acquired through observation and generalizing from

observations. Since generalization is a very tricky kind of activity, even for the professional logician or scientist, it follows that a layman may often overgeneralize from his observations, or generalize without an adequate sample of observations. We have all observed night following day with absolute regularity, and so we have accurate expectancies with regard to this fact. We have all heard thunder following lightning with absolute regularity, and so our expectancies will be quite accurate when they predict that soon after we see lightning, we will hear a thunderclap.[8]

But we may have been bitten by one dog—the bite produces pain. On the basis of that one occurrence, a person may generalize that all dogs will bite him. He sees another dog, and expects to be bitten. He becomes afraid. If we know that the dog which he fears has never bitten anyone—in fact the dog has no teeth—we would say his expectancy was inaccurate and his emotional response was inappropriate. But appropriate or inappropriate, a person's emotional responses will be predicated on his expectancies, and his expectancies have been grounded on his own experiences with paired stimuli, conditioned and unconditioned. When he observes the conditioned stimulus, he expects the unconditioned stimulus is near, and he will respond emotionally to the conditioned stimulus. When someone responds with fear or hostility to some object which does not evoke those responses in us, we can assume our expectancies with respect to the object differ from his. If we interpreted the stimulus as he does, and if we had had similar experiences with stimuli of that sort, then we too might display a similar emotional response.

From all of this we may conclude that conditioning, the pairing of neutral stimuli with stimuli that affect us pleasurably or painfully, goes on unremittingly from birth until death; that we continually acquire, revise, and abandon expectancies; and that our emotional responses are elicited by (conditioned) stimuli which have been interpreted by the person in such a way that they acquire signal, or predictive properties.

IDENTIFICATION AND EMOTIONAL RESPONSES. A psychologist or layman can readily observe close similarities in emotional habits within a family or between two close friends, or spouses. Father and his sons all display similar emotional responses to politicians, salesmen, women, animals, etc. A woman, before she became married, responded emotionally after the fashion of her mother and siblings; after several years of marriage, her parents and siblings notice she no longer feels about things the way she used to—she has "changed." She has come to share some of the emotional habits of her husband, and he in turn has acquired many of hers, so that his former bachelor friends notice striking differences in him. He is no longer amused by the same things, angered or afraid of the same things as he was when he was one of the boys.

The mechanism responsible for the acquisition of emotional responses which resemble those of someone close is *identification*. Identification is a learning process by means of which an individual, A, reproduces in his own stable behavior repertoire, characteristics of person B.[9] It may be a conscious, deliberate attempt to imitate the valued traits of another person or it may be an unconsciously purposeful emulation. It is not known whether emotional habits are acquired through direct identification, or whether the similarity in emotional habits between two persons derives from identification with each other's values, expectancies, and attitudes. Nevertheless, it can be asserted that either directly or indirectly persons acquire certain of their emotional habits by means of identification.

SOCIALIZATION AND EMOTIONAL RESPONSES. A sociologist or anthropologist observes that most members of a given social class or of a society share many emotional habits in common. These emotional responses differ, however, from the modal emotional responses of people in other classes or societies.

It is likely that part of the total socialization process—the efforts of parents, teachers, and others concerned with the molding and shaping of modal personality for a society—is devoted to insuring that the growing and developing children will acquire the appropriate emotional habits. It is desired that most members of a group perceive and interpret aspects of the world in a uniform way and react with similar emotional responses to those objects. This uniformity is probably achieved through formal education—the child knows that pain and fear are associated with danger, and so his elders and instructors teach him to interpret many things as dangerous. It may also be achieved through training-experiences within the family which have the effect of conditioning most members of the society in a uniform way to certain classes of stimuli.[10]

Probably most of the prejudices, fears, likes, etc., of a given society derive, not from direct and individualized conditioning experiences but rather as a consequence of socialization experiences and identification with the emotional experience of significant persons in the family or peer-group—who in turn resemble other members of society at large.

EVALUATING EMOTIONAL RESPONSES

When once we have learned to observe, record, and describe a person's emotional responses to life situations, it becomes possible to evaluate these responses. But the question arises, "What criteria shall we use for evaluating emotional responses?" Obviously, there are many criteria possible: intensity of response, similarity of responses to those made by other people, etc. The choice of criteria depends largely on the specific purpose for which evaluation is to be made. The criteria which appear to be of greatest value in a discussion of healthy emotionality are those of *rationality* and *consciousness*.

Rational affects are deemed to be a crucial indicator of overall personality health. When affects are irrational, as in the case of phobias, irrational hostilities and affections, and irrational guilts, a person's capacity to achieve need-satisfactions in acceptable ways is gravely impaired. We may regard the capacity to respond with rational affects as a positive personality-hygiene value.

In an earlier chapter (Chapter 2), it was pointed out that only when motives are conscious can a person select his behavior in such a way as to implement them. Emotional tensions are motives which influence behavior selection; when the tensions are conscious, the person is able to select and control his behavior. When affects are unconscious, the probability is increased that the person will act in ways which he did not consciously intend. It follows that the capacity to recognize one's own emotional tensions accurately is a positive personality-hygiene value (see also Chapter 10, on the real self).

RATIONAL AND IRRATIONAL AFFECTS. If a person became afraid in the presence of a robber holding a loaded gun, we would agree the situation objectively is dangerous, and we should call his fear rational. The term *rational affects* [11] will be reserved for those emotional responses which are associated with accurate expectancies and efficient reality-contact. Rational affects are valued by the personality hygienist as indices of personality health. But most of us carry with us emotional habits which do not make sense to another observer, or to ourselves. Thus, we may become angry with no apparent adequate provocation; we may like someone when he has done nothing to warrant this like; we may fear dogs and insects, when we know from scientific evidence there is absolutely no danger. The term *irrational affects* will be used to refer to this class of emotional responses, responses which do not appear to have adequate provocation, or which do not make sense to the person himself—he can find no adequate explanation for them. Irrational affects are generally interpreted as symptoms of unhealthy personality in general, or as signs of unhealthy emotionality in particular. Let us inquire further into their nature. The problem to be solved here is not that of explaining the manner in which irrational affects have arisen; there is no reason to doubt they were acquired after the fashion of all emotional responses. The main puzzle seems to lie in how they came to be inexplicable to the person himself. Most affects make sense to the person who has them: he fears dogs because he has been bitten; he is angry with his brother because his brother has often broken his toys. The affects which do not make sense may interfere radically with the person's life, causing him to restrict his behavior considerably or to behave in appropriate ways.

The mechanisms which probably explain irrational affects are the following:

1. REPRESSION: The individual has forgotten the events which resulted in his acquiring an emotional response to some class of objects. The only record that such conditioning did take place is the emotional response itself. Thus, a person may become angry at all red-headed persons, and not know why. It could be that long ago, he had been unfairly and cruelly treated by someone with red hair. The memory for the original traumatic experiences has long been repressed but the affect still remains. Possibly if the person were able to recall and "abreact," or experience a "catharsis" of his feelings with respect to the original trauma, his automatic hostility toward red-haired persons might disappear.[12]

2. REDINTEGRATION: [13] The original conditioning experience involved the association of many conditioned stimuli with the unconditioned stimulus. All of the conditioned stimuli save one may have lost their power to evoke the emotional response. This one remaining stimulus may have no necessary causal connection with the unconditioned stimulus; at the time of conditioning, the neutral stimulus just happened to be present with all the others. The person retains his emotional response to this stimulus, and does not know why. This tendency to react to some small part of a very complex whole situation as if it actually were the whole situation is called redintegration.

3. SYMBOLIZATION: Language is comprised of symbols that have *shared* meanings. However, a person may construct his own *idiosyncratic* symbols of events and objects past and present. Many of the stimuli for irrational affects may actually be remote symbols of the original unconditioned stimulus; the verbal connections between the unconditioned stimulus and its symbol may have been repressed. Freud explained phobias—irrational fears—in these terms. In one case,[14] a small child dreaded walking in the streets of Vienna because there were horses all about. He dreaded horses, although he had had no traumatic experiences with any particular horses. Analysis of the child's early history revealed that he had much repressed hostility toward his father, with the dread of retaliation by the father for these hostile wishes. The horses had come to symbolize his father, and he was able to keep his feelings toward his father repressed by "displacing" these feelings to horses. The apparent connecting link which made this phobia-development possible lay in the fact that the favorite game which the child and his father played together was "horsy."

4. OVERGENERALIZATION: Many irrational affects derive from the logical fallacy of *overgeneralization*. A person might have been affected pleasantly or unpleasantly by some object or person. Following this experience, he may generalize very broadly, so that he comes to expect similar treatment for good or ill from all objects or persons who even vaguely resemble the original. It is apparent that simply subjecting the expectancy to reality-testing will usually be sufficient to enable the person to discriminate between those objects

which will affect him and those which, though apparently similar say in appearance, actually differ in basic and fundamental ways from those which will produce the desired or dreaded impact. The common dread of snakes and beetles; the tendency to like or dislike people on first sight; these emotional responses probably derive from overgeneralization.[15] Often, when a person acts on the basis of these overgeneralizations, he gets into some kind of difficulty; as when an employer who trusted a given man, hires another man just on the basis of "liking his looks" (the new man resembles the trusted employee). The new man, however, may actually be a crook. Looks and actual behavior have no correlation with each other, athough we all have been conditioned to expect certain kinds of behavior from people on the basis of their facial characteristics [16] and body build. We look at a thin-lipped woman, and describe her as highly moral, expecting puritanistic behavior from her. We look at a fat man,[17] and expect jollity from him. We are often wrong in such expectancies, as experience will attest.

ACHIEVING RATIONAL AFFECTS

The capacity to feel, to respond emotionally in life situations, is a personality-health value for many reasons. Emotional tensions add a rich dimension to our experience, making life fuller and more meaningful. Try to imagine how drab life would be without affect of any sort. In addition, emotional responses serve very useful signal and motivating functions for a person, warning him of what to expect, and motivating him to do something either to avert the expected event or to hasten its arrival, as in the case of cues which portend pain or pleasure.

But the signal function of affects is of value only when the affects are rational. Irrational affects actually interfere with the attainment of gratifications. We will give a general rule for the attainment of rational affects, and then illustrate this rule with discussions of anxiety, hostility, and guilt.

The rule may be stated as follows: *In order to attain rational affects, it is necessary (a) to admit that one has the feeling in question and (b) to subject the cognitive aspects of the emotional response (the expectancies) to reality-testing.* If this is done, the person will fear only those things which realistically are dangerous; he will worry and feel anxiety only when events actually forecast impending danger to values; he will become hostile only when he has actually been insulted, threatened, or thwarted.

ACHIEVING RATIONAL ANXIETY. Irrational anxiety is known to play a very crucial role in the development of symptoms of unhealthy personality. Rational anxiety, on the other hand, serves a useful biological function to the person, warning him of actual danger to his assorted values.[18] Let us describe the general principles for the attainment of rational anxiety:

1. THE PERSON MUST FIRST EXPERIENCE HIS ANXIETY AND RECOGNIZE IT AS SUCH. This is not so simple as would appear at first glance. Anxiety is very often effectively repressed by a person, so that he is hardly aware that he has it. Or it may be warded off by all manner of effective avoidance measures,[19] so that he seldom experiences it. Yet, if the person were directly confronted by the anxiety-provoking situation, he might become overwhelmed with anxiety. The recognition and direct experiencing of anxiety is difficult to achieve in such instances; in fact, it may be necessary for a person to seek help before he can recognize his own anxiety. An expert personality diagnostician or therapist may be able to discern the indirect symptoms of unconscious anxiety and help the patient re-experience his anxiety.

2. THE PERSON MUST SUBJECT HIS WORRIES, OR EXPECTANCIES, TO REALITY-TESTING. Anxiety usually has a cognitive component, namely, *worrying*. Worry is really another term for expectancy, in this case, expectancy pertaining to painful events. Worry may be only momentary, or it may be unremitting and ceaseless. In order to insure that the worry is warranted, it is important for the anxious person to make a realistic appraisal of the probability that the dreaded events will come to pass. Such an appraisal will, in many instances, disclose that the worry is groundless and that the anxiety is thus irrational.[20] In such cases, the irrational anxiety may disappear. In cases where worry continues despite knowledge that the worry is groundless, it can be assumed that the content of worry is symbolic, that the person has anxieties which are still unconscious.

In illustration of these steps, let us assume that a person becomes anxious each time he confronts a crowd for purposes of making a speech. He worries in advance that he will make a fool of himself, or that he is a fool already and will expose himself when he speaks.

Once in the situation, he expects the people will judge him harshly, or ridicule him.

There are many ways in which he can test the validity of his expectancies. First, he can look into the origins of his worries. He may find that on one occasion he made a speech, and people laughed at him. From that one occasion, he generalized to all future occasions. "They laughed at me once, they'll laugh at me in the future." Often, such a logical analysis will dissipate the anxiety, and eliminate the worry.

The person may discover through such analysis that he is assuming all people are identical in cruelty with the few who laughed him off the platform the first time he spoke. Observation may disclose there are clear differences between the group he is about to address and the group who laughed at him. Observing the difference may effectively banish anxiety.[21]

It may not be desirable for the person to lose his anxiety entirely, for anxiety can be a very useful motive insuring that a person will work hard or take sensible precautions against danger. But there seems to be little danger that any person will ever succeed in completely eliminating anxiety from his life, unless he remains "doped" with tranquilizing drugs all day every day. If he can rid himself of his irrational anxieties, that will be a worthwhile achievement beyond which he need not strive.

Oddly enough, a person may have potential anxiety about facing a group without awareness of the fact. He has never had occasion to confront one and hence cannot recall ever being anxious. He may have all of the false expectancies about groups, but he will never have occasion to test these because he has never experienced the anxiety which would be provoked in the group situation. Only an expert observer might be able to infer from observations of his compulsive avoidance of group situations, that he has unconscious anxiety connected with groups. Obviously, the person with unconscious anxiety must experience it before he can go through the procedures that will be effective in rendering anxiety rational. Much of the effort of the personality therapist treating neurotic patients is aimed at helping a patient to recognize and experience his anxieties, when they have been warded off by means of repression and other defensive activities.

Parenthetically, it may be noted that excessive frequency of anxiety-reactions is an undesirable and unhealthy thing. Reality-testing will serve to reduce the frequency with which a person is threatened. Another factor which also serves to reduce anxiety is the increase of one's skill-repertoire. The more one is autonomous and skilled, the less there is to worry about in life. Autonomy and reality-contact thus appear to be among the factors which will reduce the frequency of anxiety-reactions.

Unfortunately, not all persons are able to follow the steps which produce rational anxiety. Instead of striving to recognize and experience their anxiety, they avoid situations thought to be anxiety-provoking; they may drink alcohol so that they don't feel their anxiety; they may gulp tranquilizing pills. Such persons are most likely to move in the direction of unhealthy personality, or remain in their present unhealthy state.

ACHIEVING RATIONAL HOSTILITY. Our society largely condemns hostility as a bad thing.[22] Most of us feel guilty and become anxious whenever we are hostile. We are afraid that if people know we feel hostile toward them, they will reject us. From an early age, we are encouraged to eliminate hostility from our emotional life, with severe punishments whenever we fail to control hostility as we should.

The upshot of training of this sort is that many of us are provoked to hostility by many situations and persons, and repress the feelings. Then, neither the offending person, nor we ourselves are aware of the hostility. It becomes unconscious hostility, and it leaks out in all kinds of ways. The person with unconscious hostility may be very sarcastic toward others; he may bump into people, forget promises and intentions, undermine others' self-confidence—all without any conscious intent to hurt them. From time to time, the hostility may break through into near-homicidal outbursts, and a usually gentle (repressed) person may commit a bloody hatchet murder, or otherwise run amok. When do we become hostile? There are only a few general sorts of instigators:

1. INTERFERENCE WITH GOAL-DIRECTED ACTIVITY.[23] We get angry when someone stands in our path, or prevents us from reaching our goal.

2. WITHHOLDING DESIRED NEED-OBJECTS. When we need money, or

affection, or sexual gratification, and someone withholds these things from us, we become hostile. In fact, whenever we are dependent on another person for different kinds of gratification, it is likely we will experience much hostility toward them from time to time, when they don't immediately gratify us, or when they let us down. The reader may be aware of the intensity with which he has sometimes felt hostility toward his parents, spouse, boss, or others on whom he is dependent for many things.

Because of fear or guilt, we may repress (rather than merely suppress) the hostility which has been provoked by the persons on whom we are dependent. When this occurs, the dependent individual will be incapable of perceiving and judging his father, leader, or other dependency-object in a realistic manner, since he cannot criticize him realistically—as it would have the significance of hostility. And so he is likely to *idealize* the object of his dependency, perceiving him as perfect, without flaws—the possessor of magical powers and unlimited strength. All of the hostility which belongs to the object of dependency is likely to be turned inward, in the form of guilt-feelings, or feelings of inferiority; or the hostility may be "displaced"—directed toward other persons.[24]

In one study, the present author[25] showed that intense moral indignation—hostility toward violators of the social mores—was correlated with an inability to express hostile criticism toward the parents. Those persons who displayed the most intense hostility toward bohemians, graft, sex perversion, etc., were persons who were least able to express criticism of their parents' traits.

3. VIOLATION OF IDEALS. We all have acquired standards of neatness, morality, decency, kindness, and when a person acts in opposition to these concepts of how things ought to be, we become hostile.[26] Of course, the more rigid these standards are, the more often will the person become hostile.

When is hostility irrational? It is irrational when it appears to be too intense, in a competent judge's opinion, in comparison with the provocation; in other words, when there does not appear to be adequate provocation for the hostility. A person may explode with hostility when his meal is ten seconds late, or a mother may become enormously irritated when her child gets some mud on his shoes. It must be admitted there are no precise norms to enable us to judge accurately whether or not a hostile reaction is warranted, but certainly crude norms exist in our society, since many of us express surprise when someone gets hostile over something which appears to be trivial.

Some notion of the extent of hostile reactions, and the stimuli which provoke them, is provided by Cason's classic catalogue of "common annoyances." [27] He collected thousands of cases of annoying stimuli, which ran the gamut from bad breath to uneven windowblinds. One must suppose that an annoyance, or hostile reaction, is irrational when it not shared by many people.

It may be said that the personality hygienist would not regard a person as healthy who was absolutely without hostility. Hostility serves a useful purpose in everyday life. It helps get things done which need to be done, as with moral indignation over slums and cruelty to children. Further, expression of hostility in relations with close friends or family lets these people know and understand how their behavior affects you. If they know what offends you, they can either change their behavior or leave you.

The personality hygienist would regard it as desirable to eliminate irrational hostility, however, since it complicates life considerably. There are two major steps which must be taken in order to achieve rational hostility:

1. THE PERSON MUST EXPERIENCE AND RECOGNIZE HIS HOSTILITY. As with anxiety, this is not always so easy, since we have such strong taboos against experiencing hostile affect. Many of us are unconsciously hostile toward parents, spouse, friends, boss, children, siblings, for reasons indicated above. These persons provoke hostility because of their behavior, but we may not dare to express this hostility toward them openly; indeed, because of strong personal taboos against hating one's family and others, we may have repressed the hostility so effectively we simply are not aware of it. Many a patient undergoing personality therapy is shocked when the therapist examines his behavior and tentatively suggests the patient has a good deal of hostility provoked by and directed toward mother, father, siblings, or wife.

2. THE PERSON MUST SUBJECT HIS HOSTILE REACTIONS TO REALITY-TESTING. This step really involves an attempt to determine why the person experiences hostility in response to the provocations which

occur. If it becomes apparent the hostile reaction is an irrational one, then steps may be taken to eliminate the tendency to react in hostile fashion. If, on the other hand, the hostile reaction seems warranted, and appropriate to the instigation, the person can perhaps come to express his hostility in appropriate fashion.

To illustrate, let us imagine that a person becomes hostile, irritated, or annoyed each time his wife straightens his tie, which she does daily. Possibly, he is not aware, fully, of his own irritation, or at least of the stimulus for it. Self-examination may disclose the precise instigator of his hostile reactions in his wife's behavior. When he is fully able to state in words "It makes me angry to have my wife straighten my tie," he may then say: "But that's really silly, to get so intensely furious about something so trivial. I wonder why I react that way?" Further self-scrutiny may disclose that such attentive behavior reminds him of some of the more overprotective and overcontrolling behavior of his mother, which he disliked intensely when he was younger. Simply making this discovery may be enough to eliminate the hostile reaction—it just no longer occurs when his wife fusses with his tie.

Naturally, not all hostile reactions will be so easy to banish through such analysis, but almost any person can eliminate some by such procedures. But even this procedure is impossible unless the person is able to feel and recognize his own hostilities and identify the stimulus for them.

Excessive hostility, whether conscious or unconscious, rational or irrational, is an indicator of unhealthy personality. When a person is chronically in a condition of hostility, his relationships with people will be seriously impaired, his ability to do productive work handicapped, and his physical health itself may suffer. Excessive hostility can be reduced by rational attempts to determine the causes and by undertaking steps to eliminate these causes. If a person becomes hostile because of chronic provocation in a dependency-relationship in which he is embroiled, he might take steps to achieve greater autonomy. If he is encountering too many interferences with his goal-directed activities, he might try to achieve greater skill so as to be better able to avoid or overcome these barriers. If his hostility derives from excessively rigid standards, it might be possible for him to alter his expectations and demands for perfection in himself and other people.

ACHIEVING RATIONAL GUILT. Many of us experience intense guilt feelings over apparently trivial breaches of conscience or of other standards for conduct.[28] Thus, some individuals, if they are simply a minute late for an appointment, or if their room is untidy, or if they tell a little white lie, become overcome with an onslaught of guilt. Very often, the guilt may have been repressed and manifests itself in indirect ways without being fully experienced as such.

Guilt itself is a desirable human emotion, in the sense that it enables us to recognize when we have done wrong, when we have violated our own consciences and the mores of society; there is no personality-hygiene value in eliminating the capacity to feel guilt. But irrational guilt may completely destroy a person's enjoyment in living, and so it should be eliminated or reduced when possible.

It is true there are no precise criteria available for judging whether or not a given guilt-reaction is irrational, but as with hostility and anxiety, crude norms seem to be available in our society. If the guilt-reaction seems disproportionate to the instigation, in the opinion of an expert personality therapist or in the opinion of a distinterested friend, then the individual can at least tentatively assume his guilt-response is irrational.

How can irrational guilt be replaced by mainly rational guilt-reactions?

1. THE PERSON MUST FIRST EXPERIENCE HIS GUILT, AND RECOGNIZE IT AS SUCH. Again, it is common that guilt, like hostility and anxiety, may be repressed and manifest itself only in disguised ways, e.g., chronic self-depreciation, inferiority feelings, avoidance of close relationships with people, vague depression, etc. The person must reverse the process of alienation from his real self and acknowledge his guilt when it occurs. Such acknowledgment makes it possible to determine whether the guilt reaction is rational or irrational; that is, to undertake reality-testing of the guilt-reaction attempts to alter it.

2. THE PERSON MUST SUBJECT HIS GUILT-REACTIONS TO REALITY-TESTING. Upon recognizing that he feels guilty about something, the person can seek to determine precisely what it was that provoked him to guilt. If it appears that he has gravely violated some deeply-

affirmed ethical precepts, then he can acknowledge his guilt and seek to make amends, or otherwise deal with it. If, on the other hand, the guilt-reaction is made to something quite trivial, the person might be able to recognize he is judging his behavior to-day from standards appropriate to his childhood years, which are no longer appropriate. Very often such recognition alone is sufficient to eliminate the guilt.

In illustration: a person may feel vaguely guilty each time he kisses a girl, so that he doesn't enjoy the kiss. His fiancée may notice he kisses only occasionally and then in a very perfunctory manner. If she would like more affectionate display, she may ask him why he avoids kissing and why, when he kisses her, he seems uncomfortable. The man may only then recognize he has had guilt-feelings about kissing. If he puts it in words, "kissing makes me feel guilty," both he and his girl can begin to evaluate the reaction and try to understand its origin. To kiss one's fiancée is not taboo in our society, and so it might be agreed that his guilts over kissing her are irrational. Then, the man may come to realize that early in childhood he was taught (deliberately, or accidentally) by his mother to regard kissing as immoral. In his later years, he no longer believed kissing was immoral, but the early teaching persisted because it was unrecognized.

PERSONALITY THERAPY AND THE ATTAINMENT OF RATIONAL AFFECTS. After a person has undergone effective personality therapy, his friends may observe striking changes in his emotionality. Things which frightened him so that he avoided them, no longer do. Things which annoyed him beyond endurance now do not affect him in the slightest degree. He may now display quite open hostility in situations where formerly he squirmed with suppressed resentment. It may further be noticed that he seems to be able to enjoy himself more, without guilt—that fewer of the good things in life are taboo for him.

The reason for these observed changes is the fact that intense personality therapy is about the best—possibly the only—means for promoting the recognition of one's emotional responses, and for subjecting these to reality-testing measures. The therapy-relationship is one in which the patient interacts with a participant observer, the therapist, who does not react to the patient as do people in everyday life. When the patient displays anger, affection, guilt, anxiety, etc., the therapist does not react with counterhostility, counteraffection, scolding, or reassurance. Instead, he tries to help the patient recognize his feelings, the stimuli for these feelings, the origins of these feelings, and the rationality of these feelings.

BEHAVIOR UNDER EMOTIONAL TENSION

Thus far, we have been primarily concerned with the emotional responses themselves. Let us now examine the behavior which emotional tension gives rise to. It may be said that emotional tensions function in the same fashion as need-tensions or wishes—they give rise to instrumental behavior which has for its aim either (a) the production in the self of certain desired emotional tensions or (b) the changing and riddance of unwanted emotional tensions. In the second instance, the reasons for wanting riddance of the felt tensions may be that the tensions interfere with efficient work or rational thinking, or they may threaten a person's relationships with others upon whom he is dependent for various reasons. He may not want his spouse, parents, or boss to know he has hostile feelings toward them, lest he be rejected or punished. Or, the feelings in question may not be wanted because they conflict with and threaten a person's self-structure; his self-concept does not include the notion that he is a person with such feelings; or the feelings in question may be opposed to the individual's self-ideal and conscience.

In the first instance, actively seeking to induce certain emotional tensions in the self, the reason may be a desire to escape from the boredom of rationality and everyday work; or it may be that these sought after feelings were pleasantly experienced in the past, and the individual wants to re-experience them for the sheer joy of feeling them again. Thus, an airplane ride may have induced feelings of omnipotence because it was a thrilling but safe danger; or someone may have said or done very nice things to you, and you want to bathe yourself again in the wonderful feelings induced by the praise, the caresses, or the nurturance.

EMOTIONAL TENSION-SEEKING BEHAVIOR

A person may actively seek out danger for the thrills it gives him, or simply to prove his lack of cowardice. Psychoanalysts give the name *counterphobic character* [29] to individuals who may be ridden with fears which their pride will not allow them to acknowledge. They appear to be engaged in a never-ending demonstration of their own daring and courage; they might be called chronic and compulsive heroes. Such a compulsive pattern of behavior must be judged unhealthy on a number of grounds. The counterphobic tendency in a person may bring him into situations beyond his capacity to handle, thus endangering his life or health. Common sense would have deterred another person, but not the counterphobe. In addition, the counterphobe, by refusing to acknowledge his own basic timorousness, is becoming further alienated from his real self, and he is doing nothing toward the end of understanding his fears and seeking to reality-test them.

Another common variety of tension-seeking behavior is to be found in the sex-addict. He (or she) strives for the frequent experience of sexual tension and orgasm. There is nothing unhealthy per se in the quest for sexual gratification. A compulsive quest for sexuality, however, may be undertaken as an escape from boredom, inferiority feelings, or other causes. It is judged unhealthy because the quest for sexuality results in ignoring other important values, such as healthy interpersonal relationships, productivity in work, and the constructive management of the problems which were responsible for compulsive sexuality in the first place.

EMOTIONAL TENSION-REDUCING BEHAVIOR

Given the fact of emotional tension produced by some stimulus, what does the person do with these tensions? In principle, there is a limited number of alternatives, and each of these has implications for personality health. The alternative reactions of a person to emotional arousal are: (a) immediate uncontrolled expression and release, (b) suppression of emotional behavior, and (c) repression of emotional tension.

IMMEDIATE EXPRESSION OF EMOTIONAL TENSIONS. This is the characteristic pattern among young children when they have been provoked to emotional tension. They express it immediately, with little if any motor control. They laugh, cry, strike out, jump up and down, throw tantrums—in short, they appear to be almost out of control. It is as if their cerebral cortex had been dethroned from rational control over behavior and their entire organism is being directed by "explosions" of subcortical brain structures, viz.: the hypothalamus.

On the positive side, immediate expression of emotional tensions in this uncontrolled manner is effective in getting rid of the tensions. They are given expression, and once out, the person is able to proceed on a more controlled and less tense basis. On the negative side, immediate expression is undesirable especially in an adult, because:

1. Society condemns uncontrolled expression of emotion in an adult on a purely normative and moral basis. Thus, the adult who throws tantrums, or who cannot control his emotions is viewed as an immature person, who cannot be trusted with important responsibilities.

2. In the process of uncontrolled emotional expressiveness, the person is "out of touch" with external reality. He does not perceive the world with accuracy—indeed, he is not interested in the external world during his tantrum. Further, he does not protect other important values at the time he is in the throes of an "affective storm." He may break things which he values; he may say or do things which cost him his job, his marriage, his reputation.

SUPPRESSION OF EMOTIONAL BEHAVIOR. Emotional control is made possible through the gradually acquired ability of a person to pick and choose responses to a situation (emotion-provoking or otherwise) that are compatible with the largest number of important values. This picking and choosing in turn is predicated on the ability to postpone immediate responsiveness, to delay responding in order to allow time to reason, plan, or think. A young child cannot do this because he has not yet learned how, and because his nervous system has not yet matured to the point where it is physically possible for him to tolerate tension and inhibit motor expression.

When once the nervous system has matured to the point where delay and purposeful planning are possible, then suppression of emotional behavior becomes possible. There are no precise norms available for the age at which control becomes possible and for the quantity of tension which a person can be expected to tolerate without exploding into expressive behavior; however, it can be expected that the ability increases from infancy up to maturity, and then declines with approaching senescence.

Let us now examine some of the implications of emotion-suppression for personality and physical health.

PHYSICAL CONSEQUENCES OF EMOTION-SUPPRESSION. When a person is provoked to emotional tension, widespread changes occur throughout his body, in consequence of heightened autonomic nervous-system activity. If expression is possible and available to the person, in the form of muscular activity, weeping, laughing, sexual behavior, then the physiological processes will shortly be restored to normal.

If no release is possible, if the person suppresses for a long period of time, then the physical events which constitute part of the emotional response will be prolonged. If the prolongation is marked, it is possible that the functions and even the structure of inner organs may be permanently impaired. The field of psychosomatic medicine is devoted to just such a study, the study of the effects of emotionality on the health of the physical organism.[30]

PSYCHOLOGICAL CONSEQUENCES OF EMOTION-SUPPRESSION. Suppressed emotional excitement is a factor which interferes with rational activity in many ways. Reich coined the term "emotional plague"[31] to describe the far-reaching impairments of logical reasoning and accurate perception which are produced by prolonged suppression of sexual and emotional tension. It is as if all of the will-directed energy of a suppressing person is being utilized in holding back affect, with a resultant diminution in the amount of energy available for commerce with reality.

In addition to the effects on rational thinking, emotion-suppression appears to interfere with efficiency of skilled behavior. One cannot play the piano, repair machinery, or knit with efficient speed and dispatch when one is full of unexpressed fear, hostility, grief, or laughter.

Finally, it may happen that the cumulative effects of suppression may eventuate in such a strength of tension that control becomes impossible, and the person explodes with expressiveness of a much more violent nature than would have been the case had he reacted much earlier. Many persons have committed murder, and other acts of destructiveness when they could no longer fully suppress conscious hostility.

Let us draw a distinction between healthy and unhealthy emotion-suppression. In anticipation, we may say that there are occasions when suppression is compatible with personality health and other occasions when it is not. The following discussion may help us to judge whether or not suppression of emotion is healthy.

HEALTHY EMOTION-SUPPRESSION. Let us first assert that for an adult, at least, the capacity to suppress emotional expression and to delay immediate responsiveness is a capacity which is not only valued by moralists, it is also valued by personality hygienists. But the personality hygienist may differ from the moralist in that *he affirms the value of the capacity to express emotional tensions just as much as the capacity to suppress them.* The healthy personality displays neither immediate expression nor chronic suppression of emotion exclusively. Rather, he displays a capacity to choose between the alternatives of suppression and expression. When it will not jeopardize important values, he will express his feelings freely, in an almost unrestrained fashion: he may laugh with gusto, cry without restraint, express anger with intense verbal outpour. If other values would be endangered by such emotionality, he is capable of suppressing his feelings and carrying on with whatever instrumental behavior is in process at the time of emotional arousal. He displays what psychoanalysts call ego-strength and what other psychologists call stress-tolerance. In the long run, however, this regime of *selective suppression and release* insures that the person will not suffer from the effects on his body and on his ability to perform produced by prolonged emotion-suppression; and he will not needlessly endanger his job, his reputation, his self-respect, and other important values, by heedless emotional explosions. In short, he can suppress when he chooses, and he can let go when he chooses—and it is he who does the choosing.

UNHEALTHY EMOTION-SUPPRESSION. Emotion-suppression becomes unhealthy when it is prolonged, for any reason. The person who habitually and chronically suppresses his emotions generally does so because of fear of the consequences which might follow emotional expression. It often happens that a person's very fear of emotional expression is itself an irrational fear, based on overgeneralization from certain unpleasant occurrences in the past. Perhaps he was severely punished, or lost his job, in consequence of an emotional outburst. From this one event, he may have generalized to the effect that "all emotional expression is dangerous, or bad." The upshot may be that he comes to suppress his feelings—though he is fully aware of them—without discrimination.

The longer-range consequence of chronic suppression *may* be psychosomatic illnesses (provided other necessary and sufficient causes are present), such as elevated blood pressure, mucous colitis, asthma, peptic ulcers; or they may include chronic fatigue (it consumes energy to suppress hostility and other strong feelings), muscular aches and pains, migraine-like headaches; or it may result in impaired work- and study-efficiency, inability to concentrate, impaired reality-contact, and impaired relationships with people. In connection with the latter, most of us value in our friends and loved ones at least some ability to express feelings. The chronic suppresser is often derogated as a "stick," or "stone-face," or an "iceberg"—someone who is "less than human."

REPRESSION OF EMOTIONAL TENSIONS. A person is said to repress his emotions (a) when he takes active steps to avoid experiencing certain affects, and (b) when confronted by a stimulus adequate to induce an emotional response, he denies (and believes his own denial) he is experiencing any emotion in particular.[32] Repression in the first instance is achieved by regulating one's life so that one will never encounter the objects known to induce certain feelings, and also by refusing to think about, or remember, objects or events which might induce unwanted feelings. Repression in the second instance appears to be achieved by means of some form of self-deception or denial—as if the person says to himself, and believes, "I am not angry (afraid, sexy, amused, etc.)." Or, in order to rid his awareness of the unwanted emotional tensions, he may think about things and perform tasks that induce feelings incompatible with the emotional tension which is not wanted. Thus, a small child, confronted by a fear-inspiring dog, might say, "Nice puppy"—puppies evoke tender feelings, not fear in the child. Or the nervous and timid speaker at a banquet, who is afraid he will be ridiculed, may address the audience as "My friends." If he believes that they are his friends, his fear will evaporate.

Repression is generally undertaken automatically and unconsciously by a person, although it is possible consciously and deliberately to attempt it, because (a) the emotional tensions serve to trigger off strong anxiety over the anticipated consequences of expressing them, and (b) the emotional tensions conflict strongly with the person's conscience and self-ideal—if he admitted he had these feelings, he might have to change his concept of himself, with accompanying losses in self-esteem.

In most, if not all instances, a personality hygienist condemns repression of emotional tensions as unhealthy. The main reason for this condemnation lies in the fact that in spite of repression, the feelings exist—or at least the capacity to experience these feelings remains present and unchanged. When feelings have been provoked but are not recognized by the person, they produce effects both physical and psychological in nature. In Chapter 2, we discussed some of the ways in which unconscious feelings (and needs) manifest themselves in thinking and behavior. In addition to the psychological consequences, repressed affects produce the same effects on the body as do consciously suppressed feelings, only the person is not aware that he has these feelings.

When feelings have been repressed, more or less successfully, it is not only the person himself who is unaware of their presence. Other persons as well will not know how the person really feels. Thus, a husband may irritate his wife for years by certain of his habits. She, however, may have repressed her annoyance and hostility. Then, at some future remote date, she leaves him, or becomes overwhelmed with uncontrollable rage at some trivial annoyance. Naturally, the husband is surprised and shocked. If she had openly vented her feelings long ago, he might have altered his behavior easily and without any complaint.

One of the most important tasks in personality therapy, and in the treatment of so-called psychosomatic illnesses, is that of aiding the patient to recognize his own feelings—to "unrepress" them, to experience and express them fully. This uncovering process generally is met with strong resistance on the part of the patient, however, since the experience of these feelings is quite threatening to security and to self-esteem.

Factors Which Promote Chronic Suppression and Repression of Emotional Tensions

In view of the fact that chronic suppression and repression of affect produce such unhealthy consequences, we shall inquire into some of the factors which are responsible for the adoption of these unhealthy patterns.

DEPENDENCY UPON OTHERS. When a person must depend upon the affection and support of others for the solution of his problems and the satisfaction of his needs, he is thrust into a situation which promotes both suppression and repression. So long as he is in the dependent role, and needs the other person's good will, he must do nothing or express nothing which will incur the displeasure of his dependency-object. Thus, a child, an employee, or an inadequate person must withhold honest expression of feelings, and express (or pretend to feel) only those affects which will improve his status in the eyes of the dominant one. Most of us have had the fantasy at one time or another of telling someone with whom we have been closely associated in a dependent role just how we really feel toward them. Some people, on achieving autonomy, wealth, or courage, come right out and express their long-withheld feelings. Sometimes, the dissolution of a dependency-relationship will remove only the motives for suppression, so that the person vents feelings he has long been aware of. Sometimes, however, with the break-up of the dependency-relationship, long-standing repressions will be undone, and the person will himself be shocked and surprised at the intensity and nature of feelings which well up for expression.

EXCESSIVELY STRICT CONSCIENCE AND SELF-IDEAL. A person may chronically suppress or repress certain emotions, not only for external reasons, such as avoiding rejection or criticism, but also to conform with the demands of conscience. A person may have acquired values which make his self-esteem contingent upon the exclusion of certain feelings and emotions, not only from behavior but even from consciousness. He can accept himself only as kind, pure, generous, strong, etc., and so he must repress all those feelings which would produce guilt or a threat to his self-concept if they were recognized.

ACHIEVING HEALTHY EMOTIONAL BEHAVIOR

The behavior undertaken by a person when he is aroused to emotional tension is healthy when (a) it is effective in reducing or changing the present tension-level and -quality to one which is more desired, and (b) when the emotional behavior does not jeopardize health, self-esteem, or any other things which are valued by the person.

We pointed out above that selective suppression and release of emotional tensions form the desired pattern from the personality-hygiene standpoint. This pattern calls for the capacity to control one's behavior under relatively high degrees of tension. It presumes ego-strength [33] in the person, such that he can refrain from explosive, uncontrolled outbursts if he chooses to, but at the same time, he can also let loose his feelings when he wants to.

What factors promote ego-strength, since this appears to be the most important capacity in the attainment of healthy emotional behavior? One such factor is autonomy, the possession of a high degree of skill and competence in many areas, so that the person is not obliged to be overly dependent on others (which we saw to be a factor promoting chronic suppression and repression). Security is another factor, whether it is the by-product of diverse skill, or an assured source of income. Insecure persons are very prone to anxiety, and they may dread expressing their feelings because they believe that if they do so, they may lose status, their job, or friendships. Reality-contact can also promote healthy emotional behavior; the person can determine realistically what values are at stake in an emotional situation and what dangers are associated with suppression and expression of feelings.

Autonomy, security, and reality-contact appear to make it possible for a person to choose how he will react under emotion, rather than reacting in a stereotyped manner with "explosions," with repression, or suppression.

SUMMARY

The role of emotion in personality health and physical health has long been recognized by physicians, psychologists, and laymen.

In order to facilitate a discussion of emotion, we draw a distinction between emotional arousal and emotional release. *Emotional tension* (or *affect*), refers to the change in inner experience produced by some stimulus which affects us in pleasurable or unpleasant ways. Emotional tensions are given assorted names: anger, fear, anxiety, depression, etc. They are part of a more complex emotional response which includes, with affects, certain neurophysiological responses, and certain patterns of activity of the voluntary musculature. The term *emotional behavior* is used to describe behavior which a person engages in when he is motivated by emotional tension.

Habitual emotional responses—*emotional habits*—are acquired through the mechanisms of *conditioning, identification,* and through *socialization experiences.* In conditioning experiences, a person acquires *expectancies* which become important determiners of his subsequent emotional responses. Accurate expectancies are an important determiner of rational affects, which are valued by the personality hygienist.

Irriational affects are emotional responses which do not appear to be appropriate to the stimulus or situation. The person himself does not understand why he responds emotionally, when he has irrational affects. Repression, redintegration, symbolization and overgeneralization are factors which produce irrational affects.

Rational affects are achieved through conscious recognition of one's own emotional tensions and through the activity of reality-testing the cognitive aspects of the emotional response, the perceptions and expectancies. The means whereby rational anxiety, hostility, and guilt are achieved are discussed to illustrate the attainment of rational affects. Personality therapy is discussed as a means of promoting rational affects in people.

Emotional behavior is classified into two broad categories: emotional-tension-seeking behavior and emotional-tension-reducing behavior. Examples of the former are counterphobic characters, and "sex-addicts."

Three broad patterns of tension-reducing behavior were discussed and evaluated with respect to their "health." They included *immediate expression, suppression,* and *repression of emotional tensions.* Of all these, *selective suppression and release* was regarded as the pattern most compatible with healthy emotionality in particular and personality health in general.

Dependency upon others and an *excessively strict conscience* were discussed as factors which promote *chronic suppression and repression* of emotional tensions. Factors which promote *healthy emotionality* include *autonomy, security,* and *efficient reality-contact.*

NOTES AND REFERENCES

RECOMMENDED READINGS ARE MARKED WITH AN ASTERISK (*)

*1. While most of the concepts in this chapter are defined in the text, the reader will get a richer understanding if he reviews basic materials. See for example, Ruch, F. L., *Psychology and life,* 4th ed., New York, Scott, Foresman, 1953, Ch. 6.

2. There is as yet much controversy and much ignorance about the neurophysiological basis of affects. Probably the "feel" of emotion is produced both by sensory awareness of the visceral changes which occur and by an "upward discharge" of the hypothalamus to the cerebral cortex. See Arnold, M., "An excitatory theory of emotion" in Reymert, M. L., *Feelings and emotions: the Moose-heart symposium,* New York, McGraw-Hill, 1950, pp. 11–33. Also, Gellhorn, E., *Physiological foundations of neurology and psychiatry,* Minneapolis, University of Minnesota Press, 1953, Ch. 14. These authors attempt to answer the question of what kinds of neural activity mediate the physiological and psychological phenomena which constitute emotional tension. There is growing evidence to verify the assumption that different affects, viz.: fear, anger, depression and pleasure are mediated by different patterns of neurophysiological functioning. *Cf.* Arnold, Magda B., "The physiological differentiation of emotional states," *Psychol. Rev.,* 1945, **52**, 35–48. Ax, A., "The physiological differentiation between fear and anger in humans," *Psychosom. Med.,* 1953, **15**, 433–442. Stevenson, I. and Matthews, R. A., "Fact and theory in psychosomatic medicine," *J. nerv. ment. Dis.,* 1953, **118**, 289–306. Stevenson, I., "Physical symptoms during pleasurable emotional states," *Psychosom. Med.,* 1950, **12**, 98–102.

3. Many of the signs of autonomic activity can be detected only with the use of a sensitive instrument called a polygraph, which registers minute changes in the electrical activity of the skin, muscles, and in the brain, some of which are indices of autonomic functioning. "Lie detection" involves the use of a polygraph to register emotion-provoked changes which occur when a person has lied to a questioner. With a poker face, he can mask his inner feeling of guilt or panic, but if these affects exist, the polygraph will often register physiological signs of their expression.

°4. Cf. Pavlov, I. P., *Lectures on conditioned reflexes,* New York, International Publ., 1928. Also Gellhorn, E., *op. cit.,* Ch. 15.

°5. Hull, C. L., *Principles of behavior,* New York, Appleton-Century-Crofts, 1943. Skinner, B. F., *The behavior of organisms: an experimental analysis,* New York, Appleton-Century-Crofts, 1938.

°6. Cf. Watson, J. B. and Rayner, R., "Conditioned emotional reactions," *J. exp. Psychol.,* 1920, 3, 1–14. Also Jones, M. C., "A laboratory study of fear: the case of Peter," *Ped. Sem.,* 1924, 31, 308–316; Liddell, H. S., "Conditioning and emotions," *Scient. Amer.,* 1954, for discussions and illustrations of the conditioning of emotional responses. See also Mowrer, O. H., *Learning theory and personality dynamics,* New York, Ronald, 1950, Ch. 1–5, for experimental and theoretical analyses of fear and anxiety.

°7. See Mowrer, O. H., *op. cit.,* Ch. 2. In Ch. 9 and 10, Mowrer expounds his two-factor theory of learning, which is relevant to the problem of how emotional responses are acquired.

8. Rotter, J. B., *Social learning and clinical psychology,* New York, Prentice-Hall, 1954, pp. 165–183, for a technical discussion of expectancy.

9. See Mowrer, O. H., *op. cit.,* Ch. 21 for an analysis of identification in terms of learning theory. The present author borrows heavily from Mowrer's discussion of identification. A paper by a psychoanalyst which is closely similar in approach to Mowrer's is Hendrick, I., "Early development of the ego: identification in infancy," *Psychoanalyt. Quart.,* 1951, 20, 44–61.

10. Mowrer, O. H., *op. cit.,* Ch. 16.

11. This term is adapted from Mowrer, O. H., *op. cit.*

12. The psychoanalytic method of undertaking personality therapy seeks, among other things, to help a patient discover the origins of many of his irrational affects, to abreact these, and thus to be bothered no more by them.

13. This concept was used to explain some of the phenomena in war neuroses by Hollingworth. See Hollingworth, H. L., *The psychology of functional neuroses,* New York, Appleton-Century-Crofts, 1920.

°14. Freud, S., "Analysis of a phobia in a five-year-old boy," in Freud, S., *Collected papers,* Vol. III, London, Hogarth, 1953.

°15. The importance of making discriminations is well brought out in Dollard, J., and Miller, N. E., *Personality and psychotherapy: an analysis in terms of learning, thinking, and culture,* New York, McGraw-Hill, 1950, Ch. 19.

16. Cf. Secord, P. F., Dukes, W. F., and Bevan, W., "Personalities in faces: I. An experiment in social perceiving," *Genet. Psychol. Monogr.*, 1954, **49**, 231–279.

17. For centuries, a correlation between body build and personality traits has been postulated. The layman commonly believes in such a relationship. A sophisticated study of the relations between physique and certain personality traits (temperament) is Sheldon, W. H. and Stevens, S. S., *The varieties of temperament*, New York, Harper, 1942.

18. Cf. Freud, S., *The problem of anxiety*, New York, Norton, 1936. Freud outlines systematically the role that anxiety plays in the genesis of neurotic symptoms. See May, R., *The meaning of anxiety*, New York, Ronald, 1950, for an excellent analysis of the constructive as well as destructive role that anxiety plays in human life. See also Mowrer, O. H., *op. cit.*, Ch. 18–20.

19. It seems likely that rigid character traits—"character armor"—are acquired during the process of personality growth as means of avoiding anxiety. See Reich, W., *Character analysis*, Part II, New York, Orgone Institute Press, 1949.

20. Cf. Dollard, J. and Miller, N. E., *op. cit.*

21. Many of the interpretations by a psychoanalytic therapist are made so as to help a patient see that he is reacting to things in the present as if they had characteristics of things from the past.

22. Whiting and Child showed that American parents treat aggression in their growing children with much more severity than do parents from many other societies. See Whiting, J. W. M. and Child, I. L., *Child-training and personality*, New Haven, Yale University Press, 1953, pp. 98–102.

23. See Dollard, J., Miller, N. E., Doob, L. W., Mowrer, O. H., and Sears, R. R., *Frustration and aggression*, New Haven, Yale University Press, 1939.

24. The so-called "authoritarian personality," a person who is highly dependent upon authority-figures for direction, support, and protection, is notoriously hostile toward the authority-figure, but at an unconscious level. He is said to manifest ambivalent attitudes toward authority. See Adorno, T. W., Frenkel-Brunswick, Else, Levinson, D. J., and Sanford, R. N., *The authoritarian personality*, New York, Harper, 1950. These investigators observed, not only signs of unconscious hostility toward authority-figures, but also evidence for overidealizing authority-figures, and displacement of hostility toward minority-group members.

25. See Jourard, S. M., "Moral indignation: a correlate of denied dislike of parents' traits," *J. consult. Psychol.*, 1954, 18, 59–60.

26. See Jourard, S. M., *op. cit.* Also Cason, H., "Common annoyances: a psychological study of every-day aversions and irritations," *Psychol. Monogr.*, 1930, **40**, No. 2. (Whole No. 132). Jourard's "moral indignation scale" was suggested by Cason's list of "annoyances," which, on analysis, all appear to be violations of a person's concepts of how things "ought to be."

27. Cason, H., *op. cit.*

28. See Chapter 11 for a fuller discussion of guilt.

29. Cf. Fenichel, O., *The psychoanalytic theory of neurosis*, New York, Norton, 1945, pp. 480–485.

°30. A good introduction to the field of psychosomatic medicine is Alexander, F., *Psychosomatic medicine*, New York, Norton, 1950. The most complete review of the bodily changes associated with emotion is Flanders-Dunbar, Helen, *Emotions and bodily changes*, 4th ed., New York, Columbia University Press, 1954.

31. Reich, W., *op. cit.*, Ch. 12. See Lazarus, R., Deese, J., and Osler, Sonia F., "The effects of psychological stress upon performance," *Psychol. Bull.*, 1952, **49**, 293–317. This paper reviews experimental studies of the impact on cognitive and performance activities of experimentally-produced emotional tensions.

32. See Chapter 13 for a more detailed discussion of repression.

33. The term ego-strength originated with the psychoanalysts, but it is gaining increasing usage among psychologists who do both clinical work and personality research. Cf. Jourard, S. M., "Egostrength and the recall of tasks," *J. abn. soc. Psychol.*, 1954, **49**, 51–58. Also Barron, F., "An ego-strength scale which predicts response to psychotherapy," *J. consult. Psychol.*, 1953, **17**, 327–333. These studies, and others, illustrate the manner in which the construct ego-strength is utilized in research work. In clinical work, the psychologist and the therapist are often called upon to make estimates of the strength of the patient's ego. Various indices are commonly employed, viz.: estimates of reality-contact, ability to tolerate delay and frustration, etc.

QUESTIONS FOR REVIEW AND EXAMINATION

1. Define emotional tension, emotional behavior, emotional responses, and emotional habits.

2. In what ways do we acquire our emotional habits?

3. What is the influence of expectancies on emotional responses?
4. What is a rational affect? An irrational affect?
5. What factors are responsible for irrational affects?
6. How may rational affects be achieved? Illustrate with anxiety, hostility, and guilt.
7. What are the major varieties of emotional behavior?
8. Why are chronic suppression and repression of emotions unhealthy?
9. What factors promote chronic suppression and repression of emotion?
10. Use the concepts in this chapter to describe and evaluate emotional responsiveness and emotional behavior in someone you know.

CHAPTER 5

Healthy Sexual Behavior

Sexuality is a source of rich pleasure, but also, a source of profound difficulty for many persons in our society. A person's attitudes toward sex, his knowledge about it, and his modes of sexual behavior all have marked consequences for the health of his overall personality. It behooves us, then, to examine sexuality in some detail and to establish some criteria for assessing it from a personality-hygiene point of view.

If we look at sexual behavior from the standpoint of the empirical scientist, we observe much variety in sexual behavior within our society, and in other societies. Marked differences in sexual aim, sexual object, sexual stimuli, and modes of sexual behavior can be found at different age levels, for men and women, different social classes, educational levels, etc. Kinsey has documented the range of variability in sexual behavior most thoroughly for men and women in our society.

But it should be asserted that not all that exists in the realm of sexual behavior is acceptable to the social mores; nor does it accord with the standards of personality health. We may ask: "What limits on the range of sexual behavior mark off what is socially acceptable, or moral? What limits mark off what might be regarded as healthy?"

120

Let us first define some technical terms which will serve us throughout this chapter, and then attempt to answer these questions.

DEFINITION OF TERMS

SEXUAL TENSION: An easily recognized quality of feeling which the layman generally refers to as "sexual feeling."

SEXUAL RESPONSE: An arousal of sexual tension which is instigated by a sexual stimulus.

SEXUAL STIMULI: Any objects or stimuli which induce an arousal of sexual tension in a person. In animals, certain odors and movements manifested by the female constitute sexual stimuli for the male. Among humans, sexual stimuli include tactile stimulation of erogenous zones, and various stimuli which have acquired the capacity to induce sexual arousal through learning. These learned sexual stimuli are called *symbolic sexual stimuli*.

SEX OBJECT: Any object with which a person behaves sexually so as to obtain a climax, viz.: another person, or in perverse cases, an animal, or a fetish of some kind.

EROGENOUS ZONES: Areas of the body, the stimulation of which produces erotic, or sexual tension. They include the genital organs, the mouth and lips, the breasts and nipples in women, and several other body parts as well.

SEXUAL AIM: [1] The conscious goal or purpose for which a person undertakes sexual behavior. It is synonymous with motive. Examples of sexual aim include the desire to conceive children, the desire to achieve pleasure, the desire to give pleasure, etc.

ORGASM, OR CLIMAX: The experience of intense pleasure associated with certain reflex activities in the genital organs, consequent upon their being suitably stimulated. In the adult male, the climax is accompanied by the release of spermatozoa in the seminal fluids. In the female, the climax does not release any reproductive secretions.

SEXUAL BEHAVIOR: Sexual behavior is instrumental behavior which is undertaken in order to achieve sexual gratification. In adults, sexual intercourse is the most common form of sexual behavior, although there are other means available for the attainment of a climax, viz.: self-manipulation and "petting."

THE SOCIAL RESTRICTIONS ON SEXUAL BEHAVIOR

In every society, strict taboos on sexuality are imposed. These taboos are concerned with the age at which sexual behavior is considered appropriate, the definition of appropriate sexual objects, the legal and moral conditions under which sexual behavior is condoned, and the definition of acceptable aims and behavior.

Our society appears to condemn sexual behavior in all circumstances save those of marriage. Thus, the following may be regarded as forbidden activities for members of our society. When they occur, they are punished or, at the least, induce guilt in the average person who practises them:

1. Masturbation.
2. Premarital sexual intercourse.
3. Extramarital sexual intercourse.
4. Sexual contact with animals.
5. Sexual behavior with a partner of the same sex (homosexuality).
6. Sexual behavior in an adult with a child for a partner.
7. Oral-genital, and anal-genital union.

In spite of the strict legal and moral limits which our society imposes on sexual behavior, there appears to be a considerable degree of violation of these mores, as Kinsey's exhaustive studies have shown.[2] Many personality hygienists would agree that some modification of our sexual mores is warranted, on the premise that their strictness contributes to widespread guilt, unnecessary repression, and even to the development of assorted patterns of unhealthy sexuality, for example, the perversions.

Some authorities, notably the psychoanalysts, hold the view that some form of difficulty with sexuality contributes actively to the development of neurosis and other forms of personality illness.

As time passes on, our concepts of acceptable sexual behavior may change gradually. At the present time, our sexual mores may be said to be relatively restrictive, at least in comparison with those of many other societies.[3] In Sweden, for example, it is assumed that unmarried couples will have sexual relations. There seem to be no strong taboos against such intimacy.

THE DEFINITION OF HEALTHY SEXUAL BEHAVIOR

Sexual behavior is healthy when it is effective in securing sexual gratification for the individual and yet at the same time accords with the social mores and the individual conscience. This definition is highly general and requires considerable elaboration. Let us discuss healthy sexuality from the standpoint of *aim, conditions for arousal,* and *behavior.*

HEALTHY SEXUAL AIMS

Most personality hygienists would concur that the aims most compatible with overall personality health seek to:

1. Achieve pleasure for the self.
2. Give pleasure to the partner.
3. Express love and depth of affection for the partner.
4. Conceive children.

In a healthy marriage, these aims will doubtless all exist. It should be stated that the above listing of sexual aims in no way implies a hierarchy of their importance. What is more likely is that at various times each of these aims will assume a priority of importance. In order to provide a broader perspective for viewing the healthy aims, let us consider some sexual aims which might be regarded as unhealthy. In theory, it is possible to engage in sexual behavior for a nearly infinite number of subjective goals, or motives. We shall limit our discussion to a few of the more common unhealthy aims.

UNHEALTHY SEXUAL AIMS

We shall select for discussion the following: (a) sexual behavior *as reassurance,* (b) sexual behavior as an *opiate,* and (c) sexual behavior as an *exchange commodity.*

SEXUAL BEHAVIOR AS REASSURANCE. Among males in our society, it is not uncommon to find grave doubts concerning adequacy, sexual potency, or general competence as a man. Sexual behavior is a very primitive and basic proof of one's masculinity, and so a man might seek numerous sexual experiences to demonstrate his prowess to himself. So long as he is able to continue his "conquests," he can maintain his self-esteem; if any factor such as illness or enforced abstinence prevents him from maintaining a certain level of sexual activity, he is likely to undergo feelings of depression, inferiority, or anxiety.

A woman might have grave doubts concerning her attractiveness to males and her "womanliness." Where this is the case, she might become promiscuous in her sexual behavior, with the aim of reassuring herself that she is indeed attractive and desirable.

The use of sexual behavior as reassurance is deemed unhealthy in these cases because it does not get to the root of the feelings of inadequacy which motivate the need for reassurance.

SEXUAL BEHAVIOR AS AN OPIATE. Sexual gratification is a very basic, biological kind of pleasure. For many persons, everyday life may be quite "gray" and devoid of many meaningful satisfactions. Their work may be boring and their relationships with people superficial and unsatisfying. Under such conditions, a person might engage in very frequent sexual relations, or masturbation, as a kind of compensation for the emptiness of everyday life. Again, such a use or aim of sexual behavior is unhealthy because it does not get to the root of the difficulty. Instead, the sexual pleasures may so "tranquilize" the person that he loses some of the impetus for efforts that could change the circumstances responsible for the suffering, boredom, and emptiness in his life.

SEXUAL BEHAVIOR AS AN EXCHANGE COMMODITY. A person might engage in sexual behavior as a means of getting things he believes cannot be gotten in any other way.

The most obvious example of sexuality as an exchange commodity is provided by the practice of prostitution. The prostitute sells sexuality for money.

Less obvious examples, but apparently quite common ones, may be provided through the study of many marriages. A wife, "starved" for affection and tenderness, may engage in sexual relationships with her husband when she does not really want to, because she feels it is only through such submission that she can gain her husband's affection.

In one case (mentioned later in this chapter), a frigid wife would abstain from sexual intercourse with her husband whenever she

wanted to force him to grant her wishes for a major household purchase, a trip, etc. She would "submit" only after her husband came
around to her point of view.

The use of sex as an exchange commodity runs counter to our
social mores. In addition, we can regard it as unhealthy because
such a means of getting things precludes personality growth. While
it may he a relatively easy way to get money, obedience, or affection, there are other ways of achieving these ends which are much
more compatible with personality growth, ways which call for new
learning on the part of the individual.

HEALTHY CONDITIONS FOR AROUSAL

An adult man or woman in good physical health can generally be
aroused to sexual tension by direct stimulation of the genitalia. However, sexual arousal in our culture is much more complicated than
this. Because of typical upbringing and training, most persons have
psychological conditions which must be met before sexual arousal
will occur. Unless these conditions are met, attempts to induce sexual
responses will fail and will induce instead feelings of disgust, guilt,
anxiety, or indifference.

The personality hygienist would view a person as healthy from
the standpoint of conditions for sexual arousal if he or she was
capable of becoming aroused sexually in a context of a socially approved sexual situation, that is, marriage. Within a love-relationship,
many of the emotions which block sexual arousal are likely to be
missing, e.g. guilt, or anxiety about "being found out." Consequently,
if a man and woman in a marital situation are capable of arousing
each other to sexual tension, through caresses, terms of endearment,
and expressions of love, they would be deemed sexually healthy.
Now let us consider some of the unhealthy conditions for arousal.

UNHEALTHY CONDITIONS FOR SEXUAL AROUSAL

A failure to respond sexually to the usual symbolic and direct
forms of sexual stimulation is generally referred to as *frigidity* in a
woman and *impotence* in a male. The most common psychological
causes of these conditions are emotions incompatible with sexual

responsiveness, such as guilt, anxiety, or disgust. Thus, a woman may have many irrational fears associated with sexuality. The stimuli which would arouse a healthy person serve only to induce guilt, anxiety, or disgust in this woman. Likewise, a male may have various irrational fears pertaining to sexuality which preclude his becoming aroused even under conditions where there is no rational basis for these fears. Such fears usually stem from early training and experiences with sex, and they may be read about in almost any treatise concerned with neurosis or personality therapy. For such persons to become capable of sexual responsiveness, it is necessary that the incompatible emotional responses to sexual stimuli be removed by some means.

Some persons will respond sexually to stimuli not generally regarded as sexual symbols in our society. The homosexual, for example, is a person who fears, is repelled by, or is indifferent to persons of the opposite sex; he can only be aroused by members of the same sex. The fetishist is aroused by the objects of his fetish and not by a receptive partner of the opposite sex. The sources of these deviations are to be found in an intensive study of the life history of the persons who suffer from them. There is no evidence that deviant sexuality is innate, or caused by endocrine disturbances, except in rare cases.

SACRED AND PROFANE LOVE

Many persons, because of overly strict sexual training, are unable to fuse the tender and sensual aspects of love.[4] They are unable to respect and care for the same person toward whom they experience sexual feelings. Thus, a man may marry a woman because she has many exemplary traits of personality and character but he is unable to become sexually aroused with her. He may be quite potent with other women whom he does not respect. Similarly, a woman may admire and respect her husband, but not be able to respond sexually to him; with a lover (who is quite unsuitable as a marriage partner), she may find herself sexually responsive.

This state of affairs is quite common in our society. Freud thought it was a derivative of an "unresolved oedipus complex." That is, a man might have chosen as a spouse some woman who bore certain resemblances to his mother. Sexual feelings are tabooed toward the mother; it is as if the man transferred many of the same feelings and attitudes from his mother to his wife. The woman might likewise transfer many of her attitudes and feelings from her father to her husband.

Although the oedipus complex may in part account for the inability of many persons to be sexually responsive to a person whom they admire and respect, another factor may be the belief that sex is a basically degraded kind of activity. This is a conception many persons acquire during the process of being socialized. They feel that sexual intercourse degrades both themselves and their partners. Consequently, they can be responsive and sexually competent only with a person whom they believe to be morally or socially inferior to themselves. In their marriage, they may display marked sexual maladjustment and discontent.

HEALTHY SEXUAL BEHAVIOR

Sexual behavior is healthy when it is effective in achieving a healthy sexual aim, yet is in accord with the social mores and the self-structure of the individual. If the aim is to achieve a climax for the self and the partner, the healthy personality will display the capacity to achieve these ends. If the aim is to express love and esteem for the partner, the healthy personality will behave sexually in ways which convey these sentiments. Among healthy personalities, sex is a source of much satisfaction and enjoyment, with considerable freedom in the choice of modes of sexual behavior.[5]

Among some persons, the conscience may impose certain restrictions on the varieties of sexual behavior which are theoretically available. Thus, certain modes of sexual stimulation, caressing, and sexual intercourse may be deemed desirable by one partner in a marriage and distasteful or ugly by another. Such incompatibilities in values and ideals may produce dissatisfaction with the sexual relationship between the spouses. It becomes apparent we cannot consider sexual behavior apart from the self-structure of the individual. We are obliged to state that healthy sexual behavior more or less presumes a healthy self-structure in the individual.

With respect to modes of undertaking sexual intercourse, it is compatible with personality hygiene principles to assert that any sexual behavior mutually acceptable to both partners may be deemed healthy. Some spouses find their sexual relations become rather boring, but feel if they change their mode of intercourse, they will be doing something perverse. Most experts in the field of sex would agree that varying the styles of intercourse is quite compatible with personality health and social normality.

PATTERNS OF SEXUAL BEHAVIOR THAT ARE SOCIALLY UNACCEPTABLE

Let us discuss some patterns of sexual behavior which deviate from the social ideals.

MASTURBATION. The practice of masturbation is well-nigh universal among members of our society and yet it runs counter to the social mores. This implies many persons undergo acute moral conflicts at some time during their lives because they masturbate. The personality hygienist is not in a position to make moral judgments about masturbation, but he can offer some natural-scientific comments about it.

Many parents will instill erroneous beliefs into their children's minds concerning the supposed effects of masturbation. The child may be told that this practice will weaken him, will destroy his mind, make him insane, or render him impotent later in life. So far, there is no evidence to support these beliefs. Some parents even make dire personal threats to their children in connection with "self-abuse." [6]

Children with strict training in regard to masturbation will have severe guilt-feelings because they cannot withstand the impulse to masturbate. These guilt-feelings often produce undesirable consequences in the form of feelings of inferiority and worthlessness. Some children become so threatened by the supposed consequences of masturbation that they completely repress sexuality. Such a means of handling sexual feelings can lead to serious personality illnesses.

In time, the sternness with which masturbation is condemned will likely be mitigated. More and more parents are beginning to regard masturbation as a rather natural part of growing up; they may attempt to discourage their children from masturbating, but they no longer punish it with severity. Some parents even overlook it completely.

PREMARITAL SEXUAL INTERCOURSE. The social taboos are most strictly directed toward this pattern of sexual behavior. The reasons behind the taboo are partly moral, and partly practical, e.g., the possibility of pregnancy, venereal disease, etc. Almost everyone in our culture has been raised to regard premarital sexual relations as morally wrong. Yet, there is increasing evidence that the taboo is being bypassed by a steadily growing number of young people. Among some teen-age groups, the fact of virginity is regarded as a sign of inferiority.

Again, the personality hygienist cannot comment on the moral issues that are at stake. He can only observe the consequences of conformity or nonconformity with the mores for overall personality health. Many of the practical reasons for avoiding premarital relationships are less pressing than they were at an earlier stage in history. Methods of avoiding conception are becoming increasingly known and understood, both by married and unmarried persons. These methods do not guarantee 100% effectiveness, but they reduce the probability of conception following sexual intercourse. Venereal disease is becoming less common than it once was, and so this reason for premarital continence is becoming less urgent. This leaves the moral grounds as the main basis for enjoining chastity on young unmarried people.

SADISM, MASOCHISM, VOYEURISM, AND OTHER PERVERSIONS. As a consequence of various life-history events, some persons can attain a climax only through inflicting pain, receiving pain, peeping, or other deviant means.[7] Such individuals are generally found to display *other aspects of unhealthy personality* besides unhealthy sexuality.

THE RECOGNITION OF HEALTHY SEXUALITY

When would a personality hygienist evaluate a person's sexual behavior as healthy? Let us present what appear to be the most salient attributes of healthy sexuality.

ACCURATE KNOWLEDGE ABOUT SEXUAL FUNCTIONING. A person with a repertoire of accurate beliefs about sex: its anatomy, physiology, relationship with reproduction, etc., will be more likely to achieve healthy sexuality than an ignorant person. Accurate information is readily obtained from books, from parents, teachers, and physicians; yet, there are many persons who have not availed themselves of even rudimentary knowledge pertaining to sexuality, because of shame or guilt. Unfortunately if a person does not have accurate knowledge, he will probably have an assortment of false beliefs concerning sexuality. These can lead only to difficulties in sexual adjustment.

AN ATTITUDE OF ACCEPTANCE TOWARD SEXUALITY. A person who regards sexuality as a natural and healthy part of living is more likely to achieve healthy sexuality than a person who views it as basically evil. The healthy personality is neither ashamed nor afraid of his sexual tensions; he may exercise self-control by suppressing any sexual behavior which violates his ethical system, but he does not try to exclude sexuality from his life as a dangerous or nasty phenomenon.[8]

THE INTEGRATION OF SEXUALITY WITH OTHER VALUES. The healthy personality views sexual gratification as an important condition for happiness, but sex is integrated in a harmonious way with other values. Although sexual gratification is not deemed to be the most important condition for happiness, it is not relegated by a healthy individual to the realm of the unimportant. For the healthy personality, sex can contribute richly to his overall happiness and effectiveness in living; he would not regard sexual gratification as more important, however, than personal integrity or love.

EVALUATING SEXUAL BEHAVIOR IN SELF AND OTHERS

There are no absolute health standards for sex, but some useful general guide-lines are available. Let us consider sexuality as it may appear in the infant, the child, the adolescent and the young unmarried adult.

SEXUALITY IN INFANCY.[9] Young infants (two years of age and younger) can sometimes be observed exploring and manipulating their genitalia. Their parents may become anxious when they observe this. It can be asserted there is little ground for alarm in connection with such activities; the most general interpretation that may be made is that the infant is in process of discovering his body.

SEXUALITY IN CHILDHOOD. Children from about three onward will touch or manipulate their genitalia when resting in bed, or occasionally when they are at play with other children. The most relevant interpretation is that the children have discovered the pleasurable sensations which self-manipulation can produce, and they tend to seek this pleasure from time to time.

Unless such activity is excessive, the parent is advised to avoid making an emotional issue out of it. If the child shows many signs of unhealthy personality, such as inability to get satisfactions out of his relationships with his family and friends, then it may be that masturbation is serving as a compensatory mechanism. Under these circumstances, the parent is advised to seek professional advice from a pediatrician, or a child psychologist.

SEXUALITY IN ADOLESCENCE. Sexual tensions are very strong during adolescence, and sex poses intense problems to the average adolescent. He will generally experience acute conflicts between his desire to conform with the morals pertaining to sexuality and his intense desires for relief from sexual tensions.[10]

Many adolescents are able to resolve the conflict by engaging in masturbation, regarding it as a sort of necessity. Masturbation is not entirely guilt-free for them, yet their guilt-reactions are not too intense or burdensome. Others find they cannot accept themselves if they masturbate and can maintain self-esteem only if they abstain entirely.

SEXUALITY IN THE UNMARRIED ADULT. Marriage is seldom possible in our culture before the late teens or early twenties, and so many young adults have problems connected with their sexual tensions. Again, since moral issues are at stake, the personality hygienist cannot offer advice very authoritatively. The moral precepts of our society may be restrictive from a cross-cultural point of view, but they represent one of the realities with which all of us have to come to terms.

Young adults are quite sexually responsive and it troubles them as to what they should do—should they seek relief through masturbation, should they engage in pre-marital sexual intercourse, or should they strive to abstain? The personality hygienist can assert there is nothing unhealthy about experiencing sexual arousal; the person's sexual behavior cannot be judged healthy or unhealthy in isolation, however. What he does (or avoids doing) must be assessed with respect to overall consequences for the whole of personality and for other values.

THE MANAGEMENT OF SEXUAL TENSIONS

Let us consider the various ways in which a person can deal with his sexual tensions, once they have arisen, or have been provoked, and attempt to provide criteria for evaluating these.

IMMEDIATE RELEASE OF SEXUAL TENSIONS. A person may find it impossible to delay or to postpone sexual gratification, so intense or urgent do his tensions and desires feel. Consequently, he may seek release in any way which is immediately available to him. The quest for immediate release reflects an inability on the part of the person to impose voluntary control over his impulses. This inability to impose control is likely to result in sexual behavior which may jeopardize many important values. If the person seeks sexual release with a partner, he may choose that partner only on the basis of immediate availability, ignoring other important criteria for the choice of a sex object. Thus, the person chosen may be quite unsuitable because of age differences, ill-health, intelligence-level, or social class. Probably many unwanted pregnancies, instances of venereal disease, hasty marriages, rapes, and other undesirable occurrences derive from the inability to tolerate delay in the attainment of sexual gratification.

If the person seeks relief from urgent sexual tensions through masturbation, and if he has strong taboos with respect to this practice, he will probably experience intense guilt-feelings and feelings of inferiority. His life becomes something of a vicious circle of sexual arousal, masturbation, self-hate, dissatisfaction with his everyday life and relationships with people, compensatory sexual desire, etc.

In an adult, the inability to tolerate delay in sexual gratification, so that the sexual behavior conflicts with other values, is often an indicator of unhealthy personality. It is probable that with more permissive sexual mores, or with a change in the social conditions responsible for delaying marriage, some of the problems associated with immediate sexual release would disappear.

REPRESSION OF SEXUAL TENSIONS. Repression of sexual tensions is likely to occur in persons who have excessively strict consciences with respect to sexuality and in persons who have come to fear sexuality in general. Repression of sexuality manifests itself in various ways, for instance, in (a) an absence of any conscious sexual wishes or desires, or (b) a denial of any sexual intent. All of us repress sexuality at various times and in various situations because we have been trained to observe and accord with certain taboos, e.g., the incest taboo. Most of us would become quite upset or threatened if we became sexually aroused by members of our immediate family. Yet psychoanalysts have shown that such feelings have occurred at one time or another in all our lives; however, we found this so threatening to self-esteem and security that we repressed sex within the family circle.

Repression of sexual desire in the right times and places is compatible with personality health, provided the repression is not too general. Social living would be impossible if persons were chronically aroused sexually by unsuitable sex-objects. Imagine being sexually aroused all day, every day, every year. But if sexuality has been totally repressed, many unhealthy consequences ensue. The repressor carries a virtual "well" of unconscious sexual desire, manifested in unpredictable and uncontrollable ways, in accidents, gestures, unwitting sexualization of interpersonal relationships, etc. Chronic unconscious sexuality disturbs the person's capacity to work effectively, and it disturbs his relationships with people by making him unduly defensive or autistic. The psychoanalysts assert that repressed sexuality contributes to the development of neurosis and other patterns of unhealthy personality.

The worst danger associated with a total repression of sexuality is the fact that from time to time the repression may be overcome. This may occur when the sexual tensions become too strong, or when the energy required to maintain the repression is decreased, e.g.—in fatigue, or intoxication. On such occasions, the represser may engage in impulsive sexual behavior, or he may become overwhelmed with guilt and anxiety without really understanding why.

CHRONIC SUPPRESSION OF SEXUAL BEHAVIOR. A person can be fully aware of his sexual tensions, but suppress sexual behavior for a number of reasons: fear of disease, pregnancies, guilt, unrealistic ideals, and other causes. He will likely remain in a condition of chronic sexual tension.[11]

Chronic sexual tension will produce many undesirable effects. The most obvious is unhappiness and a sense of frustration. In addition, the suppresser will be plagued by chronic sexual fantasies so that he cannot concentrate on his work. His relationships with people will be impaired for a number of reasons, viz.: he may not be able to appraise the feelings of others with accuracy, or he may be irritable and short-tempered.

Suppression of sexual behavior is unhealthy when the consequences to which it leads are unhealthy, and when the reasons for the suppression are unrealistic and unwarranted. The ability to suppress, however, is a desirable ability, as we shall see in the next section.

SELECTIVE SUPPRESSION AND RELEASE OF SEXUAL TENSIONS. Roback defined character as the principled inhibition of instinctive behavior.[12] The healthy personality displays character in this sense. He is fully cognizant of his sexual needs and desires, but he has affirmed a set of ethical precepts with respect to sexuality and strives actively to accord with them. When the criteria for ethical sexual behavior are not met, the healthy personality though aware of his sexual tensions will suppress sexual behavior. If the ethical criteria have been met, he will be able to engage in sexual behavior which implements his various sexual aims. He will arrange his life so he can obtain full sexual gratification when he is aroused, but in ways that accord with his sexual ethics.[13]

SOME DETERMINERS OF HEALTHY SEXUALITY

Healthy sexuality in an adult is no accident, nor is it a natural phenomenon. It is rather a product of determining factors. Some of the factors likely to play a role in determining sexual health are (a) the nature of sexual instruction and training, (b) early sexual experiences and their consequences, (c) the self-structure, (d) availability of suitable sex-objects, (e) a wide repertoire of other satisfactions, and (f) the capacity to establish love relationships.

Unlike many of the lower forms of animal life, humans have to learn how to behave sexually, and they have to learn when it is socially appropriate to become sexually aroused. Some of this learning results from deliberate parental instruction of children. Much of this instruction in our society is negative; it consists in admonishments about what is taboo. Children are told not to masturbate, not to display their bodies; in fact, from an early age, many children are actively trained to be ashamed and afraid of things pertaining to sex. Because many parents are embarrassed or tense about sexual matters, their children may be afraid to ask questions about their sex organs, or about reproduction. The children may then acquire many false beliefs concerning these matters.

Healthy sexuality is most likely to be promoted if the sexual instruction which the children receive is matter-of-fact, accurate, and in response to the children's curiosity.

EARLY SEXUAL EXPERIENCES AND HEALTHY SEXUALITY. Healthy adult sexuality is most likely to be achieved against a background relatively free of fears and guilts pertaining to sex. Many children have undergone severe punishments for childhood masturbation or sexual experimentation. These punishments have made sexual situations a stimulus for emotions incompatible with healthy sexuality. The severely punished child may, if other contributing factors are present, develop impotence, frigidity, various perversions, and similar unhealthy patterns. Healthy sexuality will be promoted if the parents handle the children's deviations from their own sexual ethics with kindness, understanding, and with explanations which the child can understand.

Thus, if a child is observed to be masturbating, the parents should let the child know why they do not want him to continue this activity if they don't like it. They should not tell lies about the results of masturbation; if need be, they can just say that it is not nice, and they would like him to stop. If the relationship between the parents and the child is a healthy one, the child will gradually acquire the standards and ideals which the parents would like him to have. Failures to accord with these ideals should be viewed as signs of immaturity in the child, not as signs of moral turpitude and worthlessness.

THE SELF-STRUCTURE AND HEALTHY SEXUALITY. Healthy sexuality is prevented by an unhealthy self-structure. An individual may acquire a self-ideal which deplores and condemns sexuality. In order to maintain self-esteem, such a person develops a self-concept that includes the assertion, "I am a person who does not have sexual feelings." For him, sexual arousal would constitute a threat. To avoid or remove threat, the individual is obliged to repress his sexual feelings.

If a person has been able to acquire and maintain a healthy self-structure, he will recognize and accept his sexual feelings when they are aroused. In addition, his self-ideal is not so restrictive that it precludes the possibility of guilt-free sexual behavior. As a general rule, it can be said that any factors which promote the development of a healthy self-structure will also promote the development of healthy sexuality.

AVAILABILITY OF SUITABLE SEX-OBJECTS. When sex-objects appropriate to a person's age and status are not available, he may make a *deviant* object-choice in his quest for sexual gratification. It is not uncommon for homosexuality to occur among students in an all-male or all-female school; among prisoners in jails, camps, and penitentiaries; among sailors. In rural areas, where the population is scanty and the opportunities for marriage are limited, sexual contacts with animals may occur.

The incidence of deviant object-choices could be reduced if appriate sex-objects were available to persons living under these conditions. It should be asserted, however, that not all cases of perversions stem from the lack of availability of more socially appropriate sex-objects and further, not all persons living under such conditions develop these perversions.

A WIDE REPERTOIRE OF OTHER SATISFACTIONS, AND HEALTHY SEXUALITY. The probability of attaining and maintaining healthy sexuality is increased if a person is gaining many satisfactions in the other realms of life. Adequate sexual relationships will promote a person's ability to function satisfactorily in his work, his leisure, and in his nonsexual relationships with people. The reverse also appears to be true; if a person is able to derive satisfaction from his work, his leisure, and his relationships with people, he is likely to be better able to achieve healthy sexuality. A person filled with unresolved need-tensions arising from other areas of his life may try to compensate for his other frustrations by means of sexual activity. He may be demanding more of sexuality than it can deliver. And further, the burden of nonsexual tensions which he is carrying may prevent him from performing adequately in a sexual situation. A tense, thwarted person can't be a relaxed, effective sexual lover

LOVE AND HEALTHY SEXUALITY. Many barriers to healthy sexuality will not arise in a healthy love-relationship. If a person has the capacity to love another person, he will doubtless have the capacity to achieve healthy sexuality within the context of that love-relationship. Loving involves knowing the object, caring for the object, behaving in ways which will promote the growth and happiness of the object, and making the self known to the object. If a couple have been able to establish such a relationship, then neither will be afraid or ashamed to make needs and desires known to the other. Each wants to please the other and to promote the happiness of the other. At the outset of marriage a loving couple may not achieve full harmony and mutual satisfaction in sexual relationships, but in time, they should be able to accommodate to each others' changing needs and wishes.

If they are afraid or ashamed to convey their deepest feelings, needs, and desires to each other, it is easy to see how dissatisfactions will soon arise; and the dissatisfactions will not be brought out in the open and discussed. It might be said that the richest sexual satisfactions can only occur in the context of a love-relationship, where the communication barriers between the partners are reduced to a minimum.

UNHEALTHY SEXUALITY AND PERSONALITY THERAPY

The individual with unhealthy sexuality generally suffers. The nature of the suffering will of course vary with the nature of the sexual deviation from health. The sexual represser and suppresser suffers from prolonged sexual privation, from guilts, and anxieties. The person with deviant sexual behavior may suffer from fear of punishment and possibly losses of self-esteem. The impotent husband and the frigid wife suffer from disturbances in the overall relationship with the spouse.

As a consequence of their suffering, persons with unhealthy sexuality may be motivated to seek professional personality therapy. While assistance cannot always be guaranteed, yet often guidance, instruction, or more intensive personality therapy may be effective in removing some of the obstacles to healthy sexuality.

A woman undertook therapy because of marked difficulties in her relationship with one of her children. During the course of therapy, it was discovered she could not be sexually responsive to her husband. She merely endured the sexual aspects of marriage. Indeed, she used sexual compliance as a means of controlling her husband. It was soon discovered her lack of responsiveness derived largely from attitudes acquired from her mother. Her mother had instructed the patient to view sex as dirty. The patient, when she became aware of the origins of her attitudes, came to see them as silly. Her lack of responsiveness vanished, and with it vanished also a lack of zest in the marriage, a lot of tension, and finally, the difficulties in her relationship with her child.

OUR SEXUAL MORES AND HEALTHY SEXUALITY

One implication which may be drawn from Kinsey's findings is that not many people in our society are able to achieve healthy sexuality. It will be recalled that the guiding definition of healthy sexuality is "the ability to achieve sexual gratifications in ways that are socially acceptable and in accord with the individual's self-structure."

Most persons in our society have been socialized in ways which impel them to espouse our current sexual mores. Yet Kinsey showed that most of the subjects whom he interviewed had violated, or were violating, the mores with respect to sexuality. It is possible that a certain proportion of those who conformed to the mores strictly were not obtaining enough sexual gratification to make them happy. Could we conclude from this line of reasoning that healthy sexuality is a rarity, and that normal or typical sexuality either is out of line with the mores or else fails to bring happiness to the individual? [14]

Sexual mores are a social necessity. There is no society which does not impose some form of restriction on the sexual behavior of its members. But there are some societies where guilts and anxieties pertaining to sexuality do not appear; where sex is not a problem. Some extremists have suggested that our society needs a "sexual revolution" [15]—that the solution to man's ills and unhappiness is to overthrow the sexual mores and to substitute absolute freedom in sexual behavior. This is impossible, and it is not known what undesirable consequences would follow from such license anyway. A more sensible view would appear to be somewhat as follows: gradually, with the passage of time, our mores may change, bringing them more into accord with human practice. Certainly we have come a long way in the past fifty years, in that sexuality is no longer a taboo subject for study or discussion. As more is learned about sexuality and its role in personality health and illness, socialization practices with respect to sexuality may be expected to change, and with these changes there may be expected the gradual modification of the sexual mores.

SUMMARY

Sexual tension refers to the easily recognized sexual feelings. A *sexual response* refers to the association between some stimulus and sexual tension. A *sexual stimulus* is any stimulus which evokes sexual tensions in a person. *Erogenous zones* are areas of the body which, when stimulated, give rise to sexual tensions. *Sexual aim* refers to the motive or purpose for which sexual behavior is undertaken. The terms *climax and orgasm* refer to the experience of intense pleasure which is produced by sexual behavior. *Sexual behavior* is any behavior undertaken for the purpose of achieving a climax or other sexual aim.

Every society imposes strict taboos and restrictions on sexuality. In our society, almost all forms of sexual behavior are prohibited except actual sexual intercourse between married couples.

Healthy sexual behavior is behavior which is effective in securing sexual gratification for the individual and accords with the social mores and the individual's self-structure. *Healthy sexual aims* include the giving and receiving of pleasure, the expression of affection for the partner, the conception of children. Examples of *unhealthy sexual aim* include reassurance, compensation for other frustrations, and the use of sexual behavior as a means of getting other valued objects.

A person is said to display *healthy conditions for arousal* when he or she is sexually responsive to the typical forms of sexual stimulation, that is, stroking of erogenous zones, terms of endearment, etc. Persons who are unresponsive to typical methods of stimulation are generally regarded as frigid (if female) or impotent (if male).

Quite commonly in our society, persons are unable to express respect and affection for the same person to whom they are sexually responsive. Thus, they may respect their spouses, but are sexually inadequate with them; they can be sexually effective only with a person whom they do not admire or respect.

Healthy sexual behavior is any kind of sexual activity which is mutually acceptable to the partners, and which achieves the various sexual aims. Many sorts of sexual behavior which would be viewed as perverse if they were an end in themselves are regarded as healthy and acceptable within the context of a healthy love-relationship.

A number of patterns of sexual behavior are regarded as socially undesirable, although they are quite common in our society. These include masturbation and premarital sexual intercourse. At one time these activities were tabooed for apparently scientific reasons; masturbation was thought to lead to insanity, and premarital sexual relationships actually did lead to many unwanted pregnancies and venereal disease. At the present time, these reasons for taboo have lessened in urgency. Therefore, the main reasons for enjoining these practices are moral ones. Other patterns of sexual behavior more universally regarded as unhealthy are sadism, masochism, voyeurism, and other perversions.

Some *signs of healthy sexuality* in a person include *accurate knowledge about sex*, an *accepting attitude toward sex*, and *the ability to integrate sexuality with the overall value-system of the person*.

Sexuality in infancy and childhood are to be regarded as natural and not to be severely punished. If sexual behavior is excessive during these stages, the parents are advised to seek professional guidance. Sexuality in adolescents and unmarried adults was briefly discussed. It was pointed out that problems relating to sex during these stages, and their solutions, must be evaluated with respect to their consequences for overall personality health.

Immediate release, repression, and *chronic suppression* of sexual tensions were all viewed as unhealthy means for the management of sexual tensions. *Selective suppression and release* was viewed as the healthy mode of control.

Some of the factors which promote the development of healthy sexuality were discussed. Personality therapy was recommended for cases displaying unhealthy sexuality. Our current sexual mores were briefly discussed.

NOTES AND REFERENCES

RECOMMENDED READINGS ARE MARKED WITH AN ASTERISK (*)

*1. An extensive discussion of sexuality, organized around the concepts of "sexual aim" and "sexual object," is Freud's classic work, *Three contributions to the theory of sex*. See Brill, A. A., *The basic writings of Sigmund Freud*, New York, Modern Library, 1938, pp. 553–629.

*2. Kinsey, A. C., Pomeroy, W. B., and Martin, C. E., *Sexual behavior in the human male*, Philadelphia, Saunders, 1948. Also, Kinsey, A. C., Pomeroy, W. B., Martin, C. E., and Gebhard, P. H., *Sexual behavior in the human female*, Philadelphia, Saunders, 1953.

*3. See the comparison of socialization practices with regard to sexuality in Whiting, J. W. M., and Child, I. L., *Child training and personality*, New Haven, Yale University Press, 1953, pp. 77–91. In a survey of 34 societies, they found only 2 other societies with more severe sexual training practices than their American sample.

4. An elaboration of this and other related points may be found in Freud's "Contributions to the psychology of love." See Freud, S., *Collected papers*, Vol. IV, London, Hogarth, 1953, pp. 192–235.

*5. Maslow has described sexuality as it occurs among "self-actualizing people." See Maslow, A. H., *Motivation and personality*, New York, Harper, 1954, Ch. 13.

6. Huschka compiled a number of parental reactions to their children's masturbation. Many of these reactions were quite brutal and sadistic. See Huschka, M., "The incidence and character of masturbation threats in a group of problem children," *Psychoanal. Quart.*, 1938, 7, 338–355.

7. A classic catalogue of sexual deviations is von Krafft-Ebing, R., *Psychopathia sexualis*, 12th ed., New York, Pioneer Publications, 1947.

8. Reich speaks of a "sex-affirmative" super-ego in the genital character.

Reich, W., *Character analysis,* New York, Orgone Institute Press, 1948, p. 167.

9. See the empirical studies of Spitz with regard to infantile sexual be-havior. Spitz, R. A., and Wolf, Katherine M., "Autoerotism. Some empirical findings and hypotheses on three of its manifestations in the first year of life," *Psychoanalyt. Stud. Child,* 1949, III-IV, 85–120.

10. Mead showed that a sexually conflicted adolescence is not innate, as was once believed, but is rather a by-product of the culture. See Mead, M., *Coming of age in Samoa,* New York, Morrow, 1928.

11. The psychoanalysts regard sexual suppression as a causal factor in the "actual neuroses." See Fenichel, O., *The psychoanalytic theory of neurosis,* New York, Norton, 1945.

12. Roback, A. A., *The psychology of character,* 3rd ed., Cambridge, Sci-Art Publishers, 1952.

13. Reich, W., *op. cit.,* p. 165. Reich speaks of an "orderly libido economy" in this connection. The genital character alternates between sexual arousal and sexual release, with no neurotic factors causing him to suppress sexuality chronically.

14. Freud's opinion was that adherence to the sexual morality of his time contributed to "nervousness." See Freud, S., "Civilized sexual morality and modern nervousness." In Freud, S., *op. cit.,* Vol. II, pp. 76–99.

15. Reich, W., *The sexual revolution,* New York, Orgone Institute Press, 1945.

QUESTIONS FOR REVIEW AND EXAMINATION

1. Define sexual tension, sexual response, sexual stimuli, sex-objects, erogenous zones, sexual aim, orgasm, and sexual behavior.

2. What are some different sexual aims? What are healthy sexual aims? Unhealthy aims?

3. Specify and illustrate healthy and unhealthy conditions for sexual arousal.

4. What are some indications of healthy sexuality?

5. What are the major ways in which persons deal with their own sexual tensions? What is regarded as the healthy management of sexual tensions?

6. What are some of the determiners of healthy sexuality?

7. Use the concepts and section headings in this chapter as guide in describing and evaluating sexuality in yourself.

CHAPTER 6

Healthy Interpersonal Behavior

Man cannot live in complete isolation from his fellow man; in fact, there is reason to believe that complete solitude will make a person inhuman and insane.[1] At odd moments, of course, people wish they could be absolutely alone—when they are full of exasperation, or when they wish to have an opportunity for contemplation,[2] or to "find themselves"—but for the most part, we have no desire to be completely divorced from our fellow man.

Why do we need other people? What do we need them for, and what do we need from them?

A very general answer would be that an individual needs other people to behave in certain ways so he will be better able to achieve his valued ends. The concept *dependency* describes man's need for his fellows. We may well ask, "What do we depend upon other people *for?*" The obvious answer is we depend on other persons for all those satisfactions and necessities we are unable to provide by ourselves. Let us examine some of the more common bases for dependency upon others.

DEPENDENCY

INFANTILE DEPENDENCY. A newborn human infant is among the most helpless of living organisms. The repertoire of instrumental action which the human infant can perform is limited to a few automatic reflexes: swallowing, defecating and urinating, crying, and gross motor movements. For sheer survival, the infant needs other people—parents, or parent-surrogates—to behave in ways which will bring all manner of need-objects to him. The mother must provide food, and arrange the environment so that the child will stay alive, relatively free from pain, and able to grow. As the child develops physically, so that he becomes more capable of learning, he needs other people as identification models, so he can become increasingly socialized. He needs to hear people talk, for example, so he can learn to talk. He needs, in his early days, a lot of mothering [3]—caressing, holding, and social stimulation; there is evidence that without such close mothering, his physical development will be impaired, and his social development will be deviant. Spitz [4] noted, for example, that the smiling response should be elicitable from an infant between the ages of two months and six months; where it is not, it is almost prima facie evidence something is missing in the child's environment that is interfering with the child's development, or something is present which should not be. The child needs other people to reward and punish him, so he can learn to behave in socially acceptable ways. He needs to be in contact with peers, other children his age, so he can learn to compete, co-operate, play games, etc. Other people are thus seen as the means for the attainment of many ends: physical survival and health; the learning of many skills important in the solution of problems and the gratification of assorted needs; and the learning of attitudes, values, morals and social roles, essential in defining the child's membership in varied groups.

ADULT DEPENDENCY. The adult, by virtue of a vastly increased skill-repertoire, is much more self-reliant than the infant or young child, but he still needs other people for many reasons. Most of the satisfactions which make life worthwhile in fact can be gratified only in relation to, or with the co-operation of, other people.

TECHNICAL DEPENDENCY. In a society so complex as ours, no man can ever hope in his lifetime to encompass all the skills necessary to solve all his problems and gratify all of his wants. The jack-of-all-trades can no longer master every problem in living which he will encounter. Division of labor and specialization in knowledge and technique is enormously developed in the Western world, so each man is dependent upon many other people for their specialized skill and knowledge.

The question may be asked, "How can an individual get the other person, who has the needed skills, to utilize them in his behalf?" In our society, this is generally accomplished on a quid pro quo basis; the needful individual "buys" the knowledge or skill from its possessor with money, or anything else that is deemed of value equivalent to the skill. In some instances if the skill or knowledge is very scarce, the possessor will set high or unusual prices for the purchase of his skill-commodity.

SELF-ESTEEM DEPENDENCY. The adult may need other people to behave toward him in certain prescribed ways in order to maintain his self-esteem. Thus if a person has acquired a "self-ideal" which specifies, essentially: "I am not a worthwhile self-respecting individual unless other people (in general, or else certain classes of people) admire me, or listen to me seriously, or just plain like me," then it becomes apparent that he needs them to behave in the requisite ways. When they do not, he will be overwhelmed with feelings of inadequacy, worthlessness, or what is commonly called depression.[5] In our society, almost everyone's self-esteem is strongly determined by the presence of approval or accepting-responses from others; but there is also great variability to be found in just how a person needs others to act toward him in order to maintain self-esteem. These individual differences stem from individual differences in life experiences. To illustrate: the author knows several men who feel depressed and inadequate if an attractive woman does not seem to be favorably impressed by their appearance and behavior. A patient undergoing personality therapy had a very curious set of conditions which had to be met, in order that he might experience self-esteem. It was necessary that his father, *and only his father*, approve of his behavior. When the needed approval-response was obtained from his father, the patient would be elated, happy, and would hold himself in very high esteem. At the faintest indica-

tion of paternal disapproval, the patient would be literally overwhelmed by self-hate, depression, the conviction that he was a
worthless individual, and he would very seriously consider destroy-
ing himself. No one else could affect him this way.

The reader might well ask himself this question: "How do I need
other people [be specific in referring to other people, e.g., my
mother, father, spouse, boss, friend, etc.] to behave toward me in
order that I continue (or begin) to feel self-esteem?" The answers
should provide considerable illumination to the motives for much
behavior which occurs in the presence of those people. Very often,
in order to obtain the needed behavior from the other, the individual
has to "buy" it, with behavior that conforms with the other's demands and expectations. This means that wherever there is a conflict between one's own wants and the other's demands, the wants
must be sacrificed; when they are acceded to, the consequence is
that the other withdraws the needed praise or approval, and the
person loses self-esteem.

SECURITY DEPENDENCY. Security has been defined in many varying
ways. In this context, security means the belief that everything one
values and needs is safe from threat. People need and value many
things for many reasons. So long as the need- and value-objects are
available and assured, the person is secure. Anything which threatens
to remove, or restrict, the availability of the need- and value-objects
provokes insecurity, or more precisely, *anxiety*. Anxiety always implies the anticipation of pain, or some form of unpleasantness; in
this context, the pain or unpleasantness is produced by deprivation
of the need-objects. It is, literally, "frustration-anxiety," the apprehension of frustration.

Since other people can provide us with many things we need and
value, then to that extent, we are dependent on these other people
for our security. In the words of Blatz,[6] we are to that extent "de-
pendently secure." As long as the other people are willing and able
to act in ways that satisfy our wants (wants which we cannot satisfy
by ourselves), then we are secure. Anything which threatens the
relationship with the "dependency-object" will provoke anxiety in
the dependent person. He cannot satisfy all his wants by his own
behavior; he needs the other person. If the other person is not
available, or is no longer willing to act in need-satisfying ways, then

the dependent person faces the prospect of deprivation, frustration, and all their attendant pain.

As with self-esteem dependency, the individual whose security is dependent upon the intervention of other people must buy their skill, knowledge, or needed behavior in assorted ways. He must conform with their expectations and demands; he must get them to like him; in more general terms, he must govern his behavior by their wishes so as not to jeopardize his friendly relationships with them.

In our society, there are many satisfactions which are possible to achieve *only if other people in general like you*. This objective state of affairs makes "likeability" a trait of fundamental importance to the individual and the experience of being disliked a near-catastrophe. When one is disliked, it may have the consequence of making many valued ends and many want-satisfactions completely inaccessible. Riesman's "other-directed" character is the logical outgrowth of the social conditions which make each of us dependent upon others for important need-satisfactions. Since other people will "come across" only if they like us, then we come to seek their approval and affection just as we seek money: not for its own sake, but for what it will enable us to acquire. And so in our society, people dread being disliked just as they dread financial bankruptcy, and for the same reasons.

AFFECTION-DEPENDENCY AND PASSIVE LOVE-DEPENDENCY. We can draw a distinction between active love and passive love. Active love means the lover behaves toward the object of his love in ways which will promote happiness and growth in the object. Passive love means the individual is the receiver of another person's loving behavior. In a later chapter, we shall devote more attention to active love (Chapter 8); in the present section let us confine our remarks to passive love.

It can be asserted that passive love is a basic requirement for personality health and for happiness, and it is obvious we are dependent upon other people for their love. We need the love of (selected) other people. One of the reasons we pursue affection so assiduously is that affection in another person is a signal that loving behavior will be forthcoming from them. Love-dependency is a form of dependency which is quite compatible with personality health. In our culture, we place such great emphasis on the positive value of independence and autonomy, we are likely to overlook the fact that the need for love is a healthy need, and its satisfaction does not necessarily rob a person of his identity or independence. Indeed, a person deprived of passive love will find difficulty in relating to other people in socially acceptable and personally satisfying ways. Or, he may become quite indiscriminate in his quest for persons to love him.[7] Later in this chapter we shall devote more time to a discussion of affection.

IDENTITY-DEPENDENCY. A person's sense of personal identity may be defined as a conviction, or belief he *is* somebody, that he has characteristics which set him off from other people.[8] In order that the sense of identity be strengthened, it is important that other people recognize, appreciate, value, encourage, and react to these individual idiosyncrasies. When other people react to an individual on a *formal* basis, when they see him as simply one member of a broad class or category of people, they actually de-individualize the person. Such behavior makes him feel much less an individual person and much more the embodiment of his social role. For example, a wife may be perceived and reacted to by her spouse as "the wife": "I'll have to ask the wife." For him, she is a wife, not a person. A recruit in the army soon learns that his personal idiosyncrasies, so lovingly recognized and catered to by his mother, are ignored by his sergeant; for the latter, he is just another G.I. And the army chef cooks for "the men"—not for John, Bill, and Arthur.

The sense of identity is an important aspect of personality health; a person could not be called healthy if he lacked a sense of identity or if he suffered a weakened sense of identity. But it is clear the sense of identity is strongly dependent upon the reactions of other people to the self. If others will not recognize and respond to one's idiosyncrasies, the person loses palpably in the sense of identity, and feels much less a person. We conclude that people are dependent upon others for the reinforcement of the identity-sense.

DIRECTION-DEPENDENCY. Personality hygienists place a positive valuation on autonomy, one aspect of which is self-direction (or more literally, real-self direction). By this is meant the person makes his own decisions; he follows his own will, and not the will of others. But it happens that people become, in consequence of certain kinds of life-history experiences, "alienated from their real selves." When this has occurred, the individual loses the sense of being self-directing, and he will experience the need for some source of direction other than his own will. Psychologists have come to recognize certain patterns which emerge from self-alienation. From among these patterns of behavior direction, let us discuss *authority direction* and *peer-group direction*. The authority-directed character, or *authoritarian character*, is an individual who feels lost unless he is in a position subordinate to some authority-figure.[9] The directing agents for his behavior might be his parents, his superior officer in the armed services, or his boss. The peer-group-directed character has substituted the will of his peers for his own; he strives to ascertain what others do in a given situation and allows their example or their wishes to be his guide to conduct. He is the compulsive conformer which Fromm[10] and Riesman[11] have described; more recently, experimental psychologists have begun investigating his traits in more detailed fashion.[12]

We can assert that while direction-dependency is very widespread in the population at large, the personality hygienist does not regard it as a healthy pattern.

Summary. A person needs others to solve problems for him which he cannot solve through his own independent problem-solving behavior. He needs other people to act in ways which will satisfy those wants he cannot satisfy through his own independent behavior. He needs other people to behave toward him in those ways which will enhance his self-esteem and keep him secure, that is, free from the danger of frustration, hostility, or more generally, the dangers attendant upon being disliked or rejected by others. He needs people to reinforce his sense of identity and to provide direction to his behavior. He needs to feel loved.

In terms of our earlier discussion of needs, we regard certain response-patterns of other people as important need-objects for an individual. The person must acquire an appropriate instrumental behavior repertoire to obtain these need-objects when they are wanted. His instrumental behavior with people must conform at least roughly with social mores and with the values of his own conscience, if he is to be adjudged a healthy personality.

INTERPERSONAL BEHAVIOR

We shall assign the name *interpersonal behavior* to instrumental action undertaken by a person in order to obtain a response from another individual which is wanted or needed for various purposes. As with all instrumental action, we can evaluate interpersonal behavior as effective or ineffective, healthy or unhealthy.

HEALTHY INTERPERSONAL BEHAVIOR. Interpersonal behavior is healthy when it produces satisfactions for the individual and yet accords with his self-structure (see Chapter 9) and to some extent with the social mores. But healthy interpersonal behavior is not effortful, or contrived and planned, as moves in a game of chess, or behavior which aims at impressing somebody.

Healthy interpersonal behavior is *spontaneous* (not premeditated), *expressive of the real self of the individual, versatile,* and *flexible.*[13] This implies there are few inner barriers to interpersonal behavior in the healthy personality. He can act pretty much as he feels and wants; in the long run, he gets what he needs from people—or at least from the people whom he desires as friends or close associates. Because of his honesty in interpersonal dealings, the healthy personality may also have a number of people who actively dislike him. The healthy personality is not liked by everyone; indeed, he does not pursue popularity as a goal in itself. Instead, he behaves in accordance with the depths and totality of his real self; in consequence, his interpersonal behavior is likely to be quite diversified and flexible. Natural and unpretentious might be adjectives describing the interpersonal behavior of the healthy personality.

In contrast, unhealthy interpersonal behavior may be contrived and deliberate, or ineffective.

UNHEALTHY INTERPERSONAL BEHAVIOR. Unhealthy interpersonal behavior fails to secure satisfactions for the individual, or else it secures satisfactions to the detriment of other important values such as integrity, honesty, growth, etc. Let us first discuss ineffective interpersonal behavior.

INEFFECTIVE INTERPERSONAL BEHAVIOR. Literature abounds with examples of persons who do not know how to act, or cannot act in ways which will make people like them. The wallflower, the "obnoxious character," the sycophant—these are well-known illustrations. Why does a person act in ways which alienate people from him, and why does a person not act in ways which will bring him affection, admiration and love? Naturally, there are many possible explanations, and so we shall content ourselves with but few of the more obvious factors which promote ineffective interpersonal behavior.

1. INACCURATE OTHER-CONCEPTS. If a person does not know what other people are like, or if his other-concepts are erroneous, then it follows he cannot know what kinds of behavior will evoke friendly feeling. Consequently, he may assume wrongly that such and such a way of behaving will evoke affection when in fact it provokes only disgust or scorn.

2. INACCURATE INTERPERSONAL PERCEPTION.[14] An inability to interpret accurately the facial and behavioral cues of others' feelings may promote ineffective interpersonal behavior. Thus, a person may believe his behavior is quite fitting, and so he blithely continues acting in a manner which is making his audience squirm with discomfort. He does not interpret their behavior and subtle emotional expression accurately and assumes he is being well-received. "Feedback," that is, knowledge of the consequences of one's behavior, is an important condition for learning. The person who is unable to interpret accurately the emotional reactions of others to his own behavior is lacking in one of the important conditions for learning interpersonal facility and skill.

3. IRRATIONAL ANXIETY. Past experience may have produced a dread of behaving in certain ways, so that these modes of acting are suppressed. Yet the suppressed behavior patterns may be the very ones which, if manifested in his present life situation, would bring rich gratifications to the person. Thus, he may have been severely rejected once when he displayed spontaneous affection for another person. The experience was so traumatic for him he suppressed any tendencies to express spontaneous affection for other people. But it happens that openly expressed affection is one of the most efficient means of eliciting affection-responses from another person. The consequence of suppressing affection may be that the suppresser is obliged to suffer an extreme lack of affection. Any other interpersonal behavior which has been suppressed because of

irrational anxiety will have the consequence of limiting the person's behavior repertoire, and hence will limit the range of gratifications which he can obtain in relationships with other people.

4. EXCESSIVELY STRICT CONSCIENCE AND SELF-IDEAL. Strict morality and unrealistic pride may so limit a person's interpersonal behavior that he cannot act in ways which provoke friendliness in others. In order to be free of guilt and to maintain self-esteem, he maintains a strict and rigid adherence to some behavioral code. The consequence may be that people find him cold, aloof, stilted, and uncommunicative. The overly proud and the overly moral person will thus have to face the consequences of a friendless and empty interpersonal existence.

5. EXCESSIVE PRIVATION. If a person is starved for food, sex, affection, fame or other gratifications, he may pursue these goals at the expense of his own dignity and integrity, as well as the integrity of others. Under high deprivation, the individual perceives others as means to his ends or obstacles to the pursuit of his ends. A person under strong need-tension is less able to perceive others' needs and reactions accurately, and is likely to manipulate others to obtain what he needs. In the long run, the manipulation will provoke dislike and alienation.

CONTRIVED INTERPERSONAL BEHAVIOR. The term contrived refers to the fact that the person behaves, not in accordance with his real self—as he really feels and wants—but rather he behaves toward others so as to produce some desired reaction in them. He is insincere, and is not always aware he is insincere. In so contriving, he suppresses, or represses his real self (thus becoming increasingly self-alienated); further, he tends to perceive the other person, not as a human being, but rather as a problem, or a machine. Finally, in so doing, he is making a machine or commodity out of himself.

A number of personality hygienists have called attention to contrived interpersonal behavior. Fromm speaks of the "marketing" character [15] in this context, and Riesman describes the "other-directed character." [16] The charming psychopath, so well described by Cleckley,[17] provides another example of contrived interpersonal behavior. In these instances, the authors are noting the very common and unhealthy tendency to manipulate the self to impress others in order to obtain popularity, good jobs, etc. These goals are obtained at the expense of inner integrity and honesty, and even health.

The contriving insincere individual, often without conscious awareness, is placing popularity and "success" at the peak of his value-hierarchy. He is selling his soul (his real self) to achieve it. He strives to determine what kind of behavior the other person likes, and then pretends to be the kind of person who habitually behaves in that way. The net consequences are that the other person formulates an inaccurate concept of the individual, and the latter finds it a growing burden to maintain a variety of conflicting and false public selves (see Chapter 9). And finally, he may come to feel he has acquired friends on false pretenses—if people found out what he was really like, they might ostracize him.

The major factor responsible for habitually contrived interpersonal behavior is the belief, conscious or implicit, that to be one's real self is *dangerous;* that exposure of real feelings and motives will result in rejection, punishment, or ridicule. Such a belief stems from experiences of punishment and rejection at the hands of the parents and other significant persons. In order to avoid punishment in the future, the child represses or suppresses his real self in interpersonal situations and learns to become a contriver: an other-directed character. Of course, more serious outcomes are possible, too: neurosis, psychopathic personality, etc.

One of the aims of personality therapy is to help the patient become aware of the extent to which his interpersonal behavior is contrived, that is, selected to please others or to achieve desired effects, but at the cost of repression of the real self. Friends and intimates of a patient who has undergone personality therapy often notice his modes of interpersonal behavior have changed strikingly; his behavior is no longer contrived and pretentious. Rather, he seems to act toward others just as he feels.

HOW HEALTHY INTERPERSONAL BEHAVIOR IS ACQUIRED. Healthy interpersonal behavior is effective in securing desired, satisfactory responses from others, and yet it is spontaneous, expressive of the real self of the person and congruent with the self-structure of the individual. How is this valued state of affairs achieved? The fortunate person who has been "raised right," who has been able to obtain rich satisfaction of basic needs during the process of growing up, and who has not been obliged to repress his real self, will doubt-less have acquired healthy interpersonal behavior patterns as a habit. Healthy interpersonal behavior is natural to him.

But what of the people with ineffective or contrived interpersonal behavior patterns? How can they alter their interpersonal behavior in a healthy direction?

In principle, the transformation of unhealthy interpersonal be-havior into healthier forms of behaving calls for insight, recog-nition of the role one's own behavior plays in producing unwanted responses in others, or in failing to produce wanted responses in others. This insight is hard to gain, since it is so easy to place the blame for one's unhappiness on the miserable personality of others. Further, *it calls for the ability to discern the difference between effortful, contrived behavior, and spontaneous, real-self behavior;* this disinction is impossible until real-self behavior has actually oc-curred. In most cases, a person requires the assistance of a trained therapist to recognize the difference between contrived and real-self behavior.[18]

A mother complained to the present writer that her children and her husband did not like her. She suffered considerably because of this lack of love and affection. It soon became apparent she was not loved because her usual behavior toward spouse and children in-volved criticizing and trying to change them. When she recognized a connection between her habitual modes of behaving toward her family and their dislike for her, she experienced considerable anxiety and threat and tried hard to avoid examining her own behavior; she persisted in shifting the blame for her unhappiness to her family's "selfishness and lack of consideration." In time, with the therapist's assistance, she was able to see clearly how she behaved toward them and she gained some understanding as to why she behaved in those ways. Finally, she was able to relate to all members of her family in a more relaxed "real self" manner. Her family then freely gave her the affection and love she longed for.

INTERPERSONAL BEHAVIOR PATTERNS AND CHARACTER. Erich Fromm [19] defines *character* as the "[relatively permanent] form in which human energy is canalized in the process of *assimilation* and *socialization*" (p. 59). *Assimilation* refers to instrumental action which secures various need-objects of a nonpersonal sort, e.g., food and money. *Socialization* refers to interpersonal behavior—behavior which has as its aim the securing of various kinds of needed responses from other people.

Character is a concept which refers to the habitual instrumental behavior repertoire of a person—assimilation referring to the recurrent modes by which a person relates to things, and socialization referring to the habitual ways of behaving with people. Fromm classified character into broad categories named, respectively, the "receptive orientation," the "hoarding orientation," the "exploitative orientation," the "marketing orientation," and, finally, the "productive orientation." Socialization patterns, that is, patterns of interpersonal behavior, differ markedly in these various types of character. The receptive character limits his interpersonal behavior to that range which gets love and support from others, he strives to become lovable so other people will give him what he needs. The hoarding character shows predominantly interpersonal behavior which keeps people at a distance, so they can get little from him. The exploitative character displays predominantly force or cunning in his interpersonal behavior, getting what he needs from others by these means. The marketing character is a person who "experiences himself as a commodity, and his value as 'exchange value.'" His main aim in interpersonal behavior is to cultivate those traits which pay off in economic success. If money is to be earned by having a pleasing personality, then he strives to cultivate a pleasing personality; if money is to be earned when one appears industrious, then he strives to give the impression of industry.

The productive character corresponds in our terminology with the healthy personality. The productive character strives, through his own efforts, to produce what he needs through his own behavior. In interpersonal behavior, he actually produces his own satisfactions by behaving toward others in ways which will satisfy them and thus make them willing to satisfy him.

Other authors have constructed characterologies, which consist in a description of types.[20] Thus, the psychoanalysts speak of the oral character, the anal character, the phallic character, and finally, the genital character. Rank[21] classified people into types: the normal, the neurotic, and the creative. Riesman[22] grouped people according to the source of direction for their behavior: the "tradition-directed" character, the "inner-directed" character, and the "other-directed" character. Each of these types may be "anomic" (maladjusted, or confused), "adjusted" (feeling no inner conflict), or "autonomous" (real-self directed—the person has found tradition, conscience, or others' will to be synonymous with his own will).

These characterologies are useful means of classifying different kinds of interpersonal behavior. Want of space precludes our doing more than mentioning them here; the serious student is advised to consult the appropriate sources directly. We will assert, however, that these character types do not exist as pure cases. Like healthy personality, they are hypothetical extremes which are useful as base lines against which to compare living persons; a sort of standard against which comparisons can be made with actual behavior.

Yet, there is a case to be made for constructing these character-ologies. It is true that persons develop consistencies in their instru-mental behavior in general and their interpersonal behavior in par-ticular. The very fact of predictability in interpersonal behavior attests to this. A character-description of the single case has many important uses, in interpersonal relationships. Our other-concepts actually are composed of generalizations about the modal behavior of the other person, especially his interpersonal behavior. Thus, we describe John as the "kind of fellow who will tell his boss what he thinks of him," or we describe Mary as "the kind of girl who behaves with gentleness and consideration for other people's feelings."

We may define a healthy character as a person whose total reper-toire of interpersonal behavior patterns meets the criteria for healthy interpersonal behavior (see above).

It is obvious, however, that not all the component interpersonal behavior traits of a person will be healthy; the person may, for example, be able to gratify his needs for esteem from others but he cannot seem to obtain love. He may relate to one person in a healthy way, but to others in his social milieu he may display either ineffective or contrived interpersonal behavior. Further, some of his interpersonal behavior patterns may be quite rigid and resistant to change. Let us discuss these rigid interpersonal habits or, as Reich terms them, *character armor*.[23]

CHARACTER ARMOR: RIGID INTERPERSONAL BEHAVIOR PATTERNS. We may regard a person's interpersonal habits, his habitual modes of behaving toward other people, as a kind of record of interpersonal problems which he has encountered in the process of growing up. Each interpersonal pattern was presumably learned as a means of gaining affection and approval from significant others, or as a means of avoiding or escaping punishment, criticism, or rejection. Adopting the terminology of learning-theory, let us refer to the habits which secured affection and approval as *interpersonal reward habits;* the term *interpersonal avoidance habits* will describe those modes of relating to others which were learned as means of warding off expected punishment and criticism.

From students of the learning process, we learn that reward habits are generally more amenable to extinction and to alteration than avoidance habits; the latter appear to be much more rigid, and resistant to attempts at alteration.[24] These generalizations were predicated mainly on studies of learning in rats, but there is little reason to doubt they hold up for human learning. In fact, most of the interpersonal behavior which psychotherapists call "ego-defensive" may be regarded as instances of interpersonal avoidance habits. Reich called the attention of psychoanalysts to a phenomenon which he called *character-resistance;*[25] in psychoanalytic therapy, the patient is obliged to relate to the observing therapist all that passes through his mind. Analysts noted that patients developed various resistances to the enjoinder they must speak all they think and feel. Character-resistance referred to subtle ways of relating to the therapist which served to bypass the free-association rule; further observation led Reich to note the character-resistances were but special cases of the more general concept, character-armor. Character-armor may be regarded as the sum total of an individual's interpersonal avoidance habits.

The reader can detect instances of character-armor in himself if he will strive to discern some consistency or pattern in the way he behaves toward say, his mother. If he is very respectful toward his mother, and tries to alter this way of behaving, he may become aware of considerable anxiety; in order to reduce the anxiety, he may find it necessary to revert back to the pattern of respect.

Character-armor—rigid interpersonal habits—is an obstacle to the attainment of healthy personality. Rigid interpersonal habits impel a person to behave toward others in ways which are inappropriate to the feelings, wishes, or traits of the other person; in spite of their inappropriateness, the individual cannot abandon or alter these rigid habits, and so his potential gratifications in interpersonal relationships are reduced.

A special problem in personality therapy is that of "loosening the character-armor." [26] What this involves is attempts on the part of the therapist to lead the patient, who has sought help because of some neurotic symptom, such as an obsession, or an hysterical complaint, *to regard his interpersonal habits as symptoms.* Up to this time, the patient may have taken his interpersonal behavior for granted, never bothering to examine it. Once he begins to examine it, he becomes extremely self-conscious, self-analytical, and usually quite anxious. The consequence is the person no longer relates to others in the smooth, long-rehearsed, automatic ways he previously did. Instead he is obliged to suppress his automatic reaction-patterns and to attempt to replace them by newer, more flexible and appropriate interpersonal behavior. Although this entire process is accompanied by much anxiety, it is intended that the patient should learn healthy interpersonal habits, ways of behaving predicated on accurate perception of others, which are more spontaneous, flexible, and expressive of his real self.

THE PROBLEM OF CHARACTER-EVALUATION. Character-evaluation involves observing the interpersonal behavior of a person, or of oneself, until it becomes possible to discern most of the repertoire of interpersonal habits. Then, each of these may be evaluated. This involves ascertaining whether or not the pattern is healthy, or unhealthy. If it is unhealthy, it can be determined whether it is ineffective in securing satisfactions, or whether it is contrived or rigid. It may happen that a person, after evaluation, will be found to display healthy interpersonal behavior toward his closest friend, ineffective and rigid behavior toward his teacher, contrived behavior toward his boss, and so on. The development of this applied field awaits the efforts of interested investigators.

AFFECTION AND INTERPERSONAL BEHAVIOR

We have pointed out already that affection is one of the need-objects a person can gain through interpersonal behavior. Affection is valued for its own sake, as a determiner of self-esteem, and also because it is an important means to many other need-objects. What are the consequences of not getting it? Are there healthy and unhealthy ways of getting it? Let us inquire into some of the answers to these questions.

CONSEQUENCES OF RECEIVING AFFECTION-RESPONSES. A considerable amount of attention has been paid by students of child development and of personality to the role of affection in personality development.[27] Personality hygienists are unanimous in asserting that unrestricted affection is as important to optimum personality development as food, shelter, or medical attention. The experience of being liked by significant others makes it possible for the growing person to like himself, and to express affection openly to others. Both these responses are important indices of personality health.

To the adult, being liked will certainly contribute to an increase in self-esteem and to a feeling of security—but the identity of the other person must not be overlooked. It feels different to be liked by one significant person, or class of persons, rather than another. It feels different because of the different meanings associated with different people. Nobody wants to be liked by criminals, if he is not a criminal himself; in fact, he is likely to become uneasy if it becomes known among polite society that criminals like him. People will wonder what he has done in order to earn the affection of criminals. A young male will feel more pleasant if he is liked by an exquisitely beautiful woman, than if he is liked by an ugly girl of unsavory reputation.

The pleasant feelings associated with being liked stem from two major sources: the increase in self-esteem which follows the receipt of affection responses and the anticipation, or expectation, that many important wants and valued ends will be satisfied or obtained in the near future. In our discussion of emotions (Chapter 4), we pointed out that expectancies play an important role in determining the emotional response to some object. Fear and anxiety are associated with the anticipation of pain; the pleasant feelings associated with being liked stem from the prediction that the liking-responses shown by the other person are a signal that your wants will be gratified in the future with the collaboration of that other person.

CONSEQUENCES OF NOT RECEIVING AFFECTION-RESPONSES. A life history marked by scarcity of affection-responses is characteristic of all mental illness.[28] As a student examines psychiatric literature, or studies case histories in abnormal psychology, he finds with regularity that the patient has seldom felt loved, or liked. Criminologists have found that in most instances of criminal behavior, the offender had a childhood and adult life which was poverty-stricken with respect to affection—nobody liked, or likes him. Ribble, Spitz, Goldfarb,[29] and others, have observed that psychiatric afflictions are a regular consequence when children grow up in an atmosphere devoid of affection.

A bountiful supply of affection-responses is a necessary precondition for the development of healthy personality. Why should this be the case? Why do people need affection in order to grow into adults who are happy, and with whom others can live in harmony? Probably because affection-responses serve the function of a "pay-off" for the pains and frustrations associated with socialization. The socialization process largely entails learning to forego immediately gratifying, impulsive behavior, and such suppression is intrinsically unpleasant. The child "paid" for these pains with affection-responses becomes willing to forego immediately gratifying impulsive behavior, and is able to learn socially acceptable behavior. The reasons why affection acquires "pay-off" value is a problem in learning theory; affection is an example of *secondary reinforcement*.[30]

The adult in our society who doesn't receive enough affection from others (the amount which is sufficient differs between persons), generally *suffers*. He regards himself as unworthy or inferior, and feels there "must be something wrong with him." He is generally anxious; he anticipates all manner of dire events at the hands of "hostile" people, which includes everyone who withholds the symbols of affection from him. In our society, not to be liked seems to symbolize "being hated" by others, rather than neutrality on the part of others.

The person who is not liked enough may react in a variety of ways. He may become vengeful and aggressive, and "move against people," as Horney puts it. Or, he may "move toward people," striving compulsively to please, in order to seduce others into giving him the affection responses which he so desperately needs. Basic anxiety, the feeling of helplessness and loneliness in a potentially hostile world, is perhaps the best term to describe the general consequences of an insufficiency of affection as this is experienced by people in our society.[31]

QUEST FOR AFFECTION-RESPONSES IN AN OTHER-DIRECTED SOCIETY. Riesman[32] has documented the thesis that our society is becoming increasingly populated by other-directed characters, people who behave, not in accordance with their own feelings and will, but rather who do what others expect of them. They do this compulsively, even to the point of losing the ability to know what they want or feel (self-alienation, as Horney describes it). The reasons for the quest for affection are being sought by sociologists and psychologists alike, and they are probably complex.

One possible psychological explanation for the compulsive quest for affection is suggested by Maslow,[33] as an implication of his theory of motivation. He asserts that human needs are arranged in a hierarchy, and higher needs will emerge into tension only when lower needs have been gratified. Love needs, which we construe as the need for affection responses from other persons, stand higher than physical and safety needs and lower than esteem and self-actualization needs. Could we assert that the chronic need and quest for affection-responses from other people is a consequence of an insufficiency of affection earlier in life? Is it that the affection-seeker is one who has had a taste of affection, just enough to get an appetite for it, but not enough to satisfy? And that therefore, his life is oriented around the quest for affection, just as primitive societies living at a survival level have a culture oriented around the food quest?

If it is true that the compulsive quest for affection stems from "scarcity economics"—what is scarce becomes highly valued—what sociological factors promote affection-poverty during the early childhood of people?[34] What psychological factors prevent mothers and fathers from giving enough symbols of affection, caresses, hugs, endearing words, to their children to satisfy them? Could we be dealing with a sort of "daisy-chain," where the parents are inhibited in expression of affection for their children because *they* didn't get enough from *their* parents? Or could it be a by-product of unattainable ideals which the parents set for the children so that the latter never "deserve" affection? Could it stem from a fear of spoiling children, a sort of acting out of the slogan "if you let your children know that you like them, they will become disobedient, unmanageable or conceited"? Since affection-lack produces consequences detrimental to personality health, it is important to determine the factors responsible for it. Because of affection-lack, many people emerge into adult life starved for affection and willing to do almost anything in order to get it, including immoral and unethical action.

COMMENTS ON THE ABILITY TO GIVE AND ACCEPT AFFECTION. Recent evidence from observation of institution-raised children suggests that the ability to give affection, to feel affection, and to accept it comfortably, is the outgrowth, in some way not yet understood, of having been the recipient of lavish supplies of affection. The person who has been adequately loved seems better able to learn how to behave in a love-attracting way. It is literally a case of "to him that hath shall be given"; the well-loved person is more responsive to others, more able to like them and to let them know it.

If it is true that the ability to give affection and to feel it stems from having received it, then a useful and valid personality hygiene measure for parents follows: "Be open and lavish and spontaneous in the expression of affection for your children . . . just as you are not stinting and grudging in your proffering of food, clothing and toys."

The inability to give affection probably stems from a more general phenomenon—a self-structure which makes affection and all other emotional tensions threatening to the individual. Any factor which promoted the capacity of parents to feel and to express affection would be a factor which promoted healthy personality both in them and in their children.

There are some social values which operate so as to make it difficult for many persons to express affection—especially males. Men often interpret affection, either giving it or enjoyably receiving it, as a threat to their self-concept, a sign of weakness, or effeminacy. Many wives complain their husbands don't show affection; the husbands, if capable of honest introspection, might admit longing for affection, but they fear to ask for it. And they don't feel like their "hard-boiled selves" when they give it.

The author would not be at all surprised if a reader found the following experiment successful: Tell everyone you know that you like them very much. If you say this openly and sincerely to people's faces at appropriate times, they'll probably be skeptical at first (what is he after?), then cautiously they'll believe you, and finally, they will love you.[35] Such an "experiment" seems to be the essence of popular courses on "how to win friends."

Young lovers are usually so unsure of their basic likability and lovability, that they hardly believe it when their sweethearts say, "I love you," or "I like you." They need proof, sometimes incredible proof, before they will believe that another human being actually likes them. By the same token, a person will be extremely cautious in saying the words, "I like you" to another person, and meaning it, perhaps because it exposes him to the possibility of being rejected, or told that he is not liked in return.

Sometimes a person will become panicky when another shows signs of liking him. This anxiety usually stems from past experience of a peculiar sort, where to be liked meant that terrible responsibility, or domination, or pain of some kind was forthcoming. The author knows a man who is relatively comfortable and secure only when he is cordially despised by others. When people show signs of liking him, it upsets him, because it jeopardizes his concept of others as "no damn good," and would require marked changes in his modal behavior.

One might ask, "What is the difference between genuine affection and pseudo affection?" People often comment, "He *seems* to like him, but really, he doesn't." A skilled actor can certainly emit all the conventional expressive responses which signify affection (contrived interpersonal behavior), but inwardly, he feels nothing, or else some other emotion. The skilled analyst of personality usually tells the difference between pseudo and genuine affection, by studying, not the verbal and expressive signs of affection, but rather the behavior of the individual toward the object of his affection. If this behavior consistently fits the cultural stereotype of affectionate behavior, then one adjudges the feelings as affection; that is, if the person behaves in ways which help the other, or which satisfy his needs, and he does this lavishly, unstintingly, without effort, and without being asked. If, on the other hand, the person says "I like him," but acts toward him in ways which hurt, humiliate, interfere with growth, or which do nothing to promote the other person's happiness, then we conclude that the words are meaningless, or at least do not portray faithfully the person's inner feelings.

AFFECTION AND HEALTHY PERSONALITY. We have asserted that affection-responses are needed by a person for many reasons: for the maintenance of self-esteem, for promoting security, and for reassuring him that other people who like him will not withhold many other kinds of need-objects. Much interpersonal behavior that a person engages in, then, has as its aim, consciously or unconsciously, the securing of affection-responses from the other person. We can appraise this interpersonal behavior from the standpoint of efficiency, and, more generally, from the standpoint of personality hygiene. Healthy interpersonal behavior is successful in obtaining affection and acceptance from others and at the same time is expressive of the individual's real self.

Unhealthy interpersonal behavior may be inefficient, contrived, antisocial, or in conflict with the individual's real self. We would have to assess as unhealthy, then, the pursuit of affection-responses at the expense of other valued ends, such as self-esteem and growth. The quest "to be liked at all cost" is not worth the cost. Very often, in order to be liked, a person is obliged to suppress and repress many of his own feelings and wants; in short, he is obliged to become alienated from his self.

Behavior aimed at securing affection may be just plain inefficient. It may be inefficient because the seeker is so anxious that he loses control over his behavior and loses the ability to assess what responses will be effective. Many of the obnoxious behavior patterns which a patient manifests with his therapist are almost "tests" of the therapist, as well as characteristic of his relationships with many other people in his present and past social orbit. If the therapist can survive,[36] or accept these patterns without seeming to reject the patient, or to dislike him, then the patient will begin to like and trust his therapist, feel less anxious, and begin to recognize how he behaves toward the therapist and others. Finally, he may learn to behave in more likable ways toward the therapist. This ability may then carry over to other persons in his life.

We will assert that it is healthy (a) to want affection, (b) to be able to accept it without anxiety when it is genuinely offered, (c) to be able to behave toward others in ways which will elicit affection, (d) to be able to give affection, and (e) to be able to choose rationally between affection and other values. In connection with (e), affection may not be worth what it costs. However, one cannot tell this to a starving individual. Taste and the ability to make discrimination is a by-product of plenty, not of scarcity. Under extreme deprivation of any sort, canalizations, or preferences in need-objects, become relatively ineffective, and the person will take what he can get. The affection-starved individual shows a similar lack of discrimination in his choice of friends (sources of affection), and in his choice of behavior patterns which he will engage in in order to get affection. It is not uncommon for persons to rob, cheat, kill, degrade themselves, swallow their pride and steal, in order to be liked by somebody.

Affection is not the only need-object which can be obtained through interpersonal instrumental behavior. In fact, it is convenient and valid to think of another person as a "cafeteria-display" of actual and possible need-objects of varied kinds. We already touched on the fact that other people possess skills which we need; all kinds of material need-objects which they will give us only when appropriately paid, either in money or in conformity with other conditions which they impose; affection; self-esteem-enhancing responses. Let us examine in more detail the role an individual's needs will play in influencing interpersonal attractions and repulsions.

OTHER NEEDS AND INTERPERSONAL BEHAVIOR

We can regard another person as an animated collection of need-objects. The other person's appearance, his status, his values, his modal behavior, all can serve as need-objects at one time or another to a given individual. As need-tensions come and go, the traits of the other person acquire positive valence, negative valence, and neutral valence. The securing of need-objects possessed by the other person presents a continual challenge to an individual; he must learn the appropriate instrumental behavior patterns which will be effective in obtaining the needed responses from the other person. In a sense, we can regard many of the personality traits of an individual, his recurrent modes of relating to other people especially, as a record of his past relationships with others. These interpersonal habits represent his solutions to past problems, problems which involved his learning effective ways of getting what he needed from the other person. Thus, a persistent habit of politeness, or of deference, may tell the observer that in order to get what he needed from others, the individual was obliged to behave politely, or deferentially. A strongly aggressive individual may reveal to the observer that, in order to get what is needed from others, it was necessary for him to take it by force. It should be possible to infer many of the needs of a person by studying the characteristics of the other people whom he likes, dislikes, and is indifferent to.[37] Further, it should be possible to make valid predictions about whom an individual will like,[38] whom he will choose as a friend or spouse, how long a friendship will last, or a marriage, on the basis of knowledge about what the individual needs in order to maintain security, self-esteem, etc.

Let us illustrate some of these points. We will discuss the role of certain needs on the choice of friends, fiancées, fellow-workers, etc.

NEEDS AND THE CHOICE OF FRIENDS.[39] A person will choose as a friend that individual whose characteristics will satisfy his varied needs. A very passive and helpless individual will be attracted by competent and highly skilled persons. A man with strong sexual tensions will be attracted toward women who seem willing to serve as potential sexual partners. A person with shaky self-esteem will like those people who seem to hold beliefs about him which correspond with his self-ideal rather than with his self-concept. A social climber will be indifferent to persons of his own social class, but will be strongly attracted to someone who comes from a higher socio-economic class.

One can regard the behavior of one person in front of another as a variety of advertising, or of wares-display. In a very short time, each person will size up the other with respect to his suitability as a potential need-satisfier. One looks the other over, and sees signs in his behavior which indicate "This fellow will be a good companion on a camping trip; a sympathetic audience when I am in trouble; a good source of jokes; a rich source of money to borrow; he can introduce me to the right people." The other person, in turn, might see the first as "a guy who knows all the answers; a first-rate technician; someone who can show me a lot about getting along with people." If each has what the other person needs for assorted purposes, then a more lasting friendship might develop out of the encounter. If, on the other hand, either sees, or thinks he sees signs which point to various frustrations, the relationship will not be cultivated. Thus, one of the individuals might think he sees a certain intolerance for some of his own modal behavior; in order to save himself from future frustrations, he will terminate the relationship, or tell the other, "I know you don't like certain kinds of behavior, and I happen to behave in those ways."

Friendships and love affairs generally begin with such a period of mutual exploration, or diagnosis. The initial attraction which brought the two people together may have been the result of such factors as appearance, or behavior samples which constitute possible need-objects. For example, in a crowded room, you might overhear a person expressing tastes in music just like your own. A girl might see some boy whose appearance corresponds with her most romantic dreams of a lover. Once two persons meet, however, the process of diagnosis really begins. Each looks the other over, asks questions, sounds out the other's values, biases and attitudes, and tries to make formulations concerning the other's modal behavior. These formulations are often grossly wrong. On the basis of this diagnostic behavior, a decision may be made to spend more or less time with the other individual.

NEEDS AND THE MAINTENANCE OF FRIENDSHIPS. So long as no external factors interfere, a friendship will endure (or a marriage, or any other association between two persons) only as long as the behavior of each partner provides more satisfactions than it does deprivations or frustrations. As soon as the needs of either are satiated; or as soon as either partner withholds the need-objects required by the other, then the relationship will no longer have any "cement" to hold it together.

NEEDS AND INTERPERSONAL AVERSIONS. Just as a person can be seen as attractive insofar as his behavior will serve as need-objects to the chooser, so can he be repulsive for the same reasons. If your self-esteem is dependent upon being chosen as a friend only by the "best" people, you will be repelled by the "not best." A person who values manners will be repelled by the uncouth. A prude is repelled by a satyr. Whether or not you will be indifferent or repulsed by another person seems to be a function of the relevance of that person's traits to your needs. If his behavior interferes with or prevents need-satisfaction, you will dislike him.

FRIENDSHIPS AND INTERPERSONAL BEHAVIOR. As one studies the relationship between two friends, one observes recurrent behavior patterns. One may note, for example, that one partner is forever giving in to the other's demands. The behavior which occurs in a friendship may be interpreted on a quid pro quo basis. It may be assumed that each party is attempting to maintain the good-will and affection of the other in order to insure that the other will continue to supply need-objects. When two people come to know each other well, they know not only what the other needs in order to make him happy, but also what will hurt the other person. So long as each is behaving in a satisfying way toward the other, all is well. But when one partner holds back, or interferes with the satisfactions of the other, then it is not uncommon for virtual sadism to ensue. The deprived one knows the weak spots of the other, and he will find these unerringly. No one can hurt a person so well and so deeply as can a friend, and no one can provide such profound satisfactions to a person as a friend.

NEEDS AND THE CHOICE OF ROLES. An individual will enact many roles in his relationships with others. He may be obliged to play the role of husband, father, son, employee, boss, etc. Each social role a person adopts carries with it certain prescriptions concerning how he must, or should, behave. Naturally, as a person plays any role, *he is obliged to suppress all behavior which is not relevant to the role in question.* If, for example, the role of son requires the person to display only respect, obedience, and submission, then the son must suppress all rebellious, hostile, or self-assertive behavior. A person may avoid certain roles, or strongly resist having the role thrust on him, when the behavior required by that role threatens his self-structure, or else interferes with the satisfaction of important needs. Thus, a person may reject the role of husband, because such a role will require him to assume responsibility for others, and he may believe he is incapable of holding down a job. Marriage may require him to give up a close relationship with his mother, or with some friends, and since he needs those relationships in order to maintain a sense of identity, security or self-esteem, he will avoid marriage.

Some roles dovetail nicely with the needs and values of the person, allowing him to find many important satisfactions. Thus a man may seek out the role of the leader, or the follower, because these roles require him to engage in interpersonal behavior which guarantees him safety, satisfactions, and self-esteem.[40]

Although an adult person has a certain freedom in his choice of roles, there are some roles which are ascribed to him by society, because of sex, age, and the social group into which he has been born. As with all roles, the sex-role, the age-role, and the roles that are assigned because of group-membership involve restriction and prescription of certain behavior-patterns. The idiosyncratic needs of the person may be satisfied or thwarted by these roles, and so a discussion is warranted of *assigned* roles and personality health. Healthy personalities can meet their needs as they enact roles.

SEX-ROLES. One's sex is determined at the instant of conception, but masculine and feminine behavior and personality are *culturally* defined and determined. Each person has got to learn, or be trained in, his sex-role. Each society differs in its concept of masculine and feminine behavior, as Mead has so convincingly demonstrated.[41] She showed that in three New Guinea tribes, there was considerable difference from tribe to tribe in the typical male and female roles. In one group, the Arapesh, men and women alike were passive, "maternal," co-operative, and nonaggressive. In the Mundugamor, a tribe geographically close to the Arapesh, men and women alike were fierce, cruel, aggressive, and self-assertive. A third tribe, the Tchambuli, showed a different pattern of sex-typing. The men were passive, dependent, individuals who spent their time cultivating the arts, while the women were assertive, and had to cultivate the gardens and make a living.

In America, rigid definition of sex-roles is gradually breaking down. Thus, many middle-class men take an active role in child-care, in housekeeping, while their wives do many things which once were deemed to be a male prerogative: they keep the budget, spend the money, and work at occupations that formerly were strictly male. In some European countries, male and female behavior contrasts in certain ways with the American concept of masculinity and femininity. Thus, in Latin countries, a man can comfortably kiss another man and he can cry openly without shame. But these men might look askance at the American woman who likes to wear trousers. For them, women belong in dresses.

In order to "wear" one's sex-role comfortably, a person has to be trained into it. Yet, some men have been reared in ways that promote the development of traits ordinarily regarded as effeminate; they may also have acquired, in process of growing up, the cultural concepts of the male role. Therefore, they find it a strain to "be a man." In acting in manly ways, they are going against their (acquired) "nature." But if they were to act in the ways which were most natural for them, they might experience a considerable threat to their sense of identity as a man and expose themselves to much ridicule. The same considerations apply to women. The individual who has acquired a rigid concept of male and female roles may experience a high degree of inner discomfort and conflict. If he acts just as he feels, he may undergo a threat to his self-concept. If he acts in accordance with his sex-role, he may suffer from considerable frustration of strong needs for self-expression. Some individuals are so insecure about their sexual identity that they must "overprotest." Instead of being content to be manly, they must be "super-manly," they exaggerate their manly traits as if to convince themselves and others that they are indeed men. If anyone questions the masculinity of such a person, he may become dangerously aggressive. His life involves a continual quest for reassurances of his own masculinity. A woman who questions her own femininity may adopt the same adjustive procedures.

A common occurrence is that of role-conflict. Sociologists have pointed out that this is becoming increasingly common, especially among women, as our social system undergoes changes. The woman is obliged to be a housekeeper, a glamor girl, and a stimulating companion to her husband. It may be difficult for her to do justice to all of these roles, so that she comes to doubt her identity as a woman.[42]

Some women, as the psychoanalysts have pointed out, are very resentful of the woman's role in society, and envious of the apparent freedom and more privileged position of the male in our society. This pattern has been metaphorically described among the analysts as "penis-envy." Mead has showed that just as women may envy the male, so may men envy certain female prerogatives, especially their role in the bearing of children. In this connection she speaks of "womb-envy." [43]

Since sex-roles are relatively fixed by society, each person, man and woman, must find ways of fitting himself to his sex-role, of coming to terms with it. Some men and women find their sex-role too constraining, and they adopt many of the patterns of the opposite sex, both sexually and behaviorally. It is not uncommon in large cities to find colonies of male and female homosexuals, in which there may be found highly effeminate men and quite masculine women.

The healthy personality is able to redefine his own personal sex-role in ways that dovetail better with his needs. Consequently, he has greater freedom to express and act out his real self and is much less easily threatened. Thus, a healthy man can do many things that might be deemed effeminate by other men, and yet he will not experience any threat to his masculinity. He may wash dishes, change babies, perform jobs such as hairdressing or ballet, and yet still feel manly. A rigid concept of one's sex-role can promote the development of unhealthy personality.

AGE-ROLES. Each society expects a progression of behavior in its members, a progression that will keep pace with the person's chronological age. If a person is keeping pace with his age-roles, he is said to be mature. If he is behind other people his age, he is said to be immature, or *fixated*. If he reverts to behavior characteristic of a younger age, he is said to display *regression*, and if he shows a premature development of traits expected from older persons, he is said to display *precocity*. As with sex-roles, age-roles may conflict sharply with the person's needs. He may not be ready to progress to the next age-role when the time for it comes. Or, he may enforce conformity with his age-role on himself, at considerable cost in satisfactions.

By the time an individual has become an adult, as this is defined in his culture, he acquires a vested interest in regarding himself as mature. Yet, need-gratifications may be possible only if he behaves in immature ways.

The healthy personality feels sufficiently secure about his identity as a mature adult that he can regress when he wants to, or when he feels like it, without any marked threats to self-esteem or to his sense of identity. A person who is insecure about his maturity may strive to convince himself and others that he is mature, and avoid any regressive behavior like the plague. Thus, some men may not allow themselves to be taken care of even when they are gravely sick, because it would imply that they had regressed. Some women may refuse tenderness and solicitude from a man, because of the implication that they are not independent adults.

INTERPERSONAL BEHAVIOR AND PERSONALITY DIAGNOSIS

Clinical psychologists, psychiatrists and laymen are often confronted with the problem of making meaningful statements about somebody's personality. For example, it may be important to ascertain whether or not a given person will be suitable as a candidate for some position, or whether a person will be suitable as a spouse. A careful study of the interpersonal behavior repertoire of the individual will provide invaluable information about the person's needs, his values, and his probable responses to certain future situations.[44]

In studying interpersonal behavior, what kinds of questions are the most helpful as guides to observation?

The crucial questions may be stated as follows:

1. With what kinds of people does the person seem to feel safe? How does he need people to behave in order that he will feel safe?

2. How does he require people to act in order that he will continue to feel self-esteem?

3. How does he behave in the presence of other people? What behavior occurs, and what behavior does not occur, in the presence of various classes of people? What aspects of his real self can he communicate to others, and what aspects does he hide?

4. What roles seem to give the person the richest satisfactions and which role gives him the greatest frustrations and deprivations?

5. Whom does the person hate, and why? Whom does the person like, and why?

Block[45] undertook an intensive study of the interpersonal behavior patterns of a young woman. He asked her to show which interpersonal behavior patterns were typical of her, and which were not typical, in her relationships with her bosses, her fellow-secretaries and close friends. He found, naturally, that certain interpersonal behavior patterns were included and others excluded in each of these classes of interpersonal relationship. We are not so interested in his specific findings as we are in the method which was employed for studying interpersonal behavior. It is a systematic approach to a study of interpersonal behavior which shows great promise as a research tool. It is only when consistencies in interpersonal behavior can be recorded and measured that research can then be undertaken into such things as the determiners of these patterns and the correlates of the patterns. Further, this approach offers great promise as a means of constructing a newer, more fruitful way of classifying unhealthy personalities than the present psychiatric classification system. We might find, for example, that those persons who exclude a great deal of behavior from their interpersonal relationships suffer a good deal from anxiety, guilt, or from sheer deprivation of all kinds of satisfactions. Or, we might expect to find that those persons who include too much in their interpersonal relationships experience a good deal of "social maladjustment." Like any new approach to the study of personality, the interpersonal method must be used a good deal before any definite conclusions can be drawn concerning its ultimate value. At the present time, however, it seems to offer great promise, and is being used in a wide variety of research problems.

One could, for example, infer the more chronic needs of an individual by studying his interpersonal behavior. One could also determine the values, or the content of the conscience of an individual, by recording samples of his interpersonal behavior. Harry Stack Sullivan, the late interpersonal psychiatrist, urged personality therapists during their therapeutic sessions to seek to determine what the patient does and doesn't do in his dealings with people.[46] Such information affords invaluable insight into the origins of the patient's interpersonal difficulties and the consequences of these difficulties. We might view the interpersonal method as a systematic application of Sullivan's enjoinder.

SUMMARY

Man needs his fellow-man for the gratification of many needs and for the attainment of human status. In these senses, man is dependent.

More specifically, man is dependent upon others for survival during his infancy. As an adult, he depends upon others for technical assistance, for self-esteem, for security, affection and passive love, for his sense of personal identity, for direction, and many other valued ends which cannot be achieved in solitude.

The term *interpersonal* behavior is used to describe the behavior of one person in relation to another. Healthy interpersonal behavior is *spontaneous, versatile, flexible,* and *expressive of the real self* of the individual.

Unhealthy interpersonal behavior may be *ineffective* in securing satisfactions from others for the individual, or it may be *contrived. Inaccurate other-concepts, inaccurate interpersonal perception, irrational anxiety, excessively strict conscience and self-ideal,* and *excessive privation* are all factors which promote ineffectiveness in interpersonal behavior.

Contrived interpersonal behavior appears to derive from a basic fear of acting out one's real self.

Healthy interpersonal behavior may be acquired through optimum upbringing experiences, or through effective personality therapy.

The term *character* refers to the more or less stable patterns of interpersonal behavior which a person has learned. *Character-armor* refers to rigid interpersonal habits which have been acquired under conditions of *avoidance-learning,* in contrast with *reward-learning.*

An extensive discussion of affection is given, showing the importance of affection for overall personality health.

Needs help to determine a person's choice of friends, the maintenance of friendships, interpersonal aversions, and role-behavior. Interpersonal behavior is discussed, finally, as a basis for making diagnoses about personality in general.

NOTES AND REFERENCES

RECOMMENDED READINGS ARE MARKED WITH AN ASTERISK (°)

°1. The reader perhaps has known people who live far away from other people, or who never interact with others, and he may have noticed that such individuals seem "odd"—different in their values, emotional reactions, etc., from the average person. Fromm regards interaction with others as a sine qua non for being *human.* Cf. Fromm, E., *The sane society*, New York, Rinehart, 1955, pp. 30–36. For an account of *desocialization* and its bearing on "behavior pathology," see Cameron, N. and Margaret, Ann, *Behavior pathology*, New York, Houghton Mifflin, 1951, Ch. 16.

2. Maslow notes that "self-actualizing people" have periodic strong needs for privacy and solitude. Cf. Maslow, A. H., *Motivation and personality*, New York, Harper, 1954, pp. 212–213.

*3. See Ribble, M., *The rights of infants*, New York, Columbia University Press, 1943. This small volume is devoted to a discussion of what the infant needs a mother *for*, and what he needs *from* a mother, in order optimally to grow. Rene Spitz, a child psychiatrist, has undertaken some interesting research on mother-infant relationships, and their consequences. See Spitz, R., "Hospitalism," in *Psychoanalyt. Stud. Child*, I, New York, International University Press, 1945.

4. Spitz, R., "The smiling response: A contribution to the ontogenesis of social relations," *Genet. Psychol. Monogr.*, 1946, 34, 57–125.

5. Horney has called attention to the various conditions which must be met in order that a neurotic person will not unleash upon himself a veritable onslaught of self-hate. See her *Neurosis and human growth*, New York, Norton, 1950, Ch. 5. Fenichel also has indicated how neurotics come to depend, for the maintenance of self-esteem, on "external sources of supply." See Fenichel, O., *The psychoanalytic theory of neurosis*, New York, Norton, 1945, pp. 387 *et seq.*

6. Blatz, W., *Understanding the young child*, Toronto, Clarke, Irwin, 1944, Ch. 9.

7. See, for example, the discussion of "self-effacing" people in Horney, K., *op. cit.*, Ch. 9.

8. The child psychoanalyist, Erikson, has recently been calling attention to the role of the sense of identity in personality growth. Cf. Erikson, E. H., *Childhood and society*, New York, Norton, 1950. See also, by the same author, "The problem of ego identity," *J. Amer. Psychoanalyt. Assoc.*, 1956, 4, 56–121. Jeanne Watson, in an ongoing study, sees interpersonal behavior (sociability) as a means by which identity is defined. Watson, Jeanne, "Sociability as a medium for definition of the self." (Mimeographed manuscript, 1956, Committee on Human Development, University of Chicago.)

*9. See Fromm, E., *Escape from freedom*, New York, Rinehart, 1941, pp. 141–178, for a discussion of authoritarianism. For an empirical study of authoritarian characters, see Adorno, R. W., Frenkel-Brunswick, Else, Levinson, D. J., and Sanford, R. N., *The authoritarian personality*, New York, Harper, 1950.

10. Fromm, E., *op. cit.*, pp. 185–206.

°11. Riesman, D., *The lonely crowd*, New Haven, Yale University Press, 1950—the discussion of the other-directed character.

°12. Cf. Crutchfield, R. S., "Conformity and character," *Amer. Psychologist*, 1955, **10**, 191–198.

13. These characteristics are not just "pulled from the air" by the author. Maslow finds these characteristics in his "self-actualizing" persons, and many practising therapists look for these properties in their patients' interpersonal behavior as indices that therapy has reached a successful outcome.

14. Steiner, I. D., "Interpersonal behavior and accurate social perception," *Psychol. Rev.*, 1955, **62**, 268–273. In this article, Steiner analyzes the role played by accurate "social perception" in "interpersonal competence" and group efficiency. "Social perception" is the term currently used to describe the means by which knowledge about others (other-concepts) is acquired. See the next chapter for a more exhaustive analysis of other-concepts.

15. Fromm, E., *Man for himself*, New York, Rinehart, 1947, pp. 67–82.

16. Riesman, D., *op. cit.*

17. The "psychopathic personality" is often seen as very charming, and well-liked. This is probably a by-product of the fact that the psychopath is not restricted in interpersonal behavior by his conscience to the same extent as most people. In consequence, he can behave in very contradictory ways with different people in order to "charm them," and yet he will not feel any guilt over the inconsistencies in his behavior. Cf. Cleckley, H., *The mask of sanity*, St. Louis, Mosby, 1941.

18. Cf. Horney, K., *op. cit.*, Ch. 14, for a discussion of therapy from the standpoint of "self-realization."

19. Fromm, E., *op. cit.*, pp. 54–118.

°20. See Notcutt, B., *The psychology of personality*, London, Methuen, 1953. His discussion of typology (Ch. 4) is unsurpassed, in the present writer's opinion.

21. Rank, O., *Will therapy, and truth and reality*, New York, Knopf, 1945.

22. Riesman, D., *op. cit.*

23. Reich, W., *Character analysis*, New York, Orgone Institute Press, 1949, pp. 40–76.

24. Cf. Keller, F. S. and Schoenfeld, W. N., *Principles of psychology,* New York, Appleton-Century-Crofts, 1950, p. 315. These authors state: "Our present knowledge, gleaned mainly from animal study, indicates that *the extinction of an avoidance response is often extremely difficult,* even in well-controlled experimental situations." (My italics.)

25. Reich, W., *op. cit.,* pp. 40–51.

26. Reich, W., *op. cit.,* pp. 67–76.

*27. John Bowlby has written extensively on maternal deprivation and affection-lack. See Bowlby, J., "Maternal care and mental health," *Bulletin World Health Organization,* 1951, 3, 335–534. Also, his popular book, *Child care and the growth of love,* London, Penguin Books, 1953.

28. Bowlby, J., *op. cit.* Check index of both volumes under heading of affection.

29. Ribble, M., *op. cit.* Spitz, R. A., *op. cit.* Goldfarb, W. His studies are summarized in Hoch, P. F. and Zubin, J. (ed.), *Psychopathology in childhood,* New York, Grune & Stratton, 1955.

30. The words, gestures and actions which signify affection and approval are thought to acquire their meaning to the individual through the association of these signals with more "primary" stimuli, such as caresses, food, etc. See Wolfe, J. B., "Effectiveness of token-rewards for chimpanzees," *Comp. Psychol. Monogr.,* 1936, 12, 1–72, for an example of an experiment which demonstrates secondary reinforcement with animals. Probably the same principles, or at least similar ones, will account for the effectiveness of words and gestures as rewards and punishments at the human level.

31. This analysis is a paraphrase of Horney's writings. See Horney, K., *Our inner conflicts,* New York, Norton, 1945.

32. Riesman, D., *op. cit.*

33. Maslow, A. H., *op. cit.,* Ch. 5.

34. Dr. William Rhodes, of the Georgia State Department of Health, undertook a study in 1955 of mothers who deprive their children of adequate care. He has collected a number of reports from visiting public health nurses which cite instances of neglect that amaze the middle-class reader. In one instance, a nurse reported that a young infant had been left on a pile of sacking, naked, for several weeks. The mother fed the child occasionally, but never cleaned it or picked it up.

35. However, such an experiment, if carried out in "cold blood" and with-

out genuine feelings, would be a very low form of fraud, in the writer's opinion.

36. Cf. Redl, F. and Wineman, D., *Controls from within*, Glencoe, Illinois, Free Press, 1952, pp. 59–62.

37. The Szondi test represents an attempt to apply this connection between needs and the valence of objects for a person to the problem of personality-testing. The subject is shown a series of facial photographs of patients from mental hospitals in Europe. Szondi assumed the psychopathology of the patients was somehow expressed in their faces, and that if a subject showed a preference for schizophrenic faces, it reflected the presence of some schizophrenic trends in his own personality. This assumption does not enjoy experimental verification.

°38. See Newcomb, T., "The prediction of interpersonal attraction," *Amer. Psychologist*, 1956, 11, 575–586, for a cogent discussion of this point, with some experimental data.

39. There have been hosts of studies aimed at the discovery of the personality characteristics which are typical of individuals with high sociometric status. See Northway, M. L., Frankel, E. B. and Potashin, R., "Personality and sociometric status," *Sociom. Monogr.* No. 11, Beacon House, 1947, for one review of the literature on this subject. The present author reported a study which showed that those children in a summer camp who were the most highly chosen by the other children were the most active and highly skilled participants in the camp program (unpublished manuscript).

A line of research which awaits the eager investigator is an inquiry into the relationship between the needs of the chooser, and the traits of the person being chosen.

°40. There is an extensive literature on role-theory. The interested student will find an excellent introduction to this area in Lindzey, G. (ed.), *Handbook of social psychology*, Vol. I, Cambridge, Addison-Wesley, 1954, Ch. 6.

°41. See Mead, M., *Male and female*, New York, Morrow, 1949. This is an excellent discussion of cultural variation in sex-typing by a leading anthropologist.

°42. See Parsons, T., "Age and sex in the social structure of the United States," in *Essays in sociological theory*, Glencoe, Illinois, The Free Press, 1954.

43. Mead, M., *op. cit.*

44. An entire system of personality theory and personality research has

been developed out of this approach. See Leary, T., *et al.*, *The interpersonal diagnosis of personality*, New York, Ronald, 1956.

45. Block, J., "The assessment of communication. Role variations as a function of interactional context," *J. Pers.* 1952, **21**, 272–286.

46. Sullivan, H. S., *The psychiatric interview*, New York, Norton, 1954.

QUESTIONS FOR REVIEW AND EXAMINATION

1. List some of the major needs for which people are dependent upon others for gratification.

2. Define what is meant by interpersonal behavior; healthy interpersonal behavior; unhealthy interpersonal behavior.

3. Why is contrived interpersonal behavior unhealthy?

4. What are some of the determiners of unhealthy interpersonal behavior?

5. How is healthy interpersonal behavior acquired?

6. What is "character"? "Character-armor"?

7. Why is affection such an important need-object for humans? What happens when people are deprived of affection beginning at an early age?

8. How do needs influence our choice of friends? The maintenance of friendships?

9. Why are some roles more desirable to a person than others?

10. How does the study of interpersonal behavior help us to understand personality?

11. Describe and evaluate interpersonal behavior in someone you know on the basis of the concepts employed in the present chapter.

CHAPTER 7

Healthy Interpersonal Relationships

Psychotherapists are becoming increasingly concerned with the problem of evaluating interpersonal relationships.[1] In their professional work, they seek to establish a relationship with their patients which will have the consequence of changing the patients' personalities in the direction of health. In their diagnostic appraisals of patients, they pay special attention to the patient's relationships with his parents, spouse, friends, boss, and other people with whom the patient is involved. On the basis of standards which are not very clearly defined, they pass judgments of this sort: "He has a healthy relationship with his brother, and a very unhealthy relationship with his wife, father, boss and sister." Let us now ask some questions: "When is a relationship between two people healthy? What are the characteristics of a healthy relationship?" We could state that two individuals with healthy personalities would undoubtedly establish a healthy relationship, but this answer really begs the question and tells us nothing about the relationship itself. Let us introduce a guiding definition of a healthy interpersonal relationship.[2]

A relationship between two people may be called healthy when:

180

1. Each partner has an accurate concept of the other's personality: each one knows the values, needs, goals of the other. Each knows the usual reaction-patterns of the other.

2. Each partner likes the other, or at least likes more of the other's traits than he dislikes.

3. Each partner feels concern for the happiness and growth of the other.

4. Each partner acts in ways which will promote the happiness and growth of the other.

5. Each partner can communicate honestly his thoughts, feelings, wants, memories, beliefs, opinions, to the other, and does so. Neither partner is defensive in the relationship—afraid to say what he wants, thinks, or feels about anything under the sun. Each wants to be known by the other, and actively strives to make himself known.

6. The demands or expectations which each partner imposes on the other as conditions for the continuation of the relationship are feasible, mutually agreed upon, and consistent with the values and happiness of the other.

7. Each partner respects the right of the other person to be self-determining, to do what he wants to do, including terminating the relationship.

It should be obvious that the foregoing set of characteristics applies primarily to adult friendships and love relationships. In assessing other relationships, some of the criteria would have to be modified. But if these criteria are useful and valid, we should be able to study interpersonal relationships and come to conclusions about their health. Suppose we found all of these characteristics present in a relationship between a husband and his wife. What should we observe as by-products of this relationship? We should find that the husband, if asked how he feels about his wife, will assert that he likes her very much and likes to spend a lot of time in her company. We should find that he knows her idiosyncrasies very well. He will admit, if asked, that there are some of her traits that he doesn't like, although he likes more than he dislikes. We should find that it troubles him when his wife is unhappy, dissatisfied and discontented; more than this, we should find him actively engaged in attempts to make her happy and contented. We should find that he can express anger and irritation toward his wife as well as affection. Further, we should find that he could talk about all manner of things to her—even things which we might think humiliating or embarrassing. We should also find that he respected his wife's honest differences in opinion, values, and interests.

This should give the reader an idea how criteria of health can be applied to assessment of a given interpersonal relationship. The health standards serve as a guide in observing a relationship; they tell the observer what to look for in the relationship, and what standards to compare his observations with.

Let us now turn to the problem of explaining how a healthy interpersonal relationship is developed. It is obvious that a healthy relationship with another person does not spring into existence with the first meeting between two people; it is rather an end-result, a goal for a relationship.

Almost all lasting relationships between people begin with initial attraction between them. (Of course, some begin in indifference, and others with mutual hostility.) This initial attraction is a function of the needs of each person. When an individual meets another person, he sees that other person as a source of satisfactions and frustrations. If the other person has traits or characteristics which can serve as need-objects for the individual, he will be attracted to him, he will like him. When two people meet and are mutually attracted, however, they do not yet have accurate knowledge of each other. Their other-concepts will comprise accurate as well as autistic beliefs and expectations. Much time must be spent in further observations of the other person, continually testing present impressions before we could assert the couple "knew" each other. Frequently, getting to know the other person better results in termination of the relationship. Since accurate knowledge of the other person is such an important condition for the establishment of a healthy relationship with him, let us devote attention to study of other-concepts: how they are acquired, and how accurate other-concepts are achieved.

ACCURATE OTHER-CONCEPTS AND HEALTHY INTERPERSONAL RELATIONSHIPS

The term self-concept refers to an individual's beliefs about his own personality; the term *other-concept* refers to beliefs one holds concerning someone else's personality. We can evaluate a person's other-concepts in terms of accuracy and completeness.

Formulating an other-concept is no different from formulating a concept of the structure of a motor, or a cow. We observe, generalize, make further observations, and then uphold, reject, or revise the generalizations. But emotions are more likely to influence observation of a person than of a motor. It is a very difficult thing to formulate an accurate concept of another person. The observer's needs, values, prejudices, hopes, and expectations, all exert a powerful influence on the activities of observing the other person and formulating conclusions (beliefs) concerning his nature, or structure. Accurate other-concepts are very difficult to achieve, but they are of utmost importance for healthy personality in general, and healthy interpersonal relationships more directly. Only when our other-concepts are accurate can we behave in ways which make the other happy, help him grow and communicate with him.[3] In more general terms, we will state dogmatically a person is healthy *only* to the extent that he has accurate other-concepts. Now let us turn to the process of forming other-concepts, and observe some of the factors which make it difficult to acquire accurate ones.

FIRST IMPRESSIONS OF THE OTHER PERSON. A number of controlled experiments [4] have demonstrated that we perceive a person in an organized, meaningful way in our first contact with him. We immediately classify him into some category, for example: male, adult, Protestant, middle-class, teacher, American-born, Yankee rather than postponing judgment, or experiencing puzzlement about him. On the basis of such an immediate classification, we then ascribe to that person all of the modal reaction-patterns, values, attitudes, motives, beliefs, which we have been led to expect from such persons.[5] The initial other-concept which we formulate of a new acquaintance thus comprises a host of expectations and assumptions. Some of these expectations and assumptions may prove later to be accurate, but for the most part they will be inaccurate. How do we get these other-concepts in such a short time? It behooves us to find answers, because these first impressions, though wrong, often last a long time. The following factors play an important role in determining other-concepts: (a) *projection,* (b) *attribution,* (c) *needs,* and (d) *social pressures to conformity.*

PROJECTION AND OTHER-CONCEPTS. Cameron and Magaret [6] distinguish between *assimilative projection* and *disowning projection*. Assimilative projection refers to the assumption by an individual that the other person is similar to him in personality-structure, in motives, values, goals, attitudes, and past experiences. The person ordinarily adopts this assumption when the other individual appears similar in age, social class, appearance, or other obvious and observable characteristics. In the usual course of events, the average person is not aware that his first impression, or his initial other-concept, is the by-product of a very rapid *observation* of the other person, a *comparison* of him with the self, and then a *conclusion* that the other person is indeed similar to the self. Often enough, the traits imputed to the other person through assimilative projection are sufficiently accurate to enable meaningful communication with him and to enable appropriate interpersonal behavior to occur. This accidental accuracy in first impression results from similarities in personality that stem from similarities in socialization. Yet, there is enough variation in people's life experiences, variations which produce differences in personality, to produce errors in first impressions. Hence the very common experience of "being wrong about the other person," of having "sized him up wrongly."

Disowning projection refers to the assumption that the other person is different from the self; but more than being different, there is implied the notion the other person has all the traits the observer deems repugnant and objectionable. Disowning projection is described later as a mechanism for the defense of the self-concept.[7] The disowning projector represses certain objectionable characteristics in himself and imputes them to the other person. Indeed, the traits which one sees in the other person one would be most reluctant to acknowledge in the self. Disowning projection is thus a means of maintaining an invidious difference between the self and the other person. If one's self-esteem is dependent upon the belief (a) that one is perfect and highly moral, and (b) that other people are inferior to the self in these respects, then one will need to believe that other people do have all manner of morally reprehensible motives and traits.

A man may need to believe he is without hostile impulses. He may need, for various reasons, to believe he is morally superior to other men. Therefore, to maintain self-esteem, he will repress hostile strivings in himself, but he will be very quick, even eager, to see signs of hostility in other men. On first meeting someone he will believe the other person is just waiting for an opportunity to engage in hostile, malicious activities—yet the person in question may actually be very warm, friendly, and unselfish.[8]

Disowning projection will play a role in the formulation of other-concepts primarily when the person has a very strict conscience and when his self-esteem is strongly dependent upon his belief that he is different from, or superior to, other people. Many people have very bizarre concepts about the personality of minority-group members, foreigners, etc., which derive in part from disowning projection. They also derive, however, from the popular folklore of the society in which we live.

Psychiatric literature has many examples of unhealthy personalities whose other-concepts seem indeed to be the consequence of disowning projection. Thus, a person who represses sexuality will believe other people are full of sexual desires. If he becomes able to acknowledge his own sexuality, he may then begin to change his other-concepts. Rogers found that patients who completed psychotherapy successfully manifested pronounced changes in their other-concepts; specifically, they showed a decrease in the difference between their self-concepts and other-concepts.[9]

ATTRIBUTION AND OTHER-CONCEPTS. Attribution is defined as *the assumption by a person that some new individual whom he has encountered for the first time has traits identical with those of a significant person from his past.*

The psychotherapists called attention to this phenomenon in various ways. Freud used the term transference [10] to refer to the observation that a patient would behave toward the psychoanalyst as if the latter had characteristics of the patient's father, or spouse. Sullivan coined the term "parataxis" [11] to describe the same facts (*para*: strange, or distorted, and *taxis*: pertaining to classification; literally, distorted classification).

When you meet another person, you may see characteristics in him which are apparently similar to traits of your mother, former teacher, the family domestic, or a childhood friend. The characteristic which leads to this assumption of similarity may sometimes be very trivial, for example, hair-color, or voice-intonations. Yet, once the assumption of similarity is made, it is acted upon. If you liked the person from the past, you will feel warmth and trust for this new person. If the person from the past had very stern moral standards, and always condemned you, then you will feel on probation with the new person, even though you do not as yet know him. Many of the most poignant disturbances and misunderstandings in interpersonal relationships stem from attribution (as well as from projection). A young woman, after one or two failures at shy flirting with attractive men may conclude that men have one trait in common, they *all* dislike her. When she meets a new man, she assumes that he too hates her—if not at first sight, then when he gets to know her. And so she abandons all attempts to develop a relationship which might lead to marriage. Yet, the man may in fact be wildly in love with her at first sight. Her logic, if it could be formulated, runs like this: "Bill and John disliked me. They were men whom I knew ten years ago. Tom, whom I have just now met at a party, is a man. Therefore, like Bill and John, he too dislikes me."

Secord and Jourard demonstrated attribution in a picture-rating study.[12] From previous studies, it had been found that judges agreed markedly in assigning personality traits to a group of young women whose facial photographs were employed in these studies. One group of faces—young women with thin lips and plain features—regularly suggested to the judges that the women were highly moral creatures, "good mothers." Another group of faces—young women with thick lips, narrowed eyes, etc.,—regularly suggested to judges that the women were very sexy, and had loose morals. In the Secord-Jourard study, the subjects were asked to rate their own mothers on a list of traits; then they were asked to rate the personalities of the women whose faces were shown on a screen. Strong similarities were found between the personality traits assigned to the "high moral" faces and the mother-ratings; while this similarity was much less between mother-ratings and the "low-moral" faces. The authors concluded from these data that in the high-moral faces, the subjects saw some physiognomic traits which resembled those of their mothers, and hence assumed that the young women had traits just like mother's. If mother was rated as having low morals, then even the high-moral pictures were rated as low-moral.

Thus far, we have mentioned projection and attribution as determiners of initial other-concepts. In addition to these factors, the needs of the observing individual and social pressures of many kinds also can help determine the other-concepts which an individual will formulate.

NEEDS AND OTHER-CONCEPTS. Other-concepts are formulated as conclusions or inferences drawn from observations of the other person. We have shown in an earlier chapter the ways in which perception and cognition are influenced by the needs of the individual. Autistic factors strongly influence the perception of persons and the concepts of their personality derived from such "social perception." [13] A person constitutes a complex and highly ambiguous stimulus; as we have seen, needs and other subjective factors such as interests, values, and emotions, are most likely to influence perception when the stimulus is ambiguous.

We can raise this question, what does an individual need to see in another person's behavior, what does he need to believe about the other individual's personality, in order to feel safe, to be satisfied, or to maintain self-esteem? When we state the question this way, it helps us to understand why some people see evidence for certain traits in a friend, spouse, child, boss, or enemy, which no disinterested person can see. Thus, a fond wife interprets her husband's unscrupulous business activity as evidence of the trait of intelligence. She needs to believe that he is intelligent. Or an inept employee who cannot recognize his ineptitude must believe that his boss is a harsh tyrant. He can see no evidence in his boss's behavior to justify the belief that his boss is a kind and fair man. If he were to conceive of his boss in such terms, it would mean his boss was right—he, the employee, really was a poor worker—and this conclusion might produce an unbearable loss of self-esteem.

The romantic lover, of course, provides us with the classical example of the influence of needs on other-concepts. He needs a sweetheart who is perfect. He meets a woman who has one or two of the signs of perfection. Immediately, as in the Gestalt psychology examples of "closure," he fills in the missing details; he sees her as perfect, and believes she is indeed perfect. He may later be sadly disillusioned when reality—evidence—rears its ugly head and compels him to revise his concept of her.

Emotions, such as fear, or guilt, can strongly influence the formation of other-concepts. The guilty individual believes that other people hate him. The anxious individual believes other people are just on the point of hurting him, or venting hostility on him.[14]

SOCIAL FACTORS AND OTHER-CONCEPTS. Many of our other-concepts have been derived, not from intimate, firsthand observations of the other person, but rather as a result of being told by someone what the other person is like. Everyone is very free in passing judgments about someone whom they "know," to anybody who is interested in listening. These premeeting sessions have a marked influence on an individual's expectations and on his perceptions of the other person's behavior when once a meeting occurs. When one meets another person for the first time, armed with a predetermined other-concept, it is difficult for this concept of the other person to be altered. Psychologists have turned this fact to advantage in personality research and research into the phenomena of suggestion. By explaining to one group of subjects that the person who is about to address them is a very cold, harsh, mean man, the group will respond differently to his speech and behavior than another group who have been told he is warm, gentle, and kindly. Yet, the man may behave identically before both groups.[15]

Not only do we acquire many other-concepts about specific individuals from other people; we also acquire concepts about entire classes of people from our friends, teachers, parents, or associates. The stereotypes we have acquired about Negroes, Jews and foreigners strongly influence our perceptions of single members of those categories and strongly influence the other-concepts we formulate about them. The influence of others in determining our other-concepts is so strong, that we never say to ourselves when meeting a new person, "I just don't know what kind of a person he is, or what to expect from him." Instead, as the new other person behaves, we see a corroboration of the other-concept which we brought with us into the situation.

A fruitful line of study might be that of manipulating experimentally the influence of other people on the process of other-concept formation. At Berkeley, California,[16] an ingenious apparatus has been devised for the study of social conformity. Subjects are seated in individual stalls, and before them they see several rows of lights. Each row of lights is supposed to be under the control of another person, and each light in the row stands for a certain response to questions, or a certain judgment. Then problems, or questions, are directed at each subject, and he is asked to push a button which will turn on the light that signifies his answer. But before he responds, he has to wait his turn. He must watch the lights on the panel which indicate how the five or ten other people have responded, and then give his response. Actually, there are no other people. The experimenter controls these lights, and only gives the illusion that a group of people are making responses.

Suppose in this situation, the subject was required to observe the behavior of a person and then signify a rating on certain traits with his row of lights. Suppose, for example, he was asked to rate the sense of humor of a person who had just finished cracking a number of very weak jokes. The experimenter could then manipulate the lights on his panel so the person would believe nine other subjects rated the stimulus person as having a very keen and witty sense of humor. How would our subject rate the person? Previous studies in conformity suggest he would rate the person as the "group" rated him. It is difficult to go against the judgments of a group; when one disagrees with the group, one feels uncomfortably eccentric.

Because of the pressure to conform we tend to develop fairly fixed other-concepts concerning all manner of people—other-concepts which fellow-members of the group hold, and which we acquire from them. Indeed, qualification for membership in some groups such as the Ku Klux Klan, consists in affirming some peculiar other-concepts, e.g., the belief that if a person is white, he is superior to all colored people. Or a communist must affirm a certain concept of capitalists before he can gain entry into the Party.

In view of all the factors which operate so as to produce distorted and inaccurate other-concepts, how exactly does one develop accurate other-concepts? This question is very important in personality hygiene, since it is only when an individual has an accurate other-concept that he can establish a healthy interpersonal relationship. More than that, it is only as a person has accurate other-concepts that we could call him a healthy personality.

THE FORMATION OF ACCURATE OTHER-CONCEPTS. The formation of accurate other-concepts is a special case of the more general problem: how does a person acquire accurate knowledge about anything? He does so by following the scientific method of inquiry.[17]

Scientific inquiry commences with doubt, or uncertainty. The investigator asks a question about some state of affairs and formulates as many possible answers as he has the imagination or precedent to suggest. Then under conditions as rigorously controlled as possible, he makes detailed observations in order to get facts. On the basis of these facts, he upholds some one of these hypotheses and rejects all others.

In the special problem of getting accurate knowledge of another person, we are concerned with formulating beliefs congruent with the usual behavior of the individual, and with his actual personality structure. If we are to acquire accurate other-concepts, we must be glad to get as many hypotheses as we can. But we must believe none of these in advance of actual observation of the person. *It is this crucial step of hypothesis-testing that even a trained scientist overlooks in his perception of people.*

The present author knows a man who is a very rigorous scientist. This person carries out meticulously controlled experiments dealing with isolated bits and pieces of behavior in animals and humans. If I told him that reinforcement in learning was caused by brain cells moving together in order to make new contacts with each other, he would doubt me, demand endless proof and insist that I show him anatomical slides. But if I told this same man "Say, did you know that Professor X (whom he doesn't like) drowned some rats which didn't behave according to his pet hypothesis?" Although, in fact, Professor X did not, the man would without doubt reply, "He did? Why that crook! He ought to be tarred and feathered." No demands for proof or even evidence; instead, immediate belief of an untested hypothesis—a cardinal sin for scientists.

Other-concepts probably enjoy the unique advantage of being the last of the theories which an individual will test, much less abandon. A person will abandon the belief that the world is flat. He will abandon the belief that Santa Claus brings his Christmas presents.[18] He will abandon the belief that storks bring babies. But he will not abandon his present beliefs about the other person—his other-concepts. By some curious quirk of vanity, each man believes he is an expert psychologist and that his other-concepts are accurate and irrefutable. *Never has so much been believed about people, by people, on so little evidence.* It should perhaps be stated here that as a general rule, the more thoroughly one comes to know himself, the more capable will he be of knowing others. Patients who have undergone effective personality therapy report that with self-knowledge they have also gained in knowledge of others.

A Special Case—the Assumption That the Other Person Is Malleable

An important component of an other-concept is accurate knowledge concerning the other person's malleability, or susceptibility to change. Psychologists know that human nature is not fixed, that modal behavior and personality structure are quite subject to change within very broad biological limits. Psychologists even have acquired some rudimentary knowledge of the conditions under which behavior and personality will change, and they stand in a position where they can influence, or control, the rate and direction of changes in behavior and personality structure. Teachers, psychotherapists, social workers, military training personnel, all of these professional workers seek to control the process of behavioral change in other people.

Individual people often get involved in interpersonal difficulties, however, because their concept of the other person includes an *inaccurate estimate of the changeability of the other person.* They will either overestimate the changeability, underestimate the changeability, or fail to identify the variables which must be manipulated in order to produce change.

THE EFFECTS OF UNDERESTIMATING CHANGEABILITY. A person may believe that other people's behavior is a fixed, unyielding and immutable fact; nothing will change it. In consequence, he may develop compulsive, or fixed, modes of relating to others—which may have the consequence of perpetuating the undesirable behavior of the other person. For example, a man may believe that human nature is basically evil, that people are "just no damn good"; no matter what is done for them, they will remain untrustworthy, dishonest, selfish, animal-like, lustful, and everything else that is bad.

If a person with this belief has children, his child-rearing behavior will necessarily be influenced. It makes a difference to a parent whether he is dealing with a child who will turn into a savage beast unless curbed, or whether he is dealing with a malleable piece of "clay" who will become, roughly, what he is trained to become. In the former instance, child-rearing will consist primarily in a tense battle of the parent with the forces of evil that are assumed to be inherent in the child; one false step, one weak moment of unwatchfulness, and catastrophe will result.

A person may acquire the belief some one other person despises him, or is indifferent toward him, and nothing he can do will alter the other's reaction. To be sure, it can happen that other people's appraisals of oneself may be quite rigid. But it is possible for a person to produce the appraisals of him with which he feels most comfortable. This necessarily varied, and intelligently selected, interpersonal behavior will not be undertaken by the individual, however, if he believes the other person's judgments and feelings are immutable. One's concept of the changeability of others will indeed have consequence on one's behavior.

Probably many marriages have been terminated, or else endured with resignation and martyrdom, because one spouse has incorrectly diagnosed the changeability of his partner. The husband may assume his wife cannot be changed, and the wife has tried unsuccessfully to change her man. The couple then "digs in" for a life of dissatisfaction, or else they institute divorce proceedings. Many a spouse, following a bitter divorce, has been dumbfounded to observe that, like magic, the discarded partner has become everything which was desired during the marriage. The husband about whom the wife forever complained, "He is such a stodgy, unimaginative, unromantic man," becomes after the divorce a veritable movie-star hero—more attentive to his appearance, more considerate of women, more romantic and impractical. This is certainly evidence that he was capable of change, but more than this, it is evidence *he did not want to change for her,* and that *she did not know how to behave so he would want to change for her.*

THE EFFECTS OF OVERESTIMATING CHANGEABILITY. While behavior is mutable, yet there are powerful forces which militate against behavioral change. These factors include the need to feel safe, the need to maintain self-esteem, the need to maintain a sense of identity, other people's expectations, etc. Each time a person alters some accustomed mode of response, he may feel anxious about disapproving responses of others; he may lose self esteem, if his present value-system opposes the new behavior; he may fear that other people will no longer recognize him. These factors thus operate as a kind of gyroscope, restricting behavior to a certain relatively fixed range. But a man may choose a friend, or a spouse, with a view to transforming this person, like Pygmalion, into something new and different. The person, "as is," is not acceptable. A sort of silent wager is laid down, that the chooser will in time be able to change the other person. Thus, a woman may displace her zeal as a sculptress from clay to people. She chooses a bum, deadbeat, or criminal as husband, not because he is attractive the way he is, but because she believes she can change him into a new man. In theory, it is possible to arrange conditions so that a man will change his modal reaction patterns, but few laymen are so skilled they can manipulate conditions in precisely the ways which will promote behavioral and personality change. For that matter, trained psychotherapists, criminologists, and other professional personality-changers have a difficult time doing their job, since knowledge about personality change is as yet incomplete and incompletely tested. Therefore, the layman is advised not to choose friends and lovers with the aim of changing them. If the package is not acceptable the way it is, do not accept it. The major consequence of overestimating changeability of the other person is disappointment and failure in effecting the changes.

HOW TO CHANGE THE OTHER PERSON. The most effective, and the most healthy way to produce wanted changes in the other person, is *to behave toward him so he will want to change himself.* People have voluntary control over their reaction patterns to a surprising extent. It is true that people can, within limits, act as they want to act. If another person's behavior is unsatisfactory to himself, he can usually modify his own behavior so it becomes satisfactory.

If one's behavior is unsatisfactory to another person, one can usually alter the behavior so it will satisfy the other person. Naturally, it may not always be easy to alter modal reaction patterns, either for oneself or for another person, but it is surprisingly possible to achieve. From this it follows that for one person to induce stable changes in the reaction patterns of another, the most effective way is to somehow *induce the desire to change* in the other person.

The precise means of achieving this goal—the desire in the other person to act in ways desired by the first—will of course vary. In fact, there are no valid general rules which could be said to hold for all cases. There is this general proposition which can be announced, however, without too much error: if the relationship is one which provides satisfactions for both participants, where basic needs are being richly gratified, then each partner will want to please the other. Thus, the most effective means of inducing change in the other person is to behave toward him in ways which will satisfy his basic needs. Then, the wishes of the first person, within reason, and within limits set by reality and the other person's basic structure, will literally become the other person's willingly obeyed commands.

At first blush it would appear as if the person wanting the changes in the other person's behavior is "bribing" him with satisfactions. In a sense, this is true. But there is a difference between a cold, calculated attempt to bribe another person into conformity with one's wishes and a spontaneous wish that the other person, who is loved, will change. In the former instance, the one being bribed will eventually discover he is being manipulated. In the latter, the relationship is more likely to be one of mutual requests to change, and mutual compliance with the other's wishes.

It should not be overlooked that we can change another person by force, or by threats of one kind and another. This is the essence of dictatorship. While change induced by threat and sanction may be effective in the short run, it will usually be achieved at the cost of resentment and hostility toward the person dictating the terms. The dictator seldom takes into consideration, in his demands for conformity, the other needs and values of the subject. As these are violated and thwarted in consequence of the demanded change, hostility is mobilized. Whenever the subject becomes less dependent upon the other, he will rebel and terminate the relationship, or inflict violence upon the dictator.

Yet, in friendship and marriage, there is a place for threats to induce conformity. Often, the offending partner will not fully appreciate the pain he is inducing in his partner by his behavior. The offended partner, when all other means have failed, can have recourse finally to dissolving the relationship. If the offended one has indeed been satisfying many needs for the offender, then the latter will feel the pains of frustration and deprivation threatened by the separation. Should he want to preserve the relationship, he will now experience some incentive to change his ways of acting. He will, in short, want to change.

LIKING THE OTHER PERSON

In the opening section of this chapter, we asserted that one important characteristic of a healthy interpersonal relationship was the fact that each participant liked the other, or at least liked more of the other's characteristics than he disliked. Let us inquire into the *liking-response,* in order to obtain a more detailed understanding of its determiners and its nature.

THE NATURE OF THE LIKING-RESPONSE. The experience of liking somebody or something refers to a feeling, or, in broader terms, an *affective* response to a stimulus. It is probable there are characteristic physiological concomitants to the liking-response, but these are not clearly known, or understood. We can recognize the characteristic "feel" of liking someone or something, however, without difficulty. Liking is a pleasurable feeling, and is readily identified by most persons when it is present, unless the individual has repressed his feelings and emotions so successfully that he can recognize none. We may loosely define the liking-response as *a pleasant feeling which is produced when the individual is confronted by some perceptible object, idea, memory, or situation associated with satisfaction.*

It is convenient, and perhaps valid to think of the liking-response as a conditioned response, or more precisely, as the affective component of an expectancy. The object which induces the liking-response has, in the past, produced satisfaction, or is related to something which produced satisfaction. The liking-response is a sort of *preparatory set* for something satisfying to occur, just as anxiety is a preparatory set for something painful to occur.

THE CONDITIONS FOR LIKING-RESPONSES. The crucial question for this section of our discussion is, "What will a person like, and why will he like it?" In answering these questions, it will become apparent that the answers are to be found in the past relationship between the person and the objects in question.

There are two separate but related factors which determine whether or not an individual will like something. The first of these is needs, the second is ideals or values.

NEEDS AS A DETERMINER OF LIKING. Objects which an individual requires in order to produce satisfactions will be liked. In very general terms, we can assert that *a person likes what he needs to produce satisfactions.* When the need-tensions are operative, the thought, or perception of the need-objects will be associated with feelings we can readily call liking-responses. Naturally, there will be canalizations with respect to need-objects—each individual establishes preferences for some need-objects over others on the basis of past experience. We might say that each person establishes a liking-hierarchy with respect to all the possible objects which could conceivably produce satisfaction.[19] Thus, a person likes edible things; but he likes steak better than ham, and rare steak better than well-done steak. A man likes women, but he likes gentle women better than hot-tempered women, and women his age better than women much older.

VALUES AS A DETERMINER OF LIKING. The values which a person has acquired, through assorted identifications with other people during the course of his development, will help to determine what he likes. In general, a person likes those things which have the characteristics specified by his ideals. Thus, a person likes horses which resemble his concept of the ideal thoroughbred; he likes women, whose appearance and behavior correspond closely with his conception of the ideal woman. Jourard and Secord[20] showed that liking aspects of one's own body was a function of the discrepancy between the actual size of selected body parts, and the subjective ideal which each subject held with respect to size. If a woman asserted that her desired hip-measurements were 35 inches and her actual hip-measurements were 42 inches, she reported she disliked her hips. We can thus regard a person's values, or ideals, as a kind of internal measuring device, with which he always makes comparisons whenever he observes *anything.* Those things which conform closely with the ideal are liked, those things which deviate markedly from the ideals are disliked.

NEEDS, VALUES, AND LIKING THE OTHER PERSON. From the preceding sections, we can state that a person likes those aspects of another person, for example, his appearance and traits, which satisfy needs and which conform closely with values or ideals. Let us see how these factors operate as determiners of liking-responses to another person. The other person is a complex whole composed of many parts. It is true we can speak of the other-person-as-a-whole, and we can then say we like or dislike this totality; but we can also analyze the other person into parts, and experience liking-disliking responses to those parts. In everyday experience, this part-liking and part-disliking is very common. We must add, however, that we often generalize from the specific part of the person which we like or dislike to the entire personality. For example, the reader's roommate may have one particularly annoying trait, for instance, the habit of picking his toes, or belching. If asked, the reader might say, I dislike him (all of him). What he is doing is generalizing his dislike-response from the *particular* disliked response to the *total behavior repertoire* of the person; in short, to his entire personality.[21] Contrariwise, a girl may say, I like him (by implication, all of him), when in fact, all she has seen of him is some one response-pattern she likes. Psychologists have coined the term "halo-effect" to describe this tendency of generalizing a liking or disliking response from some particular aspect of a person to all of his traits.

In a friendship, or a marriage, or a parent-child relationship, each participant may be assumed to have assorted liking-disliking responses to assorted aspects of the other person. The healthier the relationship, the more detailed, accurate and differentiated the concept (other-concept) each partner will have of the other. If the relationship is a healthy one, the liking-responses, quantitatively, will be greater than the disliking responses that are induced by the traits of the other. Practically, this means the other person behaves in more ways which produce satisfactions for the first than he behaves in frustrating ways. Further, it implies that more of the other's traits correspond with the first person's values and ideals than deviate from these ideals.

We have stated that in a healthy interpersonal relationship, each person likes more aspects of the other person than he dislikes for a specific reason. It is recognized that no one person can completely satisfy all the needs, or conform with all the values of another person—at least not in all respects or for all times. For most healthy relationships, it is enough "cement" for the relationship if the ratio of like to dislike produces a preponderance of liking-responses.

It is only in unhealthy relationships, where neither partner has an accurate other-concept, that we observe total, or global, liking and disliking. The young lover, enthusiastic over meeting the answer to his prayers and dreams, tells his mother, "She's *perfect;* I like *everything* about her." It is only later, as he comes to know her better, that he discovers her imperfections (deviations from his values and ideals) and aspects of her appearance and behavior which produce deprivation and frustration instead of satisfaction.

It is only healthy to like a person-as-a-whole under special conditions: when an individual knows another person well and has quite differentiated likes and dislikes toward the other; in considering an *integrated* concept of the person as a whole, he concludes he likes the other person. This condition corresponds to Murphy's view of third-level cognition—where the object is perceived, not as an undifferentiated mass, and not as an aggregate of differentiated parts, but rather as an integration of parts which produces a whole with unique characteristics not reducible to parts.[22]

CONCERN FOR THE WELFARE AND GROWTH OF THE OTHER

An interpersonal relationship is healthy when there can be observed active concern on the part of each individual for the welfare, happiness, and growth of the other. What is meant by concern? Out of what conditions does it emerge? What do we mean by *active* concern?

It is difficult to define concern in precise, behavioral terms. Perhaps the most accurate way we can assert what is meant by the word is in the following terms: concern means a person *wants* some valued end to be obtained—it matters to him, it makes a difference whether or not the valued end is obtained. Concern for the welfare, happiness and growth of the other person means that it *matters,* it is important whether or not the other person is well, happy, and growing. He wants the other person to be well, happy, and growing.

When we say active concern, we mean that the desire, or wish for the happiness of the other is not *passively* longed for; rather, we mean that the concerned person acts. He engages in instrumental behavior, the aim of which is to produce happiness and growth, or at the very least provides the conditions for happiness and growth of the other person.[23] We shall turn to this point about active concern in a following section. For the present, we shall inquire further into the nature of concern.

A THEORY OF THE ORIGIN OF CONCERN. We generally like the other person because he behaves in ways which produce satisfactions for us. In a sense, the other person can be viewed as a supply-source of satisfactions. Experience shows us that the other person will behave in ways which satisfy us most richly *when he is himself satisfied*. Thus, we acquire a vested interest in his welfare, happiness, and growth. Concern for the happiness of the other person is a sort of insurance for one's own satisfactions. A workhorse cannot work for us when he is ill-treated. We use the horse's energy as a means for the attainment of our own goals. Thus, we have a vested interest in tending the horse's needs very carefully. We are, in short, concerned for the horse's happiness and growth, and we take active steps to promote his contentment and growth. In so doing, we insure that the horse will better be able to provide us with the means to important satisfactions.

It may offend the reader thus to be compared to a horse, yet the analogy is not a farfetched one. The other person, like the horse (though in different ways), provides us with behavior which produces important satisfactions and important need-objects. Thus, the other person may have skills which we need employed in our service. His affection-responses, or liking-responses, may be important to us as means toward a sense of security or self-esteem. His very company may serve as a source of entertainment, diversion, etc. In order for him to continue to be willing and able to provide us with satisfactions, it is important that he be happy. When he is unhappy he is much less able to anticipate our wants and give satisfaction. In order to avoid this eventuality, we learn to anticipate his wants and fulfill them. We help him when he asks for help. We help him to grow, because a mature partner is better able to provide us with satisfactions than an immature partner.

Thus, concern arises as a by-product of satisfaction, satisfaction provided us by the other person. Also, it may arise as a kind of calculated risk in cases where an individual becomes concerned with another person's happiness, but the other person is not yet a satisfier. It is only predicted that if one gets concerned, actively concerned with his happiness, he will in turn become concerned with yours, and act toward that end.

Parents are concerned for the happiness and growth of their children for a number of reasons. Happy children are signs of success in child-rearing, and this is an important condition for the self-esteem of parents. This also provides satisfactions for the parents—even security, for it is possible that the parents may need the future economic support of their children in old age.

A wife is concerned for the happiness and growth of her husband, because a happy and mature husband is a much richer source of satisfactions for her than a miserable, thwarted, and childish husband.

It should not be construed from the foregoing that all concern for others is an outgrowth of the calculated view that "if I take care of that person, then he will take care of me." A healthy personality is capable of a kind of disinterested concern for others; it simply gives him a feeling of fulfillment, or of abundance, to be able actively to care for another person. Thus, grandparents may delight in the growth of their grandchildren, whom they indulge and nurture, yet they get nothing else but the experience of fun and pleasure from watching the children's antics.

A further determiner of concern which must not be overlooked is the fact of *identification* with the other person. In a healthy interpersonal relationship, say, between spouses, one partner identifies very closely with the feelings and needs of the other. Where this has occurred, *the satisfactions of the other person are felt as deeply as satisfactions for the self.*

It appears, then, that concern for the other person is a kind of devious concern for one's own happiness and growth. This may appear offensive and selfish to the reader. Yet, with Fromm, we shall ask this question, "Why should we not be concerned about *our own* happiness and growth?" There is growing evidence to the effect that one can love another only if one loves oneself; that love of, and concern for, the self and the other person far from being mutually exclusive are actually correlated and derive from something else, a common factor which, for want of a better name, we shall call the "power to love." [24] In other words, only if one can be concerned for the self can one be concerned for the other.

People who appear to be totally unconcerned for themselves, and who instead make all manner of "sacrifices" in order to help another person (they are called "unselfish"), usually demand a terrible price in return, and usually get this price—absolute conformity with their wishes. We are all familiar with the "unselfish" mother who sacrifices all her own chances at happiness in order to help her son get through school. Would it not be ungracious if the son then, against his mother's "reasonable wishes," married a girl of *his* choice, but not his mother's? [25]

We can see that knowledge, liking, and concern for the other person all interact as factors in a healthy interpersonal relationship. If one does not know the other person, how can one like him? If one does not know him, and like him, how can one get concerned about his happiness and growth? But concern, without knowledge, is blind. One can be concerned about the other's happiness, but if you don't know what he needs in order to be happy and to grow, how can you provide him with the appropriate need-objects?

BEHAVIOR WHICH PROMOTES HAPPINESS AND GROWTH IN THE OTHER PERSON

We have stated that a healthy interpersonal relationship is characterized by behavior on the part of each participant which promotes happiness and growth in the other. What is the nature of behavior which promotes happiness in the other? What kind of behavior promotes growth in the other?

INTERPERSONAL BEHAVIOR WHICH PROMOTES HAPPINESS. Happiness is the name we assign to the subjective feeling of satisfaction and to the feelings associated with the attainment of valued ends. In a healthy interpersonal relationship, one partner actively assists the other in obtaining satisfactions. The ability to behave in ways which promote happiness in the other, of course, is predicated on knowledge of the other person and concern for the other person. One can know what the other person needs in order to be happy, but this knowledge alone will not insure instrumental action toward securing the other's happiness. One can be concerned for the other's happiness and not know what is required in order to help the other to happiness.

In addition to knowledge and concern, however, there is one important factor which must not be overlooked in the quest for the other's happiness: the behavior patterns which are required of one partner in order to promote the happiness of the other must be *available,* or at least possible for the first person to perform. That is, the requisite behavior patterns must be within the behavior repertoire of the first person; they must be consistent with the conscience of the first person; and finally, they must not be behavior patterns which will produce frustrations or important deprivations in the first person (except under conditions of a voluntary choice).

Let us illustrate. A wife may need her husband to behave in ways that will secure large sums of money, so she can buy things which will make her happy. Let us suppose the husband knows what his wife needs and is actively concerned that she get it. It bothers him that she should be unhappy. But in his present circumstances he may not be able to acquire the skills necessary to earn more money. His present skill-repertoire will enable him to earn a certain limited income, and no more. Thus he won't be able to satisfy his wife's need for more money. Let us suppose, however, that it would be possible for him to get more money by a little bit of forgery, or theft. If he proceeds to engage in these activities, he may indeed secure the money, but in consequence he may be overwhelmed with guilt. Where this occurs we could not speak of a healthy interpersonal relationship, because the happiness of one partner is achieved at the cost of immense guilt on the part of the other.

Suppose the husband could supply his wife with the money she needs for her happiness, but at the cost of depriving himself of many of the things he himself needs, for satisfaction and happiness. Again, we could not speak of a healthy relationship, unless the husband made a careful appraisal of his own values and decided *ration-*

ally that his wife's contentment was more important to him than his own immediate satisfactions.

We can see that in a healthy relationship each partner strives to act in ways which will provide satisfactions for the other person; but we cannot call the relationship healthy unless the requisite instrumental action is feasible, consistent with the value-system of each partner, and does not involve undue deprivation on the part of the active partner.

INTERPERSONAL BEHAVIOR WHICH PROMOTES GROWTH. Personality growth is defined as a *change in modal behavior and experience* so that:

1. The individual displays the behavior and reactions which are appropriate to his age-role.

2. His self-structure changes correspondingly, so that the self-concept remains accurate, the self-ideal remains congruent with social mores and with actual behavior, and the various public selves remain accurate and mutually compatible (see Chapter 9).

3. The growing person becomes increasingly capable, through learning, of a broader repertoire of effective instrumental action.

4. His behavior is increasingly directed by his real self (see Chapter 9).

How is growth promoted through interpersonal relations? It is theoretically possible for personality growth to occur in a social vacuum. As a solitary individual encountered problem after problem and solved them, learning new skills as a consequence, he would be manifesting one aspect of growth; namely, a diversification of his instrumental behavior repertoire.

But nobody lives in a social vacuum; everyone is enmeshed in a number of interpersonal relationships. Some of these relationships may be quite neutral with respect to growth; others may be quite effective in producing regression, or growth in reverse, others may prevent growth, and still others may actively promote growth. Let us touch briefly upon those relationships which are neutral, regressive, and interfering, in their effect on growth, and then examine in greater detail the relationships which promote growth.

RELATIONSHIPS WHICH ARE NEUTRAL WITH RESPECT TO GROWTH. Any relationship with another person which does not produce enduring change in his behavior and personality structure is neutral with respect to growth. Into this category of "growth-neutral" relationships we would include all brief encounters with other people for specific purposes: the brief contact with a garage mechanic fixing your car; a person sitting beside you on a train, with whom you converse about assorted subjects, perhaps sharing a drink, but that is all; or socializing at a party and enjoying the company. We should not assume, however, that brevity is the sole characteristic which defines a "growth-neutral" relationship. Some relationships with others last for years, but neither partner changes his modal reaction-patterns or his values one whit. Other relationships may last five minutes, but the partners may have been radically changed.[26] Thus, a perfect stranger may say something to you which produces a marked change in your self-concept, a marked change in your values, or a marked change in modal behavior.

RELATIONSHIPS WHICH INDUCE REGRESSION. Students of personality development have developed crude norms which describe the appropriate, or expected, range of reaction-patterns at each of several age levels. They have done no more than attempt to define the norms for expected behavior patterns which exist in each society for each age level. Thus, we can divide a total life history into infancy, early childhood, late childhood, adolescence, early adulthood, middle adulthood, late adulthood, old age, and senility. Different behavior patterns are expected in each society from persons falling into each age bracket. Sociologists speak of this kind of categorizing as *age grading*. While growth means progressive change in behavior consistent with age-norms, regression means growth in reverse.

Experimental psychologists have formulated the general proposition that frustration, or, more generally, *stress* is one of the factors which promotes regression.[27] A stressor is any factor which interferes with the ongoing course of value-pursuing activity. Thus, physical danger, illness, frustration, interference are all stressing agents, and as such, can induce regression, or growth in reverse. Adult persons will usually display childish behavior when they are ill, thwarted, or in danger.

There are some relationships which produce stresses resulting in permanent regression in one of the partners. Thus, one of the participants in the friendship, marriage, or boss-employee relationship may act in such a way that it literally "child-ifies" the other person, who otherwise can act in ways appropriate to his age. The wife may impose such impossible demands on her husband, that in attempting to implement them he is obliged to act, or is forced by stress tensions to act, in childish ways. A boss, perhaps an overweening and autocratic sort of person, may force his employees to behave like five-year-old children in order to avoid his wrath and protect their jobs. Bettelheim described the regressive behavior of concentration-camp inmates, behavior which derived from the physical stresses of prison-camp life as well as from the arbitrary behavior of the guards.[28]

Some teachers may transform students whose behavior was at first appropriate to their age, into individuals who are much less mature.

We can generalize from these illustrations and assert that most dependency relationships tend to promote regression.

We must distinguish between situational regression and more generalized, or stabilized, regression. A person may display regressive behavior only in one kind of relationship, while in all others he can act his age. A husband may behave in quite childish manner with his wife (not much differently than the way he behaved as a child toward his mother); toward other women, he may act in mature fashion. Or, an employee may act like a grudgingly obedient child toward his boss and other authority-figures, but toward his peers he acts his age.

A truly regression-producing relationship is one which produces *permanent* regression in the participant—regression which carries over to other relationships, so that other people are impressed by the juvenile, or childish behavior of the individual. Such relationships reverse a slogan adopted by many schools: "Send us the boy, and we'll return a man." Instead, some people, by virtue of their demands and their power over anyone with whom they get involved, seem to say, "Send me a man, and I'll return a boy."

In this discussion, we have overlooked the very important fact that in a healthy relationship, the participants *can allow each other to regress;* they do not necessarily demand perpetual adultness from each other. This is an entirely different state of affairs from what we have been discussing above. There is a difference between a relationship which *enforces* regression, and one which *permits* both regressive behavior and growthful behavior to occur. There is even reason to believe that genuine personality growth is not possible unless the individual is able to abandon his present modes of behaving, regressing for some time to a more infantile level of behaving and experiencing, and then progressing to an even more adult level.

RELATIONSHIPS WHICH PREVENT GROWTH. There are some relationships which continue on the unspoken condition that neither partner will change, that is, grow. Thus, a man and woman marry. Each holds a certain concept of the other that they have deliberately constructed in the mind of the other (see Chapter 9, on public selves). At the time of the marriage, his concept of her personality was inaccurate and incomplete. She did not know him as he "really" was. However, he believed she was a person who possessed characteristics and traits which he needed in a wife. He believed she had all the traits of an ideal wife. If either behaved contrary to expectation then the other would be disappointed, would feel let down, and deceived: "You are not the person I married, or the kind of person I want to stay married to." In order to preserve their marriage (for whatever satisfactions it does provide), each partner would strive to remain unchanged; each partner might believe that a change in personality would result in the dissolution of the marriage—a consequence which is dreaded. Such a marriage prevents growth.

A bachelor, living with his parents long after his peers have been married, does not grow. His present behavior repertoire may be acceptable to his parents; they are willing to support him, cook his meals, do his laundry, and they make no demands on him he cannot readily fulfill with long-rehearsed facility. For him, further growth is contingent upon his moving away, exposing himself to new challenges, and to new people who make new demands upon him.

Some parents actively prevent growth in their children, either through ignorance, because they do not place a value on their children attaining maturity, or because their own self-esteem is dependent upon playing the parental role. So long as their child is getting satisfactions out of the child-role, he will not break away and expose himself to growth-promoting influences.

EXCESSIVE DEPENDENCY AND UNHEALTHY INTERPERSONAL RELATION-SHIPS. When a person is involved in a relationship with another person such that his growth is blocked, and he is obliged to act in ways repugnant to him, we may ask, "Why is the relationship not terminated?"

We have touched on an answer to this question in a preceding section, where we pointed out that even though he may be frustrated in many ways, and prevented from growing, the individual may be *dependent* upon the other person for important satisfactions. It is because the *individual believes he is unable to obtain satisfactions elsewhere,* that he may submit to humiliating, frustrating, and growth-interfering relationships with another person.

Thus, an employee unable to get a job elsewhere may put up with all kinds of degradation at the hands of a martinet-like boss; a lonely person, unable to find anyone else to like her, may put up with all kinds of misery-producing behavior from her friend, so that she will not again face the awful prospect of loneliness.

In view of the unhealthy consequences of dependency, it will repay us to inquire into some of the factors which will minimize dependency and maximize the likelihood that healthy interpersonal relationships will be established.

PROPHYLACTICS AGAINST UNHEALTHY INTERPERSONAL RELATIONSHIPS

SKILLS, KNOWLEDGE AND COMPETENCE. If dependency increases the likelihood that unhealthy interpersonal relationships will be established, then it follows that competence, knowledge, and skill will decrease dependency upon others. The skilled individual is "independently secure," as Blatz [29] puts it. This does not mean his relationships with others will be healthy by axiom; but independent security will leave him much freer to dissolve any interpersonal relationships which do not give him enough satisfactions to make them worth-while. His relationships with others will be entered into and maintained out of free choice. Humphrey Bogart, the late movie actor reputedly said, "The advantage of being rich is that you can tell any s.o.b. to go to hell." A similar advantage is possessed by the person who has so many skills as to be relatively autonomous. The autonomous person still needs other people for many of the satisfactions which make life worth living; but he can afford to be discriminating in his choice of friends, spouse and bosses. He will choose them not simply because they possess what is desperately needed, but because they have other characteristics in addition to those immediately needed, characteristics which will insure a broader base of gratification throughout the duration of the relationship.

Dependent persons are notoriously indiscriminate in their choice of friends and spouses.[30] Their urgent needs impel them to see in the other person only those traits which are relevant as objects for their needs. Consequently, they "fall in love" with persons who have what is needed; but the objects of their "love" (dependency) may demand an exorbitant price for giving it, and further, their other traits, less salient at first, will inevitably emerge from the background when the urgent needs of the dependent one are partially gratified. The dependent person may be literally shocked at what else came in this package of "need-objects" which he "bought" when he entered into the relationship.

A RICH GRATIFICATION HISTORY. If a person has enjoyed a life rich in satisfactions, it will be possible for him to choose his friends and lovers with more discrimination.[31] At the time of commencing some relationship, he is much less likely to be starved—for affection, approval, sex, material things. He will have been able to find gratification for many of these needs prior to commencing a permanent friendship or a marriage. Consequently, he is less likely to "fall for" the first person who has what he needs and seems willing to give it to him. Many a person is so starved for affection, appreciation, or sexuality, that the first person who provides him with these, he will marry or befriend, only to find as his need-tensions subside somewhat (allowing other needs and values to emerge into tension), that the other person lacks other important qualities.

It follows from this that nobody should establish long-term relationships in a state of starvation of any kind—whether it be affection-starvation, approval-starvation, status, hunger, etc. Under those conditions, the starved person's judgments will be faulty. Other values and needs remain in the background, and all he can see in the other person is an opportunity for immediate gratification. The other person is a complex thing, made up of many parts. Even though these other aspects are not considered during the initial appraisal, yet they go along with the "package." One can liken many a marriage and friendship to the case of purchasing an automobile solely because it has a pretty color, without considering such additional values as comfort, durability, power, etc.

AUTONOMOUS SELF-ESTEEM. By autonomous self-esteem is meant the fact that one's self-esteem is determined mostly by *one's own evaluations of one's behavior.* This kind of autonomy probably results from early relationships with parents which produced a healthy self-ideal, or conscience (see Chapter 11). A healthy self-ideal comprises "shoulds," self-expectations and demands, which are feasible and flexible; conformity with them produces and maintains self-esteem. If the parents were affectionate, consistent, reasonable in their demands on the child, and in addition provided the child with an "identification-model" which could be readily followed, the child will probably develop a healthy self-ideal.

A person with such a healthy self-ideal is much less dependent upon external sources for his self-esteem. He can accept himself, without requiring a continual flow of reassurance, appreciation, affection and flattery, from other persons. He is not starved for favorable attention, feeling depressed and unworthy when it is not forthcoming from others. He may enjoy being appreciated by others, but his self-esteem is not wholly dependent upon these outside appraisals. He is much less likely, then, to fall for the first person who seems to like him, and who flatters him for his accomplishments. Further, he is much less likely to govern his behavior so that it will insure a continuous supply of external appreciation. He can, to a higher degree, do what he wants to do, rather than do what he must do in order to please others.

FULL AND HONEST COMMUNICATION

The question we have been exploring is, "How must one person act so as to promote the growth of another person with whom he is involved in a relationship?"

Actually, the most basic answer to this question describes be-

havior which is itself a property of a healthy interpersonal relationship, namely, *full and honest communication.*

Full and honest communication between two people will result,
inevitably, in an *impasse* between them. An impasse is defined here
as a situation where one participant needs something from the
other (in order to produce happiness or satisfaction), which the
other person cannot or will not provide. Impasses block the further
growth of a relationship toward the goals listed in the definition of a
healthy interpersonal relationship (see page 181).

There are only a few interpersonal situations which produce impasses. These are: (a) a demand, or need, is regarded as unreasonable, or impossible of fulfillment, by the second person; (b) the first
person cannot, or will not, clearly state exactly what his wants or
needs are; (c) the second person cannot recognize the needs of the
first person.

The symptoms of an impasse in an interpersonal relationship are
such phenomena as recurring hatred, irritation, boredom, dissatisfaction, restlessness, withdrawal of concern for the other.[32]

Open and honest communication creates impasses; but it is also
the necessary condition for the healthy resolution of impasses. Let
us digress for a moment from our discussion of impasses, and examine some of the barriers to full communication between two
persons involved in some relationship.

BARRIERS TO OPEN COMMUNICATION BETWEEN TWO PERSONS. Why
will one person withhold certain actions, thoughts, opinions, wants,
feelings, or memories from another? The general answer to this question is as follows: the individual who is holding back does so because he fears the expected consequences of his disclosures. He may
fear the other's opinion of him. He may fear rejection, criticism, or
ridicule.

Another factor which interferes with open communication is the
self-structure of the participants. An individual may be afraid to
acknowledge to himself that he has certain feelings and wants; if he
acknowledged them, it would threaten his self-concept and occasion
a loss of self-esteem. Hence, he will repress his feelings or wants,
and the other person may never know of them.[33]

THE RESOLUTION OF IMPASSES. Impasses are created when one
partner acts in ways which thwart the other, or when one partner

does not act as the other partner needs him to act. An *open impasse* exists when the demands are clearly stated and the refusal to comply is clearly stated. A *covert impasse* exists when the demands are felt, but have not been openly stated, or when each partner tacitly agrees to avoid an open conflict in demands, in order to keep the peace. It should be obvious that only open impasses can be resolved in a growth-promoting way by intent.

The simplest case of an interpersonal impasse consists in one person *expressing an open wish or demand* that the other person do something, or stop doing something, which the other person *refuses* openly. The simplest case of impasse-resolution consists in either (a) the person withdrawing the demand, (b) the other person complying with the demand, or (c) some compromise between (a) and (b).

A resolution to an impasse can be judged for its effect on growth. If it results in a valued change in the behavior repertoire of the person, or if it results in a healthier self-structure (see Chapter 9), then we can regard the solution as a growth-producing one. If, on the other hand, the solution simply crystallizes the present behavior-repertoire and personality-structure of either partner, or if it interferes with growth or involves regression, then we must adjudge the solution of the impasses as unhealthy.

The compulsive avoidance of impasses and compulsive avoidance of interpersonal conflict is unhealthy. A person may avoid impasses by refusing to make demands, or he may avoid them by compulsively acceding to the other's demands. Open conflict is always preferable to covert guerrilla warfare, because it can result in a more open and rationally-considered solution, at least in the long run.

Thus, in a healthy relationship, each partner feels free to express his likes, dislikes, wants, wishes, feelings, impulses, and the other person feels free to react with like honesty to these. In such a relationship, there will be tears, laughter, sensuality, irritation and anger, fear, baby-like behavior, etc.

The range of behavior, feelings, and wishes which will be brought out into the open is not arbitrarily limited. In fact, one gauge to the health of a relationship is the *breadth of the topics of conversation, the range of feelings which are openly expressed,* and *the range of activities which are shared.* In each case, the broader the range, the healthier the relationship.

UNHEALTHY RELATIONSHIPS AND BEHAVIORAL RESTRICTION. In an unhealthy relationship, much is taboo. The relationship continues only on the premise that certain aspects of behavior will be excluded. Thus, a marriage may continue only so long as criticism of one partner by the other is avoided. Or a friendship may continue only so long as neither partner brings up certain topics of conversation, for example, sex, war, politics, family affairs, etc. One gauge which psychotherapists use in order to determine whether or not their patients are approaching health is the freedom of expressiveness of the patient toward the therapist. Can he express affection? hostility? criticism? sexuality? boredom? dislike? Can he express these feelings and attitudes toward others and not be afraid to accept the consequences of so doing? Can he talk freely about anything under the sun to his therapist? If some topics promote tension, anxiety, or embarrassment, can he state in words that he is tense, anxious, and embarrassed?

Unhealthy communication-restriction may be found in many parent-child relationships. The personality hygienist might ask, "Can the individual admit there are some aspects of his mother or father which he despises as well as others which he likes? Or does he feel compelled to assert that his parents are perfect?" [34] The same with marriages. Can one spouse acknowledge to the other that there are some repugnant features in the other's behavior? Any factor which curbs the full and honest communication of feelings, thoughts and demands, is a factor which interferes with the attainment of a healthy relationship and encourages the development of an unhealthy one. The only exception to the above-mentioned general rule is the case where the partners have agreed, following past experiences, to impose voluntary restrictions on their own behavior and communication because they have found that when they do not impose these restrictions, more important values are jeopardized. Thus, a couple of friends may agree, following bitter and insurmountable arguments, that politics is an area which they cannot discuss, and they agree to exclude this area of discussion from their relationship.

The question is often raised by prospective spouses, "How much of my past behavior should I relate to my fiancée?" The answer to this question is as follows: if each partner wants the other to have an accurate concept of him—both of his past as well as his present personality—then he is advised to withhold nothing. If the past behavior is markedly different from the individual's present behavior-repertoire, then it provides nothing more than interesting natural history. But if the person *doesn't want* the other to know of it, then we are observing the process of constructing an inaccurate public self, one which will be difficult to maintain and one which will interfere with the health of the relationship.

HOW DOES FULL COMMUNICATION BETWEEN PEOPLE PROMOTE GROWTH? Growth in personality occurs as a consequence of meeting conflicts and impasses head-on and resolving these. Interpersonal conflicts and impasses constitute *problems* which require solution so that a satisfying relationship may be maintained or started. Whenever a person encounters a problem in his everyday living, he is obliged to vary his behavior until he discovers some mode of responding which is successful in achieving a solution. With no conflicts, with no impasses, there would be no instigation to change one's modal behavior repertoire—one would, in short, not learn. If a person had no need to keep afloat and move in water, he would never learn to swim. If he had no occasion to keep records, or to communicate by letters, he would not learn to write. If nobody made open demands upon him, he would never learn ways of behaving which would please the other person.

In interpersonal relationships, it is only when there is an open and fully felt and recognized conflict between the participants that an occasion is provided for growth, for learning new, more adequate modes of behaving. Interpersonal relationships, besides being a rich source of satisfactions for the participants, also provide a rich source of problems for each participant. The solution of these problems results either in growth of personality toward health or away from health.

Conflicts and impasses are created in interpersonal relationships *only* when each participant acts fully in accordance with his own genuine wants, feelings, and values. Inevitably, as these are expressed and acted upon, they will come into conflict with the wants, feelings and values of the other. *Accepting and recognizing the con-*

flict is the necessary condition for its resolution. Persons who strive
to avoid interpersonal conflicts in a compulsive manner are actually
doing all in their power to avoid growth and change.

Let us illustrate how full communication can create problems, and
provide the conditions for growth:

A husband, for years, has been acting in ways which annoy his
wife. She has avoided mentioning her annoyance to him, though she
feels it deeply enough. Since the husband does not know of her
annoyance, he continues to act in those ways, thus continually pro-
voking his wife. If the wife one day bursts into a rage and lets her
husband know, through this full communication, how his behavior
affects her, then at least the necessary conditions for growth are
present. The husband may modify his behavior so as to please his
wife more, and this may be adjudged growth. Or, he may with considerable vigor refuse to change; this refusal may require the wife
to modify her demands, to accept her husband's idiosyncrasies, or
to continue asserting her disapproval. At any event, the issue is now
out in the open, and a greater opportunity for resolution is now
available than when the issue was covert.

One by-product of full and honest communication between partners is *trust.* When a person knows that his friend or spouse will
always and immediately let him know what he thinks or feels about
him, he acquires the concept of the other person as honest, and he
will believe what the other person says. Most readers will agree that
there is nothing more uncomfortable and anxiety-provoking than the
situation of never knowing what the other person *really* thinks, feels,
wants. Many a patient undergoing personality therapy reports he
never knew whether his parents liked each other or him; that he can
hardly believe it when someone says nice things to him. Instead,
he feels anxiety and suspicion when someone says something nice.
In fact, it is only in personality therapy that some persons have their
first experience at full communication, when they relate *everything*
which comes to mind to the therapist.

When one does not know the real structure of the physical world,
one is naturally insecure and anxious. If we could never tell from
moment to moment, whether a flood, earthquake, or hurricane was
going to occur, we would naturally feel chronically anxious, and we
would live a life hemmed in by precautions against these catastro-

phes. But climatology has been so well cultivated, that "honest" signs of forthcoming catastrophes are readily available.

In the social world, and in interpersonal relationships, honest communication is the counterpart of natural "signs." If we believed that verbal expressions of feelings and demands from other people were *not* accurate statements of their feelings, and forecasters of their behavior, we would always remain anxious and defensive. We may not like the honest communications of the other person, but it is only when these honest communications are present that we can find ways of acting which will save whatever is valued, including the relationship itself.

Full communication between the participants in an interpersonal relationship promotes growth, then, *by creating impasses and conflicts in the relationship.* It is in the resolution of the impasses that growth of personality occurs, but without the communication, there would never be sharply defined impasses.

SOCIALLY DERIVED BARRIERS TO FULL COMMUNICATION. Although honesty in interpersonal communication is highly valued in our society, there is another socially defined value which is often more strongly affirmed than honesty. We are speaking here of the value which is placed on "saying nice things." There is an old slogan which describes this value succinctly: "If you can't say something nice about another person, don't say anything." When people conform with this semi-formal rule for acceptable conduct, they impose a constant restriction over their own communicative behavior. In close relationships, such as marriage, friendships, teacher-pupil, parent-child, etc., the recipient of "nice" evaluations can never know how his behavior really affects the other person. Further, the "nice" appraisals of him made by significant others will contribute to the formulation of an inaccurate self-concept. We shall show later (in Chapter 9) that the judgments of oneself made by significant others are an important determiner of the self-concept. If these others have lied to you about your behavior, you will acquire beliefs about your personality which are inaccurate. Many a person, the recipient of uncritical praise from parents, friends, and teachers, has come to evaluate his talents erroneously. When he encounters impartial critics of his musical or artistic ability, he is undone and overwhelmed by their criticism. When one of the participants in an interpersonal relationship represses all those opinions, feelings, evaluations which are "not nice," he is contributing to unhealthy personality in the other, and he is developing an unhealthy relationship with the other.

Another socially derived precept holds that people should not be either demanding or complaining in a relationship. As they conform with this precept, they delimit their communication markedly. A wife who would lose self-esteem if she makes demands on her husband, may refrain from so doing. Since he has no signs available that he is thwarting or depriving her of legitimate satisfactions, he will continue blithely to behave in his accustomed ways. The upshot will be that the wife will preserve her self-esteem, true enough, but the cost may be a long life of suffering, and repressed resentment. The same holds for complaints. Complaints are to an interpersonal relationship what pain or pus is to the body—a sign that something is wrong, a sign that something must be done in order to restore the valued state of affairs. If people were incapable of feeling pain, they would have little incentive to seek competent medical attention, and they might die long before their allotted three or four score of years. If complaints were not made by one participant in a relationship, the other person would have no indication that his behavior or omissions were producing dissatisfaction and unhappiness. Vigorous and honest complaints will at least create an impasse, which we have seen is the first and necessary step in the direction of adjustments. The author, in therapeutic and counseling work, has advised quietly martyred spouses to learn the art of complaining. This is not to say that complaining is valued per se; it may happen that a person complains on the basis of irrational and unrealistic needs and demands. In such cases it is to the other's advantage to rebut the complaints with as much vigor as they have been presented. This reaction insures that all sides of the issue are brought into the open where they can be more effectively resolved.

There are some needs which one or both participants may feel ashamed of, or condemn, because of social mores. Thus, a wife may be ashamed of her longings to be "fathered" by her husband from time to time. If she is ashamed of it, she will never ask her husband (subtly or openly) to behave toward her in a paternal fashion, and he will never learn of her need. The wife may then develop a strong hatred of her husband for not being a mind-reader and sensing her need, and she will be obliged to repress the hatred, too. This will produce an impasse which is insurmountable because it is covert. But the wife may be assuming without warrant that her husband would condemn her for longing to be an infant. Perhaps he feels unnecessary to his wife and would welcome the opportunity to act as she needs him to act. But because of assimilative projection, the wife presumes that if she were to ask him to cuddle her he would laugh at her and reject her. One ounce of reality-testing might correct this misconception.

DEPENDENCY: A BARRIER TO FULL COMMUNICATION. We have already touched on this theme in other contexts, but it warrants restatement in the present setting. A helpless person may dread full communication with the one upon whom he is dependent, because he fears the other will withdraw his support. The dependent employee doesn't tell his boss how he feels about him out of dread he will be discharged from a job he needs. The dependent wife doesn't tell her husband all her feelings, needs, thoughts and opinions, because she fears he will leave her. The dependent friend doesn't tell his buddy what he thinks and feels, because he fears he will be abandoned. Any factor which promotes dependency, and interferes with the attainment of independent security, is a factor which interferes with full communication.

AN EXCESSIVELY STRICT CONSCIENCE: A BARRIER TO COMMUNICATION. A conscience which is excessively strict may prevent a person from acknowledging his thoughts and feelings to himself as well as to the other person. If the individual with a strict conscience communicates openly to the other person, he will not only suffer agonies of anxiety concerning the reaction of the other person, but also agonies of guilt and self-hate.

Thus, a person may condemn certain kinds of sexual activities, but yet experience a strong impulse toward just that kind of sexual activity. Merely to admit it openly to himself might be the occasion for profound guilt. To admit to the spouse what one longs for would produce guilt, and dread that the spouse would sue immediately for divorce. Yet, if the person were able to by-pass the defense of repression, and express what he wanted despite his guilt and anxiety, he might find that (a) his spouse welcomed this new source of satisfaction and, (b) upon open scrutiny and evaluation of the moral precept, it might be possible to revise or modify it, thus enabling acceptance of this aspect of the personality.

An excessively strict conscience can thus interfere with interpersonal communication and with the opportunity to establish a healthy interpersonal relationship.

COMMUNICATION AND THE REAL SELF. The "real self" is a term which Horney used to refer to "that central inner force, common to all human beings, and yet unique in each, which is the deep source of growth . . ." (p. 17). In another context, she speaks of the real self as "the most alive center of ourselves . . . it engenders the spontaneity of feelings. . . . It is also the source of spontaneous interests and energies . . . the capacity to wish and to will . . ." (p. 157).[35]

We can redefine the *real self* in more clear-cut terms. By real self, first of all, we are referring to *subjective experience* which only the person himself can observe directly, since he is the one who is experiencing it. The immediate subjective experience which the term real self refers to comprises *feeling* (affection, anger, anxiety, guilt, etc.) and *cognitive content* (memories, perceptions, or, more generally, thoughts). *Wants and wishes,* as these are consciously experienced, are also an integral component of the real self: a wish to hurt somebody, a longing to disagree with someone, or a desire to eat, sleep, make love, etc.

Let us now raise the question, *how much of his real self is a person willing to convey—through words, and through action—to another person?*

In a healthy interpersonal relationship, an individual is willing and able to communicate *all* of his real self to the other person. It must not be forgotten that the real self refers to the subjective, or private aspect of a person's behavioral repertoire. Anybody can see what a person *does*. Nobody, without the co-operation of the individual himself, can discover what a person is thinking, feeling, or wanting. The person himself must be willing to translate his thoughts, feelings, and wishes into words and/or actions, before the other individual can have an accurate idea of the person's real self.

For that matter, the individual himself may strive to ignore, or to repress his real self. Where this has been successfully accomplished,

Horney speaks of *alienation from the* [real] *self.* She sees the process of neurotic development, or unhealthy personality development, as having its origin in active "moves away from the real self." [36]

Thus, a person may ignore his "real" feelings, wishes and wants, and try instead to feel what he is supposed to feel; want what he is supposed to want; think what he is supposed to think. By whom, or what is he "supposed" to think, feel and want? He feels compelled by his conscience, by "duty," or by the expectations and demands of other people to think, feel, and want in certain restricted ways. Failure to think, feel and want what he is supposed to, will produce guilt, or anxiety. That is, if the individual confronts and acknowledges his real feelings, thoughts and wants, as these arise *spontaneously*, he will then experience self-loathing, guilt, or the dread that significant others will reject and despise him. The person who has become "alienated from his self" is a person who is afraid or ashamed of his real self. Discontented as he thus is with his real self, he strives to destroy it, bury it, change it, ignore it—in short, he does everything with his real self but recognize it, accept it, and act in accordance with its promptings. As Horney views it, psychotherapy, or personality therapy, has as its goal the undoing of the process of alienation from the self. The therapist tries to confront the patient with his real self, and to help him accept it and to view it with compassion and concern rather than fear and revulsion.

Personality therapy is undertaken by means of communication between one person with an unhealthy personality who is called the patient, and an expert called the personality therapist. The therapist tries to encourage his patient to communicate his real self to him. He avoids criticism, he avoids punishment, and tries to minimize all of the common barriers to full communication. Freud introduced the technique of "free association" into the mechanics of therapy. He imposed a "fundamental rule" upon the patient; the patient was required to do one and only one thing—report *everything* which passed through his mind during a therapeutic hour. The reader is asked to try this. Pick someone who is close to you, and start, with ruthless honesty, to report in uncensored fashion *everything* which enters your mind for one hour. You will find that you start off well enough, but soon, a resistance will be encountered. Your mind will go blank. Or something will come up which you would rather die than utter to another human being. Freud found that if each resistance was studied and interpreted to the patient, the process of free association would continue until the patient might just as well be pronounced cured, because he would have finally established a healthy interpersonal relationship with his therapist. He would have experienced the process of communicating his real self immediately —*in statu nascendi* (which may loosely be translated to mean expressing his private thoughts, feelings and wishes the very instant they were "born"; i.e., the very instant they popped into the person's mind).

Whitaker and Malone accomplish the same aim—helping a patient discover his real self, accept it, communicate it, and love it—by encouraging the patient to *speak his fantasies aloud to the therapist*. The therapist may encourage this activity by speaking aloud his own fantasies which he experiences during the therapeutic hour with his patient.[37] It should be apparent that one's fantasies, determined as they are by needs and feelings (see Chapter 2) will reflect one's real self with utmost nakedness. Again, the reader is asked to select some friend, and in his presence, speak aloud all the fantasies or daydreams which he develops in the presence of his friend. Probably embarrassment and guilt will drastically limit the kinds of fantasies which the reader will allow himself to construct.

We can construct a rough scale for communication: a scale which ranges from statements that have only a remote connection with the real self, to statements which may be direct expressions of the real self but which are increasingly difficult to utter. Thus, the following verbal communications from one person to another will illustrate:

REMOTE FROM REAL SELF, EASY TO DISCLOSE

"It is now raining" (a reference to the "objective" world).

"I am hungry" (a reference to the "subjective" world, and actually an honest statement of felt tensions).

"I wish that I could be a baby again."

"I hate you, and wish that you were dead."

"I love you deeply, and with passion."

CLOSE TO REAL SELF, DIFFICULT TO DISCLOSE

As a general rule, only *selected* aspects of the real self can be communicated to another person with comfort: those aspects which are consistent with (a) the self-concept, (b) the conscience, (c) the social mores, (d) the public self that has been constructed apropos the other person and, (e) the other person's actual concept of you. Messages which deviate from these restrictions will not be readily conveyed to the other person. There are some unhealthy personalities which are so repressed that the individual will communicate only *impersonal* messages to other people, and he will block, or "clam up" if any question is directed at him concerning his personal feelings, wishes, opinions, etc.

The healthy interpersonal relationship is one in which each participant can readily communicate his real self to the other.

REALISTIC AND FEASIBLE DEMANDS
ON THE OTHER PERSON

In a healthy interpersonal relationship, the demands which each partner imposes on the other as conditions for the continuation of the relationship are realistic, mutually agreed upon, and consistent with the values and happiness of the other. What does this prescription imply? What is a realistic demand?

As we have seen, interpersonal relationships are entered into as a means toward the ends of happiness, satisfaction, and growth. Each partner needs the other to act in certain ways in order to attain those ends. In most friendships, or marriages, the participants are willing to accede to the requests, demands, and needs of the other. But it can happen that one of the partners has unusual needs—needs deriving from an atypical life history. That person needs the other to act in atypical or perhaps impossible ways in order to produce satisfactions. Where one partner has unusual needs, or where each has an inaccurate concept of what the other is capable of doing, the demands may be unrealistic and impossible of fulfillment. There is a distinction between a demand which is difficult to conform with, and one which it is impossible for the other to fulfill. In the case of the former, accession may well contribute to growth. In the case of the latter, it may either be physically impossible of fulfillment, or it may cost so much that other values would have to be sacrificed, thus making it unworthwhile.

Thus, a sweetheart may demand of her lover that he abandon his work in order to spend all of his time with her. Or, a mother may demand a straight "A" average from a child of below-average intelligence. In these instances, the demands cannot be met. Growth would not consist in one person conforming with the other's demands; rather, growth would be promoted if the individual refused to conform and strove instead to show that the demands were unrealistic. If these attempts were successful, and the demanding one accordingly adjusted his demands to bring them into reasonable limits, then we could assert that the one who modified his demands had grown.

In a healthy relationship, each partner has an accurate concept of the other's personality—a concept which includes accurate estimates of ability and accurate knowledge of the values and morals of the other person. Demands upon the other which are realistic are demands which are predicated on this knowledge.

A partner in a healthy relationship would not deliberately introduce a demand on the other which would result in unhappiness for the other. But in accordance with the principle of open communication, even unreasonable demands should be openly asserted, so that the other can know of them, and rebut them with vigor. It is only through the open expression of these demands that an opportunity is provided whereby the demands can be assessed against knowledge of the other person.

The personality hygienist can utilize the demands which one participant makes of the other in their relationship, as an index of the personality health of the participants and as an index of the health of the relationship. As an impartial observer, he can compare the demands with the ability of each participant to fulfill them, and make judgments about their realistic or unrealistic nature.

Insofar as possible, in a healthy relationship there will be a close congruence between the demands which one partner imposes on the other and the latter's self-demands. If the partners share many values in common, this will likely be the case. It is as if the wishes of one partner are accepted as a *value* by the other—to be fulfilled if possible.

RESPECT FOR THE OTHER'S RIGHT
TO BE SELF-DETERMINING

Ours is a democratic society in which relative autonomy of the individual person is seen as a high value. Self-determination is a trait valued by the society at large and by personality hygienists. This emphasis upon the autonomy of the single person contrasts with concepts of the ideal man which are held in other societies. Thus, it could be said that in Nazi Germany, the ideal man could be described, not as the "autonomous man," but as the "obedient man," obedient to the leaders of the State. Nazi parents raised their children toward this goal of obedience; Nazi wives admired husbands who showed unflinching obedience to superiors and condemned those who were so "weak" and "selfish" as to put private interests above those of duty.

In a healthy interpersonal relationship, each partner will theoretically place a strong positive value on the autonomy of the other, and further, will value the goal of growth toward self-actualization of the other. When these values are clearly stated, it becomes apparent that many other values can readily conflict with them. In a marriage, for example, a husband may refuse his wife's request for a divorce because he values public opinion more than her growth. A parent may force unwilling compliance from the child so as to maintain self-esteem. In each case, we observe a lack of respect for the individual needs of the other person. This is a subtle point, but one which warrants full elucidation because of its importance.

In a healthy relationship, each partner wants the other partner to do *what he wants to do*. Certainly, friends or spouses choose one another because of similarities in values; i.e., similarities in what each wants to do. In our society, because of the high value placed on free will, few spouses would want the other to remain married unwillingly. What we are here saying is that a sign of a healthy relationship is present when each participant shows an active concern for the *preservation of the integrity and autonomy of the other*, even when this involves at some time the dissolution of the relationship. If a divorce, or the break-up of a friendship, or leaving the parent's home, or quitting a job, is an important means of promoting growth and increasing autonomy, then in a healthy relationship, the other person will want this to occur.

Very often a concern and respect for the other person's right to integrity and autonomy involves some pain. For that matter, to be concerned with *one's own autonomy* may often involve a good deal of social pressure—especially in those instances where one's wishes differ from those of the majority of people. The "nerve of failure" as Riesman and others have called it, is rare. By this is meant the courage to continue to assert one's difference from the mass of other people, despite economic and social pressure to conform, and to wipe out the differences between the self and others.[38]

In a healthy interpersonal relationship, the autonomy of the other person is as jealously nurtured as is one's own. The healthy personality would rather dissolve the relationship than continue it at the cost of the other person's autonomy.

HEALTHY CHOICE OF OTHERS

Whether or not a given choice of a friend, close working partner, or spouse has been a healthy choice can be determined only by observation of the subsequent relationship through time; "time will tell."

A healthy interpersonal relationship is one which provides for more satisfactions than frustrations, and which encourages, or does not interfere with, the personality growth of either partner. Naturally, only time will enable the judge to decide if a marriage or friendship has developed into a healthy one.

It is possible, however, to make choices of friends, employees, working partners, and spouses, in ways that will increase the probability of the relationship moving in a healthy direction. The guiding philosophy of choice would be to state, as clearly as possible, (a) the needs and values of the choosing person, and (b) the traits of the person being chosen in as detailed a fashion as is practicable. If choices are predicated on such a broad base, the chances are greater that they will be fortunate choices. Naturally, though, there are many purely technical problems involved in specifying the needs and values of the chooser, and in describing accurately the traits of the person being chosen. Since these are psychological problems, or problems within the professional realm of the psychologist, one can sometimes obtain professional help in making judicious choices of a partner in important interpersonal relationships. Thus, to an increasing degree, employers are hiring competent psychologists to assist them in choosing employees. No longer will an employer engage a worker on the basis of technical skill alone. He will strive to determine many of the prospective employee's personality traits, so that the people whom he hires can relate one to another in at least nonfrustrating ways, if not positively satisfying ways.

In a less technical setting, one's family and present friends serve as a kind of investigating committee to examine and pass judgment on a lover's choice of a spouse. "Lovers are blind," it is assumed with some validity; and so the well-intentioned family and friends try to examine all the fiancée's traits which have been ignored as "unimportant" by the love-blinded youth. He may have fallen in love because of some one need-related trait, and ignores all the rest of her characteristics. The uninvolved others look the girl over from many other standpoints, looking at such things as her health, her income, her religion, her attitudes and values, her tastes, etc. If these judges know the overall needs and value-hierarchy of the young lover, they may be able to see she has attributes which make her unsuited to him. He may or may not pay attention to their advice.

Optimally, of course, in anything so intimate as marriage, the couple should explore each other, perhaps for a long time, so that each will come to know the other's traits before they become legally committed to one another. This is unromantic, however, and seldom done; the longer-range consequence is either divorce or a long life of tortured martyrdom. But even more, each person may strive to *hide* many of his characteristics from the scrutiny of the other, because he needs the other person and is afraid he will be rejected should the other person find out these traits. And so a courtship, instead of being a period of mutual real-self-exposure and study of the other, becomes a period of mutual deception, and construction of false public selves. Many a person has experienced tragic disillusionment with his spouse when once the ceremony has been completed and the marriage begun. Even more tragic, however, is a longer-run consequence—that of striving to conform with a false public self which has been constructed during the courtship. The "perfect lovers" in the Chocolate Soldier found their relationship too idealistic, too perfect—it was a strain; and so the nobleman married the maid, with whom he could be himself, and the girl of high degree married the bourgeois chocolate-soldier innkeeper for the same reason.

SUMMARY

Healthy interpersonal relationships have seven main characteristics:

1. Each partner has an accurate concept of the other's personality.
2. Each partner likes more of the other's traits than he dislikes.
3. Each partner feels concern for the happiness and growth of the other.
4. Each partner acts in ways which will promote the growth and happiness of the other.
5. Each partner communicates fully with the other.
6. Each partner imposes reasonable demands and expectations on the other.
7. Each partner respects the right of the other to be self-determining.

An accurate concept of the other person's personality (accurate *other-concepts*) is achieved by accurate observation of the other person. First impressions of another person are generally inaccurate, in consequence of *projection, attribution, needs,* and *social factors* such as pressure to conform with others.

People are *changeable.* Underestimating and overestimating the changeability of others can impair interpersonal relationships. Another person can be encouraged to change by so gratifying his basic needs that he will *want* to change.

The *liking-response*—liking aspects of the other person—*is a function of needs and values.* We tend to like those aspects of another person which gratify our needs, and which accord with our values and ideals.

Concern for the other person's happiness and growth is a by-product of concern for the self; a happy and mature person can more fully gratify us than a dissatisfied and immature person.

Behavior which promotes happiness in the other person is predicated on knowledge of and concern for the other person. *The behavior which promotes growth* in the other person rests on full, honest communication. Some relationships are *neutral* with respect to growth, others *induce regression, some prevent growth. Excessive dependency* is seen as a factor which promotes unhealthy interpersonal relationships. *Skills, a rich gratification-history,* and *autonomous self-esteem* are seen as factors which promote the development of healthy interpersonal relationships.

Full and honest communication, so important to promoting growth, leads to *impasses.* An impasse exists when one person needs something from the other which the latter cannot or will not provide.

Impasses are resolved when the "needy" one withdraws his demands, or when the other person accedes to these demands.

In unhealthy relationships, not only is communication restricted, but so also is behavior of all kinds restricted. Dependency and an excessively strict conscience are seen as barriers to full communication, along with certain socially determined barriers. *In a healthy relationship, the "real self" of each partner is made known by each to the other.*

In healthy interpersonal relationships, the *demands* which each makes on the other are *open, reasonable, and compatible with the health and happiness of the other.*

Each participant in a healthy interpersonal relationship *respects the will of the other,* and seeks to encourage the other to be self-directing.

A healthy choice of a friend, or spouse is discussed.

NOTES AND REFERENCES

RECOMMENDED READINGS ARE MARKED WITH AN ASTERISK (*)

1. This interest in the systematic study of interpersonal relationships is commonly attributed to Harry Stack Sullivan, who defined psychiatry, not as the study of mental disease, but rather as the study of interpersonal relations. For the most recent statement of his viewpoints, see Sullivan, H. S., *The interpersonal theory of psychiatry*, New York, Norton, 1953. It should be asserted, however, that Moreno, with his "sociometric" methods of study-

ing groups, long anticipated Sullivan as a formal student of interpersonal relationships. See Moreno, J. L., *Who shall survive?* Washington, Nerv. Ment. Dis. Publ. Co., 1934.

2. These criteria borrow heavily from Fromm's characterization of "productive love," which includes the attributes of knowledge, care, responsibility, and respect. See Fromm, E., *Man for himself*, New York, Rinehart, 1947, pp. 96–101. Ackerman has developed some specific criteria for determining whether or not a marital relationship is healthy. Ackerman, N. W., "The diagnosis of neurotic marital interaction," *Social Caswk.*, 1954, April.

3. Steiner has analyzed some of the experimental work in "social perception" and in group behavior, and concludes that accurate social perception (which results in accurate other-concepts) will promote "interpersonal competence and group efficiency" under certain specific conditions which he cites. See Steiner, I. D., "Interpersonal behavior as influenced by accuracy of social perception." *Psychol. Rev.*, 1955, 62, 268–274. Dymond showed that the spouses of a happy marriage knew how their partners would respond to a psychological test with greater accuracy than unhappily married spouses. Dymond, R., "The relation of accuracy of perception of the spouse and marital happiness," *Amer. Psychologist*, 1953, 8, 344. (Abstract.)

*4. Asch, S. D., "Forming impressions of personality," *J. abn. soc. Psychol.*, 1946, 41, 258–290. See also Gollin, E. S., "Forming impressions of personality," *J. Pers.*, 1954, 23, 65–76.

5. Secord, however, found that facial features (physiognomy) were more important determiners of trait-ascription than occupational stereotypes. In one experiment, he showed a group of subjects several facial photographs, and the supposed occupation of each person's face was indicated, e.g. banker, minister, etc. He expected that as he switched occupational labels, the traits which were ascribed to each person would be changed. Instead, he found that his subjects were rating personality traits on the basis of facial features rather than on the basis of occupational labels. On pursuing this line further, he conducted some highly original studies of the facial characteristics which will induce subjects to agree in assigning personality traits to persons on the basis of facial appearance. See Secord, P. F., Bevan, W. Jr., and Dukes, W. F., "Occupational and physiognomic stereotypes in the perception of photographs," *J. soc. Psychol.*, 1953, 37, 261–270. Also, by the same authors, "Personalities in Faces, I. An experiment in

social perceiving," *Genet. Psychol. Monogr.*, 1954, **49**, 231–279. Secord has continued this program with a number of collaborators, and has published, to date, about nine separate studies.

*6. Cameron, N. and Magaret, Ann, *Behavior Pathology*, New York, Houghton Mifflin, 1951, pp. 381–387. See Lundy, R. M., "Assimilative projection and accuracy of prediction in interpersonal perceptions," *J. abn. soc. Psychol.*, 1956, **52**, 33–38 for an empirical study which is related to our discussion of assimilative projection.

7. See pp. 339–341 of this volume.

8. In 1954, a Negro male was brought to trial on the testimony of a white woman that he looked at her with the apparent "intent to rape"—she displayed disowning projection.

9. Rogers, C. R. and Dymond, Rosalind F. (ed.), *Psychotherapy and personality change*, Chicago, University of Chicago Press, 1954, pp. 90, 98.

10. The word "transference" may be found in any and every book which treats of psychoanalytic therapy, whether written by Freud, or any other analyst.

11. Sullivan, H. S., *op. cit.*, 28–30 (footnote).

12. Secord, P. F. and Jourard, S. M., "Mother-concepts and judgments of young women's faces," *J. abn. soc. Psychol.*, 1956, **52**, 246–250.

*13. "Social perception" is an area of intense investigation at the present time. A convenient summary is available to the serious student in Lindzey, G. (ed.), *Handbook of social psychology*, Cambridge, Addison-Wesley, 1954, Vol. II, Ch. 17: The perception of people (by Bruner, J. S. and Tagiuri, R.).

14. Murray's early experiment with young girls illustrates this. He asked girls to describe the picture of a man before and after they had played a very spooky children's game called "murder." The subjects saw more scary and evil characteristics in the man after the game than they did before. Murray, H. A., "The effect of fear upon estimates of maliciousness of other personalities," *J. soc. Psychol.*, 1933, **4**, 310–329. Krech and Crutchfield provide many examples of the influence of needs and emotions on the concept of other persons. See Krech, D. and Crutchfield, R. S., *Theory and problems of social psychology*, New York, McGraw-Hill, 1948, pp. 88–94. Ch. 5, 6, which provide fundamental information on beliefs, will make this section more meaningful for the serious student.

15. The influence of other people's opinions upon our own judgments and

other-concepts is a special case of the more general phenomena of suggestion, hypnosis, and propaganda. See Krech and Crutchfield, *op. cit.* for an intelligent discussion of suggestion and propaganda, and White, R. W., *The abnormal personality*, New York, Ronald, 1948, Ch. 5, for a discussion of hypnosis.

*16. Crutchfield, R. S., "Conformity and character," *Amer. Psychologist*, 1955, 10, 191–198.

17. Dewey, J., *Logic: the theory of inquiry*, New York, Holt, 1938, Ch. 4, 6. These two chapters outline clearly, although in rather turgid prose, the fundamentals of scientific inquiry, as these are applied to everyday living as well as in the laboratory.

18. But not too readily. G. Brock Chisholm stirred up public furor with an address which he delivered as a William Alanson White Memorial speech, in which he was deploring the fact that parents will lie to children about such things as birth and Santa Claus. Newspapers all over the country and Canada picked up his remarks about the Santa Claus myth, and the public berated him for trying to destroy a happy illusion. See Chisholm, G. B., "The psychiatry of enduring peace and social progress," *Psychiatry*, 1946, 9, 1–36, for his actual remarks.

19. Clyde Coombs has developed some highly sophisticated methods for determining and measuring liking-hierarchies. See his Chapter 11 in Festinger, L. and Katz, D., *Research methods in the behavioral sciences*, New York, Dryden, 1953, pp. 491–492.

20. Jourard, S. M. and Secord, P. F., "Body-cathexis and the ideal female figure," *J. abn. soc. Psychol.*, 1955, 50, 243–246. See also, by the same authors, "Body-cathexis and personality," *Brit. J. Psychol.*, 1955, 46, 130–138, for a more extensive discussion of these themes. In these technical papers, the words "cathexis-response" may be understood as synonymous with "liking-disliking"; thus, "positive cathexis" means liking, and "negative cathexis" means disliking.

21. This tendency (generalizing from some aspect of a person's behavior repertoire to the entire personality) is very much like one of the primitive ways of thinking and explaining— the so-called "law of pars pro toto." See Werner, H., *The comparative psychology of mental development*, Chicago, Follett, 1948, p. 423.

*22. The serious student should read carefully the sections of Murphy's text which deals with the "levels" of cognitive activity. See Murphy, G., *Personality: a biosocial approach to origins and structure*, New York, Harper, 1947, pp. 342–346.

*23. This section draws heavily from Fromm's discussion of "productive love." Fromm, E., *op. cit.*, pp. 96–101.

*24. Fromm, E., *op. cit.*, pp. 129–141. Fromm's discussion of "selfishness, self-love, and self-interest" is a classic which the student should read in entirety.

*25. Howard, S., *The silver cord.* This play should be read by all students as part of a liberal education. It treats of "mom" before Philip Wylie and E. Strecker handled this theme.

26. The English film, "Brief Encounter" illustrates this theme nicely.

27. Mowrer provides an astute analysis of the concept of regression, and cites one of his rat studies to illustrate some of the conditions under which regression occurs. See Mowrer, O. H., *Learning theory and personality dynamics*, New York, Ronald, 1950, Ch. 13.

*28. Bettelheim, B., "Individual and mass behavior in extreme situations," *J. abn. soc. Psychol.*, 1943, 38, 417–452.

29. Blatz, W., *Understanding the young child*, Toronto, Clarke, Irwin, 1944, Ch. 9.

*30. See Horney's descriptions of the person who "moves toward" people, and her discussion of the "self-effacing solution" in, respectively, Horney, K., *Our inner conflicts*, New York, Norton, 1945, Ch. 3; and Horney, K., *Neurosis and human growth*, New York, Norton, 1950, Ch. 9. These chapters provide excellent illustrations of dependency.

*31. This discussion borrows heavily from Maslow's concept of "gratification-health." See Maslow, A. H., *Motivation and personality*, New York, Harper, 1954, pp. 115–117.

32. The discussion of impasses was suggested by the recent work of Whitaker and Malone which the present writer sees as the most significant development in individual psychotherapy after Freud's. It is a difficult work for an undergraduate student to read, however. Whitaker, C. A. and Malone, T. P., *The roots of psychotherapy*, New York, Blakiston, 1953. A superb discussion of impasses in psychotherapy is provided in Whitaker, C. A., Warkentin, J., and Johnson, Nan, "The psychotherapeutic impasse," *Amer. J. Orthopsychiat.*, 1950, 20, 641–647.

33. A more technical discussion of communication and its vicissitudes is provided in Ruesch, J. and Bateson, G., *Communication, the social matrix of psychiatry*, New York, Norton, 1951. See also Ruesch, J., "The therapeutic process from the point of view of

communication theory," *Amer. J. Orthopsychiat.*, 1952, 22, 690–700.

34. The present writer showed that those subjects who were least able to admit any dislike or criticism of their parents showed the highest degree of moral indignation. Jourard, S. M., "Moral indignation: a correlate of denied dislike of parents' traits," *J. consult. Psychol.*, 1954, 18, 59–60.
35. Horney, K., *Neurosis and human growth*, New York, Norton, 1950.
36. Horney, K., *op. cit.*, Ch. 6.
37. Whitaker, C. A. and Malone, T. P., *op. cit.*, pp. 202 ff.
38. The courage to be oneself, though different, is a message which has been eloquently expounded by Nietzsche, Rank, Riesman, and Tillich.

QUESTIONS FOR REVIEW AND EXAMINATION

1. What characteristics describe a healthy interpersonal relationship?
2. How are accurate other-concepts acquired? What factors promote the development of inaccurate other-concepts?
3. What are the chief determiners of the liking-response?
4. What is concern? How is it acquired?
5. What factors facilitate interpersonal behavior which promotes growth and happiness in the other person?
6. How can interpersonal relationships promote regression, or prevent growth?
7. Why is excessive dependency unhealthy?
8. What factors operate so as to minimize dependency upon others?
9. What are some common barriers to full and honest communication with another person?
10. What is an interpersonal impasse? What are some healthy and unhealthy solutions? How does one decide whether or not an impasse-solution is healthy?
11. How does full and honest communication between persons promote growth?
12. Describe and evaluate as fully as possible the relationship between two people, using this chapter as a guide.

CHAPTER 8

Love and Healthy Personality

Love is a phenomenon of peculiarly crucial interest and concern to the personality hygienist. Loss of the capacity to love, or failure to develop it, is one of the most universally agreed-upon signs that personality health is impaired. Freud once remarked that *lieben und arbeiten*, loving and working, were the crucial signs that personality health had been achieved, through growth or through therapy.

Yet love is among the least understood of all human phenomena, and is the least studied by investigators of human behavior and experience. We do not yet have an applied science or a pure science of love.

One of the reasons for the difficulty in arriving at an understanding of love is the ambiguity with which love is defined, and the diversified ways in which the concept love is employed in speech. A woman loves her fiancé, her mother and father, her country, fudge, swimming, bone chinaware, and many other things besides. She "falls" in love; she *longs for* love, she *gives* love, she *makes* love, she *feels* love, etc.

Fromm[1] has been almost singular among writers on the subject by defining love in behavioral terms. In his work, love is not a passion or emotion; rather, it is a way of *behaving* toward the love-

233

object. A love-relationship exists when a person behaves toward the love-object in ways that convince an objective observer that the lover *knows, cares for, respects,* and *feels responsibility for* the object. Unless there is knowledge, care, respect, and responsibility, there is no love.

This is a definition of love which has some promise of doing justice to what is commonly called love, and which at the same time will enable more precise study of the conditions of love and its characteristics.

THE DEFINITION OF LOVING BEHAVIOR

Let us modify Fromm's definition of love in a way which will conform more closely with the concepts already utilized in the present volume. For us, love is an *adjective* which describes behavior, as it does for Fromm. We shall speak of *loving-behavior*. Loving-behavior is distinguished from other kinds of instrumental behavior by its *motives* and by its *consequences*. We can speak, with Fromm, of the "power," or capacity, to love. It should be possible to evaluate whether or not loving-behavior is *effective* in achieving its aims, and it should be possible to assess loving-behavior from the standpoint of personality health.

Loving-behavior refers to all action undertaken by a person with the conscious aim of promoting the happiness and growth of the object.

It is not enough, however, that the lover wants to promote happiness and growth; he must want to promote these values in his object for their own sake, as *ends in themselves*. We make this point because it is possible for a person to engage in behavior which looks like loving-behavior, but the reasons for undertaking it are ulterior —the person wants to make his object happy to impress him favorably, or to win a friend he can use. Loving-behavior cannot be defined as such unless the lover *enjoys* doing whatever is necessary to make his object happy, unless he does these things *freely*. A near-synonym for loving is *giving*.

ACTIVE LOVE AND PASSIVE LOVE. Loving-behavior, as we have defined it, is synonymous with *active* love. *Passive* love refers to the process of being loved by someone else, of being at the receiving end

of an active lover's efforts to make one happy and to help one grow.[2]
Thus, we can speak of a person who *loves* somebody, and *is loved*
in return by the other person. Or, one can love one object without
the love being reciprocated. When love exists between two persons,
we shall speak of *mutual love,* and we mean that each participant
in the loving-relationship is actively engaged in promoting the happiness and growth of the object. Obviously it is possible for nonmutual
love to exist.

EMOTIONS, MOTIVES, AND LOVING-BEHAVIOR

Since loving-behavior is instrumental behavior, we can inquire
into its motives. As we have seen, the motive basic to love is a desire to give, to do whatever will be effective in promoting happiness
and growth in the object; where the very act of giving and doing
is free from other, ulterior motives. It is giving for the sake of the
loved one. There is no compulsion or duty in love. Loving-behavior
cannot be commanded or ordered; the lover is not doing his duty
to his object under threat of punishment or guilt. He is, par excel-
lence, doing what he *wants* to do when he loves. The loving act
may be regarded almost as the acme of free choice.

But we think immediately of powerful emotions when we speak
of love: affection, lust, longing, tenderness, romance. What is the
relationship between such emotional responses and love?

EMOTIONAL RESPONSES AND LOVING-BEHAVIOR. When we love another person (or an animal, or our country), we *identify* ourselves
with the object.[3] Since the lover is very concerned with the happiness and growth of the object, he will himself *feel* the pleasures and
pains, the dangers to and the happinesses of his object *as if they
were his own.* It is as if he had extended the "contact-surface" of
his mechanisms for feeling and experiencing. He reacts emotionally
to the events which affect his object as well as to the events which
affect him personally.

Just as the lover becomes angry when someone hurts or insults
him, so he becomes angry when something hurts his object. Just
as he is happy at his own successes, and rich need-gratifications, so
is he affected by the successes and gratifications of his object. Just
as he is concerned about his own growth, so is he concerned for the

growth of his object. *Identification, empathy,* and *sympathy* are thus all involved in loving. Empathy involves the correct interpretation of cues which reflect the feelings and wishes of the object.[4] Identification—becoming like the object for longer or shorter intervals of time —makes sympathy (literally, feeling *with* the object) possible.

Experiences which affect the object provoke emotions in the lover. These in turn serve as important *motives* for loving-behavior. Under the impetus of emotional tensions provoked by whatever has affected the object, the lover strives to do those things which promote happiness and reduce unhappiness in the object.

SEXUALITY AND LOVING-BEHAVIOR. Sexual behavior is a rich source of happiness and gratification for the self as well as for the object. There are many love-relationships, of course, where sex is out of place: in the love of parents for their children, or in the love of a woman for her close girl-friend. But in a love-relationship where sexuality is socially and personally sanctioned, for instance in marriage, sexual behavior can be regarded as one of the patterns of loving-behavior—it is indeed behavior which makes the object (and the self) happy. Sociologists interpret the sexual act as a *ritual,* not unlike religious behavior; it has the function and consequence of cementing the "solidarity" of a small group—the married couple.[5]

It should be pointed out that there can be sexuality without love, and there can be love without sexuality. We would not call sexual intercourse which was desired by one partner but not by the other an expression of loving-behavior. And we could call it a love-relationship between a man and his friend, male or female, when there was active concern for happiness and growth, but no sexuality in the relationship.

THE OBJECTS OF LOVING-BEHAVIOR

We have seen in what loving-behavior consists; we can assume that any human has the *capacity* to love someone or some thing if he is capable of behaving at all. But there remains the question of the *choice* [6] of an object toward whom a person will devote his power to love, i.e., his power to satisfy, make happy, and help grow.

In principle, a person can choose almost anything and anyone as the object of his loving behavior, if he wants to love at all. But it is well-known that when choices are made from among a variety of possible alternatives, the motivations for the choice may be very complex, and sometimes unconscious. As the psychoanalysts say, choices are "overdetermined"

A person may choose another person as the object of his freely given loving-behavior on the basis of certain estimable characteristics of that person. In this connection, we can speak of *canalizations* [7] of the need to love; a person acquires preferences for possible love-objects in advance of his actually finding them and then loving them. It should be stated that we recognize a difference between a person as a *source* of love and gratification for the chooser, and a person as a possible *object*, or target, of giving and loving. One might be attracted to someone else on a dependent, passive basis— you expect that person to give you lots of satisfactions; but one may also be attracted to the other because the other appears to be "worthy" of your love, or the other person just seems to elicit from you the desire to give.

SOME COMMON CRITERIA FOR THE CHOICE OF A LOVE-OBJECT

HELPLESSNESS AND NEED. One may be moved to love another because the other seems to be helpless and in need of loving-behavior. Thus, most people find that it is easy for them to love small children, helpless animals, without necessarily expecting anything in return.

CONFORMITY WITH THE LOVER'S IDEALS. A potential lover may have constructed certain ideals of appearance, personality and behavior which a potential love-object must conform with before the lover will devote his power to love to that object. The concepts of the "ideal wife" and "ideal husband" may be the most crucial determiners of whom a young man or woman will select, or "fall in love with." The young adult observes the "passing parade" of potential spouses, and when he observes someone who accords with his ideals, he may then pursue this person as the object of his present and future loving-behavior. There is considerable cultural stereotypy in the characteristics which define the beautiful and/or ideal person who will be one's love-object, but there may be much individual variability as well. Langhorne and Secord,[8] in one study, showed that unmarried college males sought a "pleasing personality," tenderness and consideration, moral uprightness, and a complex trait which included health, emotional maturity, stability, and intelligence. Any clinician or personality therapist may be quite aware of some of the deviations from the norm in the choice of a love-object. Freud [9] described a class of men who were most attracted to women who were the "property" of another man, or whose fidelity and sexual propriety were questionable. The author knows of men who can love, or who seek to love only women who are much older, or much younger. The range of possible variability in object-choice is remarkable. The reasons for this variability probably stem from life-history experiences which deviate somewhat from the modal life-history experiences of the average male and female. Thus, the man whom one woman is attracted to as a potential love-object may be repugnant, or fear-inspiring to another.

THE ABILITY OF THE LOVE-OBJECT TO RECIPROCATE LOVE. A person may not experience the desire to love another person *until and unless* the other person shows clear signs of a desire to love first. In other words, the person can be moved to love if and only if he has been first assured that he is loved. It is almost as if the would-be lover is afraid to risk possible rejection of his or her loving-behavior, or else is not willing to love unless there is some guarantee that the love will be returned.

RATIONAL CHOICE OF A LOVE-OBJECT. This discussion applies mainly to marriage, where mutuality of love is almost a sine qua non of a successful and happy marriage. In our culture, the custom obtains that would-be spouses must first "fall in love" with each other, before they consider marriage. The process of falling in love is itself a nonrational phenomenon, probably based on strong need-deprivation of a sexual sort. When a person in our culture is in love, he and she display most of the characteristics associated with deprivation, viz.: preoccupation with the need-object, "overestimation" [10] of the value of the object, a desire to possess and "consume" the object so as to appease the hunger, etc. In fact, what is called romantic love might better be called a special variety of hunger, for it is not love. Romantic love becomes active loving when the lovers actually behave in ways which will produce mutual gratifications and happiness, and which will promote growth in each other. The hunger to "be loved" may serve as a factor which brings people together. But whether or not love can emerge from romantic love depends on the actual loving-capacity of each partner, and the *actual* suitability of each person's traits for promoting happiness and growth in the other.

To fall in love, or to be in love, is exciting and fun. But the healthy lovers are those who postpone commitment one to the other in marriage until there has been an opportunity for reality-testing to occur. The romantic lover is inclined to construct autistic concepts of the object: to idealize, to underrate the importance and relevance of other traits in the object for his future happiness, to overlook genuine shortcomings and deficiencies which signify an inability to love, etc.

Since we value romance as well as active love in our culture, it might be said that a rational choice of an object for loving has been made when the other person does induce romantic affect in oneself, but who also possesses the actual personality-structure and traits which the lover *can* love; the object also has the personality-structure and traits which will insure that the love will be mutual.

Concretely, this means that the person who is "in love" must soberly ask himself the question, at some time prior to marriage, "Can I make this person happy, and can I help her to grow, in the long run? Can she make me happy, and help me to grow?" Obviously, the more reality-based the answers are to these questions, the more likely is it that a rational choice will be made.

FACTORS WHICH PROMOTE AN UNHEALTHY OBJECT-CHOICE

Let us consider some of the factors which will impair the capacity of a person to make a rational object-choice.

CHRONIC STRONG NEEDS. An individual with strong, unsatisfied needs will be likely to perceive other persons in an autistic fashion.[11] He will seek satisfaction of his immediate needs, and ignore other traits of the object that are important to his growth and *overall* happiness. In consequence, he might choose a person for a love-object who can gratify this need. He doesn't realize he has other needs and values that will emerge into importance when the present needs have been satisfied.

Thus, the inadequate man who needs to be taken care of and to have decisions made for him, may fall in love with a dominant woman. Eventually, he may outgrow his need for dominance and require other modes of behavior from the woman. If she cannot

change her ways of behaving toward him, an impasse may arise
which will result in termination of the relationship.

Or, a man may be attracted only to women who are "owned"
by another man—the fact of being the property of another man constitutes their appeal.[12] And so he pursues and wins such a woman.
Once he has won her, he then might "look her over," as it were, and
find that she doesn't have what it takes to make him happy. His
need, if it can be called such, is to prove himself a better man than
others—and if the psychoanalysts are correct, it may be an outgrowth of an unresolved "Oedipus complex."

LACK OF SELF-KNOWLEDGE. The person who is alienated from his
real self, whose self-concept is inaccurate, may be said not to know
what he needs from another person to make him happy, or to help
him grow. Since his choice of a love-object is not based upon consideration of these important factors, it will be based on other
criteria which are irrelevant to growth and happiness. Thus, he
might choose a possible wife just on the basis of appearance alone
—because other people regard the woman as desirable. He doesn't
know if he really desires the woman; rather, he wants her because
he believes he ought to. This would be the case with the other-
directed character described by Riesman. Or, he may choose a
woman as a possible mate because his parents, or his conscience,
demand he make that choice.[13] Again, he is ignoring, or is ignorant
of, his own needs and wants. It is not rare for a person to fall in
love, court, and marry someone, and then, much later, come face to
face with his real self and wonder, "How did I ever get joined to
this person?"

LACK OF KNOWLEDGE OF THE OBJECT. It was pointed out earlier[14]
that there is only one way to acquire an accurate other-concept:
that is, to observe, to come to tentative conclusions, and then continuously to modify these conclusions as more observations are
made. This calls for time to make many observations of the behavior
of the object in a wide range of life-situations.

When this procedure has not been adopted by the would-be lover,
then it follows that his concept of the object will be autistic, or inaccurate. That is, it will be based on need-selective observation,
attribution, disowning or assimilative projection, hearsay, or other
mechanisms which guarantee inaccurate other-concepts.[15]

The experience of falling in love, with its accompanying intense needs and feelings, is without exception an experience which occurs in relation to an *inaccurate* concept of the object. The romantic "lover" does not know his object. He doesn't know if he can love her, nor if she has what it takes to love him. She (or he) is a *construct,* a creation of the needs and fantasies of the lover. Marriages contracted while romantic affect is high and intense may either break up later, or become incompatible with growth and happiness of the partners—unless by accident each partner happens to have the traits or the flexibility to love the other in a healthy way. When the romantic affect "wears off," each partner may then discover (possibly with a shock) that they have needs which they were not aware of at the time of the marriage-ceremony, and which the other person cannot fulfill; nor can they gratify the needs of the other person.

LOVE AND PERSONALITY HYGIENE

We have stated that the ability to love *actively* is a personality-hygiene value, and that the person who cannot love is "sick" in basic ways. By the same token, the person who is afraid or unable to *accept* love may be regarded as sick. Since incapacity at loving and at accepting love is regarded as a psychiatric symptom, let us inquire into some of the conditions of loving.

THE NEED TO LOVE ACTIVELY AND THE NEED TO BE LOVED PASSIVELY. We are born helpless, and so we need to be loved. We must be the love-objects of our parents if we are to survive in the physical sense. There is evidence that we need to be loved in order to grow in a psychological sense as well. Sheer physical care is now known to be insufficient as a determiner of healthy personality growth. Unless the child has received loving care, including emotional displays of affection, and attention to his idiosyncratic needs, he is likely to grow in deviant ways. Spitz,[16] for example, showed that children raised from birth in a foundling home, with adequate physical care but no personalized attention from a mother-figure, were retarded in physical growth, were less resistant to disease, and were retarded in their overall "developmental quotients," compared to infants raised by their own mothers. Goldfarb [17] showed that institution-raised children, by the time they reached adolescence, were severely handicapped in their ability to relate to others on an emotional and loving basis. Ribble [18] saw a lack of "adequate mothering" as a causal factor in the development of infantile *marasmus*—a rare disease in which the infant literally wastes away. And Spitz [19] showed that "anaclitic depression" in infants was the by-product of separation from the mother. It would appear to be definitely established that in infancy and early childhood, passive love is needed both for physical growth and for optimum personality growth toward health.

It is doubtful if anyone ever completely loses the need to be loved passively. The strength of the conscious longings for passive love, however, is probably related to the amount of passive love-indulgence which a person has experienced. If from early infancy, a child has had no passive love, he may grow into a psychopath who is incapable of active loving, and who experiences no conscious longings for passive love. If, on the other hand, the child has had a "taste" of passive love, just enough to learn that it feels good but not enough to satisfy, then he may develop what Levy called "primary affect hunger," [20] and pursue passive love for the rest of his life at all cost.

It seems likely that the ability to love actively is an outgrowth of having one's passive love-needs gratified earlier in life. There is a logical basis for such a statement, as well as empirical grounding. A person whose needs are greatly thwarted is a "hungry" person, seeking to be filled. When one is empty, one can hardly give. Active love seems to rest on the "economics of plenty" rather than on "scarcity economics." [21] The healthy lover is as one who is "filled," and who gives freely to his objects, not only because of the object's need, but because of the lover's abundance. He gives out of the joys of giving with no preconceived notion of getting something in return.

No one, however, is that "full" that he can love endlessly without receiving loving-behavior in return. In mutual love-relationships, if the partners have chosen wisely, each can give freely what the other needs, and each receives in return, freely given, what is needed for happiness and growth. Thus, it is doubtful if a parent could actively love young children without receiving love from the spouse, or from the children, or from some source. It is doubtful if a personality therapist could meet the needs of his patients if he was not receiving love from his spouse or friends.

But once a person has approached mature years, society expects him or her to have the capacity and the desire to become an active lover. If the person has been sufficiently loved in the past, the likelihood will be increased that he will be able to establish a mutual loving-relationship with another person, rather than a relationship of continued passivity and dependency.

Let us try to highlight some of the factors which appear to promote the capacity to love actively as well as the ability freely to accept the loving-behavior of another.

SOME DETERMINERS OF THE ABILITY TO LOVE ACTIVELY

RICH NEED-GRATIFICATION IN THE PAST AND PRESENT.[22] As a general rule, the person who experiences rich need-gratification will be in a position to become an active lover. He is not obliged to devote all of his efforts to personal need-satisfaction. He can afford to use some of his time, skills, and energies for other people's happiness and growth.

AN AFFIRMATION OF THE VALUE OF LOVE. If a person has acquired a strong sense of the worth and value of love in and for itself, then he will undoubtedly seek out opportunities to love. His self-esteem will be based, at least in part, on his ability to love actively. In other words, unless he is involved in an active loving-relationship, he may feel less than whole and fully "actualized"—less than a whole person.

HIGH FRUSTRATION-TOLERANCE. Loving another person often involves deprivation of some of one's own needs. The more fully developed is the lover's ability to tolerate periods of privation, the better able will he be to love his object.

SELF-LOVE. Fromm has pointed out, in an important essay,[23] that love of self and love of some other person are not mutually exclusive, as was long believed. He states emphatically that one can love another only if one loves oneself. "Love of self and love of other are conjunctive, not exclusive." The rationale behind this precept may be stated in these terms: to love oneself means that one will be concerned with his own growth and happiness and will behave in ways which implement these values. Self-loving, in a real sense, gives one actual practice in loving; to the extent that others are similar to the self, then these ways of acting which constitute self-love will make another person happy if they are directed to that person. Self-love makes one attentive to one's own needs and probably increases one's sensitivity to the needs of others; if one has experienced needs and gratifications, one can visualize more vividly what the object's needs and gratifications feel like.

It should also be pointed out that healthy self-love is an outgrowth of having been loved, by parents, and other significant persons; [24] and we have shown that the experience of having been loved promotes one's active-love capacity.

When one ignores or hates oneself, one is less likely to be able to love others. The self-hater is unable to love others because he usually claims total obedience from those for whom he has "sacrificed" so much. The mother described by Sidney Howard in *The Silver Cord* [25] was such a martyr, who "loved" her sons more than she did herself—she sacrificed her own happiness on their (unasked) behalf. All she wanted in return was complete conformity with her wishes and demands, which is incompatible with genuine love. Rather, it is a subtle form of dictatorship.

Indeed, psychoanalysts regard excessive "unselfishness" as a neurotic trait, while such personality hygienists as Maslow [26] and Fromm [27] place a positive value on "healthy" selfishness. This is no more than a recognition on the basis of clinical experience and careful observation that the person who is concerned for his own growth and happiness will have acted so as to promote it; in consequence, he is a better person, and better able to give. He has more to give in active love, more "self." And since "self" is, in the last analysis, all that is or can be given in love, it follows that the more self one has to give to the object, the more gratification will the object receive from such a gift.

A DIVERSIFIED PERSONALITY-STRUCTURE. The broader the behavior repertoire a lover has, *the more diversified will be the kinds of needs of the object which he can gratify through his loving-behavior.* This breadth, of course, presumes that the individual has no inner barriers, such as an unhealthy self-structure, to the full use of his entire behavior repertoire. If he has, then he will experience threat whenever he is about to behave in a loving manner, and so he will suppress the loving-behavior.

A HEALTHY SELF-STRUCTURE.[28] If the lover has a self-concept, a self-ideal, and public selves which permit him to function at the real-self level, then his loving capacity will be promoted (see Chapter 9). In other words, the lover will have access to all of his behavior potential. He will not be obliged to exclude some ways of behaving in his love-relationships because of the need to defend an unrealistic self-concept or to conform with a false public self or an excessively strict self-ideal and conscience.

Thus if the object wants tenderness, affection, domination, etc., the healthy lover will be able to sense these needs and behave in a gratifying way without a sense of forcing, faking, or threatening himself. Indeed, if the healthy personality is defined as the individual who can gratify his needs by behavior which is personally and socially acceptable, then *the healthy lover can be defined as the one who can gratify the needs of the object by means of behavior which is personally and socially acceptable.*

In principle, the more diversified the personality-structure of an individual and the healthier his self-structure, the broader the range of persons whom he can effectively love. Practically, however, the healthy lover probably prefers to seek an object who has an equally diversified personality and healthy self-structure, since his needs may require just such a person to love him. Anyone with a less differentiated personality would be less able to meet his needs.

REALITY-CONTACT. It takes accurate knowledge of the object to be able to love effectively; the person with autistic other-concepts will generally be unable to love in a way which meets the needs of the object. As Fromm has pointed out, the lover must *know* his object. Very often, a person may suffer a handicap in love because he cannot interpret accurately what his object needs, in spite of his willingness to provide it if able.

SECURITY—FREEDOM FROM IRRATIONAL FEAR AND ANXIETY. Probably fear and anxiety are among the factors most responsible for impairment of the capacity to love. The fearful person is much more likely to be dependent to a morbid degree on his object; he

may give, not out of love, but out of fear of being ridiculed, or rejected. The more secure a person, the more likely will he be able
to employ his whole self in loving.

A person may withhold much loving-behavior because of unwarranted fears. Thus the author has observed a man who would not
display signs of affection to his wife, on the unwarranted assumption she would scorn him as a weakling. In his past, he had learned
to suppress and to repress open affection as a means of being safe.
He expected women to interpret open affection as a sign the man
was weak and easily exploited. In truth, his wife was yearning for
affection from him.

REASONABLE IDEALS FOR THE LOVE-OBJECT. Before a person can
actually love some object, the object must be available and chosen.
It may happen that a person constructs such impossible ideals and
expectations as conditions for expressing his own love, that no
human could ever hope to qualify. He may then engage in an endless and fruitless quest for the "worthy" and "perfect" recipient of
his love. Of course, he will never find this paragon, or else he will
experience perpetual disillusionment. If it happens that a person
has married on grounds other than love, he may place such stringent
conditions on his love that it is never given. The spouse doesn't
"deserve" his love, and must meet his impossible demands for perfection before it will be given.

It becomes apparent that one can love only if one's demands and
ideals with respect to the object are within the latter's capacity to
conform. Reasonable demands and ideals apropos the object are
likely to be held by a person who holds reasonable demands and
expectations of himself.

EMANCIPATION FROM PARENTAL DIRECTION. When a person cannot
direct his behavior in accordance with his real self, his capacity to
love his object may be impaired. A person who is not alienated from
his real self will be better able to govern his loving-behavior in
accordance with the needs and wishes of his object and with his
own real feelings and wishes. But if the person still suffers from an
"unresolved oedipus situation," or if he behaves so as to please his
parents, his capacity to love may be reduced markedly. The reason
for this lies in the fact that much of the behavior which might be
necessary to promote happiness in the spouse may be tabooed or

condemned by the parents, and the individual cannot displease his parents. The psychoanalysts have shown that much of the sexual difficulty in marriage, viz.: impotence and frigidity, derives from a failure to emancipate the self from parental control, and a failure to withdraw unconscious sexual interest in the parents. It is as if the spouse cannot devote love and sex to the partner, because unconsciously love and sex "belong" to the opposite-sexed parent.

EMANCIPATION FROM "INNER-DIRECTION." Riesman's concept of "inner-direction"[29] describes the individual whose behavior is governed, not by the real self, but rather by the need to conform with a very stern conscience. If one of the spouses, or both, are inner-directed characters, their capacity to love the other may be strikingly reduced. Much of the behavior which would meet the needs of the other might induce guilt, and so must be suppressed. The consequence may be that freedom from guilt is achieved, but at the cost of misery in the self and in the love-object.

SOME DETERMINERS OF THE ABILITY TO ACCEPT LOVE

It may seem surprising to the reader that some individuals find it hard, if not impossible, to accept love which is freely given by others; yet such is the case, as any personality therapist can attest.

Some persons cannot accept the deepest expressions of the real self of another person who loves them. They find such expression cloying, or threatening, or embarrassing. When someone loves them, they become suspicious of the lover—the lover may be just pretending to love in order to disarm him and make him vulnerable. Or the lover may be trying to get the individual to do something. The person who cannot accept love may hold the false assumption that to accept love implies that one needs love, and to need love means one is weak.

We may generalize and suggest that the factors which might prevent a person from accepting love, genuine loving-behavior, from others, include (a) *inaccurate other-concepts,* and (b) *repression of the need to be loved.*

INACCURATE OTHER-CONCEPTS. Because of past experiences with people, the individual may project, or attribute motives to others which they do not in fact possess. He may assume they do not, or cannot love him. If he believes this, then he will probably misinterpret loving-behavior from others; he will believe their behavior toward him is motivated by sentiments other than active and unselfish concern for his own welfare and happiness.

REPRESSION OF THE NEED TO BE LOVED. In the past, the individual's longings for love may have been thwarted, or he may have been deeply hurt in his quest for gratification of his need to be loved. The consequence may be that he represses his need for passive love; he may, indeed, develop *reaction-formations* against his love-needs and make loud protestations of his independence from others: "I don't need anybody for anything." Such a person may actually strive to prevent other people from loving him, with considerable success in such efforts.

The healthy personality is able to accept freely given love just as he is able to give love freely. He does not demand love from his lover, as a duty for the lover. Rather, he assumes that if he is loved, the lover is giving out of free will, with no strings attached, and so he can accept it without guilt or fear.

LOVE AND DEPENDENCY

Although we have placed a positive valuation upon autonomy and self-sufficiency, this is a relative matter. In the first place, it is impossible for a person to be completely self-sufficient; indeed, attempts directed toward complete independence of everyone may be regarded as pathological, since they are likely to be predicated on a profound irrational distrust of all people.

In the second place, it is undesirable for a person not to need people for some things. People want to feel needed by those to whom they feel close. Thus, it can be said that there are occasions where actual dependency upon another person is an expression of active loving, for it implies trust and accords dignity and worthwhileness to the one who is needed and depended upon.

A healthy love-relationship probably involves two persons who are relatively self-sufficient in most ways, but who are mutually dependent one on the other for important gratifications. The love-relationship thus involves mutual giving and mutual taking, mutual needing and mutual willingness to provide what is needed.

The lover, in an important sense, needs his object, or is dependent upon his object, in spite of marked self-sufficiency in many areas. He needs his object, at least the love-relationship, in order to enrich his own gratification-experiences; he needs his object as a means of promoting his own growth; he needs the relationship so as to enrich self-esteem.

Dependency in a love-relationship is compatible with personality health when it does not involve undue suppression of the real self in either partner, and when each partner does not use the other's dependency as a means of controlling his life.

It may happen in a marriage, for example, that one spouse may use sex as a means of controlling the behavior of the other. A wife whose sexual needs were apparently less frequent or urgent than her husband's used sexual compliance almost as a club to force her spouse to do her will. We could hardly call this relationship a love-relationship. Because of the social mores, the husband was dependent upon his wife for sexual gratification, as she was upon him; but she was content with the frequency of coitus while he was not. She took advantage of his dependency and discontent to regulate his life in accordance with her often unreasonable wishes.

How Many People Can an Individual Love?

Love is activity, and there are limits upon how many things a person can do. If one devotes more time and attention to one sphere of activity, then other spheres of possible activity will suffer relative neglect. Consider an analogy. A farmer has numerous fields, numerous kinds of livestock, buildings to maintain, and a family to look after. If he spends all of his time and skill at cultivating his cornfields, then his wheatfields and vegetable plots will become overrun with weeds; his farm buildings will begin to deteriorate from neglect, and his livestock may fall victim to diseases owing to lack of prophylactic measures. In order to be an adequate farmer, he has got to apportion his time so that everything is attended to according to its requirements.

Now, a grown-up man or woman has many things to attend to, not the least in importance being the needs of the people whom he loves. Thus, the husband must earn a living and satisfy his own urges toward productivity and status, but he also wants to promote the growth and happiness of his wife and children. Often, there will be sharp and poignant conflicts experienced by the man with respect

to how he will divide himself. How much of himself should he give
to his work and how much to his wife and children? His friends?
His parents? Is there room in his life for other loves in addition to
his wife and children?

There is no simple answer to this question. The needs of the lover,
and the needs of the love-objects, have got to be taken into consideration. In addition, there will be broad individual differences
from love-relationship to love-relationship with respect to the
"amount of self" which must be invested.

In some marriages, for example, the wife is quite happy and able
to grow, with only occasional contacts with the husband, who may
be immersed in a career or travelling at his occupation. In others,
the wife may receive the loving attention of her spouse for all of
his time away from his work, and it is yet not enough to make her
happy.

Since there is a limit on how many things a person can *do,* there
is thus a limit on the number of people a person can *love.*

Many a wife has complained her husband loves his work or his
hobbies more than he loves her. If he devotes more of his undivided
attention to these than he does to her needs, then to that extent
she is correct.

The healthy personality is able, like the good farmer, to apportion
his time and his instrumental behavior, so that he is able to har-
monize his own needs with the growth and happiness of his loved
ones. This is not a simple task, but one which requires continuous
reassessment, readjustment, and vigilance.

In cases where a wife or husband loves some other person more
than the spouse, for example, a parent or a child, and the ignored
spouse does not complain, then it signifies the needs of the ignored
one are not very intense or diversified, since they are so readily
gratified. Usually, however, a spouse needs all of the partner's love
which is available, and is willing to share this loving-behavior only
with the children.

We may now provide an answer to the question, "How many
people can an individual love?" *A healthy personality actively loves
as many people as he can, without doing violence to his own growth
and happiness and the growth and happiness of his objects.*

This answer is sufficiently flexible to allow for individual differences in the capacity of the individual to love, and in the needs of objects, differences which occur between persons, and in the same individual at different stages in his life.

Thus, a healthy personality may be able to love his wife and his children, and nobody else. He may *like* many people and have many friends, but if he is to avoid spreading himself too thin, he is obliged to limit his loving-behavior to his wife and children. If he has a choice between meeting the needs of a friend and those of his family, he will select his family as the object of his loving-behavior. If, on the other hand, his family can "afford" to allow him to "spend" himself on friends (at the time, his family is not in need), then he will be able to work for the growth and happiness of his friends.

When a person's own growth and happiness are in jeopardy, his ability to love others actively is impaired. Since he can love actively only when he is happy and growing, then he will be in accord with personality-hygiene precepts if he attends to his own needs before those of others. While this may sound selfish [30]—yet it may be seen that he cannot love actively and effectively when he is less than a whole and fully-functioning person. An individual with an un-healthy personality may devote his time, attention, and money to personality-therapy, the while ignoring the needs of people who are close to him. This is desirable, since he will be a more effective lover *after* he has taken care of his own growth.

THE PRODUCTION OF LOVE FOR THE SELF IN OTHERS

It commonly occurs that an individual believes no one could ever love him and that he is powerless to induce someone to love him. This belief may stem from a childhood which was devoid of parental love and an adolescence devoid of friendship and peer-acceptance.

How does one induce others to love him? Ignoring for the time being such factors as attractive appearance, we can assert that *love begets love*. Active concern for the needs of another individual will, in general, tend to motivate the other person to become actively concerned for the growth and happiness of the giver. Unfortunately, a vicious circle often appears. The unhappy person who believes no one can love him is usually in such a chronic condition of need-deprivation that he cannot give to others freely and unstintingly. Hence, while he may be pitied by others, he is unlikely to be loved by them. How can one break this vicious circle? How can one arrange it so that the person who "hath not" love will be given love? The biblical precept, "To him that hath shall be given," seems to hold true for love.

In our society, the love-deprived individual may be able to reach a stage wherein he becomes able to love only through effective personality therapy. The professional personality therapist is, in a sense, a source of love for the deprived individual.[31] The therapist behaves toward his patient in ways which will promote growth and happiness—and this is love, albeit without romance. Through successful therapy, an individual may acquire the capacity to love others, and thus make it possible to induce others to love him.

Love and the Self-Structure

We have alluded several times to the fact that a person's capacity to love is influenced by the nature of his self-structure. Let us see more directly some of the ways in which the self-structure imposes limits on love.

LOVE AND THE SELF-CONCEPT.[32] The self-concept refers to the system of beliefs which an individual holds with respect to his personality. In general, a person strives to delimit his behavior within the framework of these beliefs. Behavior which conflicts with these beliefs generates threat, and the threat impels the individual to exclude that behavior from his repertoire, if he is to defend his self-concept. Now, love is behavior. In order to gratify the needs of the object, the lover is obliged to act in many and diverse ways. Not all of these modes of behavior will be in accord with the lover's self-concept, and will hence generate threat. What should the lover do, when he faces a conflict between preserving his present self-concept and meeting the needs of his love-object? The general answer is this: If to love his object threatens his self-concept, and if the requisite change of the self-concept is in the direction of a healthier self-structure, then he should act in the way required by his love-object and strive to alter his self-concept. If, on the other hand, to gratify his object's needs would move him further away from personality health, then he must ignore the love-object's needs.

An example will clarify this point. Let us suppose that a lover believes he is inadequate and lacks the ability to do certain things, for instance, change occupations. He may not be abjectly miserable in his present occupation but he would like to change to another. The reason he does not is because he believes he does not have the capacity to learn new skills. His wife wants him to change occupations for assorted reasons, and he wants to please his wife. He may make the change and discover in fact he does have the capacity to learn his new vocation. Thus he has altered his self-concept and met the needs of his wife.

On the other hand, a husband may need his wife to be subservient to him, in order to warrant a component belief of his self-concept that he is strong and dominant. His wife, on the other hand, has come to realize she no longer is helpless and subservient, but rather a fairly self-reliant person. She has to choose between her own growth and keeping her husband free of threat. Her choice, if it is to accord with personality-hygiene precepts, must be as follows: She must eliminate the subservient behavior from her repertoire and *be herself*, that is, act in accord with her healthier self-concept. Thus she has moved closer to personality health, but she has threatened her husband's self-concept. This throws the responsibility back to her husband as to whether he will handle the threat in a healthy way, or in a defensive and unhealthy way.

LOVE AND THE SELF-IDEAL.[33] The self-ideal refers to the individual's conscience: the ideals, values and taboos with which he strives to conform, and which he strives to approach. It will be recalled that self-esteem is a function of the extent to which a person's actual behavior conforms with his self-ideal. Failure to conform with the self-ideal produces guilt, self-hate, inferiority-feelings, hurt pride, etc.

In order to love effectively and in healthy fashion, a person must have a fairly broad repertoire of behavior patterns and roles at his disposal. The reason for this has been pointed out earlier. As his love-object's needs vary, so must his loving-behavior, if he is to promote the happiness and growth of the object. But if some of the behavior objectively required (in order to keep the object growing and happy) is in conflict with the self-ideal, then again the lover faces a rather sharp value-conflict. *Which is more important, the happiness of his object, or the maintenance of self-esteem?*

Again, we can provide a principle which would enable us to

assess a given solution to such a conflict, but there are obviously no recipes which we could offer to resolve the conflict when it arises with two given persons.

In principle, the conflict may be resolved by a decision which is the most productive of growth and happiness in both the lover and his object.

Thus, if the lover's conscience, or self-ideal is *excessively restrictive*, he may be obliged to take whatever steps might be necessary to alter his self-ideal, if he is to grow and at the same time maintain his love-relationship with his object. On the other hand, he may decide the needs of his object could not be gratified by him, since to do so would cause him to lose self-esteem. Since he believes he has a healthy conscience, he decides to affirm his values and ignore his object's needs.

In every relationship, a conflict will at some time arise between the maintenance of pride, or self-esteem (conforming with the self-ideal), and acting in ways which will please or satisfy the object. The individuals involved in the relationship may not always be able to formulate the nature of the conflict very clearly, or understand it. All that each might realize is that in pleasing the object, they "don't feel right about it," or they feel vaguely uneasy, or they are not "being true to themselves."

When a person habitually neglects his real self in this way (his values are part of his real self, as are the feelings of uneasiness which he might vaguely experience when he conforms with his object's demands or needs), the relationship is almost by definition unhealthy (see Chapter 7). A conflict between a person's self-ideal and the needs of the object is one kind of impasse, and we have seen it is not healthy to avoid an impasse by repressing one or the other aspect of it. Continuous conforming with the object's demands, while ignoring one's own pride or values, is an active move away from the real self, as Horney would put it, and is productive of unhappiness and the reverse of growth.

The only healthy way to resolve a conflict between the self-ideal of a lover and the needs of his object, is to sharpen the conflict as much and as openly as possible, so that an autonomous and responsible decision can be made by either partner, a decision which will be acted upon, and in which the decider is willing to accept the consequences. The person may withdraw the demand or seek to satisfy the need in other ways. The lover may strive to alter his self-ideal, in order to be able to satisfy his loved one without inner conflict. Or, he may elect to avoid satisfying the other, and face the consequence of the relationship possibly ending then and there. Whatever the outcome, if the impasse is openly faced and resolved in the manner suggested above, it is compatible with the precepts of personality hygiene.

LOVE AND THE REAL SELF.[34] In no other kind of relationship is it more important than in love that the participants act at a real-self level, rather than in accord with other determiners of actions; e.g. an unhealthy conscience, the expectations of others, an unhealthy self-concept, a formal role, etc. To act at the real-self level implies each partner is willing and able to announce and express unequivocally what he feels, needs, wants, expects, thinks, and is willing in addition to face the consequences of so acting. In an earlier chapter, it was pointed out that full and honest communication was the means by which impasses were created and resolved, the means actually by which growth of the self-structure was promoted.

When this openness of mutual communication is missing, the relationship cannot be called a love-relationship, but instead must be called a friendship, a habitual companionship, or something of the sort.

The love-object makes his needs known by full disclosure of his real self to the lover. The lover will know whether he honestly wants to meet these needs only if he can experience his own real self fully.

When the participants in a relationship simply enact a social role, the role of husband, wife, or teacher, without regard to their own feelings, then the relationship loses the vital and often intensely felt quality of a love-relationship.

If a wife or husband has been constructing a false public self in relation to the spouse, then their behavior will not express the real self; instead it will aim at consistency with the public self. The consequence will be that the person constructing the public self will have many unfulfilled needs, and the partner will acquire an increasingly inaccurate other-concept, or concept of the real self of the partner. In a love relationship, the partners want to make themselves known as they are.

LOVE, MARRIAGE, AND DIVORCE

When and whom should a person marry? When should a divorce occur? In this day and age, when almost one marriage in three terminates in divorce, and when the persons who remain married often feel quite trapped, or unhappy in the relationship, the questions above become crucial. It is difficult to proffer answers of a helpful sort to these questions, however, since there are many values at stake in a marriage.

The reasons for undertaking marriage in the first place are numerous and varied. Young couples enter marriage for companionship, for an opportunity to raise a family, for sexual gratification, to change their status in the eyes of the community, or, in a more general sense, they enter marriage on the premise they will find greater happiness in the married state than in the single state. They are often dismally wrong, unfortunately, as the divorce-rates attest.

In Chapter 7, we provided some criteria for assessing whether a relationship such as a marriage was a healthy one. When a marriage relationship deviates strikingly from these criteria, the participants experience the marriage as flat, dead, devoid of meaning or satisfactions, or more emphatically, they may experience the marriage as positively agonizing, stifling to the self and partner. When this state of affairs arises, action is called for, unless the participants are of the unhealthy type which seeks, or needs punishment (unconscious guilt, masochism). When there are children in the family, an additional problem is presented, since the children will require some care that will help them attain maturity and personality health.

If the partners are unable to face and work through interpersonal impasses themselves, in a growth-productive manner, then ideally each or both together should consult a personality therapist. With expert outside assistance, each partner can often be helped to grow, so that an autonomous, responsible and mutually agreed-upon reconciliation, or divorce, can be arrived at. When the partners will not avail themselves of such help, or seek it out, then the probability is high that whatever decision they make will be incompatible with their own personality health and the personality health of the children. It is an open question whether children are better off, from a personality hygiene point of view, living with two unhealthy parents enmeshed in an unhealthy marital relationship. A strong case could be constructed to show that children raised by one parent who is divorced from the other, where the divorce was a healthy one, have a greater chance of attaining personality health than the children raised in a miserable marriage.

WHEN IS A DIVORCE HEALTHY? A divorce is healthy when it becomes apparent that the changes necessary to "healthify" the marriage are just not practicable. There are limits to how much a person can change his personality structure in order to meet the needs of a partner; and often the changes which would be required to keep a marriage going would be personality changes in a direction away from health. Thus, one partner may need the other to be an absolute paragon of perfection in a moral sense, in order to be happy. No amount of feasible change could make the partner attain those ideals. Further, no amount of personality therapy is successful in altering the needs of the spouse who demands perfection. They may be too deeply rooted. Perhaps, in such an impasse, the best that can happen is divorce, in the fervent hope that each will be better able to grow when separated from the other (something which happens quite often), or that if they don't grow, and still want to marry, they will find a spouse with an unhealthy personality which complements their own.

The author has observed several instances where a marriage went "stale," and where insurmountable impasses existed between the partners. Each needed the other to be different but neither partner could comply, or wanted to comply, with the other's demands and needs. A personality hygienist could ascertain quite readily in observing the unhappy partners that neither of them came very close to the traits of a healthy personality. When a divorce finally occurred, each partner became, almost like magic, the embodiment of the desires and needs of the former spouse (perhaps out of unconscious or conscious hostility?). Then after some time, the partners would (with or without the aid of a personality therapist) move in the direction of a healthy personality. It seemed, then, that their prior relationship was a factor which blocked growth, rather than promoted it. The traits which drew the couple together into marriage in the beginning later became obstacles to growth.

In one marriage, the man "fell in love" with his wife because she was cute, childish, innocent, dependent, she lisped charmingly, etc. He evidently needed to enact a father-like role for assorted reasons, and she needed to be fathered. As time proceeded, he began to feel the need of an adult peer in his marriage, and he made this need known to his wife. She reacted always with tears, and the assertion "You don't love me any more." She could not change her interpersonal behavior. He divorced her, and remarried. She suffered considerably through the divorce, sought therapeutic help, and eventually she achieved an understanding of the reasons for her infantile characteristics; she was assisted in growing to a healthier level. She remarried, and the new marriage appeared to be a healthier one.

PARENTAL LOVE

Mother-love has been regarded by many observers throughout the ages as the prototype and ideal for love. In more general terms, parental love indeed exemplifies loving-behavior in a relatively clear-cut way. Parents are expected to know, care for, respect, and assume responsibility for, their children. Most parents want to behave toward their children in ways which will promote the happiness and growth of the children. Parental love is primarily active love, at least while the children are very young. Frequently, it is in the role of parents that many people first show an incapacity to love actively, to take care of their children without receiving anything concrete in return. A man or a woman may have been the passive recipient of parental love and of the love of the spouse. When children come along, the passive person is unable to rise to the demands of parenthood. In view of the crucial importance of parents for the personality health of children, it will repay us to inquire further into the parental role and parental love.

It is now recognized generally that the nature of the parent-child relationship strongly influences the course of personality development in the child. The clinical study of people with various personality illnesses shows with marked regularity all kinds of disturbances in the patients' early relationships with their parents. Sociologists regard the family as a kind of "socializing factory," where relatively unshaped biological raw material (the newborn infant) is brought in at one phase, and a modal personality is turned out at another.[35] There are some personality therapists who, on the basis of their experience, believe they can pick out "schizophrenic-producing" and "obsessive-compulsive-producing" mothers and fathers. The mental hygiene movement directs much of its preventive work toward parent education, on the premise that if parents have the right attitudes, and relate toward their children in the right ways, then personality illnesses will be decreased, and personality health will become more prevalent.

We may well ask the question, "How must mothers and fathers relate toward their children so as to promote the development of healthy personality?" This very question rests on the assumption, of course, that the way in which parents behave toward their children will indeed influence the latter's personality development.

Mothering and fathering behavior—the mother-role and the father-role—are largely defined by society. Each society defines these roles in its own characteristic way. Thus, Mead [36] showed how, in three primitive societies, all within a small geographical radius of one another in New Guinea, there were striking variations from society to society in male and female personality, and as well, striking variations in the way the parents behaved toward their children. Another illustration of variability in parental behavior is provided by Whiting and Child's book,[37] in which they compare the socialization practices of 75 societies in the world. Within a given society, however, there is likely to be much less variability from parent to parent in the style of relating to the children, except, of course, for differences associated with personality structure.

If we accept the view that the socially-defined modes of relating to children have the function of producing modal personalities for a given society or at least preparing children so they will eventually become modal personalities, then we can ask, "How is it that in spite of cultural pressures, some parents 'fail' to raise their children 'right'?" Many children in our society grow up to be criminals, neurotics, and psychotics. Further, since we regard the healthy personality as something different from the modal, or normal personality, "How can parents relate to their children so that the latter will become healthy?"

One way of answering this last question is to assert: If the parents establish a healthy relationship with their children, as defined in the previous chapter, then the probability increases that the children will become healthy personalities in their own right. Let us examine parent-child relationships first in the light of our criteria for healthy interpersonal relationships.

EVALUATING PARENT-CHILD RELATIONSHIPS

KNOWLEDGE OF THE CHILD. The first characteristic of a healthy interpersonal relationship consists in *accurate knowledge* of the other person. We cannot expect an infant to know the personality and needs of his parents, but we expect the parents to learn their children's idiosyncrasies and general needs.

We can assert that optimally, parents will strive to formulate an accurate concept of their child's needs. This knowledge is most crucial during the first few years of life.[38] Unless the parents understand what their child needs in order to experience rich gratification and to grow physically and psychologically, the danger is great that many of the infant's needs will be overlooked and neglected. It has only recently come to be known that infants need *more* than adequate physical hygiene, balanced food-diets, etc. if they are to grow both physically and psychologically in valued directions. It has been found they need a personalized relationship with a mother-figure, with much cuddling, caressing, vocalizing, smiling, and other kinds of behavior which used to be called "spoiling." [39] When infants are deprived of attendance to these newly rediscovered needs, they suffer in various ways and fail to develop in the direction of personality health. Thus, Ribble [40] found that actual physical development suffered if the children did not receive enough body-contact, verbal stimulation, sucking-activity, etc. Spitz [41] found general psychological development was impaired when a stable relationship did not exist between the infant and a mother-figure. Goldfarb,[42] in studies of institution-reared children, found many signs of inadequate social behavior, and inadequate emotional responsiveness to people.

If parents did not know their children needed such care, it is possible they might neglect their children in fundamental ways, in spite of a subjective desire to "do right by their children."

LIKING THE CHILD. In a healthy interpersonal relationship, the participants like each other. In healthy parent-child relationships, we should expect the parents to like the infant; and, later, we should expect the growing child to like his parents. We have seen [43] that the liking-response to some object is a function of needs and values. From this it follows parents will like their children if the latter gratify important needs for the parents, and if the children accord with the values, ideals, or expectations of the parents. Most parents like their newborn infants, in fact they like them before they are born: because the child was wanted, the infant looks cute, or resembles someone in the family. A sociologist might say that to like one's children is a cultural norm and ideal to which most members of a society have been trained.

Yet, there are parents who do not like their children, right from the time of conception. Some parents actively reject their children and express overt hostility toward them; others reject them unconsciously and display the rejection only to the trained observer, through "overprotection" and overconcern for the child.

Affection for the child serves the function of motivating all of the necessary and often burdensome time and attention which a child requires from parents. If the parents like their children, they are much more likely to attend to their wants and needs more lovingly and willingly than if they dislike them.

Affection for children is such a strongly approved and expected cultural pattern that we are likely to regard a person who dislikes children—his own or other people's—as abnormal in some way. "Something is wrong with the person who dislikes kids."

So culturally biased are we, that we take affection for children as natural, or "uncaused," and look only for the causes of disliking children. In fact, when people feel hostility for children, they may become so upset and threatened that they either repress such feelings immediately or else seek therapeutic assistance so they may be rid of such unwanted feelings.

We must remind the reader that just as hostile, or disliking, feelings toward children are "caused," so are affectionate feelings. Naturally, however, affectionate feelings toward one's children are valued both for their own sake and also because they motivate the care which is necessary for the child's optimum growth. It is because

affection is valued, then, that it becomes a personality-hygiene value
and goal.

CONCERN FOR THE CHILD'S HAPPINESS AND GROWTH. In a healthy
parent-child relationship, the parents experience profound concern
for the child's growth and happiness. Concretely, this means that
it matters very deeply to them whether or not the child is happy and
satisfied and whether the child is growing at an expected rate and
in desired directions. As we saw earlier, concern is indirectly an
outgrowth of concern for the self and also a by-product of *identification* with the object of concern, that is, the child's growth and
happiness feel to the parents like *their own* growth and happiness.
Perhaps it is in consequence of this close identification with the
child (later on, the child identifies with the parents in important
ways) that their child's contentment fills the parents with inner satisfaction.

Another determiner of concern for the child appears to be that of
self-esteem in the parents. Healthy, happy, growing children are an
important basis for the parents' self-esteem. Parents of children who
are sick, or maladjusted, experience apprehension for the child's
happiness, and they often report profound guilt-feelings and feelings
of failure as people and as parents. Child-guidance clinics are coming increasingly to recognize that a disturbed child must be treated
along with one or both of his parents, if he is to be treated effectively.
Some parents are unable to face the threat to self-esteem that a
maladjusted child represents, and so they avoid bringing him for
suitable help.

It has been the author's experience, as well as the experience of
many therapists, that the American parent's concern for his child's
welfare is so profound that many parents, long in need of personality therapy, will consent to undergo the process only after
they see that, if they improve, the children may have a better chance
of growing up in a healthy way.

European observers of the author's acquaintance jokingly observe
that in Europe children are still seen but not heard. In America, the
concern for children appears so exaggerated to them, they say "The
parents are seen but not heard; the child is the American dictator."

Whatever the truth may be in such comparisons, it can be agreed that without concern for the child's growth and happiness, the children would be less likely to grow into confident, secure, healthy adults, and so we can regard concern as a personality-hygiene value.

PARENTAL BEHAVIOR WHICH PROMOTES GROWTH AND HAPPINESS IN THE CHILD. This characteristic of a healthy interpersonal relationship is probably the crux of the present chapter: How must parents relate to their children in order to encourage or promote growth and happiness? What is the correct balance between indulgent behavior toward the child (which promotes momentary happiness or need-gratification) and restrictive behavior (discipline) which is alleged to promote personality growth toward maturity?

While no generally valid formula for parents to follow has yet been devised, we can call attention to some general principles.

Behavior which promotes happiness and growth in the child must be guided by knowledge of what will gratify the child, and what will help his personality grow concomitant with his physical growth. In short, the parents, or the "experts," must develop through research, a set of valid general laws concerning what children need from their parents, what consequences follow when they get it, and what consequences follow when they do not get it.

We can proffer some crude versions of these as yet unformulated "laws" of child-personality growth. The child must have his physical needs recognized by his parents, and gratified with their assistance. In early infancy, this calls for considerable ability on the part of the parents. The child can communicate only with gestures, cries, and "body-language," when he experiences need-tensions of various sorts. The parents must be able "to decode his language" to recognize what is missing, or what is present that is causing discomfort. Any factors which desensitize the parents to the child's "messages" of discomfort will decrease the frequency with which the child experiences "euphoria," or physical gratification. The wider the body of hypotheses which the parents can draw upon, when they are called to interpret an infant's discomfort, the more likely it becomes that they will be able to gratify the child. A child may scream because of hunger, pins sticking him, loneliness, etc. The parents must diversify their attempts to discover what is wrong, and try to provide relief. There is good reason to believe that if a young infant experiences more discomfort than he does gratification early in infancy, his subsequent personality development may be strikingly impaired.[44]

The child, as he grows, needs to experience unqualified affection and love. In the absence of this vital ingredient, the individual will suffer very low self-esteem, and will be subject to anxiety of powerful proportions. Or, the quest for affection may become the guiding principle of his entire life. Horney interprets "basic anxiety" (which is the root cause of all neurosis) as an outgrowth of insecurity and uncertainty that one is loved during infancy.[45]

The child needs his environment arranged so he will experience anxiety and fear to a minimum degree. If the child is continually frightened (an eventuality which is most likely if he is unsure he is loved), he is likely to develop *chronic* anxiety and fear, with attendant losses in his sense of confidence in himself.

The child needs praise for accomplishments which are in line with his degree of physical and psychological development. Such praise appears to contribute to a sense of self-esteem, which has important implications for interpersonal relationships.

Thus far we have spoken about indulgences which contribute to the immediate experience of gratification and happiness for the child. But, as Bettelheim[46] has pointed out, "love is not enough" for optimum personality growth toward health. The child also needs limits, discipline, and punishment in order to learn the behavior patterns which society expects of him at various age-levels. The process of personality development moves through different age grades, and the child is expected to "keep pace" with his age-mates. American parents, with their strong concern for achievement, become very upset if their children do not keep up with the Joneses' children in the age at which weaning, toilet training, acquiring friends, and learning to read all are expected to occur.[47]

Since personality growth involves the "renunciation" of the behavior patterns expected at a previous age, how can parents encourage this renunciation? Why do not people at thirty continue to behave toward others, seek the same kinds of gratification, wear the same clothing, diapers and so on, which they did when they were thirteen months old?

In principle, there are two ways of "dislodging" anyone from a position which it is desired they should vacate. One way is through *"attraction"*[48]—to tempt them to a new position which promises greater gratifications than they are now receiving. The other method is through *punishment*[49]—if their present position is rendered painful and uncomfortable, the person may vacate it in favor of a position which is less painful.

Parents utilize both methods in their attempts to promote growth of personality in their children. Most personality hygienists hold the view that the attraction methods are most desirable, since they can be effective in encouraging a child to abandon infantile levels of behaving and yet produce few of the undesirable consequences[50] of the punishment methods, e.g., *regression*.

The parents have two powerful rewards which they can give their children in exchange for the latter's renunciation of more infantile levels of functioning. One reward is a *parent's own personality*, and the other is *affection*. Mowrer has pointed out that if children like their parents, they will want to become like their parents in important respects.[51] In other words, the parents serve as an identification-model for their children. The children acquire much of their behavior repertoire and personality structure through identification with their parents. This "developmental identification" process is promoted when the parents have earned the affection and admiration of their children through nurturance, exemplary behavior, etc.

In addition to serving as identification-models, however, the parents are important training-agents. They reward their child's efforts at learning more mature behavior patterns with lavish supplies of highly valued affection and approval. Thus, they motivate the child's efforts to grow. The child comes to prize this affection and approval as one of the most important rewards which life can offer. In order to earn these rewards, children will sometimes do violence to their own personality, when the parents have placed an unwise and unrealistic price on their affection.

The parents are charged by society with the task of *imposing discipline*,[52] or limits on the child's behavior, so the child will come to delimit his behavior to that range expected from him according to age and sex. Discipline, if it is to be effective, (a) must involve explicit goals and limits, and (b) it must be consistent. From the child's point of view, it is as if he were obliged to learn a game (how to behave) which has periodically changing rules, with his parents as referees.

FULL AND HONEST COMMUNICATION BETWEEN PARENTS AND THE CHILD. In a healthy relationship, the parents will communicate their real selves to the child and will make it possible for the child to communicate his real self to them. In early infancy, of course, the child has no self to speak of, but gradually he learns to discern what is "him" and what is "not him." It might be said the child begins life and communication at the level of his real self, and may or may not lose this tendency to honest and full communication.[53] The parents may punish him for certain kinds of communication of feelings and wishes, so he may learn to suppress, even repress, these aspects of self, viz.: hostile feelings and erotic desires. The parents, in turn, may be expected to express their honest feelings and wishes with respect to the child, to each other, and to other aspects of the world. One reason why full expression on the part of the parents is deemed to be important for personality hygiene lies in the fact that such full communication *makes it possible for the children to obtain an accurate concept of their parents' personalities.* It is a wise and rare child indeed who knows his parents' personalities. In addition, full communication from the children enables the parents to formulate an accurate concept of their children.

In connection with knowledge of parents' personalities, clinicians have often noted that their patients have at best only a dim, or idealized, concept of what their parents are really like.[54] Often the children had the experience of "never really knowing what their parents felt and expected of them." If the parents express fully what they expect of the child, how they feel about him, what they like and what they disapprove of, the child has a better basis for establishing identifications and for learning parentally-approved behavior patterns.

By implication, any factor which limits the communication between parents and their children is a factor which will undermine the health of the relationship.

REASONABLE PARENTAL DEMANDS ON THE CHILD. Parents are in a peculiar position with respect to their children. The latter are almost totally dependent upon their parents for safety, affection, a sense of identity, and a sense of self-esteem. The parent's affection and approval come to be most important values in the child's life. In order to get these rewards, the child is obliged to conform with the parents' wishes and expectations. There is reason to believe, in fact, that the parental expectations with respect to the child come to be the latter's *self*-demands and expectations, in consequence of identification.

Parents usually base their expectations of their children on what society, or the "experts" say a child "should" be doing and accomplishing at some level of development. Often, these socially determined expectations may be quite feasible from the child's point of view, because he is physically and psychologically "ready" to give up less mature ways in favor of the more mature patterns of behaving.

But it can happen, and does happen often, that the parents may pitch their demands and expectations of the child way above his ability to conform; or if he does conform, he may do so at the cost of many other important values. Thus the parents may expect their child to be toilet-trained at 15 months, when in fact he is not physically ready. Nevertheless, they may devote much anxious attention to toilet-training him, making him feel rejected for his failures. Or, the parents may become anxious if the child lisps at age three—they expect more fluent speech from him—and so the three-year-old may be obliged to undergo speech therapy, the while missing out on other experiences which other three-year-olds are quite happily engaging in.

A child's failure to accord with his parents' expectations usually produces a profound feeling of failure, and even a sense of worthlessness and unlovability in the child, which may endure into adult years.

When we speak of reasonable demands and expectations, we are implying that the parents strive to reconcile the norms which pertain to children of such an age with the actual abilities of their child and with due consideration for other values, such as the child's happiness.

While some parents expect too much of their children, there are others who expect too little; they may be said to *infantilize* their children. Long past the age when his age-mates are dressing themselves, budgeting their own allowances, some children are still kept in an immature state by their parents. This pattern has been called "restrictive overprotection;" [55] it prevents the child from actually developing and using his potentialities at a time when he is ready to test them.

MUTUAL RESPECT FOR AUTONOMY. Since we value self-direction and autonomy so highly in our society, we should expect that in a healthy parent-child relationship, the parents would begin to encourage and reward its appearance in the child. Naturally, at the early stages of infancy and childhood, the parents cannot be expected to allow the child completely to regulate his own life: he does not know how to, and there is reason to expect that without the supervision and direction of his parents, he would likely become quite anxious.

Nevertheless, as the child shows signs of the ability to act on his own wishes *and to accept the consequences thereof*,[56] the parents should encourage and allow him to do so. It is only through the *experience* of action on the basis of one's own decisions and "will" that a person gradually acquires "independent security," as Blatz calls it. Parents who encourage their child in this direction, who give a child alternatives and allow him to choose between them, are encouraging the development of autonomy.

In addition to respect for autonomy in the child, the parents might also be expected to respect the individuality of the child, even to encourage it to some degree. While the child must learn to conform to some extent with his parents', and society's, demands, he might also be encouraged to learn how to use and trust his own judgment, his own values, and his own "powers" or skills. It would appear that a child who has been reared by parents who have respected his will and his individuality will in turn respect his parents' wishes and individuality, and that of other people.

Thus far, we have attempted to show how the criteria for evaluating interpersonal relationships in general can be adapted to the problem of evaluating parent-child relationships in particular. If a parent-child relationship displays these characteristics to an observer, then the probability is high that the child will develop in the direction of personality health.

Let us now focus our attention, not upon the relationship between parents and their children, but rather on *parental behavior* itself.

PARENTAL BEHAVIOR

Let us define parental behavior as *a special instance of instru-mental behavior which has as its goal the influencing of a child's growth and development in specific directions*. It becomes apparent that parental behavior can be directed toward conscious goals or unconscious goals; it can be effective or ineffective in attaining these goals; and it can be judged to be healthy or unhealthy. Before discussing parental behavior any further, let us first ask, "Why do people become parents in the first place?"

THE MOTIVES FOR PARENTHOOD. In the subhuman animal kingdom, mating occurs in instinctive fashion; the animals do not appear to have a choice as to whether or not they will reproduce their kind. The female mammal periodically enters her period of heat, and emits stimuli—visual and olfactory—which attract the males; the latter copulate with the female, with the result that impregnation occurs, and offspring are born after a variable gestation period.[57]

The human does not reproduce as soon as it becomes anatomically and physiologically possible. Certain social requirements must be met in every known society before marriage can take place. When once a couple have met these requirements and have married, sexual relationships with the aim of reproduction become socially sanctioned.

But even within marriage, conception of children is often controlled, so that children will not be conceived and born until they are desired by the married couple. We may well ask, "Why will a couple seek children?" In our society, if a married couple cannot conceive children, they will often go to great lengths to adopt a child, even to kidnap a child. Thus far, there does not appear to be any evidence to support the view that a conscious desire for children is innate, or that humans have a maternal and paternal instinct. Further, it is now possible to control conception; having or not having children can be the result of rational, and irrational, choice. Since children are often a great burden economically, and since they require drastic reorganization of the life of their parents, why do people want children?

Naturally, there may be an enormous diversity in the motives underlying any voluntary act, and so we can expect to find similar diversity in our quest for the motives underlying maternity and paternity. One reason which is often given for desiring children is that it gives the mother and father a sense of utter *fulfillment* and *completion*. It is possible that, for the mother at least, there may be some underlying endocrinological basis for this sense of fulfillment. Benedeck and Rubenstein [58] found that among women, a correlation could be found between unconscious attitudes of emotional passivity and receptivity, and the preparedness of the reproductive apparatus for conception. Much more probable, however, than the biological sense of fulfillment is a *culturally defined* sense of completion and fulfillment. It would appear that the cultural definition of the fully developed adult man and woman includes parenthood. A person may not feel "right" unless he has brought forth "issue." Some people experience the desire to have children with the full force of a biblical imperative: "Go ye forth and people the world. . . ."

In short, what we are saying is that to have children is a richly rewarding experience, eagerly sought out by most members of our society. To have children appears to contribute to self-esteem, to a sense of completeness as a person. In addition, to be married and to have children *makes one similar to one's peers*—which is a powerful motive in its own right. The married couple who are childless feel left out of much of the experience which is shared by their more fortunate friends and relatives. Much of social living is geared to the adults who have children, and so the childless couple are indeed left out of much that is richly rewarding in everyday life.

Perhaps it is saying enough, really, to say that having children lends strong reinforcement to one's sense of identity [59] as an adult man or woman.

It should not be supposed that self-esteem, a sense of completion, and a desire to conform with one's peers are the only motives for having children. There are many instances where children are sought as a kind of cement to hold together a shaky marriage. It sometimes happens a woman may encourage her own pregnancy so as to catch a husband, if she doubts her ability to attract one by more conventional means. Some people may want heirs to inherit property. Some want children so they can show *their* parents the right way to be parents.

We may take it for granted that a *desire* to be a parent is expected of adults in our society, so we are shocked if we hear someone say they definitely do not want to have children. We can further take it for granted that this desire is very strong; some people will go to great lengths to get a child to raise as their own—such as illegal adoption procedures and kidnaping.

THE GOALS OF PARENTAL BEHAVIOR. Parental behavior is instrumental behavior, and hence is directed toward goals, or valued ends. As with any instrumental behavior, these ends will be more efficiently achieved if the goals are explicit and fully conscious. At this point, we must distinguish between the *functions* of parental behavior and the *goals* of parental behavior.

The term "function" is one which is used by sociologists, whose focus of interest is the *social system* in which members play *roles.* Each role is found to have certain functions in the sense of keeping the social system going and intact, just as the liver has certain functions in keeping the overall body-system going and intact. The major function of the role of parents, or parental behavior, is that of *socializing* the children; the family is the "socialization factory" mentioned earlier in the chapter. The parents train their children so they will become modal personalities; they even instil in their children, by precept and example, the desire to become parents when *they* grow up.

The term "goal" is much more variable than that of function, and it presumes the opportunity for choice. A person can choose his goals, whereas he is much less able to select his functions in the overall social system. But society enters even into the choice of goals. In theory, a person can set up a near infinity of goals for his parental behavior; practically, he has a much smaller range of possible and feasible goals to choose from.

In practical terms, the problem of goals can be boiled down to this question, "What kind of a person do I want my child to become?"

This is a question which should be asked periodically by parents, since it can happen that their actual behavior may be instrumental toward producing a person quite different from what they had in mind. One's instrumental behavior is *always* instrumental toward some goal—but it may not be the goal which is consciously desired.

Thus, most parents want their children to become happy, healthy, successful adults. Their actual behavior toward their children may promote instead the development of miserable, neurotic failures.

Parents' goals with respect to their children's development will strongly influence the demands and expectations they impose on the children, and the nature of the discipline they set up. It is from the standpoint of the goals they hold that parents make judgments concerning the child's progress and behavior, and they reward and punish their children accordingly. If the goals are unrealistic, or difficult to attain, it may be expected that parents will punish, criticize, even reject their children—since the latter fail to accomplish these goals. A mother may hold, as her concept of an ideal child, an image of a docile, obedient, clean, polite, bookish, musical individual. Insofar as the child accords with her demands, he is given affection. But if he deviates from these ideals, he may be punished and criticized.

A mother and father may hold contrasting goals and ideals for the child's development. The mother wants the boy to be obedient, clean, musical, and bookish, while the father wants him to be virile, self-sufficient, an athlete, and a hunter. The result may be the child does not know whom to please and he becomes ridden with chronic inner conflicts.

HEALTHY PARENTAL GOALS. The parents' goals for their children may be called healthy when (a) they are *conscious* and explicit, (b) they are *feasible* of achievement by the child, (c) they are *harmonious*—that is, the parents are in agreement with each other with respect to their ideals for the child, and the ideals themselves are in harmony with one another—and (d) they are *flexible*.

When their goals and ideals have these characteristics, it becomes increasingly possible for the parents to select the ways of relating to their child, and of disciplining him, so the goals may be achieved. When it becomes apparent that the goals are inappropriate, or unrealistic, the parents can modify them accordingly.

Child-guidance experts and therapists often face the task of helping parents to *formulate* goals and ideals, and helping parents to *change* their goals and ideals. These aims of counseling are most likely to be indicated when the parents and their children are caught in assorted impasses of child-rebellion, parental-rejection, or marked dissatisfaction within the entire family.

It may be expected that as the concept of healthy personality comes to be more thoroughly worked out, child psychologists and family counselors will be better able to assist and advise parents in the formulation of goals, and in the giving of advice as to ways and means of attaining these goals. When parents hold as their cardinal goal the aim of raising their child to personality health, then it follows that they will strive to learn the ways of behaving which will implement this goal.

UNHEALTHY PARENTAL GOALS. When the parents are not aware of their goals, it can happen that there is no guiding principle to help determine how they should relate to their child. The child will then grow up without consistent discipline. If the goals are unrealistic and out of line with the child's ability to achieve them, the child may acquire an unhealthy self-ideal, and feel he is a chronic failure, unworthy of love. If the goals are unharmonious, the child may have all kinds of problems in establishing a satisfactory relationship with either parent—as he pleases one, he runs the risk of losing the approval of the other, with attendant anxiety and insecurity.

MOTHERING-BEHAVIOR

From birth onward, the mother plays a very important role in the nurturance of the child. "Mom" is the source of milk, love, and basic acceptance for the child. The mother is the prototype of the *giver*. Her *giving* role must be a comfortable and satisfying one for her, if the child is to grow in healthy directions. We can define mothering behavior as that kind of "loving-behavior" which has as its aim the promotion of happiness and growth in the child. *Mothering-behavior is healthy when it is effective in achieving its aim and yet provides the mother with more gratifications than frustrations.*

Motherhood is usually a very powerful motive (see section above), and so having a child to care for is a very basic kind of satisfaction for the mother. But caring for the child calls for a good deal of time, effort, and strength; often, it calls for marked self-privation in order to insure the child has what it needs.

"Disturbances" in mothering-behavior are coming into prominence in the field of psychiatry, and are studied as a problem in their own right. Ackerman [60] has devoted a paper to "disturbances of mothering and criteria for treatment." He lists eight determinants of the "quality" of mothering:

1. The woman's motivation for marriage and offspring; the image of the mothering role structured in her original family.
2. The quality of the woman's interaction with her child.
3. The quality of her interaction with the father of the child.
4. The quality of her interaction with her family as a group.
5. Culture patterns bearing on child rearing.
6. Constitutional factors.
7. Personality factors.
8. The mother's reaction to failure in this role.

Examination of this list gives some indication of some of the possible sources of ineffective and unhealthy maternal behavior. Thus, if the woman's motivations for marriage are not right, or if her relationships with her husband are not right, it may be expected her relationships with her child may be impaired in important ways. Ackerman goes on to point out that personality therapy with mothers must make due allowance for assistance with the maternal role, and he sets up various goals for treatment ranging from simple guidance in mothering to efforts at a "full reorganization of unconscious functions of personality as they impinge on the integration of personality into the maternal role."

The present writer has often had the experience of being consulted by a mother because of problems with the child. Further analysis of the total situation has resulted in a variety of recommendations. Sometimes it was recommended the child be sent for therapy; in other instances, it appeared the problems with the child were an outgrowth of neurosis in the mother, and she was encouraged to seek therapy for herself. In some cases, the mother and the child both appeared to be making a basically healthy protest-reaction to the neurotic behavior of the father, and he was urged to seek therapy. And sometimes it was a combination of all of these factors which was responsible for the problem which brought the mother to seek assistance.

One of the most powerful sources of difficulty in achieving gratifications out of mothering-behavior may prove to be the cultural changes in the concept of a woman's role.[61] In our rapidly changing social system, the role of woman has changed from that of housewife-mother, to something which is more complex. Women expect more of themselves than the wife-mother role, and their husbands are expecting more as well. The woman expects herself (and is expected) to have children, yet look slender and lovely; she seeks a career of some kind; she has to be a good social organizer to help her husband in his career; she is expected to participate in community affairs, etc.

These conflicting pressures on the woman may interfere with her role as mother to her children. At the present time there do not appear to be any ready solutions to these role-conflicts that do justice to all of the values at stake: the woman's overall satisfactions with her life, her husband's happiness, her children's health and happiness, the satisfaction of the woman's own mother and father with their daughter, etc. Probably each woman has to find a solution which meets her own particular total life situation.

There are many *neurotic* factors which prevent a mother from behaving toward her child in ways which are conducive to the latter's growth and happiness. Some of these include anxiety about her adequacy as a woman and mother; sexual difficulties with the husband; and chronic conflicting loyalties.

It may be seen that the maternal role is a complex one. The factors which appear to promote the achievement of healthy mothering-behavior include: (a) a strong affirmation of the value of being a mother, and (b) a rich supply of gratifications outside the role of mother, e.g., an abundance of affection and love from the father, a sense of being appreciated, etc.

A pressing problem in parenthood is that of *maternal rejection* and *overprotection*. Levy [62] has described a number of common patterns, which we can paraphrase as *indulgent* overprotection and *dominating* overprotection. In the former, the mother does not permit the child to experience the usual frustrations which help a child to grow in pace with his age-mates; he is "spoiled." In the latter, the child is directed in everything he does and is not allowed to learn self-direction. One of the factors found to underly the overprotective attitude in mothers is unconscious feelings of hostility and rejection of the children. In other words, the overprotective mother, though she may explain her overconcern as an expression of love, may basically dislike and reject her child.

CRITERIA OF HEALTHY MOTHERING-BEHAVIOR. Although we can assess the health of the mother-child *relationship* with criteria of healthy interpersonal relationships, we can also focus our attention on the mother herself and evaluate the mothering-behavior in its own right. We could say that the mothering-behavior is healthy when (a) the child appears to be healthy, happy, and growing in accordance with rough growth norms, and (b) the mother is subjectively happy and contented with her role as mother, deriving self-esteem from her "success" and not resenting unduly the drudgery which is associated with child care.

FATHERING-BEHAVIOR

In our society, the father plays a much less direct role in his child's growth and development, at least in the early stages of the child's life. His most important function when the child is very young, is that of striving to care for the needs of the mother, so that she can in turn nurture the child all the better. It should be stated, however, that many more fathers to-day are taking an active part in the care of infants—actually "mothering" their child. It is not uncommon that the father feeds the infant (with a bottle of course), changes his diapers, and cuddles, caresses, and otherwise "mothers" him.

As the child grows, the father's role changes somewhat; he may be the chief disciplinarian and he provides an important identification-model for his sons. He gives his daughters important experiences in relating to males. The relationship which he has established with his wife gives both male and female children their first concepts, and even ideals, of what marriage is like.

The father is an important source of affection, not only for the wife, but also for his children.

Some observers have noted that the father's role in the family is minor in comparison with that of the mother. To a certain extent, this is probably true. Yet, it may also be said that children who are deprived of an enduring relationship with a father, during the process of growing up, suffer in various subtle ways.

Josselyn [63] has made some relevant comments on the father's role. She states she "would challenge a concept that implies the role of fatherhood is a psychologically foreign one, artificially imposed by the culture for the survival of the race. . . . Tenderness, gentleness, a capacity to empathize with others, a capacity to respond emotionally . . . to value a love-object more than the self . . , is not the prerogative of women alone; it is a human characteristic." She goes on to state that these capacities for tenderness and love, if they are stifled in the man, may either result in overall emotional crippling, or be directed elsewhere than in his family. It does seem true that many fathers cannot express tender affection for their children, by whom they are perceived as cold, powerful, stern individuals—but they can be tender toward "outsiders."

We may describe fathering-behavior as all behavior which a father displays toward his children in his formal role of father. Healthy fathering-behavior is (a) expressive of the father's real self, (b) it gives him satisfactions, and (c) is conducive to the child's happiness and growth. Any factors, including cultural concepts of men as being emotionally cold, which restrict a father's range of emotional expressiveness toward his children, may be viewed as factors which preclude healthy fathering-behavior.

The author has known, for example, fathers who have never kissed their sons or their daughters; their emotional expressiveness is limited to righteous indignation when the child breaks some rule.

It is possible that difficulties encountered by fathers in carrying out their paternal role are produced by cultural changes in the concept of the man's role. At one time, a man was *a man* only if he earned the money, sired his children, and let the mother raise them. He was to rule his home (like a dictator), and punish his children when they were bad, and that about ended his fatherly role. More recently, it has happened that the concept of manliness has been altered, so that tender feelings, active participation in the household and in parenthood are no longer considered signs of effeminacy and weakness. Many men have not as yet incorporated these changes into their sense of identity, and so experience difficulty in relating to their children in a personalized, informal, emotionalized way. The consequence is that their children miss something, and they themselves suffer from "unused self."

Some observers fear that fathers are losing their "masculinity" by being tender, or by washing dishes. There seems to be no serious evidence to warrant this fear.

THE POWER TO LOVE AND HEALTHY PERSONALITY

In the last analysis, love may be regarded as a gift, freely and spontaneously given by the lover to his object. The object may be the self, a spouse, a child, a friend, etc. The gift which is proffered to the love-object is the *real self* of the lover. He gives of himself —he focuses his "powers" on the object—so that his object may be happier and so that his object may better actualize his potentialities. The criterion of the success of loving-behavior, which gives the lover rich satisfaction, is *perceptible evidence of happiness and growth in the object*.

From our preceding discussion, it should be apparent to the reader that love, or the capacity to love, is very important as an indication of personality health, and it is also the means by which personality health is promoted, maintained, and even achieved, in the self and in others. Any factors which hinder or prevent a person from loving are thus factors which jeopardize personality health in him, and in all of the other people with whom the handicapped individual comes into contact.

Since the real self is the "ingredient" of love—in loving-relationships, it is the real self which is given to the object—then any factor which prevents a person from knowing and expressing his real self is thus a factor which prevents love. The individual who is alienated from his real self cannot love. He cannot even love himself, since he lacks knowledge of what his real self is. The individual with a personality-illness—neurosis, psychosis, or character-disorder—is fundamentally a person who cannot love. Many patients who have undergone personality therapy report they have had restored to them, or else they have acquired for the first time in their lives, the power to love themselves and others. Probably what the psychoanalysts refer to as "genitality," or as "orgastic potency" refers to more than sexual adequacy; it may be interpreted as the power to love in the broader sense in which we have interpreted the word love; [64] the neurotic who does not "command" his sexual functions, who is "alienated" from control of his own sexuality, may be viewed as a person in whom sexuality is symbolic of all that is summed up by the term "real self." Just as he cannot give (or take) sexuality to his object, so can he not give (and take) his real self.

SUMMARY

Loving-behavior is defined as any action undertaken by a person with the conscious aim of promoting the happiness and growth of the object. The loving person behaves in these ways toward his object freely, willingly, and with enjoyment.

Active love refers to all occasions when a person behaves in loving fashion toward his object. *Passive* love refers to the process of accepting the loving behavior of another person.

The motive which is most basic to loving behavior is the desire for the object's growth and happiness. *Identification* with the love-object is probably responsible for much of the emotion which a lover experiences; he feels the pleasures and pains of his object. *Empathy* and *sympathy* both are involved in loving. *Sexuality* may be involved in loving, but love-relationships can exist where there is no sexuality, and sexual behavior can occur in nonloving relationships.

People choose a love-object on the basis of many criteria, e.g., helplessness of the object, conformity of the object with the lover's ideals, the ability of the object to reciprocate love, etc. A *rational* choice of a love-object has been made when the person chooses someone whom he *can* love, and who can act in loving ways toward him. *Unhealthy object-choices* are likely to be made when the chooser is under the tension of very *strong needs*, when he *lacks self-knowledge*, and when he *lacks accurate knowledge of the personality and needs of the object.*

Humans need *to be loved*, and they need *to love actively*, if they are to become and remain healthy personalities. Some of the factors which promote the ability to love actively include *rich gratifications of needs* in the past, *affirmation of the value of love*, high *frustration-tolerance, self-love*, a *diversified personality-structure*, a *healthy self-structure, reality-contact, security, reasonable ideals* for the love-object, *emancipation from parental direction*, and *emancipation from inner-direction*.

The ability to accept love from others may be prevented if a person has repressed his need for love, and if he has inaccurate concepts of the other person.

While excessive dependency may interfere with the establishment of a healthy love-relationship, dependency per se is quite compatible with love. In fact, without mutual dependency, there could be no love-relationships. A person can love adequately only a limited number of objects. If he attempts actively to love more than he is able to, then either he will suffer or the happiness and growth of the objects may suffer. Love *from* others appears to be promoted most directly by the fact of *loving them.*

The *self-structure* of an individual may impose limits on the range of behavior which he can include in his loving-behavior repertoire. The more the self-structure is congruent with the person's real self, the more effective will he be in loving; he will be able to behave in ways that gratify the one he loves without experiencing personal threat—anxiety or guilt.

Impasses will arise in marriage. If a couple cannot resolve these impasses in a health-promoting way, then they should seek professional help before undertaking divorce. There are some instances where a *divorce* may be necessary in order to preserve or promote personality health in one or both of the partners.

Parental love plays an important role in the personality health of the children and of the parents. *Healthy parent-child relationships* have the characteristics of healthy interpersonal relationships in general: knowledge, affection, concern, growth-provoking behavior, full and honest communication, reasonable demands, and mutual respect for autonomy.

Parental behavior is instrumental behavior which has as its goal the influencing of the child's growth and development in specific directions. The *motives* for parenthood vary widely from parent to parent. The *goals* which parents have for their children's development may vary widely. *Healthy parental goals* are *conscious, feasible, harmonious,* and *flexible.*

Mothering-behavior and *fathering-behavior* are discussed from the standpoint of health and effectiveness. Mothering-behavior is healthy when the child is growing, healthy, and happy, and when the mother is happy and contented with her role as a mother. The same criteria may be used for evaluating the "health" of fathering-behavior.

The *power to love* is regarded as an index of overall personality health. Any factor which prevents a person from knowing and expressing his real self will curtail the person's power to love.

NOTES AND REFERENCES

RECOMMENDED READINGS ARE MARKED WITH AN ASTERISK (*)

*1. The author was strongly influenced by Fromm's views on love as activity. The reader is strongly encouraged to see Fromm's remarks in Fromm, E., *Man for himself*, New York, Rinehart, 1947, pp. 96–101. Fromm extended his discussion of love in a recent work which the present writer did not examine until after this chapter had been completed. It is excellent, and should be read by the interested student. See Fromm, E., *The art of loving*, New York, Harper, 1956. The work of Sorokin also came to the attention of the present writer after the manuscript was completed. The reader is encouraged to study Sorokin, P., *The ways and power of love; types, factors, and techniques of moral transformation*, Boston, Beacon Press, 1954. Sorokin is the director of an institute at Harvard University which has been investigating "altruism" and love. It is an interesting commentary on the poor communication between disciplines, that not many psychologists have cited Sorokin's extensive work on love. Sorokin is a prolific contributor to sociology.

2. The psychoanalysts have devoted considerable attention to the contrast between "activity" and "passivity." They regard passivity as more primitive and infantile than activity, and they speak of active mastery and passive mastery with reference to a person's attempts to come to terms with the environment. Cf. Fenichel, O., *The psychoanalytic theory of neurosis*, New York, Norton, 1945, pp. 44 ff.

3. The psychoanalysts regard identification as a more primitive mode of relating to another person than love. We would state that identification plays some role in love, even at mature levels of development, for reasons which are brought out in the text. Cf. Fenichel, O., *op. cit.*, pp. 83–84.

4. Cf. Dymond, Rosalind, "Personality and empathy," *J. consult. Psychol.*, 1950, 14, 343–350, for an empirical study of empathy.

5. Parsons, T. and Bales, R. F., *Family, socialization and interaction process*, Glencoe, Illinois, The Free Press, 1955, p. 21. The authors state, ". . . genital sexuality . . . the primary 'ritual' of marital solidarity. . . ."

6. See Fenichel, O., *op. cit.*, pp. 98–99. He distinguished, as did Freud,

between anaclitic and *narcissistic* types of object-choice. In the former, an object is chosen because it provokes associations about another original object of the past, usually the parent of the opposite sex. In the latter, the person is chosen because it represents some characteristic of the person's own personality. See also, Freud, S., "On narcissism: an introduction." In Freud, S., *Collected Papers*, Vol. IV. London, Hogarth, 1953.

*7. See Murphy, G., *Personality: a biosocial approach to origins and structure*, New York, Harper, 1947, Ch. 8.

8. Langhorne, M. C. and Secord, P. F., "Variations in marital needs with age, sex, marital status, and regional location," *J. soc. Psychol.*, 1955, 41, 19–37.

*9. Freud, S., "Contributions to the psychology of love. A special type of choice of object made by men," in Freud, S., *op. cit.*, Ch. 11.

10. Fenichel states, "When a person in love estimates his partner's virtues, he usually is not very realistic; by his projection of all of his ideals onto the partner's personality, the reunion with him becomes all the more enjoyable." Fenichel, O., *op. cit.*, p. 86.

11. See Chapter 2 for a discussion of autism.

12. Freud, S., *op. cit.*, note 9.

13. When a person does not choose a spouse on the basis of his own needs and feelings, he is much more likely to choose on the basis of these other criteria. See Riesman, D., *The lonely crowd*, New Haven, Yale University Press, 1950, for a discussion of behavior which is directed by the conscience, or by others' demands, in contrast with autonomously directed behavior.

14. Cf. Chapter 7.

15. Cf. Chapter 7.

16. Spitz, R. A., "Hospitalism: an inquiry into the genesis of psychiatric conditions in early childhood," *Psychoanalytic Study of the Child*, Vol. I, New York, International University Press, 1945.

*17. Cf. Goldfarb, W., in Hoch, P. and Zubin, J. (ed.), *Psychopathology of childhood*, New York, Grune & Stratton, 1956, pp. 105–119.

18. Ribble, M. A., *The rights of infants*, New York, Columbia University Press, 1943.

19. Spitz, R. A., *op. cit.*, Vol. II.

20. Levy, D. M., "Primary affect-hunger," *Amer. J. Orthopsychiat.*, 1937, 94, 643–652.

*21. This point is well brought out in various writings of Maslow. See, for example, "Love in self-actualizing people," in Maslow, A. H., *Motivation and personality*, New York, Harper, 1954.

22. Cf. Maslow, A. H., *op. cit.*
23. Fromm, E., *op. cit.*, pp. 119–140.
24. See Sullivan, H. S., *Conceptions of modern psychiatry*, Washington, William Alanson White Psychiatric Foundation, 1947, p. 10. Murphy, C., *op. cit.*, p. 522. For an empirical study, see Jourard, S. M. and Remy, R. M., "Perceived parental attitudes, the self, and security," *J. consult. Psychol.*, 1955, 19, 364–366.
*25. Howard, S., *The silver cord.* See also, for an indictment of "Mom," Strecker, E., *Their mother's sons*, Philadelphia, Lippincott, 1946.
26. Maslow, A. H., *op. cit.*
27. Fromm, E., *op. cit.*
28. See Chapter 9 for a discussion of the healthy self-structure.
29. Riesman, D., *op. cit.*
30. Fromm, E., *op. cit.*
31. Maslow makes this point. See Maslow, A. H., *op. cit.*, pp. 305–334.
32. See Chapter 9 for a definition of the self-concept.
33. See Chapter 9 for a definition of the self-ideal.
34. See Chapter 7 for a discussion of the real self.
35. Cf. Parsons, T. and Bales, R. F., *op. cit.*, page 16.
36. Mead, M., *Sex and temperament in three primitive societies,* New York, Morrow, 1935.
37. Whiting, J. W. M. and Child, I. L., *Child training and personality,* New Haven, Yale University Press, 1953.
38. See the recent volume, Brody, Sylvia, *Patterns of mothering,* New York, International University Press, 1956, for an analysis of mother-child relations in the first six months of life.
39. The World Health Organization has underwritten a study to investigate causes of maternal deprivation. See Bowlby, J., *Maternal care and mental health,* Geneva, World Health Organization, 1951.
40. Ribble, M., *op. cit.*
41. Spitz, R. A., *op. cit.*
42. Goldfarb, W., *op. cit.*
43. See Chapter 7.
44. See Coleman, J. C., *Abnormal psychology and modern life,* New York, Scott, Foresman, 1950, pp. 116–123.
45. Horney, K., *Neurosis and human growth,* New York, Norton, 1950, p. 18.
46. Bettelheim, B., *Love is not enough,* Glencoe, Illinois, The Free Press, 1950.
47. See Riesman, D., *op. cit.*, for a discussion of the anxieties of other-

directed parents in connection with the achievements of their children.

48. This is analogous with "reward training" which the learning-theorists talk about.

49. Punishment is useful as a means of getting a child "dislodged." But, as Maier has pointed out, it may induce frustration and frustrated behavior, which are strong barriers to learning. See Maier, N. R. F., *Frustration, the study of behavior without a goal,* New York, McGraw-Hill, 1949.

50. Cf. Maier, N. R. F., *op. cit.*

51. Mowrer, O. H., *Learning theory and personality dynamics,* New York, Ronald, 1950, pp. 590–596.

°52. See Baruch, D., *New ways in discipline,* New York, McGraw-Hill, 1949, for a nontechnical discussion of discipline. See also Mowrer, O. H., *op. cit.,* Ch. 16. For an excellent cross-cultural view of discipline, see Wolfenstein, M. Some variants in moral training of children. In *Psychoanalytic study of the child,* V, New York, International University Press, 1950, pp. 310–328.

53. Cf. Cameron, N. and Magaret, Ann, *Behavior pathology,* New York, Houghton Mifflin, 1951. See especially their discussion of behavioral duplicity, pp. 109–112.

54. The "authoritarian characters" were found as well to have idealized conceptions of their parents. See Adorno, T., Frenkel-Brunswick, E., Levinson, D., and Sanford, R. N., *The authoritarian personality,* New York, Harper, 1950.

°55. See Levy, D. M., *Maternal overprotection,* New York, Columbia University Press, 1943, for an extended discussion of overprotection.

56. See Blatz, W., *Understanding the young child,* Toronto, Clarke, Irwin, 1944, for an excellent discussion of "the development of responsibility." Ch. 10.

57. See Ford, C. S. and Beach, F. A., *Patterns of sexual behavior,* New York, Harper, 1951.

58. Benedek, T., *Studies in psychosomatic medicine: Psychosexual functions in women,* New York, Ronald, 1952, p. 340.

59. See Ch. 9 for a discussion of the sense of identity.

60. Ackerman, N. W., Disturbances of mothering and criteria for treatment. *Amer. J. Orthopsychiat.,* 1956, **26,** 252–263.

61. For an analysis of changes in the woman's role, see Parsons, T., "Age and sex in the social structure of the United States," *Amer. Sociol. Rev.,* 1942, **7,** 604–616. See also Mead, M., *Male and female,* New York, Morrow, 1949.

62. Levy, D. W., *op. cit.*

*63. Josselyn, Irene M., "Cultural forces, motherliness and fatherliness," *Amer. J. Orthopsychiat.*, 1956, 26, 264–271.

64. Cf. Fromm, E., *op. cit.*, pp. 83–101.

QUESTIONS FOR REVIEW AND EXAMINATION

1. What is loving-behavior? What are its motives? What role do emotions and sex play in loving-behavior?

2. What are some common determiners of the choice of a love-object? How is it decided whether or not the choice of a love-object is rational and healthy, or unhealthy?

3. What factors promote unhealthy object-choice?

4. Is the need for passive love unhealthy? If so, why? If not, why not?

5. What are some determiners of the ability to love actively? Of the ability to accept love?

6. What role is played by the self-structure in loving-behavior? By the real self?

7. What criteria enable us to decide whether or not parents "love" their children in a healthy fashion?

8. Analyze parental behavior from the standpoint of aims and consequences.

9. Describe and evaluate someone's love-relationships from the standpoint of the concepts employed in this chapter.

CHAPTER 9

The Self-Structure in
Healthy Personality

An individual's self, or self-structure, is an important determiner of his behavior. Consequently, students of personality have devoted increasing attention to the self.[1] The self-structure an individual develops provides certain limits to his overt behavior and to his inner experience. In general, a person will strive to behave in ways consistent with his self-structure,[2] and he will delimit his thoughts, feelings, and wishes to its boundaries. Let us illustrate these points with two diagrams of an arc:

The total area of each arc represents all possible human behavior and inner experience. The narrower shaded area within the total arcs represents the *restrictions* imposed by the self-structure on the total range of possible behavior and experience. Thus, it is physically and psychologically possible for a person to cheat on an examination, or to beat up his brother, but such behavior probably lies outside the self-structure limits, and so the person will seldom act in those ways. Further, it is possible for an individual to feel lust toward his mother, or to wish for his father's death, but most of us do not experience such feelings and wishes at a conscious level; they lie outside the bounds of our self-structure.

What is this self-structure which sets limits on the freedom of our action and experience? Is it possible to observe someone's self-structure and describe it? Is it possible to evaluate the self-structure as healthy and unhealthy? How do we acquire our self-structure? Does the self-structure change? What is a healthy self-structure like? Before we proceed to answer these questions, let us first provide ourselves with some technical definitions.

THE DEFINITION OF THE SELF-STRUCTURE

In order to obtain a clear understanding of what is meant by the self-structure, we shall define some related terms: personality, and ego.

THE EGO AND THE PERSONALITY

Personality refers to the totality of an individual's behavior patterns in life situations. A description of personality is a description of how the person typically behaves in specific situations. No description of personality is complete without a description of the situations in which the typical behavior occurs.

Ego is a term long employed by philosophers to describe the "knower" and the "doer." Psychoanalysts assign a more technical meaning to the term; they regard the ego as one of the three main components of "psychical personality." For the analysts, the personality includes three major structures, or components: the *id*, the *ego*, and the *superego*. The id is unconscious, and is the source of basic urges and impulses. The ego is the part of personality in contact with external reality; it is responsible for perceiving inner and outer reality, for regulating behavior, and for controlling impulses.[3] The *superego* is synonymous with conscience; it comprises the taboos and ideals with which behavior and experience must conform.

We shall regard the ego as the agent of personality. A near-synonym for ego is the will, or more properly, the act of willing and deciding. The ego may be viewed as the agent or source of all instrumental behavior. The ego perceives, reality-tests, selects and rejects behavior patterns. It is responsible for learning, for the control and suppression of impulses. The ego is the agent of cognitive behavior. *The ego is the constructor of the self-structure.*[4]

It should be stated that the ego is a hypothetical construct[5]—it cannot be observed directly. We postulate it as a force or agent on the basis of certain observed effects. This is very similar to the concept of electricity; we cannot know or see electricity, but we know what it does, and so we define electricity in terms of its functions and its effects. Just as we can judge electric current to be strong or weak, in terms of its effects on gauges, fuses, or light bulbs, so we can judge the ego to be strong and weak, in terms of certain behavioral consequences. We may assert that a strong ego is a personality-hygiene value.

EGO STRENGTH. Psychoanalysts and clinical psychologists utilize certain behavioral signs as indices of the strength of the ego. The psychoanalysts have constructed an elaborate theory of personality pathology on the basis of variations in ego strength. The psychotic is regarded as a person whose ego strength has been severely impaired: the hallucinations and bizarre behavior patterns are interpreted as signs of "ego-breakdown." The neurotic is a person whose ego strength has partially been impaired; the symptoms of neurosis—obsessions, phobias, hysterical organ-impairments—are interpreted as attempts on the part of a weakened ego to solve problems and to gratify needs. The healthy personality has optimum ego strength, which is manifested as the ability to reconcile the conflicting demands of the id, the superego, and external social reality.[6]

In terms much more general than those employed by psychoanalysts, we may say that an individual with a strong ego is able to behave in ways which gratify his needs, and yet conform with personal and social standards for acceptable conduct. In brief, *a strong ego is the agent of healthy personality.*

Since the concept of ego strength is such an important one in clinical psychology and psychiatry, we should indicate some of the reasons for which it is generally assessed. Personality therapists often require some estimate of ego strength prior to undertaking therapy with a patient, on the premise that certain minimal degrees of ego strength are necessary before a patient can observe his own conduct, and achieve insights. Personality researchers utilize the concept of ego strength as the basis for making predictions about the outcome of certain experiments conducted with human subjects.

Some of the criteria of ego strength which are employed are:

1. CERTAIN SCORES ON THE RORSCHACH INK-BLOT TEST, for example, the percentage of accurately perceived forms. This variable may be thought to represent an estimate of the degree of reality-contact achieved by the person, and reality-contact is regarded as a sign of ego strength.[7]

2. CERTAIN MEASURES OF RIGIDITY-FLEXIBILITY IN THINKING AND IN BEHAVIOR. A strong ego is thought to possess the capacity to vary instrumental behavior when it is found that some one behavior pattern is not effective in achieving a goal. Weak egos persist in making a response pattern, even when it is ineffective; in short, weak egos display *rigidity* in thinking and in instrumental behavior.[8]

3. CERTAIN MEASURES OF STRESS- AND FRUSTRATION-TOLERANCE. A strong ego displays the capacity to carry out goal-directed activity in spite of stress, strong needs and emotions, without any disorganization of instrumental behavior. The weak ego is less able to tolerate frustration and stress. Under stress, the weak ego displays disruption in ongoing instrumental action and shows instead emotional behavior of some kind.[9]

4. MINIMAL EVIDENCE FOR THE USE BY THE PERSON OF VARIOUS MECHANISMS FOR THE DEFENSE OF THE SELF-STRUCTURE, namely, repression, rationalization, projection, reaction-formation, etc. The strong ego is able to face inner reality—his real self—without distortion, selection, or denial of what is perceived there. The weak ego will admit to himself and others only such thoughts, feelings and wishes as are compatible with the social mores, or which are flattering to his self-esteem.

In summary, it may be said that any and all of the behavioral measures utilized by psychologists as indices of "good adjustment" may be re-interpreted as ego-strength indices, since the capacity to "adjust" to one's milieu in need-satisfying ways betokens ego strength. Most of these adjustment signs, or ego-strength signs,[10] have been discovered by comparing the responses to various test stimuli of people with personality illnesses—neuroses and psychoses —with the responses of normal and relatively healthy individuals, and the responses of those who improve with therapy and those who do not. The premise for such comparisons is the theoretical assumption that if a person has developed a personality illness, it is prima facie evidence of a weak ego; if he responds favorably to treatment, his ego is stronger than the ego of patients who do not respond. The behavioral and personality tests which discriminate between "normal" and "sick" people are then regarded as different expressions or manifestations of ego-strength.

It is possible that one day, the variable ego-strength may be found to correlate with certain modes of function of the cerebral cortex in its interrelationships with lower, subcortical brain structures.[11] Probably a strong ego reflects a situation wherein the cerebral cortex maintains and retains dominance over more primitive structures in the brain, viz.: the hypothalamus (which mediates more explosive emotional behavior).

THE REAL SELF, THE EGO, AND THE PERSONALITY

Personality can be observed directly, and described in the language of traits, that is, "In such and such a situation, he is most likely to act in such and such a way." The ego cannot be directly observed by an outsider; its "structure"[12] and strength must be inferred from behavioral indices. The *real self* is another hypothetical construct which is gaining increasing usage, especially in the writings of Horney[13] and Fromm.[14] These "neo-psychoanalysts" regard the real self as the basic *inner reality:* the actual feelings, wishes, thoughts, memories, and fantasies of the person. Personality hygienists are in almost universal agreement that the ability to *know* one's real self, to *express* one's real self, and to *act* in accordance with one's real self are optimum goals for child-rearing and personality therapy. If we employ the concept of the real self in our thinking about personality and behavior, we should make such observations as the following: "He acts at a real-self level in some situations, but not in others"; "He is only pretending to like his girl-friend. Actually, he hates her." "I never know what he *really* thinks, feels, and wants."

The ego may be regarded as the perceiver of the real self. As with external reality, the ego may perceive the real self accurately, or in autistic fashion. If the ego is strong, then the individual will indeed know his real self. His perceptions and beliefs about his real self will be accurate.

In order that we shall become the masters of these concepts, let us employ them in some sentences: "His personality reflects a weak ego, he is unable to gain satisfactions through socially and personally acceptable behavior. His behavior tends not to reflect his real self. He does not act in accordance with his real wishes and feelings. His perceptions and beliefs concerning his real self are inaccurate; he has an inaccurate self-concept." The reader may see, from the manner in which the technical terms have been employed, something of their different meanings.

THE REAL SELF, THE EGO, AND THE SELF-STRUCTURE

The real self refers to the real nature of a person's feelings, wishes, and thoughts. The ego is the perceiver of this inner reality. What, then, is the *self-structure*?

The self-structure is constructed by the ego. The ego constructs the self-structure just as it constructs a set of beliefs, conclusions, and ideals pertaining to anything else that can be observed, e.g., horses, or women. A Kentucky "colonel" observes horses act, grow, perform. On the basis of his direct observation, supplemented by hearsay, tradition, and authority, he constructs a repertoire of beliefs, expectations, and ideal standards, pertaining to horses. Perhaps we could call this body of information his "horse-structure." We could describe his horse-structure after we had interviewed him concerning what he knows, believes, expects, and feels about horses. We could evaluate his horse-structure in the light of scientific knowledge; we could determine how well his various beliefs about horses meet logical standards of consistency; we could compare his ideals and standards with those of other people, etc. We could even track down the origins of many of his beliefs and feelings, by studying his life history in some detail.

If we knew enough about our colonel's horse-structure, we could probably predict many of his overt behavior-patterns with respect to horses, and we could also predict many of his feelings, wishes, and decisions as these pertain to horses.

As with the horse-structure, so with the self-structure. The self-structure is a construction of the ego. *It refers to the beliefs, percep-tions, ideals, expectations, and demands, which a person has come to formulate with respect to his own behavior and experience.*[15]

We are not born with a self-structure, any more than we are born with a horse-structure; it is acquired and constructed by the ego. We can determine the nature of an individual's self-structure, and de-scribe it, if we observe and interview the individual exhaustively enough. We can evaluate his self-structure with respect to the ac-curacy of the beliefs which it comprises, and the feasibility of the component ideals and expectations. If we know a person's self-structure, we should be able to predict and understand his behavior and experience. Indeed, it has been found empirically that when people know each other, they know each other's self-structure in considerable detail. Married couples, for example, know well how their spouses feel about themselves, what they expect of themselves, and what they believe to be true about themselves.[16]

Personality hygienists place a positive value on the construction, by the ego, of a self-structure which is *closely congruent with the real self*. What this means, fundamentally, is that a person should per-ceive his own inner experience with accuracy, without selection and distortion; he should formulate accurate beliefs about his own modal inner experience; his ideals and values should be experienced as his own, and not those of someone else; his expectations of himself should lie within the realm of possible achievement.[17] That is, his expectations of himself are formulated with due attention to his real abilities and potentials for conforming with these expectations.

When an individual's self-structure is markedly discrepant with his real self, he is said to display *self-alienation*, or alienation from his real self.

ALIENATION FROM THE SELF

Horney [18] has listed a number of indications, or symptoms of self-alienation. These include:

1. The general capacity for conscious experience is impaired; the person is living "as if in a fog. Nothing is clear, neither one's own thoughts and feelings, nor other people, nor the implications of a situation."

2. There may be a decrease in awareness or concern for the body, its

needs and feelings, or for material possessions such as a house, car, or clothing.

3. There is a loss of the feeling of being an active determining force in one's own life.

The factors which Horney sees as responsible for the process of self-alienation include:

1. The development of compulsive solutions to neurotic conflicts, such as striving for affection, detachment from others, chronic hostility to others, etc.

2. Active moves away from the real self, such as the drive for glory, strivings to live up to an impossible self-ideal, etc.

3. Active moves against the real self, as in self-hate, self-destruction, etc.

The net consequence of alienation from the self, Horney says, is that the person's *"relation to himself has become impersonal"* (her italics). More specifically, in the self-alienated person, *pride governs feelings*—the individual does not react with spontaneous feeling-responses. Instead, he feels what he should feel. Further, the self-alienated person does not feel in possession of his own energies; his powers are not his own. Another consequence of self-alienation which Horney describes is an impairment in the ability to *assume responsibility for the self*. The self-alienated person *is lacking in plain, simple honesty about himself and his life.* The lack in honesty manifests itself, she states, as (a) an inability to recognize oneself as one really is, without minimizing or exaggerating, (b) an inability or unwillingness to accept the consequences of one's actions and decisions, and (c) an inability or unwillingness to realize it is up to oneself to do something about one's difficulties. The person who is self-alienated insists that others, fate, or time will solve these difficulties for him.

Let us generalize from Horney's important contribution to an understanding of self-alienation, and re-state some of her observations in terms we have defined for this chapter.

Self-alienation means, basically, that the ego is not directing behavior according to the person's real needs, wishes, and feelings; that is, his real self. Instead, the ego is serving some "master" other than the real self. But if the real self is not the source of direction to the individual's behavior, what is the direction-source for the self-alienated person? Let us distinguish among the following sources of be-havior-direction, namely, *pride-direction, conscience-direction, authority-direction, other-direction, impulse-direction,* and, finally, *real-self direction.*

PRIDE- AND CONSCIENCE-DIRECTION. Riesman's concept of the "inner-directed character" [19] is an excellent illustration of the person whose behavior expresses the dictates of conscience and self-ideal rather than the real self. When choices for action arise, such a person experiences a conflict between what he really wants to do, and what he believes he *ought* to do. In this connection, Horney has written of the *tyranny of the should.*[20] Implicitly, such a person believes his real self is an unreliable guide to conduct, and so he represses, suppresses, or ignores, his real self. Instead of following his real self, he habitually follows some inflexible moral code, or some stringent ideals which he believes he must conform with. The net consequence of ignoring the real self in favor of the conscience and self-ideal is that the person may behave in a moral and exemplary fashion, but his real needs are ignored, and he will be perpetually thwarted.

AUTHORITY-DIRECTION. The "authoritarian character," so well described by Fromm, Maslow, and more recently by Adorno, Frenkel-Brunswik, Levinson and Sanford,[21] is a person who allows the dictates of some authority-figure to serve as the source of direction to his conduct. He strives to discern what behavior the authority-figure expects of him, and he hastens to comply. If there is any conflict between his own wishes and the demands of authority, he habitually suppresses his own, and compulsively complies with the authority's wishes. Indeed, he experiences his real self as evil, or weak—not worth considering. Fromm [22] interprets the manner in which authoritarian characters perceive authority as a by-product of real-self repression, followed by a projection to the authority-figure of all of one's own repressed "powers." Hence, the authoritarian character perceives himself as weak, and the leader as all-powerful, and possessing unusual strength and wisdom—the "charismatic" leader.

OTHER-DIRECTION. Riesman's concept, the "other-directed" character [23] describes an individual who allows the wishes and expectations of his social peers to direct his actions. The other-directed character becomes sensitized to other's wishes, and actively seeks to comply with them. The result may be popularity and acceptance, but it is purchased at the cost of knowledge of the real self, and at the cost of thwarting many basic needs.

IMPULSE-DIRECTION. Impulses and emotions are a part of the real self, just as are will and ideals. The ego has the function of reconciling the often conflicting demands of impulses, ideals, the will, and the demands and expectations of other people. An impulse-directed person is one who habitually ignores all demands upon his behavior save those imposed by his impulses and feelings. He ignores his conscience, the rights of other people—even his own long-range welfare and growth. All is subordinated to the immediate gratification of his needs and impulses, and the immediate expression of his feelings. Psychoanalysts refer to such individuals as "instinct-ridden" characters; they idealize and rationalize their drives and emotions because they cannot voluntarily control them.

REAL-SELF DIRECTION. In the instances mentioned above, the person's ego has been directed and guided by sources other than the real self. The real-self directed person is the healthy personality. His ego is sensitive and perceptive of his real self. The person affirms the value and worth of his real self. He trusts his real self as the best guide for his own conduct.[24] Consequently, his behavior is a true expression of his real self. He knows his real needs, his own values and ideals, and strives to satisfy the needs in accordance with his own values. In contrast with the other types of characters, the real-self directed person is *autonomous*.[25] His ego selects the promptings of his real self, rather than other sources of direction, as the guide to conduct.

SELF-REALIZATION: KNOWLEDGE OF THE REAL SELF

Knowledge of the real self, and action in accordance with the real self, are fundamental personality-hygiene values. How is knowledge of the real self achieved, when it is apparent that many factors militate against such knowledge, for example, pride, conscience, needs for popularity, etc. The basic answer to the question is *honest introspection*. But honest self-observation is a very difficult kind of activity, for many reasons. A person is so close to his real self that it is difficult for him to observe it with accuracy. Further, there are many factors, such as pride, which prevent us from observing many aspects of our real self. Finally, we may have repressed much of our real self, in order to maintain self-esteem, and to avoid anxiety. In all likelihood, the only means for achieving a fuller knowledge of our real selves, and to increase our ability for honest introspection, is through *intensive personality therapy*. The personality therapist strives to discern all kinds of subtle indications of the person's real feelings and wishes, and he interprets these to his patient.[26] If therapy is successful, the patient will become acquainted, often for the first time, with aspects of his real self which he had never before experienced.

If a person has loving friends and family, he may be able to obtain assistance at knowing his real self; [27] his friends and loved ones may confront him periodically with their interpretations of his motives and actions. Such honesty from one's intimates is not a substitute for intensive therapy with a trained therapist; but if a person has grown up among such honest persons, he may not arrive at such a degree of self-alienation that intensive therapy becomes necessary.

THE COMPONENTS OF THE SELF-STRUCTURE

Thus far, we have distinguished among the personality, the ego, the real self, and the self-structure. Let us investigate the self-structure in further detail. The self-structure may be broadly defined as a by-product of the cognitive activity of the ego; it is constructed by the ego, in the last analysis. It comprises three broad components, the *self-concept*, the *self-ideal*, and various *public selves*.

An individual's self-structure is seldom in the forefront of his thoughts, but it is possible for him to verbalize its contents. An observer can often determine the nature of an individual's self-structure through inference, and through direct questioning. Personality investigators have devised rather ingenious methods for making the self-structure explicit for research purposes. The basic procedure has been to develop a list of statements concerned with behavior and inner experience: "I never lose my temper"; "I have a good sense of humor"; "I have many fantasies about success," etc. The person then responds to this list in various ways, depending upon what aspect of the self-structure is under study. Thus, if the self-concept is being studied, the subject is asked to indicate which of the statements is accurately descriptive of him, and which are not. If the statements are printed on cards, the subject sorts them into piles, where one pile represents statements that are very true for him, other piles include statements which are less true, and still others contain statements which are definitely not descriptive of the person.

If the self-ideal is being investigated, then the individual again sorts the statements into piles, but this time, he is selecting those statements which would describe him if he was *the way he wanted to be*. If the public selves are to be explored, the person sorts the cards so they will describe the way he behaves in the presence of others: the way *he wants others to think of him.*

This procedure has been described in the literature as "Q-methodology," and a number of important researches have been made possible by its invention.[28]

In the last analysis, the self-structure of an individual can be formulated by an observer through asking him to describe himself as he believes he is, as he would like to be, and as he wants others to think of him. The research procedures are little more than a refinement and extension of this basic procedure.

THE SELF-CONCEPT. The self-concept comprises all the beliefs the individual holds concerning what kind of person he *is;* i.e., conclusions concerning his *modal* or typical reaction patterns to typical life situations. Although a person seldom formulates all of these beliefs, yet a sample of them can readily be obtained simply by asking a person to describe himself. Generally, he will proceed to enumerate a series of trait-names: "I am lazy, happy-go-lucky, even-tempered; I have a good sense of humor; I don't rattle easily; I am polite." It can be seen that these words and phrases refer to consistent modes of behavior. They are in a sense statistical formulations. When a person says "I am even-tempered," he is asserting that he has observed his own behavior in a broad variety of situations and over an extended period of time; during that period of observation, the person believes that very few occasions could be found when he became angry or excited.

Yet it should not be concluded that the beliefs which comprise the self-concept are all grounded in the individual's direct observations of his own conduct. Many of the beliefs that the individual holds concerning his personality have been acquired from other people—

"significant others," as Sullivan described them [29]—from parents, friends, spouse, siblings, etc. These other people have observed the behavior of the individual, and have formulated beliefs concerning his personality, beliefs which they convey to him. He, in turn, adopts or affirms these beliefs. As they believe he is, he comes to believe he is. Many of the beliefs which a person has acquired from other people are not simply statistical conclusions, free from value-judgments; rather, many of them derive from a comparison of the individual's behavior with various moral standards. Thus, parents may say to a child, "You are bad." "You are lazy." The child has no reason to doubt the veracity of his parents, so he comes to agree with them. He believes he is lazy and bad.

Since the self-concept is actually a system of beliefs, we can apply the principles of logical and scientific criticism to those beliefs. We can ask, for example, "On what evidence does the person believe he is energetic? Bright? Even-tempered? Is this belief warranted? Or is it a generalization based on insufficient data, or on a biased sample of observations?" In other words, we can determine whether or not the beliefs correspond with the individual's modal behavior.

We can inquire further as to the logical compatibility or coherence of the beliefs with one another, much as we would examine any system of beliefs with respect to its logical coherence. Are some beliefs contradictory with one another? Does a person believe that he is both kind and unkind? Honest and dishonest? Lazy and energetic? Easy-going and tense?

Examination of the beliefs which an individual holds concerning his modal behavior will often disclose many that are patently inaccurate and contradictory. Further, there may be a wide range of behavior and experience which the individual himself does not observe, or misinterprets—just as a scientist who is defending some pet theory will ignore or misinterpret "negative instances." This is done so as to avoid drawing undesirable conclusions about his personality and to defend his present self-concept.

WHAT CONSTITUTES A SIGNIFICANT OTHER? Sullivan, the late prominent American psychiatrist, accorded considerable attention to the role played by "significant others" in the acquisition of the self-structure, or "self-dynamism," as he called it. He stated [30] that the self (-structure) was made up of "reflected appraisals," appraisals of the individual which were made by "parents and significant others." The implication of his comments is clear: as the parents and significant others defined and evaluated the person, so would he come to define and evaluate himself.[31]

Another way of looking at this problem is as follows: The self-concept comprises the beliefs which an individual holds with respect to his behavior, as well as a number of moral conclusions, based on a comparison of the behavior with some moral standards. Now, a person can arrive at beliefs and moral judgments through his own independent observations and comparisons, but he can also arrive at them simply through *listening to the conclusions which another person makes, and believing the other person.* Thus, I can examine my past behavior, and assert: "I hardly ever stole anything in the past. Therefore, I can say that I am honest and trustworthy. Honesty and trustworthiness are very valuable traits in our society, and since I have them, I can also say that I am a good person." Suppose my mother then said: "Look here. You are overlooking a lot of things. Remember all the times that you stole and told lies? I believe you are dishonest, untrustworthy, and bad." Whom shall I believe? My mother, or myself?

Let us define another person as a significant other *when his beliefs and feelings about us make an important difference to us, and when he has a status which implies his opinions and judgments must be considered as authoritative.* By these criteria, it is clear that one's parents are highly significant others when one is very young—on both counts. Their opinions and beliefs about us will strongly influence the way they treat us, and further, when we are very young, our parents appear omniscient. If they say we are bad, they punish us, and we believe we are bad. What child can pit his opinion against that of his parents? Why should the child doubt his parents' conclusions?

All of us are surrounded by significant others, and we are continually modifying our self-concepts so they will accord nicely with the opinions and judgments of these significant others. When one's superior says, "You've done a nice piece of work, you're a good craftsman," one can hardly escape believing that one is a good craftsman, and glowing with pride. If one's friend says the same words, it doesn't feel the same, and it leaves one with a certain measure of un-

certainty concerning one's skill, for the friend is not really qualified
to judge.

An individual may believe that he is insane. His friends may reassure him, but they are not significant others when it comes to making
judgments about sanity. The individual will not be reassured until
he hears a qualified psychiatrist or psychologist pronounce the words
"you are sane."

THE SELF-IDEAL. The self-ideal refers to a set of beliefs which an
individual holds concerning how he *should* behave.[32] These specifications of ideal behavior usually derive from the more abstract moral
and ethical precepts which are current within the society at a given
time. The beliefs of the self-ideal can be stated as "self-expectations,"
or "self-demands." The individual expects it of himself that he will
behave with honesty, punctuality, morality. If he fails to live up to
these self-expectations, he will experience self-hatred, or guilt. (See
Chapter 10.)

The self-ideal has its beginnings in early childhood in the form of
demands and expectations which parents and other significant persons held of the child. As the child conformed with these demands
and expectations, he was rewarded and received approval. When he
failed to conform with parental demands, he was punished, and rejected. Usually, the child conformed with the parental demands for
very concrete reasons—to maximize very concrete rewards, and to
minimize very concrete punishments and reprimands. Later, the demands, or ideals came to be formulated as moral absolutes, as abstract statements of what is right and good, and what is wrong and
bad. The child gradually adopts these demands (which others have
made of him) as *his own demands on himself*. When the parents asserted to their children that they should be prompt, clean, neat,
obedient, high achievers in school, etc., they generally assumed the
children had the ability or the potential ability to conform with
those expectations. But often, the demands and expectations were
set beyond the real ability of the child to conform with them. The
child, however, again has no reason to doubt his parents. If they say
he can and should conform with their wishes, he believes them.
When he cannot, he questions his goodness, obedience, or persistence, not his parents' demands. One sees no reason to doubt that if
a mother said to her child, "You should grow wings and fly," the

child would try and try, and when he observed that no wings were sprouting, he would feel guilty and unworthy of his mother's love. He would hate himself, because he *should* be able to grow wings; Mother said so.

We can examine the beliefs that comprise the self-ideal from a number of viewpoints. We can inquire: "How possible is it for this particular person to conform with this particular ideal?" "How compatible are these ideals one with another?" "To what extent do the ideals, or expectations conform with the mores of society at large?" "To what extent are the ideals compatible with gaining physical satisfactions?" "To what extent does fulfillment of the ideals bring satisfaction?"

When once a self-ideal has been formulated (it is continuously in process of formulation and reformulation), it provides a standard in terms of which the individual appraises his own conduct (and personality). Just as a person intermittently observes his own conduct, so does he evaluate it in terms of his moral or ideal precepts. There is no self-observation which is not also a self-evaluation—a comparison between what is done and what should be done. It is only under special conditions of sophistication that an individual can attempt to observe and describe his conduct without evaluating it in moral terms.

In view of the continual self-evaluation which goes on during a person's life, it should be apparent that when the self-ideal is violated by the person's conduct—when he does not behave as he believes he should—he will hate himself, or believe he is a failure, a sinner, or just plain "no good." If he behaves as he should, he will experience self-esteem, and believe that he is a worthwhile, likable, acceptable person. The self-ideal is such an important factor in personality health, that we shall devote a chapter (Chapter 10) to fuller discussion.

THE PUBLIC SELF. Other persons who have observed an individual, formulate beliefs about his personality. They not only observe his behavior, however; they also evaluate it in terms of their own value-system. The small child soon learns that when his parents believe he is one kind of person, they punish and reprimand him; when they hold different beliefs, they reward and approve of him. Consequently, he acquires a vested interest in promulgating certain *pre-*

ferred beliefs about his personality in the minds of other people.

At this point, we must draw a distinction between the valid beliefs that other people hold concerning an individual, which constitute his "real personality," and the carefully monitored set of beliefs which the individual *strives* to *induce* other people to formulate. It is the latter which constitute the *public selves* of the individual. Students of the history of psychology will observe a close parallel between the "social self" described by William James,[33] and the present writer's concept of the public self. James states *"a man has as many social selves as there are individuals who recognize him* and carry an image of him in their mind" (italics his).

The layman's term for the public self is "wanted reputation." Everyone strives to construct a reputation with respect to his modal behavior; i.e., he carefully restricts his behavior before other persons so they cannot help but formulate the kinds of beliefs which he wants them to possess. Almost everyone in our society draws a distinction between his "public" life and his "private" life. Ordinarily, only those persons whom an individual loves or trusts absolutely are allowed to observe the full range of his behavior repertoire. Outsiders are permitted to observe only the "expurgated" edition of his behavior.[34]

The most important reason for constructing public selves of various sorts is *expedience*. It is only when others believe certain things to be true of you that they will like you, marry you, give you jobs, refrain from imprisoning you, appoint you to public office, buy things at your store, or consult you professionally. If, for any reason, other people believe undesirable things to be true of your modal behavior, they will ostracize you, jail you, etc.

A person may construct highly diversified public selves, depending upon his needs and values. The young man seeking a spouse strives to behave in ways that the girl will be likely to value and approve. He does not allow her to see the rest of his behavior, which may be tremendously discrepant with the censored version of him which she does see.

A person's public selves are usually incomplete versions of his total self, since he seldom allows other people to observe or know about *all* of his behavior. This implies that the individual knows more about himself than any one other person. It is only in principle that another person could know more about me than I know myself. If he could accompany me at all times, and if I related everything I thought and felt aloud to him at all times, then he might know me better than I know myself, for he is capable of less biased observation than I.

Very often, a person may slip during the process of constructing, or living up to, a given public self. He may want his audience to believe one thing about him, say, that he is blameless, and morally scrupulous; yet, he may forget himself, and curse, or lose his temper, and thus destroy the image he was constructing. Such experiences produce embarrassment, to say the least. The reading public has an insatiable curiosity for details which conflict with the public selves of newsworthy people.[35]

A person is generally very sensitive to the impression his behavior produces in his audience. When it appears that the other person is formulating nonpreferred beliefs about him, he will become disturbed, and say "You have the wrong impression of me. I am not like that," and he will strive, with words and action, to convey a set of beliefs he wants the other person to adopt.

With respect to the beliefs which comprise an individual's public selves, we can ask: "Do these beliefs correspond with his self-concept? Do they correspond with his modal behavior? Do they correspond with his self-ideal? Are his public selves compatible with one another? Are his public selves accurate versions of his total behavior repertoire?"

We have related in some detail the definitions of the parts of the self-structure. Let us now ask: "What difference does it make, what a person believes himself to be, or what he believes he ought to be, or what he wants other people to believe about him? Will variations in these assorted beliefs make a difference in the way in which the person behaves?" We shall answer these questions with a "yes."

THE SELF-STRUCTURE AND BEHAVIOR

A person tends to show marked consistency in his behavior. A neat individual is usually neat in almost everything he does. An honest person is usually consistently honest. A poor speller generally shows consistency in making errors.[36] A thorough person generally does everything in a thorough fashion. What factors are responsible for this observed consistency in behavior? One answer may be found in the realm of learning theory. Consistent behavior is *habitual* behavior. As a general rule, habits persist so long as they are "reinforced"; i.e., so long as they continue to be instrumental toward the attainment of satisfactions, or toward the avoidance and reduction of pain.

Another reason for consistency in behavior, not necessarily incompatible with that derived from reinforcement theory, is to be found in the theory of the self-structure. It may be asserted that *people behave with consistency in order to maintain or to justify their present beliefs about their personality*. In other words, an individual believes he is such and such a kind of person, that he "has" certain traits. He continues to behave in ways that will enable him to continue believing that he has those traits.

Why should the person *want* to continue believing he has those traits? What difference could it possibly make, whether he believes or doubts that certain trait-names describe his behavior accurately?

There are three separate, but related answers to this question. A person must believe certain things about himself, (a) in order to maintain self-esteem, or to avoid guilt and shame, (b) in order to maintain his sense of identity, and (c) in order to continue to believe he is acceptable to other people.

SELF-CONCEPT, BEHAVIOR, AND SELF-ESTEEM. Self-esteem, a variety of self-appraisal highly valued by personality hygienists as well as by the person himself, is highly dependent upon behavior which conforms with the self-ideal. So long as a person *acts* in self-approved ways, he can justifiably believe he is a worthwhile person, at least in his own eyes. Thus, we can assert that a person behaves in certain ways, not only to secure satisfaction of assorted wants, but also to verify or justify certain beliefs about his personality. He must justify these beliefs in order to maintain self-esteem.

Let us imagine that a person values the ability to speak with elegance. His self-esteem may be highly dependent upon his own ability to speak with elegance. So long as he speaks in this fashion, he holds his personality in esteem. When he speaks crudely, he despise himself. This individual literally must believe, if he is to maintain self-esteem, that he is an effective and elegant speaker. As a consequence he will strive continually to speak in this fashion. It is onl as he speaks that way that he can (a) believe he is such a speaker, and (b) hold his personality in esteem.

It may readily be seen, then, that a person actually *strives* to behave with consistency. He strives to behave in those ways which will continually verify or justify the beliefs he holds with respect to his personality. Only so long as these beliefs can be affirmed will he be able to maintain self-esteem.

THE SELF-CONCEPT, BEHAVIOR, AND THE SENSE OF IDENTITY. The sense of identity may be defined as the subjective experience of "being one's real self." Psychologists have not as yet paid much attention to this variable. Erikson,[37] a psychoanalyst, has used the term "ego identity" to refer to the identity-sense, and he mentions at least four meanings for his term: "At one time, (ego identity) will appear to refer to a conscious *sense of individual identity;* at another (time) to an unconscious striving for a continuity of personal character; at a third, as a criterion for the silent doings of *ego synthesis;* and, finally, as a maintenance of an inner *solidarity* with a group's ideals and identity" (italics his).

For us, the sense of identity is a conscious, subjective experience of "being oneself" which derives from self-observation and judgment. The person observes his actions as he goes along through life, and compares them, consciously or unconsciously, *with a standard provided by his memory of how he has been throughout the recent and immediate past.* It is as if each action of a person yielded a proprioceptive and kinesthetic "feed-back" that is judged as being "like me" or "not like me." The "me" which is referred to is the individual's self-concept.

When a person acts in accordance with his self-concept, his sense of identity is reinforced. When he acts in ways discrepant to his self-concept, he feels what we shall call *a loss of the sense of identity.*[38] It is probably verbalized by the person: "I am not myself." When a person is acting in ways counter to his self-concept, he experiences anxiety, apprehension about the probable reactions of other people to his behavior. So long as he is "himself," he can predict fairly well how others will react. When he is in process of changing his identity, he will likely experience "identity-crises" marked by intense anxiety.

Behavior which conforms with the self-concept may thus be

viewed as behavior which preserves the sense of identity; like anxiety and guilt, the sense of identity is a factor which promotes consistency in behavior, and resists change in behavior.

Another way of defining the sense of identity is to describe it as a person's *beliefs* concerning the ways in which *other people* think about him. This is not the same as the public self or personality. Public selves are preferred or valued beliefs which a person *wants* other people to have about him; personality formulations are beliefs which other people actually have with respect to the individual's behavior, independent of his wishes, knowledge, or preferences. The sense of identity, on the other hand, refers to the individual's conviction—accurate or inaccurate—of his "stimulus value," of how other people think about him. He may like or dislike, be proud or ashamed, of his identity. Yet it seems valid to assert that even a shameful identity is preferable to a person than no identity—being nobody.

Therefore, a person who believes he is bad, or unskilled, or sloppy, will tend to behave with consistency, thus continually reinforcing those beliefs, *because they constitute his identity*. It is as if being John Smith means being bad, lazy, and sloppy—but better to be John Smith than to be nobody. If he were to behave in other ways, John would feel strange, "not himself;" in order to get rid of the feeling of strangeness, he snaps back to the old ways of behaving.

Many overweight people have constructed a public self, a self-concept, and a sense of identity which are all predicated on overeating, being happy and jolly and clown-like. Such persons have a difficulty in reducing their weight in addition to that produced by hunger pangs and hearty appetite. They do not feel they are "themselves" when they are eating small meals, and they fear that should they change their body shape, they will not be known and recognized by their friends and associates. They fear the prospect of creating a new identity for themselves.

One of the determiners of fugue and amnesia is discontent with one's present identity. A change of locale and name facilitates a change in modal behavior, which in turn facilitates the construction of a new self-structure.

THE SELF-CONCEPT AND THE BELIEF THAT ONE IS ACCEPTABLE TO OTHERS. We have stated that a person must believe certain things about his personality in order to maintain self-esteem and his sense of identity. In addition, he must believe certain things about himself in order to justify the belief that he is *acceptable to others*.

Early in childhood, the individual learned that only when he acted in certain ways was he acceptable to his parents. As he consistently acted in those acceptable ways, he would come to believe he *was* the kind of person who acted that way. A child's sense of safety, or security, is strongly dependent upon the belief that his parents like him.[39] We may generalize further, and assert that any individual's sense of security is dependent upon the belief that other people like him.

Because only a certain range of behavior is acceptable to others, a person will strive to behave in acceptable ways, and hide unacceptable behavior from the public gaze, or eliminate it. So long as he does behave in acceptable ways, he can (a) believe that he is the kind of person others will like, and (b) believe that other people actually do like him. If he behaves in ways which challenge his self-concept, the person is likely to experience guilt, a feeling of not being himself, and also a sense of anxiety or insecurity—the conviction that other people will not like him.[40]

THE PUBLIC SELVES, SELF-IDEAL, AND BEHAVIOR. The public selves which a person has established, or is trying to establish, constitute an important determiner of behavior, especially in behavior which comes under the observation or scrutiny of other people. In contemporary society, where privacy and secrecy are difficult to find, this naturally includes most of a person's behavior repertoire.

A person will strive to behave before others in ways that will construct, or preserve, a set of beliefs about him he wants them to have. Riesman has [41] described vividly the changes in the contemporary American social structure which compel a person to become concerned with the opinions of others about him. His other-directed character is a superb description of a type of man, or personality-structure, which is becoming increasingly common.

In the presence of others, an individual may often behave in the ways which *they* expect him to behave, irrespective of his real feelings or wants. Since many of the satisfactions in contemporary living can be achieved only through the good-will of other people (lone wolves are no longer fashionable), the person must present at least the appearance of being an "acceptable" individual.

The public selves constructed by a person will generally correspond closely with his self-ideal. He may know with certainty that he doesn't really want to act in certain ways; he doesn't really have the opinions which he expresses; he doesn't really have the feelings which he pretends to have. Yet he must behave as if he had those feelings, opinions, and desires, because he believes that he *should* (as specified by his self-ideal), and because if he fails to act in those ways, other people will formulate undesirable beliefs about him. These beliefs will jeopardize his status, his marriage, his job, and many other things which he values highly. Behavior which conforms with the self-ideal, with other people's expectations, or with the person's public selves, rather than with a person's real feelings and wishes, all indicate some degree of alienation from the self.

Thus far, we have defined the components of the self-structure, and attempted to show how the self-structure influences behavior. Let us now pose the question, "What is a healthy self-structure?" We need a description of the healthy self for purposes of comparison with any given self-structure, in order to ascertain how healthy or sick it is.

A HEALTHY SELF-STRUCTURE

Probably the best single indicator of a healthy self-structure is to be found in an individual's threat-threshold. The more easily threatened the individual, the less healthy is his self-structure. It will be recalled that threat to the self-structure is experienced subjectively in the form of guilt, loss of self-esteem, as anxiety, or dread of being "found out," and as dread of finding out things about oneself.[42] The more accurate the individual's self-concept, and the more congruent one with the other are his self-ideal, self-concept, public selves, and real self, then the less readily can a person be threatened. We are all familiar with the person who, when his motives are questioned, becomes upset and defensive. He is striving to hide the motives in question from the viewer and also from himself. The individual with a healthy self-structure can face and admit all of his motives and feelings, and all of his past and present actions.

In more formal terms, a healthy self-structure [43] is comprised of the following components:

1. A self-concept which, at any given time, is based on the individual's real self. He has no vested interest in believing anything about his own motives or actions which is untrue. He can acknowledge to himself and to others (if need be) all of his feelings, wishes, fantasies, needs, and experiences.

2. A self-ideal which is feasible, comprising values which are roughly congruent with social mores, and which the person has had an active role in formulating and affirming.

3. Public selves which are accurate, compatible with one another, and expressive of the real self.

It is fair to state that no person ever has an absolutely healthy self-structure; rather, a healthy self-structure is a goal or value, and it is never maintained for long. The real self is in continuous process of change, as is the actual behavior of the individual. If he is to maintain a healthy self-structure, the person must continually reformulate his self-structure so that it keeps in touch with the realities of his inner self and his overt behavior. Each time the self-structure becomes discrepant from the real self, and the individual becomes aware of the discrepancy, he will again experience threat. *Whether or not his self-structure moves in the direction of health will depend upon how he has handled the threat—whether in a growth-promoting way, or in a defensive manner.*

Thus, it is not only the threat-threshold which depicts the health of the self-structure; the manner in which the individual deals with threats to his self-structure must also be considered.

A NOTE ON THREAT. Threats to the self-structure arise from inner and outer sources. Inner threat refers to all of those thoughts, feelings, wishes, fantasies, and memories which are likely to be discrepant with the present self-structure. Thus, a person may strive to avoid thinking certain things because to do so would cause him to doubt certain aspects of his self-concept.

Outer threat comprises the reactions of other people to the self. If another person holds a concept of you which is different from your self-concept, you may experience threat. If he assigns a different interpretation of your motives than the one which you want him to hold, you will experience threat. Threat is a very powerful motive. It can lead to behavior pathology, and it can lead to further personality growth in the direction of health.

VARIETIES OF UNHEALTHY SELVES

INACCURATE AND INCOMPLETE SELF-CONCEPTS. This is perhaps the most common variety of unhealthy self. A person may entertain only a limited repertoire of beliefs about his personality, refusing to acknowledge entire realms of behavior as part of him.[44] He might, for example, refuse to acknowledge the proposition that he is an aggressive person, even though he behaves often in an aggressive manner. Instead, he may believe he is basically a gentle, kindly person. When he loses his temper, he will assert that "I was not myself at the time," or else forget about it.

We are all familiar with the person who defends some cherished theory by ignoring all evidence which would refute his theory. The self-concept is very closely analogous with a cherished theory. Thus, from a strictly logical point of view, the person's beliefs about what kind of a person he is may be grossly incomplete.

In addition to incompleteness, a person's beliefs about how he behaves may be logically contradictory with each other. He may, for example, believe he is both aggressive and kind, competitive and co-operative, highly moral, and also a jolly-good-fellow—"one of the boys."

Finally, a person's beliefs may be drastically inaccurate. His beliefs about how he behaves—i.e., how his behavior should be classified —may do violence to the science of taxonomy. Thus, many people may label his behavior with his children as cruel and brutal, while he calls it "good parenthood." Or, many people might call his behavior in business sheer piracy or dishonesty, while he chooses to call it "business acumen."

One of the important aims of psychotherapy can be stated as the attempt to help a person formulate beliefs about how he behaves (i.e., what kind of person he is) which are accurate, complete, and logically compatible.

UNDULY HIGH SELF-IDEALS. The self-concept refers to the way that a person believes he acts. The self-ideal refers to his concepts of how he *should* act. The penalty for failure to behave as one "should" is *guilt*—a hatred of the behavior in question, and more than that, hatred of the total personality and of the real self.[45] When a person has acquired values or ideals which are well out of the range of human capacity to implement, he has the groundwork prepared for chronic guilt. More than that, he has the groundwork prepared for inaccurate beliefs about the self. When it is so painful to doubt certain beliefs about one's personality, one may be driven, by the need to maintain self-esteem, to formulate inaccurate and incomplete beliefs. Thus, a "tyrannical" self-ideal facilitates the formation of inaccurate self-concepts, and also promotes the chronic experience of guilt, or loss of self-esteem.

INACCURATE AND INCOMPLETE PUBLIC SELF. Like the inaccurate self-concepts, inaccurate and incomplete public selves are very common forms of the unhealthy self. People seldom allow other people indiscriminately to observe all of their behavior, or allow others to know what they think and feel about things. They monitor their public behavior carefully, in order to promote censored beliefs concerning the kind of people they are.

As a consequence of this felt necessity to promulgate highly selected concepts of their personality to others, people often develop highly contradictory concepts among different groups of people. Thus, a college student might promote the view in his home town that he is highly obedient to his parents, a conformer, etc. At college, in his fraternity, he encourages the view that he is a "devil with the ladies," a man who can hold his liquor, and a bit of a nonconformer. With one girl-friend, he behaves in ways which will promote a concept of him as the kind of person she might like to marry; with another, he presents a different conception.

None of these public conceptions of his personality correspond with the individual's real personality, with his self-concept, or with his self-ideal. As a consequence, the individual with such conflicting public conceptions of his personality will often believe he is a hypocrite (since a common value is that of consistency), hate himself for it, and live in continual dread of being unmasked.[46]

MOVEMENT OF THE SELF-STRUCTURE. A healthy self-structure probably does not exist; it is rather an ideal formulated by the personality hygienist. People differ in the extent to which they presently have a healthy or unhealthy self.

We can study an individual, however, and come to conclusions

concerning whether or not this self-structure is "moving" toward a
healthier, or less healthy, self-structure, or whether it is remaining
static and unchanging. Naturally, the personality hygienist is concerned with promoting movement toward a healthy self-structure.[47]

How do we go about deciding in what direction a person is moving, with respect to common vicissitudes of the self-structure? How do
we tell whether a self-structure is becoming healthier or less healthy?

As observers, we have to take into account the following factors:
(a) the person's actual behavior and subjective experience (his real
self), (b) the nature of his self-concept, self-ideal, and public selves,
and (c) the degree of congruence of each of these factors with every
other factor. Let us illustrate how judgments might be made concerning movement toward and movement away from a healthy self-
structure.

Peter believes the following things about his personality: that he
is a highly moral person, and according to his standards, this implies
that his behavior, thoughts, feelings, and fantasies, all conform with
social norms; also he believes he *should* be moral. Finally, he wants
other people to believe that he is moral.

Let us now imagine that careful observation of Peter's behavior
discloses that much of the time, Peter has fantasies and wishes which
are in violent opposition both to his self-ideal and to social mores,
for example, he wants to murder his wife, establish a romance with
another woman, and abandon his children. Further, when he is certain that nobody who knows him is around, he cheats on his wife,
drinks lavishly, and is not averse to petty theft.

When Peter examines *all* of his behavior, and labels it accurately,
we should expect him to experience guilt and fear of rejection and
criticism. These emotional tensions are painful, or unpleasant, and
serve as a drive to some kind of activity which will eliminate or
avoid them. What kind of activity is most valued by the personality
hygienist as movement toward a healthier self-structure? What kind
of activity is, on the contrary, condemned as movement away from
a healthy self-structure? Actually, we are restating a question dealt
with in other sections (Chapter 10: healthy and unhealthy reactions
to guilt; Chapter 4: healthy and unhealthy reactions to fear and
anxiety). In the present context, the focus of our discussion is somewhat different, however, and so the question warrants restating.

ACTIVITY TOWARD A HEALTHIER SELF-STRUCTURE

When a person experiences guilt, or fear of rejection, punishment, and ostracism, it is usually because his behavior is not consistent with his self-concept. It will be recalled that the person *must* hold certain beliefs about his personality, on pain of guilt, loss of a sense of identity, and loss of status and the approving reactions of others. In principle, the healthy reactions to guilt and anxiety, prompted by inconsistent behavior are:

1. RESTRICT BEHAVIOR AND EXPERIENCE so that they *conform with the self-concept*. This is not entirely desirable, since it implies a static self-structure, and the personality hygienist values change (growth) of the self.

2. CHANGE THE BELIEFS WHICH COMPRISE THE SELF-CONCEPT, so that they encompass *all* behavior and experience.

3. CHANGE THE SELF-IDEAL, leaving the self-concept intact. (When this can be effected, the individual's behavior does not change, but his negative evaluation of it will. He will no longer experience guilt for the behavior that formerly was culpable.)

4. CHANGE HIS VARIOUS PUBLIC SELVES, so that he strives to convey to other people, by his behavior, a set of beliefs more congruent with his actual behavior and his self-concept; he strives to get other people to know him as he really is.

Any activity which produces these consequences may be regarded as movement toward a healthier self-structure, as this was defined in an earlier section.

Throughout the course of a person's life, many of these activities take place spontaneously. People actually do change their self-concepts, self-ideals, and public selves from time to time. Changes of this sort may be experienced sometimes as emotionally charged crises, or they may occur so gradually as to be unnoticed. Many personality therapists have observed people in the process of amending their beliefs about the kind of person they really are. Generally, these alterations in the self-concept are forced upon the patient as he observes the full extent to which his actual behavior, thoughts and feelings diverge from the presently held self-concept. Probably in the natural course of events, the self-concepts change gradually, almost without the awareness of the person involved. He just realizes at one time or another that he no longer believes something about himself which he always had before, and it doesn't particularly bother him. This is most likely to occur as a consequence of identifications with persons in groups that have different values. College students living away from home are often unaware they have changed their behavior patterns, their concepts of self, and their self-ideals. It is only when they return home that their parents and former associates "hardly know them." This often produces discomfort, conflict, and embarrassment.

In a later chapter, we will inquire in more detail into the conditions under which movement toward a healthy self-structure can be promoted, even controlled. This is actually the problem of psychotherapy, or personality therapy, as the present author prefers to call it. We can anticipate this chapter, however, by stating that movement toward a healthy self is most likely to be promoted within the framework of relationships with other people. More of this later. We are merely asserting here that it is difficult if not impossible, for a person to move toward self-health without the assistance of others.

Let us illustrate at this point, with concrete examples, the above-mentioned healthy moves.

The author undertook personality therapy with a middle-aged man who complained of the following symptoms—marked sensitivity to light, and an absolute panic when in the company of other people (including the therapist).

Over a period of several months, it was discovered that, among other things, he believed (but without being absolutely certain of it) that he was intellectually superior to other people. Further, he valued intelligence, culture, and poise very highly, and demanded of himself that he manifest all these traits. As he talked about his daily round of activities, his past, his feelings and fantasies, it soon became apparent to the therapist (and to him) that his belief in his own intellectual superiority to all others was a shaky one at best. He lived in constant dread lest others outsmart him, which would prove his self-concept was without foundation. Under the impetus of panic, he could not display his really considerable background of reading and general culture. He would instead block, stammer, giggle, get embarrassed, be unable to answer questions coherently, etc. These panic-produced reactions made him hate and despise himself. He "moved away from people," as Horney puts it, and spent much solitary time in his room. In addition, he believed that his eyes betrayed his inner feelings, so he wore very dark glasses when among other people. Naturally, this made him very sensitive to light whenever he removed them. As years passed, light became a source of agony, and so he was obliged to live almost as a blind person, in darkened rooms. So much for the "presenting symptoms."

At one point, he stated: "I am a hypocrite; I am stupid; I hate myself so much I don't see how you or anyone else could possibly be concerned about me. I don't deserve to live."

In the course of time, however, he came to modify his self-concept in important ways, bringing it much more into line with his actual behavior and feelings. His self-ideal underwent marked changes, mainly with respect to the stringency of his ideals. Finally, when among others, he behaved much more in accord with his feelings, constructing thereby more accurate public selves. It could be said about him that he manifested all of the active moves toward a healthy self-structure.

Here are some quotations from his remarks which illustrate these moves: "I know that I am not the smartest person in the world, but I really am smarter than many people I come into contact with. Not long ago, I'd have died rather than put that into words. Wasn't that stupid?" "I used to think that it was the most important thing in the world to be perfect, never to make a mistake in grammar, never to state an unfounded opinion. It's funny, but now I curse quite a bit, I sometimes speak like a hillbilly instead of a cultured person, and do you know, it doesn't bother me?" "You know, I'm getting brassy. I don't seem to give a damn what other people think of me. I just speak my piece, let them know what I think, and if it satisfies me, then that's all that counts. I don't mean that I'm a wild man; don't get me wrong. I just mean that when I'm with other people, I don't feel so phony, like I'm trying to get them to think about me in a special way. I'm finding out who my real friends are."

Lest the reader get the wrong impression, these statements were made after long months of agonizing, emotion-charged sessions during which the patient talked about his thoughts, feelings, wishes, past events, fantasies, with many attempts to hide and cover up important experiences.

EGO STRENGTH, AND GROWTH VERSUS DEFENSE OF THE SELF-STRUCTURE. We have stated that the self-structure should be maximally congruent with the real self, if it is to be adjudged healthy. But the real self is a continually changing thing. One's needs, wishes, feelings, values, goals, and behavior all change with age and experience. This continual change in the real self—its "unfolding" and "becoming" [48] —poses a problem for the individual. There is always the danger his real self will outgrow his self-structure in much the same way that a person outgrows his clothes. One knows his shoes or clothes no longer fit when they feel tight, and produce discomfort. One knows that his self-structure no longer "fits" the real self when threat occurs unduly often.

When a person experiences threat to his self-structure (which is a common, even daily occurrence), he has a limited number of alternative paths to action. Which path he will take hinges greatly on the strength of his ego.

If the ego is strong, the person will acknowledge the threat, and explore the factors responsible for it. On the basis of this reality-testing activity, he may suppress the threatening activity, or repress the unwanted feelings or impulses (but through conscious choice). Or, the person may accept and act upon the threatening feelings, and strive to modify his self-concept and self-ideal so they again fit his real self. A strong ego thus facilitates growth of a healthy self-structure.

But if the ego is weak, the individual may not be able to tolerate the threat to his self-structure. Instead of striving to determine what is threatening him and why, he may, quite automatically and involuntarily, resort to actions designed to *defend and protect his present self-structure*. There is a wide variety of "mechanisms" for the defense and maintenance of the self-structure which a weak ego will adopt. In the next chapter, we shall discuss these.

SUMMARY

The self, or *self-structure*, is known to be an important determiner and director of behavior. It imposes limits on the total possible range of behavior and experience of which an individual is potentially capable.

The self-structure is not synonymous with such terms as personality, ego, and the real self.

The *ego* is defined as the *agent* of personality and of all instrumental behavior. Ego is a hypothetical construct employed by psychologists to explain certain observable phenomena. The ego is thought to vary in *strength*. A strong ego is the agent of healthy personality. Ego strength is estimated by clinical psychologists, personality researchers, and psychiatrists through the use of certain indices, or signs, including certain Rorschach-test factors, measures of flexibility-rigidity, measures of stress- and frustration-tolerance, and signs of defense-mechanisms. The strong ego is in good contact with reality, displays flexibility, a high degree of stress-tolerance, and minimal use of self-defense mechanisms.

The *real self* refers to the inner experience of the individual, his actual wishes, feelings, needs, etc. The ego is regarded as the perceiver and the agent of the real self.

The *self-structure* comprises the beliefs, perceptions, ideals, expectations, and demands which a person has come to formulate with respect to his own behavior and experience. It is a construction of the ego.

Personality hygienists value highly the ability to know one's real self, and to act in accordance with the real self. When a person does not know his real self, or ignores and represses it, he is said to display *alienation from the self.*

Alienation from the self is manifested when the person is less aware of his own spontaneous wishes and feelings, and when he feels he is not in control of his own behavior. Instead of being real-self directed, the self-alienated individual's behavior may be directed by his conscience and pride, by authority-figures, by his peers, or by his impulses.

Knowledge of the real self can be achieved only through honest introspection. Intensive personality therapy may be required before an individual is capable of honest introspection.

The self-structure is comprised of the *self-concept*, the *self-ideal*, and various *public selves*.

The *self-concept* includes everything a person believes to be true, or typical of his usual behavior and inner experience. It is acquired through self-observation and through adoption of the conclusions about the self held by significant others. *Significant others* refers to those persons, such as parents, teachers, etc., whose feelings and judgments about one's own personality are important. They have high status in relation to the individual.

The *self-ideal* includes all of the ideals and standards with which the person must conform, if he is to maintain self-esteem and freedom from guilt. The self-ideal derives primarily from the demands and ideals which were directed toward the self by significant others.

The *public selves* of an individual refer to the beliefs which a person *wants* other people to have about him. He wants someone to believe he is a liberal, and so he utters liberal cliches without believing them. He wants his wife to believe he likes her mother, and so he suppresses his dislike for her.

The various components of the self-structure influence behavior by impelling the individual to restrict his behavior and experience to the limits which they set. Failure to behave in accordance with the self-structure results in a loss in self-esteem, a loss of the sense of identity, and anxiety and insecurity about one's acceptability to others.

A *healthy self-structure* is said to exist when the self-concept is based on the individual's real self; when the self-ideal is feasible, congruent roughly with social mores, and when the person has had some role in formulating it; when the public selves are accurate, compatible with one another, and expressive of the real self; and, finally, when all three aspects of the self-structure are roughly congruent with each other and with the real self.

Such a healthy self-structure is relatively immune to threat.

Unhealthy self-structures include those with inaccurate and incomplete self-concepts, unduly high self-ideals, and inaccurate, incomplete, and conflicting public selves.

It is possible to make judgments as to whether or not an individual's self-structure is moving in the direction of health. Healthy responses to threat are those which result in movement toward a healthier self-structure. Movement toward a healthy self-structure is facilitated if the individual has a relatively strong ego. If the ego is weak, threat to the self-structure is likely to be reacted to by means of defense mechanisms—which serve the function of preserving the present self-structure, and preventing growth.

NOTES AND REFERENCES

RECOMMENDED READINGS ARE MARKED WITH AN ASTERISK (*)

*1. The study of the self by psychologists and sociologists has a history that is longer than that of experimental psychology. William James wrote most lucidly on the subject, and anticipated much of the contemporary empirical research findings with respect to the self. See James, W., *Principles of psychology*, New York, Holt, 1890; or his *Psychology: briefer course*, New York, Holt, 1892, Ch. 12. The social psychologist, Mead, has contributed richly to present-day interest and formulations with respect to the Self. See Mead, G. H., *Mind, self and society*, Chicago, University of Chicago Press, 1934. A highly articulate formulation of the theory of the self is given in Rogers, C. R., *Client-centered therapy*, New York, Houghton Mifflin, 1951. Sullivan, Fromm, and Horney have been most explicit about the self among the psychiatric group of writers.

*2. Prescott Lecky was highly influential in directing the attention of contemporary psychologists to the phenomenon of *consistency* in behavior as a function of the self. See Lecky, P., *Self-consistency: a theory of personality*, New York, Island Press, 1945.

*3. See Freud, S., *An outline of psychoanalysis*, New York, Norton, 1949, for Freud's last systematic presentation of his conception of personality structure. For a systematic account of ego-psychology, see Hartmann, H., "Comments on the psychoanalytic theory of the ego," *Psychoanalyt. Stud. Child*, 1950, V, International University Press, New York. An excellent survey of ego functions is given in Redl, F. and Wineman, D., *Children who hate*, Glencoe, Illinois, The Free Press, 1951, pp. 61–196.

4. This distinction between the ego and the self parallels that made by Symonds, P., *The ego and the self*, New York, Appleton-Century-Crofts, 1951.

*5. Cf. MacCorquodale, K. and Meehl, P. E., "On a distinction between hypothetical constructs and intervening variables," *Psychol. Rev.*, 1948, 55, 95–107.

6. Fenichel, O., *The psychoanalytic theory of neurosis*, New York, Norton, 1945, Ch. 10.

7. It was Beck who suggested employing the "form-level" on the Rorschach as an index of ego-strength. Following his suggestion,

a number of experimenters have employed this index, or some adaptation of it, in various experiments, and with varying degrees of predictive efficiency. See Williams, M., "An experimental study of intellectual control under stress, and associated Rorschach factors," *J. consult. Psychol.*, 1947, 11, 21–29; McReynolds, P., "Perception of Rorschach concepts as related to personality deviations," *J. abn. soc. Psychol.*, 1951, 46, 131–141; Eriksen, C. W., "Psychological defenses and ego strength in the recall of completed and incompleted tasks," *J. abn. soc. Psychol.*, 1954, 49, 45–50; Jourard, S. M., "Ego strength and the recall of tasks," *J. abn. soc. Psychol.*, 1954, 49, 51–58; Feldman, M. J., *et al.*, "A preliminary study to develop a more discriminating F-plus ratio," *J. clin. Psychol.*, 1954, 10, 47–51.

8. Cf. Cattell, R. B., *Description and measurement of personality*, Yonkers, World, 1946.

9. See Personnel Research Branch Technical Research Note 22, *A bibliography for the development of stress-sensitive tests*, Washingington, Psychological Research Associates, 1953.

10. Cf. Davidson, H. H., "A measure of adjustment obtained from the Rorschach protocol," *J. proj. Tech.*, 1950, 14, 31–38; Barron, F., "An ego strength scale which predicts response to psychotherapy," *J. consult. Psychol.*, 1953, 17, 327–333.

11. Cf. Gellhorn, E., *Physiological foundations of neurology and psychiatry*, Minneapolis, University of Minnesota Press, 1953, pp. 434–438.

12. The "structure" of the ego may be described as the total repertoire of instrumental behavior-patterns which a person has acquired up to any given time in his life.

13. Horney, K., *Neurosis and human growth*, New York, Norton, 1950.

14. Fromm, E., *Escape from freedom*, New York, Rinehart, 1941, pp. 256–276.

15. This definition is similar to that expounded by Rogers. See Rogers, C. R., *op. cit.*, pp. 497–510.

16. Dymond, R. F., "Interpersonal perception and marital happiness," *Can. J. Psychol.*, 1954, 8, 164–171; Corsini, R. J., "Understanding and similarity in marriage," *J. abn. soc. Psychol.*, 1956, 52, 327–332.

17. These phenomena are found to occur among patients who have undergone successful personality therapy. Cf. Rogers, C. R. and Dymond, R. (ed.), *Psychotherapy and personality change*, Chicago, University of Chicago Press, 1954.

18. Horney, K., *op. cit.*, Ch. 6.
19. Riesman, D., *The lonely crowd,* New Haven, Yale University Press, 1950.
20. Horney, K., *op. cit.*, Ch. 3.
21 Fromm, E., *op. cit.*; Maslow, A. H., "The authoritarian character structure," *J. soc. Psychol.*, S.P.S.S.I. *Bulletin*, 1943, 18, 401–411; Adorno, T. W., Frenkel-Brunswik, Else, Levinson, D. J., and Sanford, R. N., *The authoritarian character,* New York, Harper, 1950.
22. Fromm, E., *op. cit.*, pp. 174–177 (discussion of the "magic helper"). Also Fromm, E., *Man for himself,* New York, Rinehart, 1947, pp. 145–146.
23. Riesman, D., *op. cit.*
24. Cf. Rogers, C. R., *The concept of the fully functioning person.* (Mimeographed manuscript, privately circulated, 1954, Chicago.)
25. Cf. Riesman, D., *op. cit.*
26. Horney has written a book as a guide to self-analysis. See Horney, K., *Self-analysis,* New York, Norton, 1942.
27. See Ch. 7 and Ch. 8.
*28. See Mowrer, O. H. (ed.), *Psychotherapy: theory and research,* New York, Ronald, 1953, for a detailed discussion of "Q-methodology." This technique was employed in the extensive studies of therapy conducted at Chicago. See Rogers, C. R. and Dymond, R. F. (ed.), *op. cit.*
29. Sullivan, H. S., *Conceptions of modern psychiatry,* Washington, William Alanson White Psychiatric Foundation, 1947.
30. Sullivan, H. S., *op. cit.*, pp. 10, 131.
31. Jourard, S. M. and Remy, R. M.,"Perceived parental attitudes, the self, and security," *J. consult. Psychol.*, 1955, 19, 364–366.
32. The concept of the ideal self is employed in the studies cited in Rogers, C. R. and Dymond, R. F. (ed.), *op. cit.* Horney also uses the term extensively in Horney, K., *Neurosis and human growth.* New York, Norton, 1950.
33. James, W., *Psychology,* New York, Holt, 1892, p. 179.
34. The concepts of "public self" and "social role" are systematically related to each other; each involves the selection by the person of "appropriate" behavior to perform in the presence of other people. See Ch. 6.
35. Compare the versions of movie stars' private lives as these are portrayed in the popular movie-magazines, and in the "scandal-sheet" magazine *Confidential.*

36. Lecky, P., *op. cit.*

°37. Erikson, E. H., "The problem of ego identity," *J. Amer. Psychoanalyt. Assoc.*, 1956, **4**, 56–121. See also Bugental, S. and Zelen, S. L., "Investigations into the self-concept. I. The W-A-Y technique," *J. Pers.*, 1950, **18**, 483–498.

°38. See Sherif, M. and Cantril, H., *The psychology of ego-involvements*, New York, Wiley, 1947, Ch. 12, for extensive discussion of the loss of identity.

39. Jourard, S. M. and Remy, R. M., *op. cit.*

40. Horney sees the conviction that others do not like you as an important component of "basic anxiety"—the feeling of powerlessness in a potentially hostile world.

41. Riesman, D., *op. cit.*

°42. See Snygg, D. and Combs, A. W., *Individual behavior*, New York, Harper, 1949, Ch. 7.

43. Rogers and collaborators found that the subjects who profited from therapy showed essentially the characteristics indicated in the text. See Rogers, C. R. and Dymond, R. F. (ed.), *op. cit.*

44. The psychoanalysts speak of this unacknowledged aspect of the real self as the "unconscious"; Sullivan referred to it as "dissociated" aspects of the self.

45. Cf. Horney, K., *op. cit.*

46. Mowrer's theory of anxiety and the development of neurosis is related to this interpretation. See Mowrer, O. H., *op. cit.*, Ch. 2, 6.

47. This movement is interpreted as "growth." For examples of some criteria of "growth," or improvement, see Rogers, C. R. and Dymond, R. F. (ed.), *op. cit.*; Conrad, D. C., "An empirical study of the concept of psychotherapeutic success," *J. consult. Psychol.*, 1952, **16**, 92–97; Barrabee, P., Barrabee, Edna L., and Finesinger, J. E., "A normative social adjustment scale," *Am. J. Psychiat.*, 1955, **112**, 252–259.

°48. Cf. Allport, G., *Becoming. Basic considerations for a psychology of personality*, New Haven, Yale University Press, 1955.

QUESTIONS FOR REVIEW AND EXAMINATION

1. Define and distinguish among the following terms: ego, personality, real self, self-concept, self-ideal, public selves, and self-structure.

2. How is ego strength estimated?

3. Define and explain alienation from the self.

4. What factors serve to direct a person's behavior when he has become self-alienated?

5. How is knowledge of the real self acquired?

6. How is the self-concept acquired? The self-ideal? Indicate the role played by significant others in acquiring the self-structure.

7. Indicate the influence imposed by various aspects of the self-structure on an individual's behavior and experience.

8. Explain what is meant by the sense of identity.

9. Describe the hypothetical healthy self-structure, and describe some common patterns of unhealthy self-structures.

10. How does a person achieve and maintain a healthy self-structure?

11. Describe as fully as you can, and evaluate, someone's total self-structure, using the concepts employed in this chapter as your guide.

CHAPTER 10

Defense of the Self-Structure

If a person's ego is strong, it is likely his self-structure will "grow" with actual changes in his real self and in his behavior. Each time that threat is experienced, the person with a strong ego will face the threat, analyze it, and respond to it in a way which promotes further growth of his self-structure. His self-concept will keep pace with changes in the real self; and his self-ideal, public selves, and self-concept will continually be in a process of mutual adjustment toward congruence with each other and with the real self.

But no one possesses an ego of optimum strength at all times, and so we all respond to threat at least some of the time in a *defensive* manner rather than in a growth-promoting manner. What is meant by a defensive response to threat?

When a person responds defensively to any threat to his self-structure, he is actually placing a greater value upon maintaining his present self-structure than he is upon being his real self and upon his own growth. For in the last analysis, threat is the by-product of a conflict between the real self and the self-structure. Threat is experienced whenever some impulse, feeling, thought, memory, or perception conflicts with the person's beliefs about himself, with his

324

self-ideal, or with one of his public selves. It is experienced as guilt, loss of the sense of identity, anxiety about the reactions of other people, etc. And so, in order to preserve self-esteem, the present sense of identity, and the desired reactions of others to the self, the threatened individual may strive to *ignore* or *distort* the inner experiences that produced the threat. Defense of the self-structure against threat is achieved by means of ignoring and distorting the perceptions that have induced threat. When the defenses have been effective, the experience of threat is eliminated from consciousness.

WHY DEFENSIVE REACTIONS TO THREAT ARE REGARDED AS UNHEALTHY

Personality hygienists regard indiscriminate defense of the self-structure as unhealthy because of the long-range consequences which it produces. Threat is very analogous with pain. When a person experiences pain, it is a signal that something is wrong with his body.[1] If he utilizes pain as a signal, the person will take active steps to remove the causes of the pain, thus prolonging his life. If the person anesthetizes his pain, *the factors which are responsible for the pain remain active;* as soon as the drug or anesthetic wears off, pain is again experienced. Further, since no action has been undertaken against the causes of the pain, the destructive action of these causes may have progressed considerably.

So it is with defensive reactions to threat. The various mechanisms of defense are much like anesthetics; they may be effective in neutralizing or reducing the unpleasant emotions of guilt and anxiety, but they do nothing to remove the factors which are producing the threat. Consequently the defensive person becomes addicted to defenses just as a pain-evader might become addicted to aspirin, codeine, serpisil, or alcohol. Neither person has the courage or ego strength to investigate the causes of the unpleasant feelings and to take the steps necessary to remove the causes.

The person who habitually responds to threat with defense mechanisms eventually becomes alienated from his real self. He consumes energy in defending his self-structure, and hence has little left over for constructive work. His relations with people are impaired, be-

cause he does not have all of his real self accessible to him for interpersonal relationships. In time, the habitual addict to defense mechanisms may display the clinical symptoms of neurosis and psychosis.[2]

WHAT ASPECTS OF THE REAL SELF
TYPICALLY PRODUCE THREAT?

In our society, there are very strong taboos directed against three
classes of impulses, or feelings, viz: *sexuality, hostility,* and *dependency-longings*.[3] Most individuals who have been socialized in the
usual fashion internalize these taboos, and embody them in their
self-ideals. Thus, persons come to believe they should not experience
sexual impulses at any time except during marriage. They come to
believe they should not feel hostility and hatred toward anyone except violaters of the social mores. And men especially believe that
once they have grown beyond childhood, they should not admit
weakness and helplessness, and longings to be taken care of.

The self-concept and the public selves of the average adult generally include these taboos. The average person wants, even needs,
to believe he does not have socially disapproved sexual strivings,
hostile feelings, or dependency-longings; and he certainly doesn't
want anyone else to believe he experiences these unwanted feelings
and impulses.

Yet, the circumstances of life and of growth are such that, at the
real-self level, these impulses and feelings all exist in everyone.
People do become aroused to sexuality before they are married, and
they have sexual longings for persons whom they are not supposed
to be interested in as sexual partners: family members, people of the
same sex, etc.[4] People are aroused to hostility by provocations and
provokers which society does not recognize as legitimate. We all
experience hostility toward our parents, our children, our spouses,
or close friends. And no adult is so self-reliant he has not experienced
the wish to be a protected child at one time or another.

While sexuality, hostility, and dependency are not the only sources
of threat to the self-structure, yet they are very common sources. It
is not too far-fetched to assert that *every* reader of this book is defending his self-structure against the perception and acknowledgment of these feelings as well as many others.

WHAT ARE DEFENSE MECHANISMS?

Defense mechanisms are automatic, involuntary ways in which a person reacts to threatening perceptions, so that his self-structure will remain unchallenged and unchanged.[5] Whenever anything of value is threatened, the person will naturally strive to defend it. But there are realistic and rational ways of defending something of value, and there are unrealistic and irrational shortsighted ways of defending our values. If we value our body, and our body is threatened by disease, the rational means of defense is to study the disease, determine its cure, and administer this cure. The unrealistic and irrational means for defense is to ignore the pain, or anesthetize ourselves against the pain, and pretend there is no threat operative against our life and health.

If we value some theory, we can defend it unrealistically by distorting any evidence which conflicts with it, or by ignoring this unwanted evidence. The earlier discussion of *autism* (Chapter 2) gives many illustrations of this kind of autistic cognition.

The defense mechanisms are autistic means of defending the self-structure. They make it possible for a person to continue believing he is the kind of person he wants to believe he is, when there is much evidence (from the real self) to refute these beliefs.

DEFENSE MECHANISMS ARE INSTANCES OF UNCONSCIOUS INSTRU-MENTAL BEHAVIOR. Instrumental behavior has been defined as any behavior undertaken by the individual so as to achieve some valued end. Most instrumental behavior is conscious, or potentially subject to voluntary control. Defense mechanisms may be viewed as "preconscious," or unconscious instrumental behavior. The defensive individual is not aware he is defending himself against threat. As a matter of fact, once a defensive person recognizes he *is* being defensive against some threatening impulse or feeling, he may achieve voluntary control over his defensive behavior.

We say that defense mechanisms are instances of instrumental action because they are potentially subject to voluntary control, and because they are directed toward a valued end, namely, the reduction of the unpleasant experience of threat and the preservation of the present self-structure. In the language of learning theory, defense mechanisms illustrate both "avoidance" behavior, and "escape" behavior; they help a person to avoid threat and to escape it, once it occurs.

HOW DEFENSE MECHANISMS MILITATE AGAINST GROWTH. Growth may be defined as *change in a valued direction*. One of the goals of personality growth is a healthy self-structure; i.e., a state where the real self, the self-concept, the self-ideal, and the public selves are all mutually congruent. Whenever such a state of affairs exists, it can only be temporary—a sort of unstable equilibrium.[6] Any change in the real self is likely to disrupt this equilibrium, and such changes in the real self are always occurring. The self-structure grows when the necessary adjustments are made following real-self changes. But if the person defends his self-structure, then he will strive to ignore or distort the messages of his real self, thus preserving his present self-structure intact, despite its increasing alienation from the real self.

The person who defends his self-structure against change and growth is like the aging matron who keeps wearing the clothing of an 18-year-old beauty queen, in spite of increasing girth. Her girdle and corsets may be so tight that she nearly faints daily, but she will not admit her clothing does not fit. So with a defended self-structure; the underlying real self may have become so discrepant from the self-concept, self-ideal, and public selves, that the individual is really two distinct persons: the one he *believes* he is, and the one he *really* is.

If the real self could be knocked out of commission by defense mechanisms, the individual would not suffer in consequence of his defensive operations. But the real self inevitably finds its way to expression. A real self which has been excluded by defense mechanisms manifests itself through the experience of suffering, boredom, frustration, vague anxiety and guilt, depression, unconscious motivation (see Chapter 2), and the symptoms of alienation from the self (see Chapter 9); in short, the whole repertoire of clinical psychopathology with which psychiatrists are familiar in their daily practice. Clinical symptoms of neurosis and of psychosis may be regarded as a by-product of the conflict between the real self and the attempt to preserve a self-structure markedly discrepant with it.

DEFENSE MECHANISMS ARE INDICATIONS OF A WEAK EGO. A strong ego enables a person to face reality—inner and outer—without distortion or selection, and to come to terms with this reality. When the ego is weak, the person ignores reality, or reconstructs it so as to make it conform with his wishes and needs.[7] Before World War II broke out, the French believed the Maginot Line was adequate defense against any invasion. Evidently, they were unable to appreciate that the kind of threat Germany presented could not be stopped by stationary blockades. They probably ignored or distorted any evidence which carried the implication that France could easily be invaded. If the French military leaders had appreciated the full extent of danger, it would have been necessary to revise drastically their concepts of defensive warfare, and this would have required extensive reorganization of their entire army.

In the case of the self-structure, a person with a weak ego needs to believe he is the kind of person he *now* thinks he is. When conflicting evidence arises, he will distort or ignore this evidence, and thus blithely believe that nothing has changed; he *is* the kind of person he believes he is. If he were to admit the conflicting evidence, it might call for all manner of changes. And so, against evidence, he wishfully believes there is no conflicting evidence.

MECHANISMS FOR THE DEFENSE
OF THE SELF-CONCEPT

The mechanisms of defense might just as legitimately be called mechanisms for increasing self-alienation, or methods of evading growth [8]—for such are their consequences. They are modes of behavior undertaken by a person with a relatively weak ego, when threat to the self-structure arises. If they are effective, they reduce anxiety and guilt; but whenever the defenses are themselves weakened, threat is again experienced, for its causes continue to be operative. A defense is like a drug; it must be kept operative if it is to remain effective in removing discomfort. But a defense, like a drug, does not remove the causal conditions which are responsible for the pain and discomfort.

What are the major mechanisms of defense, and how may they be recognized? The person himself can seldom recognize his own defensiveness except under special conditions. The observer may be able to infer, from certain signs, both the nature of the defense, the consequences of the defense, and the aspects of the real self which are being defended against.

REPRESSION. Repression is the most basic mechanism of defense.[9] It consists in actively excluding from awareness any thought, feeling, memory, or wish that would threaten the self-structure. The represser will actively resist even thinking about any theme, or topic, if it seems likely to induce anxiety or guilt. Freud introduced the concept of repression in order to explain some phenomena which he regularly observed in his efforts to treat neurotic patients. He found his patients displayed resistance to the injunction that they speak freely about *everything* which came to mind. He used the term *resistance* to describe any and every deviation from the injunction to speak freely. The term *repression* was invoked to explain the efforts of the person to avoid, not merely speaking about embarrassing or threatening topics, but also to his efforts to avoid even *thinking* about these topics,[10] and experiencing the associated emotions and impulses.

Repression manifests itself by the *omission,* in the person's speech, emotion, and behavior-repertoire, of responses which might ordinarily be expected under given circumstances. For example, if a person has been deeply insulted by someone, and he displays no overt signs of hostility, the hypothesis can be entertained that he has repressed these feelings.

It should not be assumed that because some thought, feeling, or need has been repressed, it simply fades out of existence altogether. Rather, what appears to occur is that the repressed feelings and tensions continue to operate as *unconscious determiners of behavior* (see Chapter 2). The represser may betray many signs of his repressed feelings to a keen observer—in his dreams, accidents, slips of the tongue, etc.

An important indicator of repression is a *refusal by the person to examine and consider any other motives for a given action than the one which he will consciously admit*. Thus, a person may spank his children quite brutally, he may forget their birthdays, he never spends time with them at enjoyable activity, and he continually scolds them. An observer may gather the impression that such behavior expresses hatred and dislike of the children. He asks the father why he treats his children so. The father says, "Because I love them, and I am trying not to spoil them. I am trying to raise them right." If the observer asks him, "Could it be that you don't like your children?" the father might become quite indignant, and refuse to explore the possibility that this might be true. He is repressing his hostility to his children. To admit that he dislikes his children might threaten his self-structure to a profound and catastrophic degree.

Another important indicator of repression is *selective recall of the past*.[11] In relating aspects of the past, much may be omitted from the account. If the observer knows what has been omitted he may confront the person with these details, only to have him deny that the events occurred, or else admit them reluctantly and with much tension. It is as if he had a vested interest in forgetting these details —so as to preserve his present concept of self. Many experimental research studies [12] have shown how our recall and our forgetting are determined to a high degree by the need to maintain self-esteem and to preserve the present self-concept.

In principle, a person can repress any aspect of his real self, whether it is socially desirable or socially reprehensible. Thus, a person may repress sexual urges, hostility, etc., but he may also repress his own intellect and his own strength and resources, if these real-self aspects imply some threat to his self-structure. There is reason to believe that the authoritarian character, who exaggerates his own weakness and the strength of his hero or boss, is repressing his own powers, and ascribing them (projecting them) to the authority-figure in question. Fromm has detailed this point in his discussion of authoritarianism in everyday life, and even in religion; he has suggested that the image of an all-powerful god, in contrast with weak, powerless man, rests on man's repression of his own powers, and the ascription of these very powers to the deity.[13]

Repression is a very primitive means for the defense of the self-structure—it consists, fundamentally, in a denial that something real actually exists. The represser is denying that some aspect of his real self, past or present, actually exists. To admit that the feeling or wish exists as part of the self would call for a reorganization of the self-structure, and this may be too threatening, and beyond the present strength of the individual's ego.

Yet, repression is quite an unstable mechanism, calling as it does for unremitting (but unconscious) effort from the person. Whenever there is any reduction in the energy which is devoted to repression, there is likely to be a *breakthrough of the repressed aspects of the real self*.[14] When this occurs, the person may be incredibly threatened by feelings and impulses he did not know that he possessed. It may happen that the feelings are so intense, the person explodes into uncontrolled activity, for instance, sexual or hostile violence. Probably many of the sex and homicide crimes which one reads about in the papers—"Nobody would have expected him to do that, he was always so nice, so moral, etc."—illustrate the breakthrough of repressed feelings and impulses.

When repressed aspects of the self increase in strength, or when the energy available for repression decreases, these are the occasions when breakthroughs are most likely to occur. Thus, when fatigued, as before falling asleep, or during illness, a person may be overwhelmed with fantasies, feelings, and impulses that are shocking to him and to those who know him.[15]

Although repression is usually an involuntary and unconscious mechanism, recognizable only by its consequences of omissions in the person's behavior repertoire, it is sometimes a conscious and deliberate activity. Every reader will recall occasions when he has had thoughts, feelings, or fantasies which were fully conscious, but quite repugnant and threatening. On those occasions, he may have striven to get rid of the unwanted mental contents, by just putting them out of mind, or by trying actively to change the subject of thinking, in order to think of more pleasant things. Such efforts, if successful, may be called voluntary and conscious repression. They are quite analogous with a conversation between two persons; when an unpleasant subject comes up, the person who finds it is unpleasant will ask that the subject be changed, or else he may skillfully guide the conversation so the dangerous topics are avoided before they arise. Some persons are quite skilled at sensing when an unpleasant subject is about to be discussed; they subtly direct the talk around and away from the loaded topic.

Thus, whenever some aspect of the real self provokes threat, a person with a weak ego may repress this aspect. The repression is carried out by means of refusing to think about it, or by stopping thinking after a start has been made; or by not remembering aspects of the past; or by refusing to examine and accurately label motives for action. The reason for repression is that the self structure must be protected against threatening, conflicting elements. Repression protects the individual against anxiety, guilt, and the loss of the sense of identity.

One of the aims of personality therapy is to undo the process of repression and to help the patient face, and acknowledge, the previously repressed aspects of his real self. Patients undergoing therapy are often quite shocked by some of the feelings and wishes they find within themselves. If their egos have been strengthened during the process of therapy, however, this increased contact with the real self does not necessarily lead to overt action upon the new impulses, nor to renewed efforts at defense. Rather, the person is able to incorporate these newly experienced feelings into a more complete self-concept, and he is able to control his conscious impulses by voluntary suppression rather than automatic, involuntary, and unconscious repression.

RATIONALIZATION. Instrumental behavior is carried out usually in the service of fully conscious aims and goals. These aims are called motives. If a person is asked why he is doing something, or why he has done it, he is seldom at a loss to explain his motives. But a curious observation may be made. It is striking that whenever a person is asked why he did anything, his motives always appear exemplary, to him and to the observer. A person will seldom admit any intentions of an immoral, or antisocial sort. Yet the consequences of many actions are often discrepant with the admitted motive. Thus, a person intends to help his friend, and actually interferes drastically with his friend's success. A man loves his wife, yet his behavior toward her produces grief, pain, and discomfort for her.

For any given action that a person undertakes, it can be roughly assumed its *consequences were desired by the person*. If the aim is denied, or if the consequences appear at variance with the aim, then the observer may assume the *intent has been repressed*. The motive that the person admits may be called a *rationalization*. It is an explanation for an action and its consequences which is compatible with the individual's self-structure. The motive behind rationalization is not to give a factual account of the real intentions; rather, it is to do some justice to the need to explain conduct and yet, at the same time, protect the self-structure.

A more succinct definition of rationalization may be stated as follows: *A rationalization is an explanation of one's own motives and behavior which has been selected from among many possible explanations, because it enhances and defends the individual's self-structure.*

A rationalization is not a conscious lie. When a person rationalizes his behavior and motives, he believes that his rationalization is true. The observer only begins to suspect the person is rationalizing when he finds the same behavior could be explained by other motives than the one which is admitted, or when the consequences of action are strikingly inconsistent with the admitted aim.

If a person were not rationalizing, but rather was sincerely interested in discovering his own motivation, he would at least consider a number of different possible explanations for his conduct, and select one or more which did the greatest justice to his conscious aims and to the actual consequences of his conduct. This quest might be threatening to the self-structure, but it would insure that the person was learning his own motivations. The weak-ego person needs to defend his present self-structure. He will rationalize his motives and actions and strongly resist any attempts from others to get him to explore his motives beyond the one motive he admits.

Patients who have undergone successful therapy will find themselves acknowledging a much broader range of motives for action than they did earlier; they are much less threatened by the act of exploring freely their own motivations, and they are better able to incorporate frankly admitted motives into their broadened self-structure.

The reader can assume that any explanation which he gives for his own conduct is at least in part a rationalization; i.e., the explanation is a by-product of an unconscious selection from among many motives, the one which is most compatible with self-esteem and the self-structure. If we assume, as the psychoanalysts do, that there is an unconscious component to *all* of our motivation, then it becomes increasingly clear that rationalization is a continuous activity for all of us; our conscious motives explain only part of our behavior. Our behavior serves unconscious aims as well as conscious ones. These aims are unconscious, or repressed, *because* they conflict with the self-structure.

Let us suppose a young man asks a girl for a date. His friend suggests he is asking for a date with this particular girl because it is known she is a "heavy petter." If the young man does not like to think of himself as a sexy young man, he may be threatened by this explanation. He will indignantly insist he is dating this girl because, and *only* because, he wants to discuss the lecture they both attended. He is probably rationalizing his motives.

Rationalization may be regarded as an attempt by the person to fill in the vacuum which repression leaves. We all have a strong need to make sense of our behavior to ourselves and to others. It is intolerable for us to act without knowing reasons. And so, if we have repressed our genuine, real-self motives, we replace them by constructing explanations which go part way in explaining the conduct, but which serve the more important function of defending the self-structure. A crude rule of thumb for inferring rationalization is to ask a person to consider some motives other than the one which he admits. If he becomes intensely indignant at the suggestion, it may be provisionally assumed he is rationalizing his motives.

VERBAL REFORMULATION. There is a very subtle kind of defense mechanism which is closely related to rationalization. It is adopted usually by persons who have been well-educated and who have an extensive vocabulary. Psychoanalysts originally called the mechanism in question *isolation,* and some psychiatrists and clinical psychologists refer to it as *intellectualizing.* We shall give it a more general name—*verbal reformulation.*

What verbal reformulation amounts to, in the last analysis, is selecting words to describe one's feelings, motives, perception, and behavior, *on the basis of the feelings which they induce in the self.*[16] Thus, the same perception, thought, or motive, if stated one way, might invoke threatening feelings and meanings; if stated another way, with different language, these meanings and feelings are avoided. Let us illustrate with *euphemisms.* A euphemism may be defined as a nice way of talking about something which produces threatening feelings. Thus, some people are made uncomfortable by frank discussions about biological functions; they refer to pregnancy with the term "infanticipating," or with the French word, *enceinte*. Menstruation may be referred to as "falling off the roof," "a visitor," or "the curse." Most of us have been trained to avoid obscene words; only nasty, evil people swear. And some of the words to describe excreta are regarded as obscene; children who employ four-letter Anglo-Saxon words in reference to bodily wastes are severely punished. Even to think these words is enough to induce anxiety and threat. And so euphemisms, or technical terms may be learned as substitutes. Thus, children speak of BM, or voiding, or "dee-dee," or "tinkle," or Number Two; adults speak of urine and feces when they might be quite threatened to think or speak the Anglo-Saxon equivalents.

The mechanism of verbal reformulation—earlier called isolation and intellectualization—was discovered by personality therapists. They found that their patients, in talking about past experiences or present feelings, were avoiding any unwanted emotions by carefully choosing their language on the basis of its "feel." Thus, a patient who might break into tears if he admitted he hated his father, might relate to the therapist, "You know, I do have some antipathy against my father." If the therapist reflected back, "You mean you hated the old boy," the patient might become severely upset. A patient from a lower-class background was striving to elevate her socio-economic status. She spoke of her sexual affairs, not in the four-letter language of her partners, but rather in pseudotechnical terms: "Well, I had an intercourse with him, and then I had an intercourse with that other fellow, and an intercourse with still another man, etc."

Words are very powerful conditioned stimuli, they carry with them emotional meanings as well as cognitive ones. Jung [17] regarded certain words as "complex-indicators"—stimuli for strong but repressed emotional responses. The familiar word-association lists are illustrations of how words are associated with both cognitive and emotional responses.

It is in order to avoid the unwanted emotional tensions which some words produce that verbal reformulation is adopted as a defense. Verbal reformulation, as a defense, takes many different forms in usage. Thus, it may be manifested through chronic *understatement*. The Englishman is stereotyped as a man who might describe some horrible and terribly emotional experience as follows: "It was a bit thick, a bit of a shaky do."

Euphemisms as well might reflect defensive verbal reformulation: the undertaker is described as a "mortician" and a dead person is described as "the dear departed."

Intellectualizing, the use of technical language to describe events, behavior, and motives, often reflects defensive verbal reformulation. If the person were to use other language to describe the same things, the feelings which might be provoked would be overly threatening. One patient could not even think, must less say, the common vulgar word for *flatus.* The four-letter word, when spoken or even thought, would bring back the memory of a very painful episode which occurred early in childhood involving flatulence in a social situation.[18]

Obscenity [19] itself may be an instance of verbal reformulation for purposes of defense of the self-structure; a person may be able to accept himself only if he is rough and tough and virile, and he believes that swearing is synonymous with masculinity, or emancipation from parents. Thus, an educated person who compulsively uses profane words may be employing them to keep dependency-feelings and "sissy" feelings in a repressed status.

Verbal reformulation thus takes many forms. In a sense, this defense may be regarded as an adjunct to repression as well as a positive means of defending the self-structure against the real self. As long as the person formulates his inner experience in the particular language which he employs, he is protecting himself against the feelings and memories which other language might invoke. The unwanted feelings and memories remain repressed.

A person with a strong ego and a healthy self-structure is not obliged to limit the vocabulary with which he will think about and describe his inner experience; he can pick words and concepts, not on the basis of the feelings they induce in him, and the associations they stir up; rather, he can think and talk in the words which are the most richly descriptive of his experience.

Scientists are probably among the worst offenders in the use of verbal reformulation. In scientific work, it is important to use language which is neutral with respect to emotional meanings; emotion is deemed a barrier to effective experimentation; it distorts perception and steers thinking into autistic channels. But in everyday interpersonal relations, emotions play an important role. The scientist may be actually afraid of his own emotions, and so he depersonalizes his relationships with his wife, children, and friends, and may use the language of technical science in his interpersonal relationships outside the laboratory and the classroom.

REACTION-FORMATION. A person may defend himself against unwanted, threatening thoughts, feelings, and wishes, first by repressing them, and then by compulsively thinking, and striving to feel or the opposite. It is as if it were not sufficient for the person to free himself of threat by merely eliminating the unwanted thoughts and feelings from his mind and overt action. He can only convince himself (and others?) he is not that kind of a person if, and only if, he displays the opposite kinds of behavior in extreme degree. Reaction-formation reveals itself through the compulsive and exaggerated nature of the behavior and attitudes which the person manifests; [20] yet the repressed aspects of the real self may still leak out. Thus, a compulsively generous person may betray his repressed egocentricity and selfishness by giving gifts which the receiver does not like, or cannot use: he gives expensive cigarette-lighters to non-smokers, and bottles of expensive Scotch whisky to teetotalers. The person who is *compulsively* kind to animals betrays underlying sadism by the brutality with which invective is levelled against those who experiment with animals.[21] The devoted, overprotective mother prevents her child from growing by her exaggerated overconcern with his health and safety.[22] The guilty, philandering husband showers his wife with lavish gifts and with surprising and unusual tenderness and solicitude. The man with repressed dependency-strivings displays exaggerated self-reliance, until he gets sick, when he becomes a virtual baby. The latent homosexual displays exaggerated masculinity—he lifts weights, beats up known homosexuals, yet, when drunk, may caress his male drinking buddies.

A person with a strong ego can acknowledge the wide range of his real motives and feelings, and his behavior is much more guided by reality-contact than by the need to defend his self-structure. The weak-ego person who employs reaction-formation, displays a rigidity and an exaggeration in his everyday behavior which leads the observer to exclaim, with Shakespeare, "The lady [or man] doth protest too much, methinks." Whenever one observes exaggerated behavior of the sorts described above, one can suspect that it exemplifies reaction-formation; one can look for evidence of repressed aspects of the real self in other aspects of the person's behavior repertoire: in dreams, accidents, etc.

Aside from manifest attitudes and behavior, reaction-formation may be revealed in the actual content of the person's thoughts. It was pointed out that repression may take the form of stopping thinking, or refusing to think about threatening topics and themes. A represser may "tamp down" the repressed material by compulsively occupying his thoughts with content that is opposite in moral significance; he thinks the opposite, as it were. Thus, a person with repressed sexual strivings may frantically preoccupy himself with thoughts of a religious nature, often to an obsessional degree. He cannot rid his mind of the religious thoughts, and so his work-efficiency may be impaired. The overprotective mother who is repressing much hostility toward her child may become obsessed by thoughts that the child's health and life are in danger. A solicitous wife, who is repressing hostility to her travelling husband, may say on his return: "I couldn't sleep or eat while you were gone. I kept thinking your car turned over and you were crushed to a pulp, and your arms, legs, and head were all cut off."

PROJECTION. The ability to perceive the world accurately and impersonally is an achievement that is relatively difficult to attain. The probability is high that persons will perceive the world autistically unless they have taken active steps to reality-test their perceptions. Autistic perception is animistic, and "physiognomic." The young child, the regressed psychotic, and to some extent, primitive people, all manifest primitive perception.[23] Primitive perception is characterized by the tendency for the individual to assume that animals, trees, water, nature, etc., are personalized; that they have motives, feelings, and wishes just as the perceiver himself has motives, feelings, and wishes. The defense mechanism of projection is a special case of primitive perception. *Projection is the name given to the tendency to assume that another person has motives, feelings, wishes, values, or more generally, traits which the individual himself has.*

If a person assumes that someone else is similar to himself, the term *assimilative projection* is used to describe such an assumption.

If the person assumes that someone else has motives or feelings which are denied, disowned, or repressed in the self, the term *disowning projection* is employed.[24] Both varieties of projection manifest themselves in the perceptions and beliefs one formulates concerning another person.

Projection as such is not a defense mechanism; rather, it might be called *mis*perception of another person. Or, it may be regarded as a sort of logical fallacy—the act of formulating beliefs about another person's motives and feelings without adequate evidence. Thus, I may notice that some man resembles me in age, sex, educational level, and so I assume he is responding to some situation in a manner identical with my own response. Both of us look at a pretty girl, I notice I am pleasantly affected by the girl, and I assume that the other person is similarly affected. Further questioning of the other person may prove my assumption is wrong. I have manifested *assimilative* projection.

But suppose I have repressed any interest in pretty girls; to admit any such interest might threaten my self-structure. I may assume the other fellow is very interested in the pretty girl, but I would myself vehemently deny any such interest. I could be just as wrong. But if I assumed the other fellow was ridden with lustful feelings that I denied in myself, I would be displaying *disowning projection*. This unwarranted assumption about the other person's motives would be a defense mechanism. I would be protecting my self-concept by repressing certain feelings in myself, and assuming without warrant that other people, not I, are motivated by such scurvy drives.

The evidence which prompts the observer to suspect disowning projection is to be found in the beliefs which a person holds concerning his own motivation and that of others. One suspects disowning projection if (a) the motives imputed to others are derogatory and immoral, (b) such motives are vigorously denied in the self, (c) there is not much evidence to support the belief that the other person has the motives imputed to him, and (d) the person himself gives evidence of these imputed motives, but at an unconscious level.

Disowning projection is thus an outgrowth of repression, as are rationalization, verbal reformulation, and reaction-formation. The disowning projector really defends himself in two ways: by repressing unwanted aspects of his real self, he is directly protecting his present self-structure; by drawing comparisons between himself and others (to whom he imputes unsavory motives), so that the other person is seen to be morally inferior, he is enhancing his self-esteem.

As was suggested earlier, a person can disown and project not only unsavory aspects of his real self, he can also repress and project his own positive potentialities. Where this occurs, the person perceives himself as imperfect, weak, and base, while the object of his projection is perceived as perfect, strong, and ideal. Authoritarian characters appear to do this, as do certain lovers. Many a romantic lover has seen himself as worthless and evil, and has projected his own moral potential to his object, perceiving her as the embodiment of all that is clean, wonderful, and morally perfect. He may become disillusioned when reality sets in.

Both varieties of projection are manifested in persons with weak egos; assimilative and disowning projection are actually instances of impaired contact with social reality. Disowning projection is the only kind of projection which can properly be called a defense mechanism. Bigoted persons appear to predicate many of their beliefs about the shortcomings of minority-group members on disowning projection. They perceive themselves and their fellow group-members as free from all kinds of moral shortcomings and ascribe these shortcomings to the members of the minority group. The bigot would strongly resist any suggestion that the same undesirable traits existed in himself, although at an unconscious level.[25]

Projection is often a very subtle mechanism, difficult to detect, because it may happen that the motives imputed (through projection) to the other person are almost accurate. One can only become reasonably sure that a person is projecting if one knows the other person actually does not have the traits imputed to him, or if one knows that the suspected projector has not yet had an opportunity to know the personality and motives of the person whom he is describing.

In cases of extreme ego-weakness, e.g., in psychotic patients, projection of disowned aspects of the self may take very dramatic forms, as in delusions of persecution, and in hallucinations.

DEFENSIVE DISCRIMINATION. Perception is strongly dependent upon classification and discrimination. We classify things into categories, and assign different labels to them on the basis of perceptible differences.[26] Thus, a cat is perceptibly different from a dog, and so we give different names to animals, depending upon whether or not they have the properties associated with the concepts dog and cat.

One important aspect of normality is the ability to form categories similar to those formed by the majority of group members, and the ability to make discriminations, i.e., to notice differences among objects and situations, in socially shared ways. A person may defend his self-structure by *not* noticing differences which are apparent to others, and he may likewise defend his self-structure by *making discriminations* which no one else would make. It is the latter which we call defensive discrimination. To illustrate: A situation may be one which calls for honest behavior. The individual takes pride in his honesty. But if he stands to gain richly from dishonest behavior, he might pick out some aspect of the situation which enables him to say, and believe, *"This situation is different.* Conventional morality does not prevail here." The disinterested observer fails to see the difference. But the defensive discriminator will strongly resist any attempts that are made to show him that the situation in which he is cheating is really no different from a situation where morality prevails. Thus, some persons may be scrupulously honest in their dealings with individual persons, but they cheat the government, or large corporations without blushing. "It's different," they might say.

A person might relieve himself of fear and anxiety, if he can single out some aspect of a fear-provoking and dangerous situation which differentiates it (for him) from other, similar situations. Yet, the detached observer may notice the situation objectively is dangerous. So long as he can believe in the difference, however, the defensive individual can remain relatively free from fear and anxiety.

In extreme forms, this tendency to make discriminations which are not shared by others is a symptom of serious personality illness: schizophrenia. The schizophrenic not only classifies his experience in deviant ways, he also makes deviant discriminations.[27] Perfectly safe food may be perceived as poisonous because of some barely noticeable difference in color or temperature between the food-serving to-day, and the same food which was served yesterday. The healthy personality can tell the difference between a difference which makes a difference, and one which does not make a difference.

DEFENSIVE CLASSIFICATION. A person may classify completely different things into the same category, not because they belong together, but so as to defend his self-structure. Things are classified into categories on the basis of fundamental, or essential properties, viz.: function, structure, color, etc. One of the signs of psychiatric normality is the ability to form concepts, or to classify objects in ways that are shared by the majority of persons.[28] A loss in this ability is deemed to be a sign of schizophrenia, or of brain damage. Among persons with only moderately impaired ego strength, classification of objects, persons, or situations may be made in the service of defense rather than on the basis of real (i.e., socially agreed-upon) similarities. Thus, a person may classify persons into categories, on the basis of superficial and unnecessary similarities, because he *needs* all the members of the group to be similar to each other. He needs them to be similar so as to defend his present ways of behaving toward those persons. If he recognized individual differences among all the members of the particular class which he has constructed, it might call for self-threatening re-adjustments of his present interpersonal behavior repertoire. Thus, a person may say, "All women are alike," when it is apparent that there are important individual differences among women. But so long as he believes they are alike, he does not have to alter his present ways of behaving toward women. Or, he may believe that all Negroes are alike, etc.

Not all faulty classification can be regarded as defensive in function. Autistic classification may simply reflect impaired ego strength. We can regard faulty classification as defensive only when there is evidence to show that the person actually is protecting and enhancing his self-structure by his deviant modes of classifying.

In another context (Chapter 7) we spoke of *attribution* as a means by which inaccurate other-concepts were formed. Attribution refers to the assumption that, because a present person has one trait in common with someone in the past, then the present person has many or all of the traits which were known in the person from the past. Attribution is an instance of defensive classification. So long as one believes that the present person is similar to the past person, one does not have to learn new ways of relating to him. In personality therapy, the phenomenon of "transference" illustrates attribution and defensive classification. The therapist may be classified into the category "just like mother," or "just like father." Much therapeutic gain follows when the patient is able to know that the therapist is really different from his mother and father, in spite of superficial similarities.

PERCEPTUAL DEFENSE. Repression is really an instance of refusing to see or hear aspects of inner reality: the real self. But one can defend one's self-structure by refusing to see or hear aspects of outer reality, if such perception would result in threat to the self-structure. The psychoanalysts coined the term *denial* to describe this tendency to ignore aspects of outer reality which induced anxiety, fear, or losses in self-esteem. Experimental psychologists use the term *perceptual defense* to describe the same phenomena. Sullivan spoke of "selective inattention" in this connection. In Chapter 2, the concept of perceptual defense was discussed and documented in greater detail. In the present section, we shall only restate some of this material.

Humans seem to have a very strong tendency to ignore or reconstruct reality when reality is pain-producing. It is such a stubborn tendency that Freud spoke of it as one of the "principles" of mental functioning—the *pleasure-principle* in contrast with the *reality-principle*.[29] It is as if when there are two possible meanings which might be assigned to some perception, one pleasant but untrue, and the other true but painful, we must actually *fight* the pleasure-principle in order to arrive at accurate cognition. Thus, we do not hear derogatory remarks uttered by someone about us, even though our hearing is quite adequate to notice whispered praise. We do not see the blemishes in our loved ones, if our self-esteem rests on the premise that we have made a wise choice of a perfect mate. In extreme forms, among persons with very weak egos, we may actually see something quite clearly, but then deny we saw it, and believe the denial. For some persons the death of a loved one is so catastrophic, calling as it does for much reorganization of behavior and the self-structure, that they will not believe the person is dead.

PERCEPTUAL SENSITIZATION. If a person is habitually quite anxious, he may become quite sensitized to all stimuli which have the significance of danger. He might be able to detect their imminence and onset at very low degrees of intensity. It is as if eternal vigilance is the price he must pay, not to protect just his self-structure, but even his life.[30] Thus a person may actually perceive hostility in others long before a nonanxious individual might. He is sensitized to it, as it were. It is probably true that we have become extremely sensitized to the feelings of other people toward us, insofar as we are becoming other-directed characters (as Riesman suggests).

While sensitization may well serve a defensive function, it may actually lead us to misinterpret the motives and feelings of other people. We may misinterpret others' motives because we interpret too quickly, before enough evidence is available. Oversensitization and vigilance are similar to the behavior of the "bomb-happy" discharged soldier who reacts to each car-backfiring as if it were an 88mm shell.

ISOLATION. Much of the meaning which psychoanalysts imputed to the term isolation has been incorporated into the concept of verbal reformulation. We shall employ the word *isolation* to describe any activity which a person undertakes so as to divest a perception, thought, or act, of its threatening emotional implications.[31] Thus a person may commit some crime, or some immoral act such as sexual infidelity. If he allowed himself to think about these things freely, he might be led inevitably to guilt and condemnation of himself. However, he might be able to avoid these threatening feelings if he isolates his acts from the rest of his life. He may admit he has done these things, but he refuses to allow himself to make moral judgments. Isolation most often takes the form of refusing to evaluate one's own actions. One admits they were performed, but one does not evaluate them as other acts might be evaluated. So long as this evaluative thinking is repressed, the threatening action is encapsulated, as it were. It has no connection with the total self.

"Sunday Christians" may be viewed as individuals who employ the mechanism of isolation. All week, they may violate most of the moral precepts they supposedly affirm, but they experience no guilt, because this behavior is isolated from evaluative judgments. A term which has often been employed as nearly synonymous with isolation is "living in logic-tight compartments." As we have used the term, isolation is actually a case of repressing value-judgments so as to avoid guilt.

COMPENSATION. For most of us, success in any undertaking is an important determiner of self-esteem. But our coping efforts do not always meet with success. When we fail at some endeavor, some threat to the self-structure is the consequence. In order to rid ourselves of the unpleasant feelings of inferiority that failure might produce, we often pursue some substitute goal. The response to feelings of failure by pursuing substitute, second-best goals is termed *compensation*. Considered by itself, compensation is neither healthy nor unhealthy. We can judge compensation from a health point of view only in terms of its long-range consequences. If a person perpetually failed, and satisfied himself with second-best all his life, we would regard his compensatory activity as unhealthy, for he might always carry unconscious inferiority feelings. It would be healthier if he could lower his level of aspiration, or modify his self-ideal. But the ability to compensate is actually a healthy one, because no one meets with success all the time, in every venture.

Overcompensation is the name given to a special kind of compensatory activity. If a person has failed in reaching some goal because of some personal inadequacy, he may devote so much effort toward altering his inadequate traits that they actually become overdeveloped. For example, a person may have failed to win a certain girl because of his "97-pound-weakling" physique. Instead of compensating for this failure by pursuing some other girl, he might enroll in a physical culture course, devoting all of his time and money to the quest for a herculean, muscle-bound physique. This might be called overcompensation. As a matter of fact, experimental evidence has been gathered to show that weight-lifters, considered as a group, actually show more signs of overcompensation for inferiority-feelings, latent homosexuality, and dependency-feelings, than other comparable groups of young men.[32]

Actually, overcompensation is a special case of reaction-formation—it could be renamed "denial by overdoing."

Persons with strong egos will adopt compensation, not necessarily as a defense of their self-structure, but rather as a means of insuring for themselves at least some gratifications, after their efforts at some goal have failed. The person with a weaker ego is profoundly threatened by his failures; we can speak of compensation as a defense mechanism only when there is enough evidence to show that the person is pursuing some other goal, not to make up for missed pleasures, but rather to restore self-esteem which has been threatened by failure at some instrumental activity.

PSYCHIC CONTACTLESSNESS. This term, which was coined by Wilhelm Reich,[33] refers to an inability, or a refusal, to communicate with, or to get emotionally involved with, another person. If one has been deeply hurt in relationships with people, one might protect oneself against further hurt and losses in self-esteem by walling the self off from people. One is *among* people without being really *with* them. Avoidance of close contact and emotional involvement with others serves many defensive functions, not the least of which is the fact that others will never come to know you. Since others are never given the opportunity to observe his real self, the contactless person can entertain all manner of grandiose fantasies about himself, and these are never known or criticized by others. Horney's concept of "moving away from people" is closely similar in meaning to the concept of contactlessness.

DEPERSONALIZING OTHERS. If an individual does not allow himself to think of others as human beings with feelings, hopes, etc., he can protect himself in many ways. He may be afraid to become personally involved, and so he stubbornly refuses to pay any attention to the other person as a feeling, sensitive human being. Instead, other people are just the embodiment of their social role; they are workers, or wives, or doctors, not men and women, or *human persons*. The act of depersonalizing others may thus protect the person against guilt-feelings he might experience if he knew he was hurting others. Or, if he suffers from an inability to love, he might protect himself against such a disquieting insight through depersonalizing others.

A NOTE ON GROWTH AND AGE-GRADING. Personality *growth* refers to changes in the various aspects of personality so that the individual conforms with his successive *age-roles*.[34] Each society has its concepts of expected behavior for each age level, and socialization practices are designed to promote the acquisition of behavior patterns which are deemed appropriate to each age level. For each aspect of personality, a growth-sequence which is typical for a given society can be observed and described. Thus, the food and the eating-habits of the infant differ from those of the child, the adult, and the senile person. The sexual fantasies, objects, and practices differ from age level to age level. In our society, psychologists have made attempts to specify in explicit fashion the behavior patterns which are believed to be modal, or typical for the various age levels. Intelligence tests,[35] and growth norms such as those established by Gesell,[36] are examples of formal, scientific age-grading in our society. The psychoanalytic theory of stages in psychosexual development is another example of descriptive norms for personality development.[37] Maslow's theory of a hierarchy of needs is in a sense, a normative developmental theory.[38] Murphy's doctrine of stages in the development of perception—global, differentiated, and integrated perception—is a developmental theory.[39] Werner's distinctions between primitive and developed mental activities are illustrative of crude growth norms.[40] Fromm's distinction between authoritarian and humanistic conscience may be viewed as a rough developmental distinction.[41] The reader is urged to acquaint himself with the details of these various theories of developmental stages as they apply to various aspects of personality, for they serve as the basis for judgments which have high importance in our society—judgments about maturity, rates of growth, retardation, fixation, and regression.

At any given chronological age, it is possible to describe the various aspects of a personality, and make judgments about how mature, developed, or appropriate to that age are each of these aspects. Thus, we might study John's personality in detail, and on the basis of our observations, and comparisons with age norms, arrive at conclusions of this sort: "In terms of breadth of knowledge, John is quite *advanced* for his age. His skill-repertoire is greater than that which is typical of other sixteen-year-olds. His emotional responses, however, are similar to those usually found in five-year-olds; his emotionality is *fixated*. Also, we find that his needs appear to be fixated; he strives after goals similar to those pursued by much younger children. Whenever John meets with frustration, we find there is a generalized *regression* of all aspects of personality; his perceptions become autistic, his emotions appear infantile, his fantasies become juvenile, his instrumental behavior becomes diffuse and disorganized, etc."

From this discussion, it should now be apparent that the concepts of growth, fixation, regression, precocity, retardation, deterioration, etc., all are meaningless except with reference to age norms, or growth norms.

Growth of personality—learning ways of solving problems and satisfying needs which correspond with the ideals and expectations for each age level—is highly valued by personality hygienists. In fact, some theorists hold that all varieties of personality illness derive from either growth-resistance (fixation) or from growth-regression. The psychoanalytic theory of neurosis, for example, explains neurotic symptomatology as a case of fixation or regression in growth. Obsessive-compulsive neurosis is thought to derive from stress applied to a person who has been *fixated* at the phallic stage of development. In consequence of the stress, the fixated individual regresses to the anal level of psychosexual development. The obsessive and compulsive symptoms are interpreted as infantile attempts to master conflicts and solve problems which are appropriate, or normal, in a five-year-old, but neurotic when they arise in an adult.[42]

This lengthy digression on growth and on norms is necessary to provide a background for understanding the concepts of fixation and regression. It should be pointed out that complete and explicit age-graded norms for all aspects of personality have not as yet been formulated by psychologists. Further, a contrast must be drawn between *norms* and personality-hygiene *ideals* for each age level. As more research is done on this problem, we shall some day have, not only explicit age-graded norms for most relevant aspects of personality, but we shall also have descriptions of the *healthy* versions of each trait which might reasonably be expected for each age level. When this basic research has been accomplished, our developmental diagnoses will become much more precise, and they will enable much more effective child-rearing practices and effective personality therapy.

FIXATION AS DEFENSE. The self-structure is a very powerful determiner of *fixation* of behavior. When new problems arise for solution, then new patterns of behavior are required from the person. But new situations—the "unknown"—generally provoke *anxiety* in a person. Further, the new behavior-patterns might conflict strongly with the present self-structure. If the individual acts in the new ways

that the situation demands, he might become threatened. Therefore, he may *resist the new learning*, and his old behavior-patterns
will become more strongly reinforced—fixated.[43]

We can visualize the total personality of an individual as being
comprised of traits which differ in the degree to which they are
fixated. Some traits are quite flexible, and easily modified, while
others are stubbornly resistant to change. It is the latter which are
fixated. The fact of fixation helps us to understand why we can
often find, even in a very mature and healthy personality, some traits
which appear paradoxically juvenile, childish, or undeveloped. They
have been fixated as a defense against the threat to the self-structure which abandonment of the trait, and learning new traits, would
produce.

Thus, we may know a person who strikes us as being very mature
and relatively healthy in most aspects of personality. But he persists in relating to women in a manner similar to the way in which
he related to his mother when he was very young. This particular
interpersonal trait has been fixated; for him, other ways of relating
to women may be greatly threatening. Even though this fixated trait
might produce all kinds of problems for the man in his dealings with
women, yet he is able to keep his present self-structure intact only
as long as the trait remains unchanged.

REGRESSION AS DEFENSE. Regression means, basically, growth "in
reverse." [44] When a person regresses, it may be a highly *selective*
regression, where only one trait changes from its present form to
one which was typical of the person at a younger age; or, it may be
a more *global* regression, where all aspects of the personality become
more "primitive."

Clinical and experimental studies have warranted the generalization that regression is a reaction to stress, frustration, and deprivation. If ego strength is relatively low, the person cannot preserve his
present level of performance under stressing conditions, and so he
might come to manifest more primitive and childish reactions. Regression may be a *transient* reaction to stress, or it may be a relatively permanent, almost *irreversible* reaction. Transient regression
is very common—it happens to all of us. We may burst into tears
when we have been thwarted, but later we learn to master the

obstacles to gratification of our needs in a more adult manner. We may deliberately regress from our adult, formal roles, and become childish in our behavior just for purposes of fun and enjoyment. Actually, the ability to regress without undue threat to the self-structure is a personality-hygiene value, since it permits the individual to have fun. It is possible that the ability to regress is an important determiner of many forms of creative work.

Permanent regression is more properly indicative of a defensive process. If a person has been finding it difficult to gain satisfactions in conforming to an adult role, he may regress to some level of functioning which yields him greater satisfactions. This regression serves the function of defending the self-structure, or at least the sense of identity of the individual, and it may further defend the value of gratification-richness. If the person, through regressing, is able to force others in his social situation to take care of his needs, his regression may become permanent. If the regression is extreme, as in severe psychoses, the person is able to obtain only fantasy-gratifications; but in less severe regressions, very real satisfactions may be obtained.

It should be pointed out that regression itself may be a strong threat to the present self-structure. In order to reduce the threat which regression might produce, the individual may have to formulate elaborate rationalizations in order to justify the regression. The real reason for regressing may be a fear of inadequacy in present situations. The rationalization for regressing might be: "I deserve to be taken care of because I am sick."

DEFENSE OF THE PUBLIC SELF

The repertoire of public selves constructed by an individual is very important to him for practical reasons. It is only so long as the other person holds the desired set of beliefs about him that the individual can feel reassured his needs will be satisfied and his valued ends secured. Consequently, it is not enough for him simply to construct the public selves by appropriate behavior and verbal definition of his personality to others. Once he has constructed a public self, he is obliged to defend and maintain it. How is this done?

The most general means of defending and maintaining the public self is by means of a *selective suppression of all incompatible behavior and emotional expression*—behavior and expression which is inconsistent with the public self-structure.

Sometimes, in order to defend a public self, the individual is obliged to lie. A mother may have heard reports about her son's behavior which conflict with her concept of him. She confronts him with the report, and he denies it flatly. He does not want her to believe that he behaves in such a way.

Secrecy is more common than lying as a means of defending public selves. We can do almost anything without fear (though not necessarily without guilt), if only no one observes or discovers what we have done. The secret activities may be incredibly disparate with the public selves of the individual. The minister may operate a gambling house under a pseudonym; his wife may write spicy novels or gory detective thrillers under a pen name. Men at conventions display behavior markedly different from their usual home-town behavior, and are quite disconcerted if their family and neighbors hear reports of their conduct.

A really intelligent person can construct various public selves with ingenuity and finesse—sometimes fantastically diverse and contradictory selves. The more diverse they are, however, the greater the difficulty in maintaining them; very often persons who hold contrasting concepts of the individual may meet him simultaneously, and he is at a loss to know how to behave.

DEFENSE OF THE SELF-IDEAL

The self-ideal is comprised of values. The individual may formulate these values in various ways: as abstract propositions of right and wrong, or as very specific prescriptions and formulas which specify how he should behave in various situations. When once a self-ideal has been constructed, or "built into" a person, it becomes a fairly fixed structure, strongly resistant to change. In fact, when confronted with social pressure to change his values, a person will diligently resist all such external pressures. We might ask here, "Why will a person resist efforts to alter his values, i.e., his self-ideal?"

Consider, for example, an individual with a very pathological level of aspiration. He sets incredibly high standards of performance in situations involving competitive achievement, never attains those levels, and as a consequence believes that he is worthless, a complete failure. If only his self-ideal could be altered, his behavior and his self-concept could remain unchanged, and he would experience self-esteem, perhaps for the first time in his life. Yet, when he is urged to relax his standards, he will refuse, or else say, "I wish I could, but I can't."

One of the reasons why a person finds it difficult to examine, criticize, and alter his values is because they came from sources he dares not question—his parents, teachers, God, the Bible, etc. His values have been acquired in the context of an authoritarian relationship, and he dreads all manner of horrible consequences should he question or defy the "commands." [45] Values and ideals acquired in this way are very analogous with orders from a superior officer in the army. The private is "not to reason why," he must obey. If he has been rigorously trained in authoritarian fashion, he is likely to get anxious at the bare thought or mention of disobedience, criticism, or personal alteration of the orders. Many people deal with their self-ideal in the same fashion. For them to question their values is unthinkable. They just obey. They are afraid (for reasons unknown to them) to examine their values in the light of critical reason, and they will not brook anyone else questioning their values. In short, they will avoid thinking about, will repress, all criticism of the self-ideal and its component values and shoulds. Freud said, "As the child was once compelled to obey its parents, so the ego submits to the categorical imperative pronounced by its superego." [46]

This fear of obscure consequences, if one should examine, criticize, and change one's values, presents a powerful conserving force in the self-structure. Although the self-concept is very resistant to change, observation discloses that the conscience is even more resistant to change. A person may kill his conscience with alcohol, he may lull it with self-deceptive arguments and rationalizations, he may even repress it by refusing to think of his values, and refusing to compare his behavior with his ideals; but he will rarely change it, and then only under highly specialized circumstances. [47]

DEFENSE VERSUS GROWTH OF THE SELF-STRUCTURE

The many mechanisms for the defense of the self-structure all have the consequence of keeping the self-structure constant. If the self-structure is fixed, and resistant to change, the likelihood is great that the behavior patterns of the person will become increasingly fixated, or crystallized. His responses to life situations will become increasingly predictable, sometimes to an almost caricatured degree; people can set their watches by the individual in question.

Such fixity in behavior and in the self-structure is perfectly fine—or would be, if the environment in which the person lived was absolutely unchanging. Then like the dinosaurs, during their epoch on earth, he would be remarkably well-adjusted to his surroundings. Like the dinosaurs, he would live as long as physical health allowed, and would find a maximum number of satisfactions in living. But when the dinosaurs' environment changed, the beasts died off. Their physical structure was such that they could not alter their highly fixed repertoire of responses so as to survive. Humans living in modern cultures are unlikely to die because of rigidity in their behavior; but they are likely to experience a good deal of misery if they are unable to change. Modern personality hygienists and therapists assert that it is only as a person continues to meet new situations, and modifies his behavior and his self-structure, that he will grow. This is another way of asserting that the personality hygienist values change of behavior and self-structure of a special kind. He does not value the kinds of changes which a psychiatrist would call regressive, or psychotic. He does, however, value changes which move the person in the direction of greater productivity, of mastery over the environment (see Chapter 1 for the heuristic portraits of healthy personality), and which produce increasing congruence among the self-concept, behavior, self-ideal, and public selves.

The defense mechanisms actually interfere with personality growth, as this has been defined. They preserve, even "freeze" the individual's self-structure. When it has become unduly frozen, it becomes also brittle, and can crack. The individuals whom psychiatrists call neurotic, or psychotic, or who have "nervous breakdowns," are generally individuals who have a frozen self-structure which cracks under the pressure of too much conflicting evidence—evidence which conflicts with the self-concept, evidence which results in catastrophic losses of self-esteem, and evidence which results in the person living in dread of public shaming and ridicule.

RECOGNIZING DEFENSIVE BEHAVIOR

The preceding list of defense mechanisms does not include all that have been recognized and described by students of behavior; it may be regarded as a list of those which are relatively common. In principle, any behavior-pattern whatsoever may serve defensive functions as well as other aims. It is desirable, at this point, to suggest the means by which an observer can recognize defensiveness when he sees it.

In general, defense mechanisms are behavior-patterns which are motivated by anxiety and guilt. When they are operating, the person does not directly experience these unpleasant affects. But defensive behavior differs from positive, goal-oriented instrumental behavior in this fundamental respect. Where positive, goal-directed behavior is quite flexible within certain limits, defensive behavior is not. Any interference with defensive behavior is apt to induce anger, anxiety, guilt, depression, or other unwanted affects in the defensive individual. Defense mechanisms are like emergency measures; [48] they are the crutch upon which the individual's security hinges, that is, the security of a person with diminished ego strength. And when anyone's security and self-esteem are threatened, he will become upset. And so, the best means for ascertaining whether or not some behavior is defensive, is to observe what happens when this behavior is interfered with. If it gives rise to anxiety, hostility, depression, or guilt, then one is justified in at least suspecting that some aspect of the real self is being protected by the behavior in question.

EGO STRENGTH AND GROWTH OF
THE SELF-STRUCTURE

The self-structure is not synonymous with personality; rather, the self-structure is only a part of the total personality. If an individual's ego is strong, his self-structure at any given time is likely to be quite congruent with his real self. But again it should be stated that the congruence of the self-structure with the real self, at any point in time, is only temporary. The real self is continually changing; new needs arise, new feelings, memories, etc., crowd into conscious awareness; and usually (but not always) these new experiences induce threat, for they do actually threaten the present self-structure.

If the person has a strong ego, and if he values self-honesty, he will respond to the threat, not by defensive behavior, but rather by reformulating his self-structure. It may thus be seen that ego strength is a very important determiner of a healthy self-structure, and more generally, of a healthy personality. When we learn better ways of estimating ego strength, it may some day become possible to discover means for promoting it. The net consequence will be that more persons will achieve a healthy self-structure and healthy personality.

SUMMARY

A person with a strong ego is able to keep his self-structure in congruence with his real self, following threat, by making modifications and adjustments within his self-structure. If a person's ego is weak, however, he is likely to respond to threats to the self-structure in a defensive manner. Defense mechanisms are deemed to be unhealthy responses to threat because they do not come to grips with the cause or source of threat.

Some common sources of threat to the self-structure are *sexuality, hostility,* and *dependency-longings.*

Defense mechanisms are automatic, involuntary ways of reacting to threatening perceptions, feelings, impulses, etc., with the aim of preserving the present self-structure intact. The defense mechanisms enable a person to continue believing that he is the kind of person he believes he is, when there is much evidence (from the real self) to refute this belief. They may be regarded as examples of unconscious instrumental behavior, motivated by anxiety and guilt, and directed toward the valued end of preserving the present self-structure.

Defense mechanisms interfere with healthy *growth* of the self-structure, and they produce the consequence of self-alienation. They are symptomatic of a weak ego.

Repression is the most basic mechanism of defense. It consists in actively excluding from awareness any thought, feeling, memory, or wish which would threaten the self-structure. However, when mental contents have been repressed, they continue to influence behavior, but in unconscious ways.

Rationalization is the name given to the act of selecting from among many possible explanations (motives) for one's conduct, that one which is most compatible with the present self-structure.

Verbal reformulation is a defense which consists in selecting language to describe one's experience on the basis of the feelings which this language provokes. *Euphemisms, understatement, intellectual jargon, obscenity,* all may be employed for defensive purposes, and they serve as examples of verbal reformulation.

Reaction-formation refers to the adoption of thoughts, feelings and actions which are *opposite* in significance to repressed materials.

Projection refers to the tendency to impute one's own conscious or unconscious traits to another person. *Assimilative* projection refers to the assumption that another person is similar to the self; *disowning* projection is more properly a defense mechanism, referring as it does to the ascription of *repressed* aspects of the self to others.

Defensive discrimination refers to the tendency to perceive differences between situations which are actually similar, so as to defend the self-structure.

Defensive classification is the tendency to equate situations which really are different, for defensive purposes.

Perceptual defense refers to the tendency to ignore and misinterpret external reality in accordance with one's wishes and needs.

Perceptual sensitization describes the reduction in recognition-thresholds which is associated often with anxiety (as well as with various needs).

Isolation refers to a tendency to avoid evaluating one's immoral acts, so as to avoid guilt; these acts are thus isolated from the rest of a person's life.

Compensation refers to the tendency to pursue substitute goals when failure in one line of endeavor has produced a threat to self-esteem. *Overcompensation* describes the efforts of a person to transform some handicapping trait so that he excels other persons with respect to that trait.

Psychic contactlessness describes the tendency to avoid emotional

and communicative contact with another person so as to avoid hurt
and threat.

Depersonalizing others refers to the tendency to think of other
people, not as whole, feeling persons, but rather as impersonal
embodiments of their social roles.

Fixation refers to the adherence to particular traits or reaction
patterns owing to a fear of abandoning them so as to learn newer
behavior patterns.

Regression refers to growth in reverse—abandoning present ways
of meeting problems and satisfying needs in favor of more childish,
less mature modes of behavior.

A person defends his *public selves* by selectively suppressing any
overt behavior, or expressions of the real self which would jeopardize
the concept of himself he wants others to have.

The *self-ideal* is relatively resistant to change because the person
seldom dares to examine, question, compare, or critically assess his
own values. These values are usually experienced as authoritative
imperatives which must be obeyed and followed unquestioningly,
much like military commands.

Defensive behavior in general manifests itself to the observer as
very rigid and compulsive behavior. If it is questioned, examined, or
interfered with, the person manifests intense anxiety, guilt, hostility,
or other signs of threat.

The defense mechanisms operate so as to interfere with personality growth. A strong ego enables a person to face threat squarely
and to avoid the use of defense mechanisms.

NOTES AND REFERENCES

RECOMMENDED READINGS ARE MARKED WITH AN ASTERISK (*)

1. Cf. Szasz, T. S., "The ego, the body and pain," *J. Amer. Psychoanalyt. Assoc.*, 1955, 3, 177–200.
2. See Freud, S., *Inhibitions, symptoms, and anxiety*, London, Hogarth,
1948, for the psychoanalytical view of the relationships among
defenses and symptoms.
*3. Whiting and Child show that socialization practices in our society
with respect to these three classes of motives are very strict in

comparison with other societies. See Whiting, J. W. M. and Child, I. L., *Child training and personality*, New Haven, Yale University Press, 1953.

4. Cf. Kinsey, A. C., Pomeroy, W. B., and Martin, C. E., *Sexual behavior in the human male*, Philadelphia, Saunders, 1948.

5. See Menninger for a systematic account of the ways in which a person preserves his identity and integrity under stress. Menninger, K., "Regulatory devices of the ego under major stress," *Int. J. Psychoanal.*, 1954, **35**, 1–9. Also, by the same author, "Psychological aspects of the organism under stress. Part I. The homeostatic regulatory functions of the ego," *J. Amer. Psychoanalyt. Assoc.*, 1954, **2**, 67–106. "Part II. Regulatory devices of the ego under stress," *J. Amer. Psychoanalyt. Assoc.*, 1954, **2**, 280–310.

6. The concept of *homeostatsis*, originally used in reference to physiological functions, has been extended to describe and explain psychological stability. See Stagner, R., "Homeostasis as a unifying concept in personality theory," *Psychol. Rev.*, 1951, **58**, 5–17.

7. See Werner, H., *The comparative psychology of mental development*, Chicago, Follett, 1948, for illustrations of "primitive" cognition—indices of ego-weakness. See also Fenichel, O., *The psychoanalytic theory of neurosis*, New York, Norton, 1945, Ch. 4, for a discussion of the "archaic ego." See Nunberg, H., "Ego strength and ego weakness," in *Practise and theory of psychoanalysis*, New York, Nerv. and Ment. Dis. Monogr., 1948, **74**, 185–198.

8. See Angyal, A., "Evasion of growth," *Amer. J. Psychiat.*, 1953, **110**, 358–361, for one psychiatrist's formulations concerning the means by which people strive to evade personality growth. Whitaker and Malone have organized their book on psychotherapy around the concept of growth. See Whitaker, C. A., and Malone, T. P., *The roots of psychotherapy*, New York, Blakiston, 1953.

9. See Freud, Anna, *The ego and the mechanisms of defense*, London, Hogarth, 1937, for a formal psychoanalytic presentation of the mechanism of repression. Also, see Fenichel, O., *op. cit.*, pp. 148–151.

*10. See the analysis of repression from the standpoint of contemporary learning theory in Dollard, J. and Miller, N. E., *Personality and psychotherapy*, New York, McGraw-Hill, 1950, Ch. 12.

*11. Shaffer and Shoben provide the reader with a treatment of experimental studies that have been done on repression. See Shaffer, L. F. and Shoben, E. J., *The psychology of adjustment*, rev. ed., New York, Houghton-Mifflin, 1956, Ch. 8.

12. See Rosenzweig, S., "An experimental study of 'repression' with special reference to need-persistive and ego-defensive reactions to frustration," *J. exp. Psychol.*, 1943, 32, 64–74. Alper, Thelma G., "Memory for completed and incompleted tasks as a function of personality: an analysis of group data," *J. abn. soc. Psychol.*, 1946, 41, 403–420. Eriksen, C. W., "Psychological defenses and ego strength in the recall of completed and incompleted tasks," *J. abn. soc. Psychol.*, 1954, 49, 51–58. For a different, promising experimental attack on the problem of repression, see Eriksen, C. W. and Kuethe, J. S., "Avoidance conditioning of verbal behavior without awareness: a paradigm of repression," *J. abn. soc. Psychol.*, 1956, 53, 203–209.

*13. Cf. Fromm, E., *Psychoanalysis and religion*, New Haven, Yale University Press, 1950.

14. Freud spoke of the "return of the repressed" as one of the determiners of neurotic symptoms.

15. Bettelheim discusses the difficulty which emotionally disturbed children have in establishing ego control upon awakening from sleep. Cf. Bettelheim, B., *Love is not enough*, Glencoe, Illinois, The Free Press, 1950, Ch. 4.

16. It is well known both by clinical and experimental psychologists that words and symbols are powerful conditioned stimuli for emotional responses.

17. Jung, C. G., *Studies in word association*, New York, Moffat, Yard, 1919. See Eriksen and Kuethe, *op. cit.*, for a recent demonstration of how feelings may experimentally be associated with stimulus words.

18. See Feldman, M. J., "The use of obscene words in the therapeutic relationship," *Amer. J. Psychoanal.*, 1955, 15, 45–48.

19. Feldman, M. J., *op. cit.* See also Ferenczi, S., *Sex in psychoanalysis*, New York, Bruner, 1950.

20. Reich and other psychoanalysts view many rigid traits of character—"character-armor"—as a by-product of reaction formation. See Reich, W., *Character analysis*, New York, Orgone Institute Press, 1949.

21. Cf. a letter received by Jules Masserman from a woman antivivisectionist, quoted in Coleman, J. C., *Abnormal psychology and modern life*, New York, Scott, Foresman, 1950, p. 89.

22. See the case histories in Levy, D. M., *Maternal overprotection*, New York, Columbia University Press, 1943.

23. Cf. Werner, H., *op. cit.*

*24. This distinction has been adapted from Cameron, N. and Magaret, Ann, *Behavior pathology*, New York, Houghton Mifflin, 1951, pp. 381–387.

25. Students of prejudice assume that projection plays at least some part in the development of bigoted beliefs about minority-group members. See Allport, G., *The nature of prejudice*, Cambridge, Addison-Wesley, 1954.

*26. Cf. Dollard, J. and Miller, N. E., *Personality and psychotherapy*, New York, McGraw-Hill, 1950, Chs. 17, 18, 19.

27. See, for example, Rapaport, D. (ed.), *Organization and pathology of thought*, New York, Columbia University Press, 1951, for various approaches to the analysis of schizophrenic, or primitive thinking. See also Werner, H., *op. cit.*

28. See Feldman, M. J. and Drasgow, J., "A visual-verbal test for schizophrenia," *Psychiat. Quart. Suppl.*, 1951, Part I, 1–10, for a description of a test which measures the ability to make socially agreed-upon classifications.

29. Freud, S., "Formulations regarding the two principles in mental functioning," Ch. 1 in Freud, S., *Collected papers*, Vol. IV, London, Hogarth, 1953.

30. See Ch. 2. See also Cameron, N. and Magaret, Ann, *op. cit.*, pp. 70–74.

31. Cf. Fenichel, O., *op. cit.*, pp. 155–159.

*32. Harlow, R. G., "Masculine inadequacy and compensatory development of physique," *J. Pers.*, 1951, 19, 312–323.

33. Reich, W., *op. cit.*, pp. 316–328.

34. See Parsons, T., *Essays in sociological theory*, Glencoe, Illinois, The Free Press, 1954, Ch. 5, for a discussion of age-grading in the United States.

35. Terman, L. M. and Merrill, Maud A., *Measuring Intelligence*, New York, Houghton Mifflin, 1937.

36. Gesell, A. and Ilg, F. L., *Infant and child in the culture of to-day*, New York, Harper, 1942; see also the subsequent volumes which provide norms for various aspects of behavior up to adolescence.

*37. A good secondary source which describes the psychoanalytic theory of psychosexual development is Brown, J. F., *Psychodynamics of abnormal behavior*, New York, McGraw-Hill, 1940, Ch. 10.

*38. Maslow, A. H., *Motivation and personality*, New York, Harper, 1954, Ch. 5.

*39. Murphy, G., *Personality: a biosocial approach to origins and structure*, New York, Harper, 1947, Ch. 14.

40. Werner, H., *op. cit.*
41. Fromm, E., *Man for himself,* New York, Rinehart, 1947.
42. Cf. Fenichel, O., *op. cit.*, Ch. 14.
°43. See Cameron, N. and Magaret, Ann, *op. cit.*, Ch. 5, for an excellent and well-documented discussion of fixation.
°44. See Cameron, N. and Magaret, Ann, *op. cit.*, Ch. 8, for a thorough discussion of regression.
45. Cf. Fromm, E., *op. cit.*
46. Freud, S., *The ego and the id,* London, Hogarth, 1927, p. 69.
°47. See Mowrer, O. H., *Learning theory and personality dynamics,* New York, Ronald, 1950, Ch. 22, for a discussion of "conscience-killing." Mowrer has written extensively about the interrelations of guilt and anxiety.
48. Cf. Menninger, K., *op. cit.*

QUESTIONS FOR REVIEW AND EXAMINATION

1. What is meant by threat to the self-structure? What factors typically induce threat?

2. Distinguish between reactions to threat which constitute growth of the self-structure, and those which serve to defend the self-structure as it now is.

3. What are defense mechanisms? Why are they believed to indicate a relatively weak ego?

4. List the major mechanisms of defense, and indicate what signs are used as the basis for inferring that a person has utilized them.

5. How does a person defend his public selves? His self-ideal?

6. Try to discover instances of the various defense mechanisms in yourself or in another person, using the text as a guide.

7. Try to determine instances where your own self-structure has grown as a consequence of a healthy reaction to threat.

CHAPTER 11

Conscience and Guilt in Healthy Personality

INTRODUCTION

When a person does something which society considers wrong, he will be punished in some way. The thief is imprisoned, the liar is shunned, the adulterer is divorced, and the murderer may be executed. Each society has its set of rules that the members must obey, if they are to continue to live in that group as accepted members. The various means for producing conformity with social mores are called techniques of *social control*.[1] Social control of behavior ranges from overt force to such subtle techniques as omitting an offensive person's name from the list of people invited to a party. We can depict the impact of limits and social control over an individual's behavior by recourse to the concept of an arc:

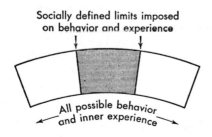

Socially defined limits imposed
on behavior and experience

All possible behavior
and inner experience

In the diagram, the total area of the arc encompasses all behavior and inner experience of which the human being is potentially capable. The shaded area within the arc indicates the range of behavior and experience which a society will recognize, value, and accept. So long as a person restricts his behavior within those limits, he will avoid punishment from the law and from his peers, and he can retain the respect and esteem of others.

The actual behavior encompassed by the social mores is the expression of that society's *value-system*.[2] The value-system refers to the more or less explicit statement of the valued goals that are pursued by the group members, and the kinds of behavior prescribed as means to those goals. Some common goals in our society are a sizable income, a high-prestige profession, a wife or husband who will be deemed desirable and attractive by our peers, etc. A person who achieves these goals in the *right* ways will enjoy a high degree of status. The person who achieves these goals the *wrong* way [3] will be judged harshly, and will not be accepted in the groups in which he desires membership.

External sanctions are not the only means by which society controls the behavior of individual persons. Each member of a society is subjected to a fairly rigorous training process—socialization—which indoctrinates him with the values characteristic of his society.[4] Each socialized person acquires a *personal value-system* which resembles the social value-system. By the time he becomes an adult, he conforms with social limits on behavior because he fears external punishments for deviant behavior, and also because *he wants to conform with his conscience.* If the person violates the group code (and his own conscience), he will experience anxiety, the dread of being caught and punished; and he will also experience *guilt,* an acute moral condemnation of himself. Guilt may be more severe than any punishment that society could mete out to an offender. Persons who could easily escape punishment for a crime have been known to give themselves up and actually beg for external punishment, just so they could be relieved of agonizing guilt-feelings.

Guilt and the conscience, when seen from a sociologist's point of view, serve the very important function of augmenting social control over behavior, and insuring conformity with the social value-system. The necessity for the external control of behavior is reduced when all the members of a society have a conscience and are capable of experiencing guilt. People with consciences control their own behavior, and strive to remain within limits which will keep them free of guilt.[5]

From a psychological standpoint, the conscience is one component of individual personality structure, and a highly important determiner of personality health and personality illness. It is meaningful to ask, "Does this person have a healthy conscience, or is his conscience unhealthy?" The problem, of course, is to determine the characteristics which earmark a healthy conscience, and those which describe an unhealthy conscience.

The conscience is a determiner of guilt and of self-esteem, both powerful motives and determiners of behavior, especially interpersonal behavior. A self-respecting individual behaves quite differently with other people than a guilt-ridden person. The self-respecter "has nothing to hide" from others; the guilty person is very defensive, withdrawn, and prone to avoid close and confiding relationships with others.

An unhealthy conscience is known to play a crucial role in the determination of neurosis and psychosis. Freud and his followers believed that neurosis was a by-product of an overly-severe but unconscious conscience (he called it the *superego*). The neurotic is obliged to refrain from certain kinds of behavior, such as sexuality; more than that, he must refrain even from thinking about or wishing to act in the forbidden ways, if he is to be guilt-free. The therapeutic aim in such cases is to help the patient to reformulate his conscience along more conscious, rational, lenient, and adult lines. If that aim can be accomplished, the patient will have no further need to repress his inner experience, because it would no longer induce guilt.

Mowrer differs with the orthodox psychoanalytic theory concerning the role of conscience in the development of neurosis. He differs also in his concept of therapeutic aims with respect to the conscience.[6] According to Mowrer, a neurotic is not a person with an overly-strict conscience, who must repress his sexuality in order to remain guilt-free. Instead, he sees the neurotic as a person who persists beyond childhood in the pursuit of irresponsible pleasures, including sexuality, and *who represses his guilt and his conscience.*

Neurotic symptoms arise as defenses against guilt, not as defenses against infantile sexuality, as the Freudians might maintain. Consequently, Mowrer claims, the aim in therapy is not to render the conscience more lenient, but to make it *conscious,* so that a person will feel guilt more acutely, and seek in future to obey his conscience rather than ignore or repress it.

Clinical experience suggests that neither Freud nor Mowrer is wholly correct or wholly incorrect. Rather, it can be found that some neurotic patients do indeed have a conscience that is too strict; in order to remain guilt-free, they must refrain from *all* pleasurable activities, including those which society condones.[7] Other patients may be found with the make-up which Mowrer has regarded as nuclear to all neurosis—they repress conscience so they can break social taboos without conscious guilt.

If we paraphrase Freud's therapeutic aim to read, "change the conscience in lenient directions," and Mowrer's to read, "strengthen the conscience, and help the person to conform with his conscience," we are thrust into an acute impasse: we find that contradictory roles are assigned to the conscience in neurosis, and contradictory therapeutic aims are proposed. This impasse can be resolved if we recognize that consciences *are not all alike* among all members of a given society. Some consciences are stricter than the society requires, some are more lenient, some are quite deviant from the social value-system, and many are highly conflicted. Further, consciences differ at various age levels; a child's conscience differs from that of an adult—although adults can be found with the conscience of a child. In other words, the conscience is a highly variable thing. We could state that if a person has a *healthy* conscience, then *healthy personality will be fostered if he conforms with his conscience.* But if a person's conscience is *unhealthy,* then conformity with it will only perpetuate or promote unhealthy personality. The healthy thing for a person to do, if his conscience is unhealthy, *is to change it.*

This lengthy introduction is necessary to provide a context suitable to the more technical discussion which follows. In the sections below we shall define conscience, discuss its origins, describe healthy conscience as explicitly as our present knowledge permits, and describe some common patterns of unhealthy conscience. In addition, we shall examine guilt and self-esteem in some detail, and attempt to specify healthy and unhealthy aspects of these two modes of response.

THE DEFINITION OF CONSCIENCE

Conscience is made up of ideals and taboos for a person's behavior. Each socialized person internalizes the *social* value-system, and acquires a *personal* value-system. The personal value-system is more comprehensive in its scope than conscience, since it defines the person's goals, his standards for judging other people, and his standards for judging himself. Conscience refers only to the values and ideals which pertain to the self. Values and ideals pertaining to other people may be similar to those pertaining to the self, but they cannot be called part of the conscience. Rather, they are part of the more comprehensive concept of the personal value-system.

In the literature on personality-theory, many terms have been employed to describe what we call conscience. The psychoanalysts use the term *superego* in this context, but superego has a somewhat different technical meaning from conscience. The superego is a hypothetical substructure within personality structure as a whole, with conscience being one of its *functions*. The literal meaning of conscience is roughly "simultaneous knowledge, or awareness"; that is, conscience means observing and judging one's own behavior and experience during the actual process of behaving and experiencing. The superego is regarded as a derivative of another psychological structure, the *ego*. The ego constructs the superego, and also the *ego-ideal*. The ego-ideal sets the goals and ideals which the ego will strive to attain.[8]

Other personality theorists [9] have employed the term *self-ideal*, or *ideal self* (in contrast to the real self, perceived self, or self-concept) to embody the facts which we are summing up with the term conscience.

In order to avoid confusion in terminology we shall use the word conscience throughout this chapter to refer to the values, ideals, rules, taboos, goals, etc., which an individual holds with respect to his own behavior and inner experience.

HOW THE CONSCIENCE IS ACQUIRED

The conscience is gradually acquired during the process of growing up by means of *identification*.[10] Identification is the name given to the process of adopting traits of some *valued model*. It is through identification that intra-familial resemblances in behavior, gesture, values, attitudes, and morals are acquired. It is through identification with the parents' value-system that the growing child acquires his personal value-system and his conscience.

The growing child begins life without a conscience. He just acts in accordance with his momentary needs and feelings. But his parents are usually watching him like a hawk, and making value-judgments about his behavior. If the child acts in ways which violate the parents' concepts of what is right, they will generally punish him. If the child fails to conform with their expectations about achievement, they may punish him, or make him feel rejected and unloved. The parents appear huge, powerful, admirable and wonderful from the child's standpoint; he wants to become like them. In order to avoid punishment, to retain the parents' love, and to acquire their wonderful attributes, the child strives to become like his parents in very many ways. He identifies with their demands and expectations of *him;* these gradually become the child's expectations of himself. In short, he comes to forbid in himself what his parents forbade. He comes to demand of himself what his parents demanded. He comes to expect of himself what his parents expected. In this manner, gradually, the conscience is acquired.

SOME CHARACTERISTICS OF THE CONSCIENCE

THE CONSCIENCE IS NOT ALWAYS CONSCIOUS. The conscience is gradually acquired beginning in early childhood, and so the individual cannot verbalize all of its component taboos and ideals. All he knows is that when he acts in certain ways he feels guilty, and when he acts in other ways he feels all right. It may happen, indeed, that a person *thinks* certain modes of behavior are perfectly all right and virtuous, but if he behaves in those ways, he experiences guilt. He doesn't know why he feels the guilt, but he feels it none the less. Since he does not know why he feels guilt, the implication is clear that certain aspects of his conscience are *unconscious*.

Furthermore, if a person always acts in accordance with his conscience, he never feels guilt anyway; in fact, he may be said to be unaware that he *has* a conscience. His conscience manifests itself only indirectly, through his automatic choice of behavior-patterns which accord with his conscience.

THE CONSCIENCE IS AGE-GRADED. Just as society expects varying kinds of behavior from a person at various age levels, so does the person make age-graded demands upon himself. The child does not expect the same performances from himself that he will when he reaches adult status. The child does not feel guilty about the same things an adult would feel guilty about. If total personality development proceeds smoothly, the conscience will change in the appropriate way at each growth stage. However, conscience-*fixations,* conscience-*regressions,* and *precocity of conscience* occur commonly, and they are important causes of unhealthy personality.

THE CONSCIENCE IS OFTEN VERY STRICT.[11] The conscience is a set of demands which a person makes upon himself. If he fails to conform with these demands, he may experience guilt, depression, or inferiority-feelings of incredible intensity. Some people would never dream of judging their worst enemy as harshly as they judge themselves when they fail to live up to some self-expectation. The problem becomes quite complicated when the self-demands are unconscious, that is, unstated in words. For in such instances, the person experiences only the guilt, and is unaware of the self-demands which he has failed to comply with. The causes of this severe self-punishment have been investigated by psychoanalysts; they have suggested that severe self-criticism reflects severe punishments and stringent demands the parents imposed upon the child when he was younger. In identifying with his parents, the child came to evaluate himself, to make similar demands, and to impose taboos upon himself similar to those imposed on him by his parents. Violation of these taboos results in a "punishment" of the self similar to the punishments the parents imposed.

THE CONSCIENCE OFTEN IS HIGHLY CONFLICTED. The conscience is acquired originally through identification with the values and ideals which others held with respect to the self. These origins may result in *conflicting* values and ideals. The parents may disagree on what they demand of their child, and so he acquires conflicting self-expectations. As the child becomes involved with other significant adults, such as teachers, ministers, relatives, maids, etc., he internalizes some of their demands on him, and these may conflict sharply with his present conscience. As he becomes involved in various peer-groups, he may adopt many of their values, which can be at variance with his present value-system. His conscience will thus comprise demands upon the self which are logically contradictory with one another. In conforming with one set of values, the person is violating another set. The result may be chronic guilt, or chronic moral indecision.

THE CONSCIENCE IS USUALLY AUTHORITARIAN. The "authoritarian character" is a person who believes authority figures are omnipotent, and must be obeyed and submitted to without question or criticism. Indeed, to disobey or to question authority is synonymous with sin for the authoritarian character; he becomes overwhelmed with guilt at even the thought of disobeying or challenging vested authority. A person may experience his own conscience in the same manner that he experiences external authority—it is to be obeyed blindly, without question, hesitation, or criticism. Fromm has named a conscience with such characteristics an *authoritarian conscience*.[12] He regards an authoritarian conscience as an undesirable thing, from the standpoint of healthy personality. An authoritarian conscience will most likely be acquired by a person reared by authoritarian parents—they brooked no disobedience and no questioning of their authority. Most persons have aspects of conscience they acquired out of the authoritarian relationship with their parents, or other significant persons. A high degree of rigidity, or resistance to change in the typical conscience reflects its authoritarian nature.

THE CONSCIENCE CAN BE REPRESSED AND PROJECTED. To repress is to refuse to think about something, or to refrain from engaging in some mental operation, such as thinking, remembering, day-dreaming, or *evaluating*. Conscience functions by means of the comparison of one's own behavior, feelings, or motives with relevant taboos and shoulds. A person may have learned to refrain from making value-judgments about aspects of his own behavior, so as to avoid the painful experience of guilt.[13] *This avoidance of making value-judgments concerning one's own behavior is what we mean when we speak of the repression of conscience.* The most vivid proof that one has repressed aspects of his own conscience is provided by experiences of the following sort: Suppose you have done something without thinking too much about its moral implications, such as stealing office supplies for home use. You feel no guilt. But then, another person discovers it, and reminds you this is theft. You become threatened, and overwhelmed with guilt. What the other person has done is to reactivate your tendency to evaluate yourself. On doing so, you feel guilt. Probably one of the more important functions of a revivalistic minister is that of reminding his congregation they have values, and they should compare their deeds with these values. He is striving to undo the process of conscience-repression, so the church members will again feel guilt whenever they violate their consciences.

A person can project his conscience as well as repress it.[14] Concretely, this involves repression of the process of self-evaluation, and *ascribing evaluations of the self to others.* Thus, a person might engage in some act, but deny it is wrong for him to do this. However, he may impute condemnation of himself to some other person, and feel without warrant that the other person is criticizing and condemning him. In extreme cases of personality illness, for example, paranoid schizophrenia, the patient projects all of his self-criticism to others, and believes that everyone is criticizing him and persecuting him.

THE CONSCIENCE CAN BE DECEIVED. A person skilled in argument and debate can persuade a gullible individual that black is white, and that wrong is right. Such a person can direct his rhetoric at himself, or rather, at his conscience. Most of us have at one time or another faced some moral conflict, where strong temptation confronted us. We took the easy path, the one which procured some forbidden pleasure for us, and stifled our self-condemnation by means of subtle self-debate. Much of our *rationalization* serves the function of duping or deceiving our conscience (i.e., ourselves as a whole person) into believing that we really have done no wrong.[15]

This list of characteristics of the conscience could be extended at some length, but it should suffice to acquaint the reader with this aspect of his own personality. Now that we have some idea about the range of variability of conscience in society, let us proceed to evaluate conscience from a personality-hygiene point of view.

THE EVALUATION OF CONSCIENCE

What are the characteristics of a healthy conscience? What are some of the more common patterns of an unhealthy conscience? These are the questions we shall attempt to answer in the following sections.

CHARACTERISTICS OF A HEALTHY CONSCIENCE

A person with a healthy conscience will follow personality-hygiene precepts if he strives to conform with it. Such conformity will have a number of consequences. It will enable the person to obtain enough basic need-gratifications to make life worth living, but in a guilt-free manner. The person will enjoy relatively high self-esteem. His behavior may be quite highly approved by other members of his social group—at least to the extent that his conscience is congruent with the group's value-system. A healthy conscience will be compatible with continual personality growth, indeed, it may be a strong motivating force toward personality growth. In view of all these important and valuable consequences of a healthy conscience, it is important to define its characteristics as clearly as our knowledge will allow. This clear definition might then facilitate the personality-hygiene goal of promoting healthy conscience-development in more people. Let us turn, then, to a listing of some of the more salient attributes of a healthy conscience.

ACCESSIBILITY TO CONSCIOUSNESS. A healthy conscience is a *conscious* conscience. The person is able, when he wants, to formulate its component taboos, ideals, and ethical precepts in words. That is, he can state his moral-ethical convictions to himself. This accessibility to consciousness is very important for such problems as *moral conflicts*. If a person is faced with a decision which he must make, he can make his decision along moral lines much more readily when his conscience is clearly stated. A conscious conscience provides the person with explicit standards in terms of which he can evaluate his own behavior in a rational manner.

When we say that a healthy conscience is conscious, we do not mean the person is always thinking about his moral standards. Most of the time, the healthy conscience will be unconscious; the person will conform with his conscience automatically. But when he does feel guilt, he will be able to determine what aspects of his conscience he has violated; and when he has to resolve some conflict, he will be able to make all of the relevant moral aspects explicit, so that his decision will be made after due consideration of the moral issues at stake.

SELF-AFFIRMED. A healthy conscience is not experienced as an "alien power" within the total personality structure, a power compulsively obeyed out of dread. Rather, it is composed of a set of ideals and taboos, each of which has been examined by the person, and *affirmed* by him so that it becomes a true part of his real self. A self-affirmed conscience is one which the person conforms with *because he wants to,* not because he is afraid of disobeying. Another way of saying this is to assert that the person feels he *owns* his conscience; it is *his.* He has had a voice in determining the rules by which he will live. He is like the citizen in a democracy who does not mind conforming with rules he has helped formulate.

FLEXIBILITY. A healthy conscience is based upon general values and ideals which remain fixed throughout life. But the specific behavior which these values call for is not rigidly defined. The person can change many of his self-demands when it becomes apparent they are no longer relevant to his present life-circumstances. Let us illustrate what we mean by flexibility of conscience: Early in life, a person may have been trained to believe that smoking is a sin. Since he wants to be considered a good person, the individual refrains from smoking. Actually, smoking may be considered to be a sin only by his parents. Later in life, the person discovers there is no necessary connection between goodness and refraining from smoking. Consequently, he may revise this aspect of his conscience, and start to smoke with enjoyment, free from guilt. He has not changed his affirmation of the overall value of being a good person; he has merely dropped one specific taboo which he earlier thought must be observed if one were to be good. Smoking has ceased to be a moral issue for him. Of course, he may still refrain from smoking, but not on moral grounds; rather, to save money, or protect his health.

The flexibility we are talking about as a property of a healthy conscience depends on freedom to examine one's specific taboos and self-expectations, to evaluate these in terms of more general values, and to abandon, change or re-affirm the specific aspects of conscience on the basis of such examination. This flexibility is most likely to be found in consciences which are *not authoritarian* in nature. Such flexibility insures that a person will be observing only those taboos which he wants to observe, and it insures that the individual's conscience will be up-to-date. That is, he will not be observing taboos or pursuing ideals in adult years that are appropriate only to a child.

MATURITY. The healthy conscience is comprised of ideals and taboos which are appropriate to the individual's present stage of overall maturity. Healthy conscience is not fixated, nor regressed to less mature levels. A person with a healthy conscience does not demand things of himself which would be more suited to a person of more advanced years, or a person with more skill, knowledge, or ability.

REALISTIC. The specific taboos and ideals which comprise a healthy conscience are formulated with due consideration for the person's actual ability to conform with these self-demands. The person does not impose taboos upon himself which no human being could be expected to conform with, viz.: absolute perfection, absolute blamelessness, absolute freedom from hostility, absolute freedom from thinking about socially tabooed activities.[16] Rather, the healthy conscience may affirm the person's right to absolute freedom to think and fantasy anything imaginable without guilt; it is only the overt behavior which would be self-condemned, and productive of guilt.

HIERARCHICAL STRUCTURE. The values which make up a healthy conscience are organized into a hierarchy of relative importance. This arrangement enables the person to make moral decisions, when conflicts arise, on a rational basis. He will be able to see what values are at stake, and make decisions which implement his most important values. Probably the value which would lie at the pinnacle of the hierarchy would be the person's concern for his own integrity and growth as a whole, with all other values assigned lesser importance. Fromm has implied this in his discussion of a *humanistic* conscience in contrast to an authoritarian conscience.[17] The humanistic conscience includes a positive affirmation of the importance of full development of the latent capacities of the self. Maslow [18] also regards full development of one's potential self as a value more important than other goals.

SOME DEGREE OF CONGRUENCE WITH THE SOCIAL VALUE-SYSTEM. The person with a healthy conscience is living among other people, and so he will be obliged to share at least some of their values, ideals, and taboos. This is not to say that his conscience must be absolutely congruent with the social mores. It may happen that the person finds his values more ethical than the prevailing mores, and so he will follow his own conscience rather than the moral expectations of his peers and contemporaries. It may be necessary for the person with a healthy conscience to be able to *resist* the efforts of others to make him conform with their moral precepts. He may even be obliged to leave some group, or locale, because of moral-ethical differences, and seek a group more congenial to his outlook, or else live on in active opposition to the group.

To state this point another way, the person with a healthy conscience may choose to conform to some degree with the mores of his group, but he will preserve a certain degree of inner freedom from the group's demands. His self-affirmed conscience is his guide to conduct, and not the expectations of others.

HUMANE. When we say that a healthy conscience is humane, we mean that the person does not treat himself cruelly and sadistically when he violates his own ethical precepts. He will feel guilt, to be sure, but it is not likely to be harsh or brutal. Rather, he will experience his moral lapses as mistakes which can be rectified by him through any suitable restitutive and expiatory measures. And he does not condemn himself outright and wholly for his lapses; in spite of his "sins," he can continue to love and esteem himself as a person, with the same compassion for his own frailties that he would show to some child who made moral mistakes. We do not kill a child who steals and lies, so it is difficult to see how it could be healthy for a person to kill himself—literally, or symbolically—for some deviation from his own conscience.

A person with a healthy conscience will have the capacity to experience guilt, but he will not likely suffer from chronic guilt. It is not implied that a healthy conscience will be highly lenient, permitting anti-social behavior. Indeed, it may be very difficult to accord with the precepts of a healthy conscience. Fromm has stated that the voice of a humanistic conscience may be only dimly heard, because it is readily masked by the authoritarian elements of conscience. As Fromm puts it, "[conscience] is the voice of our true 'selves' which summons us back to ourselves, to live productively, to develop fully and harmoniously—that is, to become what we potentially are." He points out further that guilt arising from a violation of a healthy conscience may be very difficult to identify; we might feel guilt arising from our *authoritarian* conscience when we ignore its demands in order to pursue the requirements of a *healthy* conscience.[19]

SOME INDICATIONS OF AN UNHEALTHY CONSCIENCE

If a person has an unhealthy conscience, his growth toward personality health will be fostered by efforts to change it in the directions indicated in the previous section. Let us now list some signs of an unhealthy consicence.

UNREMITTING GUILT. If a person experiences guilt chronically, and yet his behavior does not appear to an observer to warrant such guilt, it is likely that the person has an unhealthy conscience. This chronic guilt may be fully conscious, or it may be unconscious, disguised even from the person who is victimized by it. Unconscious guilt assumes many forms.[20] It may manifest itself through repetitive accidents; through repeated failures in important ventures, failures which easily could have been avoided if the simplest precautions had been taken; through habitual self-depreciation in the presence of others; through habitual, uncalled-for justifications and explanations of one's past and present actions, etc. All of these signs of unconscious guilt, as well as conscious guilt, indicate that the conscience which is responsible is unhealthy in at least some respects; it may be unconscious, too rigid, too strict, or not suitable to the person's present age level.

ABSENCE OF GUILT IN SPITE OF OBVIOUS MORAL VIOLATIONS. If a person violates many ethical precepts, and yet seems free from conscious guilt, it may be assumed that his conscience is strikingly deviant from the modal conscience. Or, he may have repressed both conscience and guilt. Psychiatrists use the term "psychopathic personality" to describe individuals who violate mores without guilt.

GUILT OVER APPARENTLY TRIVIAL LAPSES. If a person suffers an onslaught of guilt over something trivial, such as coming late to an appointment, or failing to return a borrowed book on the exact date that was promised, it betokens unhealthy conscience. His conscience is unhealthy because it is too strict, too exacting, or childish. Such a disproportionate reaction may indicate the person has repressed guilt that was induced by a very grave violation of conscience, and then *displaced* his guilt-response to the less serious crime. Edmund Bergler, a psychoanalyst, illustrated this mechanism with an analogy: "I couldn't be guilty of that murder, because I was robbing a bank on the other side of town at just the time the killing occurred."

SOME PATTERNS OF UNHEALTHY CONSCIENCE

We will describe *excessively strict consciences, excessively permissive consciences, deviant consciences,* and *conflicted consciences.* Following this discussion we shall examine a variety of ways in which people can relate to their consciences, and then we will evaluate these ways.

EXCESSIVELY STRICT CONSCIENCE. This pattern of unhealthy conscience limits guilt-free behavior more drastically than law and custom. The unfortunate bearer of such a conscience allows himself fewer need-satisfactions than other members of his social group; he expects more of himself, more difficult achievements, and a sterner morality, than his group peers. In America, it might be quite acceptable, and certainly not immoral, for a middle-class girl to smoke, take an occasional drink, neck, go to dances, etc. Her friend, with an excessively strict conscience, might want to do these things, but finds herself so ridden with guilt they are rendered unenjoyable for her. Many people have been subjected to socialization influences from parents, ministers, and other moral models, so that they must not only avoid certain kinds of activities (which are defined as wrong, or sinful), but they must even avoid thinking about such activities. Thus, many persons may have been taught that sexy, or hostile fantasies and thoughts are equivalent in sinful significance to sexual and hostile activities. In order to remain guilt-free, they must not only restrict their activities, but also their thoughts. It is probably this type of excessively restrictive conscience which Freud saw as a factor responsible for the development of neurosis, and which he sought to modify in his patients.

In terms of our arc-concept, we would depict the excessively strict conscience as follows:

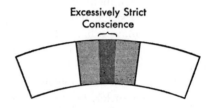

Excessively Strict
Conscience

The horizontally shaded area in the diagram represents all of the behavior patterns which are theoretically available to members of a given group, but which are taboo for the person with an excessively strict conscience; he must confine his behavior to the narrower, cross-hatched area.

EXCESSIVELY PERMISSIVE CONSCIENCE. An excessively permissive conscience is one which allows a person to engage, guilt-free, in a range of behavior broader than that which is usual or allowed by the laws and customs of the group. The person shares most of the moral values of his group, but his behavioral boundaries are broader than those of the group. It should be stated that the word excessive is always in reference to the social group in question. Obviously, what is regarded as "loose living" in one group may be regarded as strictly moral in another. In terms of the arc-concept, the overly permissive conscience would be depicted as follows:

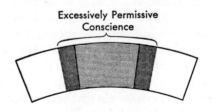

Excessively Permissive
Conscience

The persons in our society most likely to have an excessively permissive conscience (as seen from the viewpoint of the average person) are the intellectuals, or the bohemians. Such individuals conform in most respects with conventional moral standards, but they may refuse to delimit their behavior in some selected area, such as sexuality. The intellectual inveighs against "middle-class morality," all the while conforming with it in most respects, excepting sexual morality. If he is successful in his reformulation of modal morality, he may be quite capable of indulging himself in promiscuous sexuality without guilt.

Many parents, eager to apply "newer concepts of child-rearing" may inculcate an excessively permissive conscience in their children. They refuse to set and enforce limits on the behavior of their children (so as to avoid thwarting them), and inculcate a conscience (or lack of one?) which enables the children to transgress the limits of conventional morality in a guilt-free manner. The layman almost expects the children of psychiatrists and child-experts to be uninhibited and amoral, although there is little evidence to support this expectancy.

DEVIANT CONSCIENCE. A deviant conscience is one which comprises values markedly different from the values prevalent in the person's present social group. His standards for conduct may overlap in important respects with those of other people, but they will differ strikingly in other areas of activity. The goals which he considers important are not the goals emphasized by his group. His concepts of right and wrong diverge in many ways from those of the group. In actuality, the person with a deviant conscience may be evaluated in comparison with his "home group" as having a strict or permissive conscience, but with reference to the new group, he has a deviant conscience. The persons in our society who have deviant consciences are primarily first-generation immigrants. The immigrant who has not as yet been acculturated to American ways still behaves in accordance with the values of the culture from which he has come. Thus, many of the American practices seem scandalous to him, and he would be overwhelmed with guilt if he emulated them. Similarly, many of his guilt-free activities may be viewed as sinful and criminal to the American.

Another version of deviant conscience is to be found in certain groups in American society, especially groups of teen-agers. They may evolve a set of values which differ markedly in many important respects from the values represented by their parents, or by society at large. Thus, the teen-ager may have an extremely exacting and strict conscience, based on identification with the values of his gang or group. In order to maintain his self-esteem, he may feel compelled to perform all kinds of actions repugnant to the person with a modal conscience. He may lie, cheat, steal, rape, etc. These actions may serve not only to preserve his status within the group, but also to maintain his self-esteem.

CONFLICTED CONSCIENCE. This is a very common version of unhealthy conscience. It is composed of values, ideals and taboos which contradict one another. Thus, conformity with one component value requires violation of another, with consequent guilt. The conflicted conscience is developed out of identification with persons who have contrasting demands, expectations, and prohibitions with respect to the individual's behavior. A common source of conflicted conscience is parents who have different standards for judging the behavior of their children. The mother may value gentleness, submissiveness, obedience, and "womanly things," while the father affirms self-assertion, aggressiveness, muscular strength, etc. Prior to the establishment of a conscience, the child may experience considerable confusion and conflict as he strives to obtain the approval and affection of his parents. In pleasing his father, he displeases his mother, and vice versa. When once he has identified with the values of each parent, the interpersonal conflicts are changed into *intra*personal conflicts. He acts one way, in order to maintain self-esteem, only to experience guilt for the violation of contrasting values.

An additional source of conflicted conscience is to be found in the fact that very often the parental values with which a person has identified differ markedly from the values of teachers, peers, or the values of other groups with which the person is involved. He may identify with many value-systems, incorporating them into his conscience, and increasing the frequency of value-conflicts.

Some people attempt to resolve the value-conflicts by compartmentalizing their lives: they follow one set of values at work, another set in the home, another set when they are among their peers, etc. A more desirable way from the personality-hygiene viewpoint is the attempt to reconcile one's values with one another so they constitute a harmonious and hierarchically arranged system.

MODES OF RELATING TO THE CONSCIENCE

It should not be forgotten that the conscience is a part of a person's self-structure. Consequently, when we speak of "modes of relating to the conscience," we are really speaking of different ways in which a person relates to his real self. In principle, a person can relate to his conscience, or his real self, *in almost all of the ways that he might relate to another person.* Thus, one can listen to oneself, ignore oneself, obey and disobey oneself, love and hate oneself, rebel, conform, kill, aggress, worship, deceive, drug, reason with the self, etc. Since the conscience is one aspect of the self, a person can relate to his own conscience in all of these ways. Let us describe the healthy ways of relating to the conscience, and then comment upon some of the more obviously unhealthy ways of relating to the conscience.

HEALTHY RELATIONSHIPS WITH THE CONSCIENCE. Since the conscience is really the self observing, evaluating, and "talking" to the self, it is healthy for the person to pay attention and to listen. Presumably, the conscience is that part of the real self which is actively concerned with the growth and the "goodness" of the whole person, and so should be attended to. The voice of the conscience is heard, however dimly, whenever some action is being considered which will have consequences for the overall growth and moral worth of the whole person. The individual will then experience a conflict between his immediate wishes for need-gratification and pleasure, and his desire to grow, to become a better person, or to remain a good person. If the person is relating in healthy fashion with his conscience, he will listen at these times to what it has to say to him. This message will neither be ignored nor compulsively and unthinkingly obeyed. Rather, the person will "hear himself out," and strive to make a realistic appraisal of all the issues that are involved in the proposed behavior. If he discovers that no important values are being violated, he will so inform himself (his conscience), and proceed with his actions. If, on the other hand, he discerns that he will violate important values by acting in this way, he may decide to conform with his conscience. Let us call this mode of relating to the conscience *reasoned consideration.* It is obviously comparable with the reasoned consideration an adult will give to the opinions, objections, and requests that other people might express to him when he is planning some sort of activity which affects their welfare. He has to decide upon that line of action which will reconcile all of the conflicting values that may be at stake.

COMPULSIVE CONFORMITY WITH THE CONSCIENCE. This is an unhealthy pattern which is most likely to be observed in a person with an authoritarian conscience. Such a person very likely experiences himself as "split," or divided in fundamental ways; he has a "bad" self, which is impulsive, childish, selfish, and immoral, and a stern, powerful "good" self—his conscience—which orders him to suppress his bad self and to be good. Habitually, the person acts in accordance with the literal dictates of his conscience, upon pain of intense guilt for failures to conform. This pattern parallels very closely the relationship that a "good boy" might establish with very stern and autocratic parents, or that an obedient and well-trained soldier establishes with his superior officers.

COMPULSIVE REBELLION AGAINST THE CONSCIENCE. A person who has acquired a strict and authoritarian conscience may set out deliberately and systematically to rebel against it. His manifest guide to conduct might then be, "Would my conscience (meaning my parents, authorities, etc.), become shocked by such behavior?" If the answer is affirmative, he will then act in the shocking ways, even enjoying the dismay of others, and the possible punishment which he receives for acting in those ways. The compulsive rebel is not aware that in compulsively violating the social mores and his parents' wishes, he is actually violating a repressed aspect of his real self; namely, his conscience.

ANESTHETIZING THE CONSCIENCE. Fiction is full of examples of people who have taken to drink, and in so doing, have violated their consciences high, wide and handsome. Just as one might induce someone else to do all kinds of things when drunk that he would never do when sober, so can one "dissolve" one's conscience in alcohol. Alcohol appears to function as a "conscience solvent" by impairing the accuracy and precision with which the person makes (moral) judgments, and also by anesthetizing the person against the painful experience of guilt which he would ordinarily experience following moral lapses.

CONSCIENCE-KILLING. If a person is being followed, threatened, and persecuted by some accusing individual, he may resort to the extreme expedient of killing the accuser, so as forever to still his voice. By the same token, all attempts on the part of a person to suspend, repress, or eliminate the act of self-judgment and self-criticism might be construed symbolically as conscience-killing.[21] In extreme instances, a guilt-ridden person might kill himself because that is the only way that he can kill his conscience.

"SENDING THE CONSCIENCE ON VACATION." An employer who has an annoying, self-righteous partner or employee can sometimes gain temporary respite against the other's reproaches by sending him away for some period of time. In many ways, people may put their own consciences on vacation, and place a definite moratorium on moral self-criticism. For example, a highly righteous man may go on a wild spree when he is out of town at a professional convention. There is a sort of tacit agreement between him and his fellow conventioneers, that no one shall judge conduct during the convention-time by home-town moral standards. However, if some neighbor from the home town who is not part of the convention should see the man in the midst of his revels, he might become guilty as well as embarrassed.

All of the preceding ways of relating to the conscience, with the exception of reasoned consideration, may be regarded as unhealthy patterns. In the long run, these unhealthy patterns have the consequence of promoting increased alienation from the self, and of mobilizing increasing amounts of guilt. Now, let us examine the "voices" of conscience themselves: guilt and self-esteem.

GUILT AND SELF-ESTEEM

When a person behaves in opposition to his conscience he experiences guilt, just as he received punishment from his parents when they caught him behaving contrary to their expectations. When he behaves in conformity with his conscience, he experiences a heightening of the feeling of self-esteem, just as he received signs of love, and lavish praise from his parents when they observed him doing something meritorious during childhood days. Guilt and self-esteem may be regarded as the internalized version of the punishments and rewards which earlier in life were accorded the child by his parents and other significant persons.

Guilt and self-esteem are both *emotional responses* to one's own inner experience, and overt behavior. The emotional responses to *other people's* behavior which are analogous with guilt and self-esteem are moral indignation [22] and admiration,[23] respectively. Thus, when we see someone else treating an animal cruelly, we may become infuriated with that person, just as we would feel guilty for ill-treating the animal ourselves. If we see someone doing something which we wish we had the moral fortitude to do ourselves, we admire them for the exemplary deed.

As emotional responses, both guilt and self-esteem include cognitive, affective, expressive, and instrumental components. We can evaluate these responses with respect to their rationality, their congruence with social norms, with the person's age-roles, etc. Further, we can evaluate the emotional behavior which guilt and self-esteem motivate the person to perform. Guilt-motivated behavior may be adjudged healthy or unhealthy, depending upon the consequences which follow from this behavior. Self-esteem-motivated behavior likewise can be assessed with respect to its consequences. Let us examine, discuss, and evaluate guilt and self-esteem.

SELF-ESTEEM

Self-esteem is the name given to the complex cognitive-affective response which accompanies behavior in accordance with the conscience.[24] Most of the time, we are not aware of the experience of self-esteem. It peeps, or leaps, over the threshold of awareness when we have accomplished some fairly difficult task that reflects favorably upon our moral worth in our own eyes, and in the eyes of those who share our values. We most often become cognizant of self-esteem when we have lost it through some loathsome, immoral activity, or through some failure in achieving our self-appointed goals.

The cognitive aspects of self-esteem include verbal judgments of the following sort: "I am a good and worthwhile person"; "I respect myself as a person because of the way that I act," etc. The affective aspect of self-esteem is something analogous to the feelings which accompany the expectation of pleasant things. When a person has high self-esteem, he probably anticipates affection, praise, or admiration from others, and this expectancy feels good per se.

Self-esteem is rational when it derives from an accurate comparison of actual behavior and achievement with the relevant ideals of the conscience. It is irrational when the person esteems himself for traits which he actually does not possess, and achievements he has not actually performed. The extreme case of irrational self-esteem is found in the patient who is displaying a manic psychotic reaction, and in paranoid patients who believe they are someone great and wonderful.

Rational self-esteem is a personality-hygiene value, both in its own right, and also because of its influence upon the individual's interpersonal relationships. A person with self-esteem is much more likely to be able to establish healthy interpersonal relationships with others (cf. Chapter 7) than one who is chronically guilty, or plagued by inferiority-feelings.

Self-esteem is very highly dependent upon the continued receipt of affection, approval, and admiration from other persons, even in the individual with a healthy conscience. If one is perpetually criticized by others, one is likely in the long run to suffer a loss of self-esteem, even if one knows the criticism is not warranted. But a healthy personality is much more independent of external praise and approval than an unhealthy individual. The healthy personality may be said to display relatively *autonomous self-esteem*—he experiences it when he accords with *his* values, and he loses it when he violates *his* taboos. A person with a less solidly established conscience is likely to be what Riesman called an other-directed character, one whose self-evaluations and self-esteem are almost totally dependent upon a continued supply of favorable evaluations from others. The person who displays *self-esteem dependency* is much more at the mercy of people about him than the person with autonomous self-esteem; he may be subject to depressions and acute attacks of inferiority-feelings every time there is some decrease in the flow of "narcissistic supplies"—praise and love from others—upon which his self-esteem rests.[25]

A fairly stable level of self-esteem is most likely to occur in persons with a healthy conscience, who have received abundant supplies of love and appreciation during the process of growing up, and who have been able to achieve a fairly adequate number of socially valued successes throughout their life. Self-esteem is of course highly dependent upon success, that is, achieving at one's level of aspiration. The more one has achieved, the more solidly established will one's self-esteem be. Finally, under optimum conditions, self-esteem will be predicated on a *broad base* of achievements and traits, and not dependent on some one, temporary and insecure basis, such as income, or appearance.

GUILT

Guilt involves both cognitive judgments (I am no good; I am worthless), and strong affective components. No feeling is so agonizing to a well-socialized person as is acute guilt, except, perhaps, an acute anxiety attack. Since guilt is such a powerful feeling, it incites the person to do something quickly in order to get rid of its pain. As we noted in an earlier chapter (Chapter 4), we can distinguish between rational and irrational guilt, and we can recognize healthy and unhealthy guilt-motivated behavior.

HEALTHY REACTIONS TO GUILT. In principle, a healthy reaction to guilt is one which (a) gets rid of the guilt feelings and restores self-esteem, and (b) either preserves personality health or moves the person closer to the goal of a healthy personality.

There are some fundamental rules which, if followed, will insure that a person is handling his guilt in a healthy fashion. These rules may be listed as follows:

1. When guilt is experienced, *acknowledge it*. This is no more than saying that a person should pay attention to all of his inner experience, whether it be pleasant or unpleasant.

2. Following the recognition of guilt-feelings in the self, the person should strive to determine why he feels guilt. This involves a careful appraisal of whatever behavior, thoughts, wishes, or fantasies occurred just prior to the guilt-reaction. More important, it involves the necessity of making the rules and taboos of the conscience explicit, stating them in words in somewhat this fashion: "Since I feel guilty after doing that, I must hold the conviction, consciously or unconsciously, that such activity is wrong."

3. Once the relevant taboo has been put into words, the person can then *examine the taboo itself*, in order to ascertain how he

acquired it, how appropriate it is for a person in his present situation and with his present degree of development.

4. If critical assessment indicates the taboo is one which he believes should be observed, then the person can *re-affirm* it consciously, do whatever is necessary to make amends or to undo the "wrong" he has committed, and strive thenceforth to *conform with his conscience* in that respect.

5. If, on the other hand, the person discovers that the taboo responsible for his guilt is childish, or no longer relevant to his present situation, this very discovery may eliminate the guilt. The person can say to himself, and believe it, "Why, I no longer believe it is wrong to do that." He has, in effect, actually *changed his conscience*. From that time onward, he can perform, guilt-free, whatever actions he earlier had avoided because they induced guilt in him.

These steps toward the healthy management of guilt have been described earlier as *conformity with the conscience* and *changing the conscience*. That is, a person who has faced his guilt and acknowledged it, has two healthy alternatives at his disposal for the riddance of his guilt: subsequent avoidance of the guilt-inducing behavior and conformity with his conscience (which has been made *conscious*) or changing his conscience, and thus feeling free to do what earlier made him guilty.

Although we have spoken about changing the conscience, it must not be assumed this is an easy task to accomplish. There are many obstacles which make it a very difficult problem indeed. Yet it is not so difficult as to be impossible. We do know that conscience changes by itself many times during the process of growing up, usually in a way that is unconscious and automatic. As the person makes new identifications with new significant people, he often adopts many aspects of *their* consciences which come to replace the relevant taboos and rules of his own. As the person becomes involved in various groups which follow a moral code different from his present one, he may come to adopt these new codes, without any conscious conflict, or with conflict. These changes in conscience, however, are not deliberate and willed by the person. They just happen. It is the deliberate changes in conscience which probably are most difficult to achieve. Yet, if the person can make his conscience *conscious*, he will have gone a long way toward altering his taboos in the light of common sense and mature judgment. Probably one of the most effective means for changing an infantile conscience into one which is more conducive to adult living and adult satisfactions is intensive personality therapy. In therapy, the patient exposes his real self to the therapist, and in the process of self-exposure, he may verbalize many of his presently unconscious taboos for the first time. Further, he may get a clearer idea how he acquired these immature rules for conduct. Simply seeing all this *may* help the person change his conscience.[26]

What of conformity with the conscience? When is it healthy to conform with the conscience, and when is it healthy to attempt to change the conscience? The obvious answer is as follows: "If the conscience is healthy, then the guilty person should strive to conform with it. If the conscience is unhealthy, then the person should strive to change it."

UNHEALTHY REACTIONS TO GUILT. Guilt is like pain or any other kind of suffering, it motivates the person powerfully to do something to get rid of the unwanted feelings. With physical pain, a person has three alternatives. He can simply endure the pain, doing nothing to ease it. He can take drugs or anesthetics to relieve himself of pain, the while doing nothing to remove the causes which are responsible for the pain. Or, he can treat the pain rationally—seek out its causes, and do whatever is necessary, even go through greater pain, in order to alter or remove these causes.

So it is with guilt. The person experiences guilt for a reason; he has acted in some way that violates his conscience. Upon experiencing guilt, the person can endure it, anesthetize it in various ways, or deal with it rationally. The rational means for dealing with guilt were discussed in an earlier section. Here, we shall examine some of the unhealthy reactions to guilt. They are called unhealthy because they do not get at the causes of the guilt, and because they promote or perpetuate unhealthy personality.

REPRESSION OF GUILT. A person may behave in ways which violate his conscience, and then repress the consequent feelings of guilt. Repression is the name given to the process of excluding from awareness any painful or undesirable thoughts, feelings, or impulses. When a person represses his guilt-feelings, we may assume that they continue to exist and function as all unconscious motives do. That is, we may expect the unconscious guilt to influence the person's behavior in subtle and unforeseen ways; we may expect a "return of the repressed" from time to time, when either the repression is weakened or the guilt-feelings are increased in intensity. When this occurs, we would expect the person to experience an overwhelming onslaught of self-hate, worthlessness, depression, unlovability, feeling like a fake, or phony, and other like reactions. Another indicator of unconscious guilt might be the frequent recurrence of accidents that hurt the person's body, his property, or his career.

As long as the repression is effective in removing the guilt from awareness, the person can continue to act in ways that violate his moral precepts without any conscious loss in self-esteem. But he is actually compounding guilt. In the intervals when the repression is less efficient, he may review his long history of morally reprehensible conduct, and feel so full of self-hate, and so unworthy of being accepted by others, that he may commit suicide. The author has known cases where a person has repressed guilt for a long interval. When the guilt "returned," the person was so full of loathing for himself, that he became dramatically converted to a religious viewpoint, believing the religious affirmation would help him behave morally and regain self-esteem as well as the esteem of others. He has also known persons who reviewed their "sinful" pasts, evidently felt they were unsalvageable, and so they committed suicide.

THE PROJECTION OF GUILT. When a person is guilty, he despises himself. It is possible for a person to attribute his own psychological processes to another person, e.g., his feelings, thoughts, values, etc., without recognizing that he has done so. But when this projection has occurred, he believes it is the other person who has these feelings and attitudes. A person with repressed guilt will of course deny he *experiences* guilt, but he may believe very strongly that other people condemn and despise him (disowning projection). This belief will be acted upon—he lives in a world of people whom he assumes despise him—yet careful study may disclose that other people have nothing but esteem for him, since they have not seen his sins and crimes.

DISPLACEMENT OF GUILT. A person may successfully have repressed guilt for some major crime or sin against his own values, but then, for some minor omission or deed, he is overwhelmed with a guilt-onslaught which is disproportionate to the crime. Here we are probably observing the displacement of guilt. Thus, a man may have been cheating on his income tax for years, but he does not experience any conscious guilt for so doing. He may then forget to pay the paperboy, and be overwhelmed with guilt.

RATIONALIZATION OF GUILT. Rationalization refers to the selection of explanations for action which will preserve self-esteem. In one's dealings with conscience, motives or reasons for actions are all-important. One can perform an apparently immoral action, but if one's motive is pure, no guilt is felt, no matter what the results of the action. If the motive itself violates the conscience, then, no matter if the action be saintly, the person will feel guilty. Consequently, of all the motives or explanations a person could find for a given action, he has a vested interest in choosing and believing only those motives which are consistent with his conscience. Take, for example, the act of killing another man. In our society, this action violates our moral code. If a person killed another individual intentionally, because he didn't like him, he would feel guilty. If he killed a person to protect his household, he would feel less guilty. If he killed a man who was trying to kill him, perhaps he would feel proud.

Redl and Wineman [27] described some ingenious rationalizations which a group of aggressive and delinquent children used in order to justify, without guilt, a wide variety of immoral actions. These included:

1. Repression of intent: An inability to recall the original motive for performing the crime, though there was full recall of the details of the crime itself.

2. "He did it first": Though the action was wrong, the fact that another person had done such a thing evidently served as a precedent, and this precedent made the action "legal."

3. "Everybody else does such things anyway": If everybody does such things, then they can't be wrong, and so I need not feel any guilt for doing them.

4. "We were all in on it": Since it was a group activity, the responsibility, and hence the guilt, either belongs to the leader, or else to no one person.

5. "But somebody else did that same thing to me before": Because I once was the victim of such an act before, I am entitled to do the same thing to some present innocent party, without having to feel guilt for it.

6. "He had it coming to him": The wronged person was such a sinner himself, that he deserved to be sinned against; ergo, I need not feel guilty.

7. "I had to do it, or I would have lost face": Justifying one's actions on the assumption that status in a group with deviant values is more important than conformity with society's morals.

8. "I didn't use the proceeds anyway": An appeal to the "Robin Hood" mechanism. If I used the proceeds of illegally gotten money, etc., for charitable or highly moral purposes, there need be no guilt.

9. "But I made up with him afterwards": If I befriend the victim of my immoral activity, I have thus undone the crime, and need feel no guilt.

10. "He is a no-good so-and-so himself": Similar to number 6.

11. "They are all against me, nobody likes me, they are always picking on me": Since the person is living as if he is in an enemy camp, then all activity is justifiable.

12. "I couldn't have gotten it any other way": Self-exculpation on the premise that what was gained immorally was somehow the person's inviolable right; he is entitled to get it by any means.

Though these rationalizations were collected from a group of pre-adolescents, the reader might find them to be prototypes of many adult rationalizations.

One of the criteria which psychotherapists use in determining whether or not a patient has profited from the treatment is his willingness to consider seriously, and to compare with evidence, a wide range of *possible* motives for some action, rather than violently affirming some one self-enhancing motive and vigorously denying all others. The healthy personality will be less prone to such instant selectivity in the choice of possible explanations for his conduct, and will be able to entertain even guilt-provoking motives as possible explanations for his action.

WHY THESE REACTIONS ARE UNHEALTHY. When a person has repressed, projected, displaced, or rationalized his guilts away, he has not really gotten rid of his guilt. All of the factors which are responsible for his guilt in the first place are still present; his conscience still includes the taboos he has been violating, and he is continuing to behave contrary to these taboos. Consequently, it can be assumed he is continually adding to his fund of guilt, in spite of the temporary effectiveness of his defenses against feeling it. The more guilt he accumulates, the more drastic must his defenses become in order to keep it from conscious awareness. The eventual conse-

quences to these unhealthy reactions to guilt will be increased alienation from the self, increased ease of being threatened, and reduction
in the capacity for free, honest communication with others—all unhealthy consequences. Finally, it should be stated again, that these
guilt-evasion tactics are seldom effective for very long. When the
person is confronted by the full intensity of his previously repressed
guilt, he may become neurotic, psychotic, or perhaps commit suicide.

PROMOTING HEALTHY CONSCIENCE

Parents, teachers, spouses, and friends can all assume they will
have at least some influence on the conscience-development of the
children, students, spouse, and friends with whom they interact. How
can people in these roles promote the development of a healthy conscience in the individuals for whom they constitute significant
others?

One obvious thing they can do is avoid making unreasonable and
excessive demands on the other person. If the relationship is one in
which identification is likely to be fostered, then the demands made
upon the other person are likely to become internalized as self-
demands; that is, they are incorporated as part of the individual's
conscience. Thus, if the demands and expectations made of a person
have been reasonable and humane, the ground is prepared for the
development of a healthy and humane conscience.

Another factor which can promote the development of a healthy
conscience in a growing person is the presence of a healthy conscience in the significant others with whom he deals. When we
identify with another person, we may identify with *his self-expectations* as well as with his expectations of us. If his demands upon
himself are reasonable, then it is likely that we will make reasonable demands upon ourselves, following his example. A significant
other who tortures himself with excessive demands and undue strictness with himself may promote the development of an excessively
strict conscience in his child or student—even though he has never
openly called for such achievement or moral strictness from him.

Yet another factor which can help promote the development of a
healthy conscience in one's child, or friend, is to act at the real-self
level when in the presence of the child, student or friend. When this

is done, the person who is doing the identifying will be able to acquire an accurate concept of his identification-model, complete with foibles and frailties Parents often strive to hide many of their weaknesses and faults from their children, thus portraying themselves as perfect, flawless beings. The child may base his conscience upon this unrealistic model, thus paving the way for chronic guilt and inferiority-feelings; that is, he strives to become "just like Daddy," and feels worthless when he finds he has many faults which Daddy seemed not to have. It might come as a shock to the son to discover that his father probably had these faults too, but hid them from his son's gaze.

We can help another person achieve a healthy conscience in still another, more direct way, by commenting upon and evaluating his conscience from a realistic and health-oriented point of view. If we do not share our friend's ideals and taboos, we can let this be known to him, and let him know why we disagree with his moral precepts. Just the experience of hearing another person comment upon his conscience may make him conscious enough of its contents to begin to assess it critically by himself.

THE SOCIAL VALUE-SYSTEM AND HEALTHY CONSCIENCE

Our personal value-system derives from the social value-system. If the social value-system is fraught with many conflicting values, taboos, and ideals, it can only be expected that the personal value-systems and the consciences of individual members of society will likewise be conflicted. A number of observers [28] of the contemporary American scene have called attention to sharp conflicts in values at the cultural level. We all value competitive success, but we also value co-operation. We value obedience to parents, but we also value independence. We value economic self-sufficiency, but we also value government support of industry and public relief. These conflicts at the cultural level are all reflected in the personality-structure of individual members of the society. A culture which has conflicting and rapidly changing values is one which makes it difficult for its members to achieve a harmonious and healthy conscience and personal value-system. There does not appear to be any ready solution for the problem of rapid social and cultural change, even though it produces personal conflict for many people; nor is there any ready solution for the already existing conflicts in value that characterize our society. The most that can be said from a personality-hygiene point of view is that if most members of the society are raised so as to have a strong ego, they should be able to reconcile conflicting values into some more or less integrated hierarchy. One of the functions of the ego is that of reconciling conflicting demands, its so-called "synthetic function." [29] When the ego is strong, it is able to perform this function in a way which enables the person to live in a fairly satisfying, and minimally conflicted way.

SUMMARY

Each society has its characteristic *value-system*, and it enforces conformity to this system among its members by assorted means for *social control*, e.g., punishment, ostracism, etc.

Each member of a society who has been socialized will internalize a version of the social value-system which may be called his *personal value-system*. This personal value-system helps to define the person's goals, his standards for judging other people's actions, and for judging his own behavior. The *conscience* is made up of those aspects of the personal value-system which *pertain to the self*. The conscience is another factor which can enforce conformity with the social mores, in addition to external sanctions. From a psychological viewpoint, the conscience is a determiner both of guilt and self-esteem. It can promote personality illness, or it can promote the development of healthy personality.

The conscience is acquired during the process of growing up, chiefly through the mechanism of identification with the demands and expectations which significant others held of the self. These become self-demands and self-expectations.

Some characteristics of the conscience are its relative degree of unconsciousness, its variability with age, its variability with respect to strictness and freedom from conflict, its authoritarian quality, its proneness to being repressed and projected, and its susceptibility to being deceived.

A *healthy conscience* is conscious, self-affirmed, flexible, mature, realistic, organized into a hierarchy of values and ideals, fairly congruent with the social value-system, and humane.

An *unhealthy conscience* makes its presence known to an observer by such signs as unremitting guilt, absence of guilt when the behavior would seem to warrant it, and excessive guilt over trivial moral lapses.

Some common patterns of unhealthy conscience include an excessively strict conscience, an excessively permissive conscience, a deviant conscience, and a conflicted conscience.

A person can relate to his own conscience in just about all the ways he is capable of relating to his real self, or to some other person. He can show reasoned consideration for the demands of his conscience (which is held to be the healthy way of relating to the conscience), or he can compulsively conform, or rebel against his conscience. He can anesthetize and symbolically kill his conscience; and he can "put his conscience on a vacation."

Self-esteem is the emotional response which accompanies behavior that conforms with the conscience. Self-esteem is on a healthy basis if it is rational, and relatively independent of the reactions of other people to the self.

Guilt arises when one violates his conscience. The *healthy response to guilt* includes acknowledging it, determining why one feels guilty, and then either re-affirming the conscience and conforming with it, or else changing the conscience so as to permit the guilt-producing behavior to continue without guilt in the future. The conscience may be changed through new identifications, or through a critical appraisal of the values and taboos of which it is comprised.

Unhealthy reactions to guilt include repression, projection, displacement, and rationalization. These reactions are deemed unhealthy because they fail to come to grips with the basic causes of the guilt.

Healthy conscience can be promoted in others by making reasonable demands on them, or more generally, by providing a healthy identification-model for them to emulate. Another means of promoting healthy conscience-development is through a critical appraisal of the other person's conscience, as this becomes known.

Conflicting social values promote the development of conflicted personal value-systems and conscience. Since there is no ready way of eliminating conflict at the level of culture, healthy conscience-development can be promoted if most members of society have *strong egos*. A strong ego is able to integrate conflicting values into a more harmonious system, thus facilitating the promotion of a healthy conscience.

NOTES AND REFERENCES

RECOMMENDED READINGS ARE MARKED WITH AN ASTERISK (*)

*1. See LaPiere, R., *Social Control*, New York, McGraw-Hill, 1954, for a systematic account of social control. See also Parsons, T., *The social system*, Glencoe, Illinois, The Free Press, 1951, pp. 297–321.

2. See Parsons, T., *op. cit.*, for a sociological account of value-orientations.

*3. This phenomenon is one aspect of what sociologists call *anomie*. See Merton, R. K., *Social theory and social structure*, Glencoe, Illinois, The Free Press, 1949.

*4. See Parsons, T., and Bales, R. F., *Family, socialization and interaction process*, Glencoe, Illinois, The Free Press, 1955, Ch. 2.

5. Riesman calls the person whose behavior is primarily controlled by his conscience an *inner-directed character*. See Riesman, D., *The lonely crowd*, New Haven, Yale University Press, 1950.

*6. See Mowrer, O. H. (ed.), *Psychotherapy: theory and research*, New York, Ronald, 1953, especially Chs. 3, 6, for the most systematic account of Mowrer's theory of the origins of neurosis, and of the aims of therapy. Also, by the same author, "Learning theory and the neurotic paradox," *Amer. J. Orthopsychiat.*, 1948, 18, 571–610; "Symposium, 1952. The therapeutic process. III. Learning theory and the neurotic fallacy," *Amer. J. Orthopsychiat.*, 1952, 22, 679–689; "Some philosophic problems in mental disorder and its treatment," *Harvard Educ. Rev.*, 1953, 23, 117–127. A more sophisticated view of conflicting theories of neurosis is given in Waelder, R., "The principle of multiple function," *Psychoanalyt. Quart.*, 1936, 5, 45–62, especially pp. 54–55.

7. A patient undergoing personality therapy once remarked to the present writer, "I've been brought up to believe if I enjoy doing something, then it *must* be a sin, so I mustn't do it."

8. Cf. Freud, S., *The ego and the id*, London, Hogarth, 1927. Also

Fenichel, O., *The psychoanalytic theory of neurosis*, New York, Norton, 1945, Ch. 6.

9. Rogers, C. R., *Client-centered therapy*, New York, Houghton Mifflin, 1951, p. 140. Also Rogers, C. R. and Dymond, Rosalind F. (ed.), *Psychotherapy and personality change*, Chicago, University of Chicago Press, 1954.

10. For a psychoanalytic formulation of identification and the superego, see Fenichel, O., *op. cit.*, Ch. 6; for a more general learning-theory analysis of identification, see Mowrer, O. H., *Learning theory and personality dynamics*, New York, Ronald, 1950. See also Hendrick, I., "Early development of the ego: Identification in infancy," *Psychoanal. Quart.*, 1950, **20**, 44–61.

*11. See Flugel, J. C., *Man, morals, and society*, New York, International University Press, 1945, Ch. 4, 9, 11, 12, for an analysis from a psychoanalytic viewpoint as to why the superego (conscience) is often so strict.

12. Fromm, E., *Man for himself*, New York, Rinehart, 1947, pp. 143–175.

13. Cf. Mowrer, O. H., *op. cit.*

14. Fenichel, O., *op. cit.*, pp. 109–110.

*15. Cf. Redl, F. and Wineman, D., *Children who hate*, Glencoe, Illinois, The Free Press, 1951, Ch. 4, 5.

*16. Horney called such impossible ideals the "tyranny of the should." See Horney, K., *Neurosis and human growth*, New York, Norton, 1950, Ch. 3.

17. Fromm, E., *op. cit.*

18. Maslow, A. H., *Motivation and personality*, New York, Harper, 1954, Ch. 12.

19. Fromm, E., *op. cit.*, pp. 159 *et. seq.*

20. See Horney, K., *op. cit.*, Ch. 5, for an excellent discussion of the many ways in which guilt, self-hate, and self-contempt manifest themselves.

21. See Mowrer, O. H., *op. cit.*, for an elaboration of the concept of "conscience-killing."

22. See Riesman, D., *op. cit.*, for a discussion of moral indignation. Also Jourard, S. M., "Moral indignation: a correlate of denied dislike of parents' traits," *J. consult. Psychol.*, 1954, **18**, 59–60.

23. See Jourard, S. M., "Identification, parent-cathexis, and self-esteem," *J. consult. Psychol.*, 1958, **22** (in press). In this paper, positive cathexis for parents (admiration) is demonstrated to be a correlate of the extent to which the parents' personality traits and behavior accord with the child's ideals for parents' personality.

24. Jourard, S. M., *op. cit.* See also Maslow, A. H., *op. cit.*

25. Fenichel, O., *op. cit.*, Ch. 17.

26. Rosenthal demonstrated that among patients who showed improvement under therapy, there was a change in moral values in the direction of those held by their therapists. See Rosenthal, D., "Changes in some moral values following psychotherapy," *J. consult. Psychol.*, 1955, **19**, 431–436. Rogers *et al.* found changes in the "self ideal" of patients who had undergone therapy—changes in the direction of the real self. See Rogers, C. R. and Dymond, R. F., *op. cit.*

27. Redl, F. and Wineman, D., *op. cit.*, pp. 145–156.

28. Cf. Horney, K., *The neurotic personality of our time*, New York, Norton, 1937.

29. See Nunberg, H., *Practise and theory of psychoanalysis*, New York, Nerv. & Ment. Dis. Monogr., 1948, for a discussion of the "synthetic functions" of the ego, and of ego strength.

QUESTIONS FOR REVIEW AND EXAMINATION

1. Find examples of external social control over your own behavior.

2. Define social value-system, personal value-system, and conscience.

3. Contrast Freud's and Mowrer's views on the role played by conscience in neurosis, and on aims for personality therapy.

4. Discuss the conscience from the standpoint of its characteristics, and the manner in which it is acquired.

5. What is a healthy conscience?

6. What are the chief signs of an unhealthy conscience?

7. List some of the common patterns of unhealthy conscience.

8. What are the various modes in which a person relates to his conscience? Evaluate these.

9. Explain and define rational guilt and rational self-esteem.

10. What are the healthy and unhealthy reactions to guilt?

11. How might healthy conscience be promoted by parents and others? What is the connection between conflicts at the level of cultural values, and conflicts at the level of conscience?

12. Use the headings and concepts of the present chapter as a guide for describing and evaluating someone's conscience, and modes of handling guilt.

CHAPTER 12

The Body and Healthy Personality

The body plays a crucial role in personality hygiene, but it is a role which many psychologists and students of personality have overlooked. The body is the meeting-ground of psychology and physiology. An individual behaves with his body, and his behavior produces consequences for his body. His body is an important aspect of his personality structure. The body is subject to the direction and control of the ego just as the ego may be under the control and direction of bodily needs and impulses. A person perceives his body, and formulates a body-image, or body-concept. He evaluates his body as he knows it, and expresses satisfaction, dissatisfaction, or disinterest in his body. All these affectively-toned responses to the body can serve as strong motives for various kinds of instrumental behavior. The health of the body is a crucial value, both for its own sake, and also because no other values can be achieved unless the body is intact, healthy, and fully functioning. Accidents and injuries which befall the body will impose a strong influence on the personality as a whole, calling often for radical changes in the person's modes of gaining satisfactions, and even for changes in the satisfactions which will be pursued. Thus, a person who has had both legs amputated is no longer able to pursue an athletic career.

In addition to all these interrelations between the body and personality, the body may serve as a sounding-board for all of an individual's life problems. The body becomes sick when the person is unhappy, chronically conflicted, or chronically deprived of psychological satisfactions. The old precept, *mens sana in corpore sano* holds intrinsic validity. A healthy mind (personality) is likely to accompany a healthy body, and a healthy body may well be a crucial determiner of personality health.

SOME TECHNICAL TERMS. The *actual body* refers to the body as it might objectively be described and evaluated by an outside observer. The *body-concept* comprises all of a person's perceptions, beliefs, and expectancies with respect to his body's structure, functions and appearance. *Body-image* will sometimes be used as a synonym for body-concept. The *public body-concept* refers to the beliefs which a person *wants others* to hold concerning his body. The *body-ideal* includes all of the values and ideals a person has acquired with respect to his body's appearance and functions, his concept of how his body ought to be, or how he wants it to be. The *ideal body* is the culturally valued form, appearance, and mode of functioning of the body.

These terms are introduced so as to enable us to observe variability in the ways in which people relate to their body, and to permit us to make evaluations of these relationships from a personality-hygiene point of view.

THE BODY AND THE EGO

The ego is a hypothetical structure within the total personality to which is ascribed, among other functions, the role of co-ordinating and controlling the movements of the body (instrumental behavior) so that various valued ends will be achieved. Psychoanalysts speak, in this connection, of a *body-ego*.[1] One of the first signs that the ego has developed is the infant's capacity voluntarily to control the movements of his body. That is, before the outer environment can be mastered, the person has got to achieve mastery of his body. Before such mastery has been achieved, body movements are diffuse, global, undifferentiated, and not subject to voluntary control. Once such mastery has been achieved, the infant or child is able to *suppress* global, undifferentiated responses to stimulation, and respond in a discrete, controlled, instrumental manner. The ability to co-ordinate eyes, hands, and mouth is probably among the first signs that the ego is developing. Psychoanalysts refer to each separate achievement of voluntary control over the musculature and the perceptual apparatus as an *ego-nucleus.*

As physical maturation proceeds, the child gradually acquires increasing mastery over his body, and is able to make it perform according to his will. By the time adulthood has been reached, the person, if suitably trained, may be able to achieve such levels of bodily control as are found among athletes and dancers. The contemporary modern-dancer, the flamenco dancer, the exponent of Hindu, Balinese, or rock-and-roll dancing, all display a body-ego which has been developed to a relatively high degree.

The loss of control of body functions and body performances is usually experienced as a very threatening catastrophe by most persons. Not to be the master of one's body—its movements, needs, and functions—is a loss of the most basic level of control. An adult who loses voluntary control over his appetite, or over his bowel and bladder sphincters, will feel deep shame, and will lose confidence in himself.

THE BODY AND THE SELF

The self-structure of the average individual includes beliefs and ideals pertaining to the body as well as beliefs and ideals with respect to behavior. The body-concept, or body-image [2] is an integral part of the self-concept. The self-ideal includes values and ideals which pertain to the appearance and functions of the body; it encompasses the person's body-ideal. The public selves which a person constructs include, not only beliefs which the individual wants others to affirm with respect to his personality, they also include beliefs the person wants others to hold concerning the appearance and functions of his body. In order to construct and maintain his *public body-concept,* the individual will clothe himself in preferred ways, use assorted padding, camouflage, corsetry, cosmetics, and other means for looking his best, the way he wants other people to see him. Further he may hide all signs of actual illness, if he wants people to believe him healthy.

THE BODY AND SECURITY

When a person is secure, he is relatively free from anxiety. Insecurity manifests itself as worry and anxiety about expected pains and catastrophes. Since the body is such a highly valued object, it may become the object of anxiety, or else the source of anxiety about other expected threats. The appearance of the body is the means to many highly valued ends in our society. From this it follows that if a person's appearance is not attractive, his access to these ends may be limited, and he may suffer anxiety about the prospects of gaining these ends. Some of the ends toward which appearance is instrumental, especially among young people, is acceptance by one's peers and attractiveness to the opposite sex. The ugly and unattractive person generally has a more difficult time winning friends, and in being popular with the opposite sex, than the person with a pleasing appearance. One reflection of the importance of beauty in our culture is the annual beauty-contests which take place. Women compete with each other for the title of the most beautiful woman of the year, and rich prizes go to the winner.

That one's appearance may be the source of anxiety has been demonstrated in a number of empirical studies. Secord and Jourard [3] showed that *body cathexis* (the degree of acceptance of one's body) was correlated with measures of anxious body-preoccupation and of security. In other words, the more that a person accepted his body, or liked it, the more secure and free from anxiety he felt. Persons with a high measured degree of anxiety tended to be dissatisfied with their bodies.

Anxious overconcern with the body is called *hypochondriasis*. The hypochondriac is an individual who is continually preoccupied with his health, who complains about all manner of vague or specific aches and pains, and who may make the rounds of doctor's offices, dose himself regularly with laxatives, vitamin pills, sedatives, and other medicines. It is generally found that hypochondriacal anxiety with respect to physical health is a substitute for, or a displacement of, anxiety that derives from other sources: repressed hostility, sexuality, or achievement-problems. The hypochondriac evidently finds it less threatening to think about and worry about his health than to think about these other problems. Health-preoccupation takes his mind off his basic problems, as it were.

A person might become excessively concerned and anxious about his or her appearance. This is most likely to occur among persons who use their appearance as the means toward acceptance, toward the enhancement of social status, or as the means of attracting attention to the self. The name *narcissistic overconcern* seems appropriate to describe this pattern. Such a person will fuss over appearance beyond the point of diminishing returns, and will become panic-stricken whenever a wrinkle, gray hair, or change in weight appears.

Hypochondriasis and narcissistic overconcern both may be viewed as *unhealthy* responses to the appearance and functions of the body. They are unhealthy for a variety of reasons. They fail to solve the problems which are basically responsible for the anxiety in the first place. Furthermore, while the person concentrates so much attention on himself and his body, he neglects many other values which are of importance to a healthy personality, for instance, productive work, and healthy relationships with other people.

Concern for one's health and appearance are both compatible with personality health, but healthy concern does not place other legitimate concerns in jeopardy. If the healthy personality becomes physically ill, he will take any necessary rational steps to restore his health, or to improve it, but then he will turn his attention to other matters. Furthermore, he will live in accordance with a habitual health-regime—adequate diet, rest, etc.,—which maintains his health without requiring too much conscious attention and worry.

With respect to appearance, the healthy personality will take whatever steps are necessary to look his best, and then he will take his appearance for granted. He does not rely totally on his appearance as a means to valued ends. He can gain friends, professional success, and attract a spouse, not by appearance alone, but by genuine achievement and by means of his usual modes of behaving toward others.

THE BODY AND SELF-ESTEEM

A high degree of self-esteem means that a person accepts and approves his overall personality. There is a considerable amount of systematic and clinical evidence to show that one's *appearance* is an important determiner of self-esteem, both among men and women.

A number of studies have shown that "self-cathexis" [4] (a technical term roughly synonymous with self-esteem) is correlated with body-cathexis. In other words, persons who accept their bodies are more likely to manifest high self-esteem than persons who dislike their bodies.

One reason for this correlation lies in the fact that the self-ideal includes a set of ideals pertaining to the appearance of the body, the so-called *body-ideal*. Each person has a more or less clear-cut concept of how he wants to look. If his body actually conforms, in dimensions and appearance, with his concept of an ideal body, he will then like his body. If, on the other hand, his body deviates from his body-ideal, he will tend to reject and dislike his body.

In one study of college women,[5] it was found that the ideal body-proportions (which all girls in the sample shared) were five feet five inches for height, about 120 pounds for weight, and 35 inches, 24 inches, and 35 inches for bust, waist, and hips respectively. The girls liked their dimensions if they coincided with these ideals, and disliked them increasingly as they deviated from these ideals. The actual measurements of the girls were slightly larger than these ideals, on the average—except for bust size, where the average size was slightly smaller.

A comparable study of college males [6] showed that acceptance of the body was related to *large size*. While the women all wanted to be slightly smaller in dimensions than they actually were, the men mostly aimed at larger size; they wanted to be taller, with broader shoulders and chests.

It is evident that the body-ideals of the subjects in these studies are closely related to the cultural concept of an *ideal body*.

THE BODY-IDEAL AND THE IDEAL BODY. Each society has its idiosyncratic concepts and standards of personal beauty.[7] The Bushman native on the Kalihari desert, for example, places a value on having enormous hips and buttocks, while in America, the desired hip-measurements are much slimmer. The American woman wants to have large (but firm) breasts, a small waist, and narrow hips, and she wants to be relatively tall. In other societies, the standards of feminine beauty differ from this stereotype. In days gone by, the American glamor girl was considerably heftier than our present beauties. Old pictures of burlesque queens look to the modern eye like advertisements for a reducing salon.

The cultural concept of an ideal body has consequences for personality hygiene, since the cultural ideal determines the personal body-ideal, and since conformity between the actual body and the body-ideal helps to determine overall self-esteem. If a man or woman in our society is not able to conform with the ideal-body concepts of his society, he is very likely to face problems growing out of diminished self-esteem. If the ideal-body concepts in the society are highly restrictive, and difficult for many people to conform with, the implication is that many people will suffer self-esteem losses.

The widespread dread that many people have for aging may be an outgrowth both of the rigid concept of an ideal body, and the role of the body's appearance in gaining valued ends and in determining self-esteem. While a rational degree of concern for appearance is compatible with personality health, too much concern may indicate that the individual's self-esteem is founded on *too narrow a base*. Under optimum conditions, an individual will predicate his self-esteem on a variety of grounds, e.g., achievement, social status, ethical behavior. Attractive appearance is thus only one of many determiners of self-esteem. The healthy personality can face and accept the inevitable changes in appearance that are associated with aging without losses in self-esteem or in the sense of security. He (or she) does not feel that when youthful beauty is gone, so goes personal worth. He believes, in the words of a homely twelve-year-old girl at a summer camp, "After all, beauty is only skin. Be a beautiful *person,* and don't worry so much about how you look!"

SOME OUTGROWTHS OF THE CULTURAL CONCEPT OF THE IDEAL BODY

Because the cultural concept of the ideal body is so rigid, and yet so widely adopted by people as their personal body-ideal, a number of anxiety-loaded problems have become a part of our society's preoccupations.

OBESITY. Probably the number one appearance problem in contemporary America is obesity. This is also, of course, a health problem, since overweight people are much more susceptible to certain fatal diseases than thinner people. But the cosmetic aspects of obesity are just as acutely felt and worried about as the physical health aspects. America is the only country in the world where overweight is a public health problem; where food is abundant, yet a slender body is a cultural value.

Obesity usually is, of course, the result of eating too much. Overweight people seem unable to control their food-intake to a level which will enable them to lose weight. When a person wants to stop some behavior-pattern, but finds that will power is ineffective, it is evidence that unconscious motives of great strength lie behind the behavior in question. The overweight person is overeating for reasons other than sheer hunger. The act of eating is serving more functions than simply replenishing the body's energy supplies and maintaining physical health.

Clinical studies of chronically overweight people have shown that they have unhealthy personalities.[8] They may, for example, be unable to derive satisfactions from their relationships with people, or from their work. They may be starved for love, but unable to get enough love from parents, friends, or spouse, to satisfy them. Consequently, rather than live a life devoid of gratification, they resort to a very primitive and basic type of satisfaction—that provided by an overly full and rich meal.

A chronically overweight person is not unlike a chronic alcoholic, in that he is addicted to a practice which is harming him at the same time that it relieves anxiety and provides him with immediate gratification. Like an alcoholic, the obese person might make daily, renewed vows to taper off, but he never seems to achieve this end. In some cities, groups of obese people organize as do the members of Alcoholics Anonymous; they are all dedicated to the aim of reducing, and they lend each other moral support in adhering to reducing diets. Where intensive personality therapy is not available, and when medical aid for appetite suppression has proven ineffective, such groups are probably the most effective means for achieving a weight loss. However, unless the conditions, medical or psychological, which are responsible for the excessive appetite are removed, the person will be obliged to remain dependent upon his group membership in order to preserve his weight-loss once it has been achieved.

SKINNINESS. Just as we deplore fatness in our society, so do we pity the "skinny" person. Chronic underweight due to undernourishment is a fairly simple malady to remedy, if suitable food is available. But many persons are overly thin in spite of available food, and even in spite of a sizable caloric intake. The reasons for an inability to put on weight are most likely medical reasons and so we cannot comment intelligently upon these. But sometimes the medical reasons, such as overactive thyroid glands, or a finicky appetite, derive from more basic *psychological* causes. An intensive personality diagnosis might disclose many unhealthy personality traits in the chronically thin person. In such instances, personality therapy which produces changes in the ways the person relates to the world, may produce as a side-effect a desirable increase in weight. Sometimes simply changing the amount of exercise that the person habitually takes will suffice to stimulate appetite and promote a weight gain.

BREAST-CULTIVATION. Men in our society are highly breast-conscious, and many men equate sexual attractiveness in a woman with a prominent bosom. Since most women want to be considered attractive to men, they consider a flat bust to be a handicap. The reasons for this cultural emphasis on the breasts are not readily determined. Some anthropologists and psychoanalysts believe it is a derivative of painful weaning experiences undergone by male children in our society. Probably, however, the reasons are more complex.

Nevertheless, most women want to have prominent breasts, and if they have not been naturally endowed with them, they may strive to cultivate them by assorted exercises such as are advertised by health clubs, or they will wear brassiere-padding of one kind or another.

There is nothing intrinsically unhealthy in a woman who wears "falsies" in order to appear beautiful. Personality health is assessed in terms of a number of different criteria, including what the person does to, with, or for her body. So long as males deem breasts to be an index of attractiveness, then women, to the extent that they want admiring male attention, are justified in doing all that is practicable to gain that end.

NOSES. We even have rigid cultural ideals pertaining to noses. The ideal nose is not the majestic protuberance of a Cyrano de Bergerac; nor is it the proud, delicately curved sweep of an aquiline "beak." Instead, it must, at least in the woman, be a short, medium-width, uptilted "snub," so that an onlooker can see the nostrils. Many women feel their facial beauty is marred because their nose differs from this stereotype, and so they undergo plastic surgery in order to achieve the valued snub. Whether or not "nose-bobbing" is a healthy thing to do depends on its consequences for the total personality. Some persons may undergo a healthy personality change following the operation, while others may go through life feeling they are a fake; they haven't really accepted the new nose themselves.

FACIAL WRINKLES. The appearance of wrinkles in the facial skin, and on the neck, is an inevitable part of aging. Yet many women, especially, become panic-stricken at the first appearance of a wrinkle. This panic derives from a dread of being old, and from an over-emphasis of the importance of appearance as a basis for security and self-esteem.

The problem of aging is not a simple one, and an entire medical specialty—geriatrics—has been devoted to a many-faceted study of the problems faced by the aging person. We can do no more in the present context than mention this field *en passant*.

The person who panics at wrinkles, and goes to any length to regain, at age forty, the complexion of a sixteen-year-old, is an unhealthy person. Such an individual might well seek to find more stable sources of self-esteem than facial appearance.

GENITALIA. People have all kinds of problems in connection with their sexual organs. Some men feel they are inferior if they have what seem to be small genital organs. There are cases on record where an entire neurotic personality structure began in consequence of the belief that the sex organs were smaller than those of other men. There is no necessary connection between male adequacy in sexual performance, and genital size. There is no necessary connection between "manliness" and the size of genitalia.

In many ways, people in our society are very prudish, almost ashamed about having bodies with reproductive and eliminative functions. Many persons become panic-stricken at the prospect of being seen nude, and may actually avoid a medical examination if it requires that the genitalia be exposed.

Some women, at least at an unconscious level, may envy not only the apparently privileged social position of men, but they may also display what the psychoanalysts called "penis-envy"—they resent not having been born males, and they may reject their own feminine role in consequence.

Because of cultural taboos pertaining to sexuality, many persons acquire very unreal concepts both of their own genitalia, and that of the opposite sex. These unreal concepts may involve notions that the female organs are dangerous and castrating, or that penises are destructive weapons. Some women may acquire attitudes of disgust, resentment and shame over their menstrual functions, and isolate themselves through the duration of their period—as is done in some primitive societies.

MUSCLE-CULTIVATION. In response to the cultural ideal of a muscular male, many sedentarily occupied men will undergo strenuous weight-lifting and body-building courses so as to become "muscle-bound." There is nothing inherently healthy or unhealthy in such efforts. They are healthy if they result in an improvement of appearance, vigor and health without loss of other values. They are unhealthy if they are expressions of unnecessary compensation or overcompensation for other kinds of deficiencies and inferiorities.

A HEALTHY BODY-IDEAL

A person's body-ideal can be assessed with respect to its healthy or unhealthy implications. An unhealthy body-ideal is one that is rigid and unchanging, and which includes dimensions and characteristics that are impossible for the individual to conform with. Thus, we observe an unhealthy body-ideal in a woman who, at age forty, feels she is ugly and unattractive because she no longer looks the way she did when she was nineteen. If she devotes extreme attention to her appearance and neglects other values, we should be obliged to adjudge her body-ideal as unhealthy. Similarly, a young man with a slender physique who rejected his body-appearance because he was not heavily muscled and proportioned like a football hero, might be said to have an unhealthy body-ideal.

A healthy body-ideal is one which is not too discrepant from the cultural concept of an ideal body, but *which is revised by the person himself, so as to make allowances for his own, idiosyncratic dimensions and features.* With increasing age, a healthy personality will modify his body-ideal, so that he can continue to regard himself as reasonably attractive at each stage in life. He does not aspire after an impossible (for him) degree of beauty. Rather, at each stage in life, he strives to look his best, and then lets the matter drop so as to attend to other important concerns.

THE BODY-CONCEPT

A person's body-concept includes all of his perceptions, beliefs, and knowledge concerning his body: its appearance, functions, limits, and inner structure. As with any other concept—one's concept of self, of other people, of animals—the body-concept may be accurate or inaccurate, complete or incomplete. An accurate body-concept is a personality-hygiene value.

An accurate body-concept implies that an individual perceives, interprets, and formulates beliefs about all aspects of his body with accuracy. When the body-concept is accurate, it provides the individual with a rational foundation for taking adequate care of his body's needs, its health, and its appearance.

Accuracy of the body-concept is achieved by all of the means employed to arrive at reality-tested knowledge in general: through observation and through continual verification of conclusions, and through contact with reliable authorities and sources of knowledge. But many persons have been taught erroneous beliefs about diet, needs, health requirements, and the like. Further, a person may become so alienated from his body (as part of the more general process of self-alienation) that he loses the capacity to "listen" to his body.

Thus, some people may fail to recognize that inadequate diet, excessive amounts of exercise, insufficient rest, and excessive self-indulgence, are gradually weakening their bodies. Because of an inaccurate body-concept, such people fail to learn how to take suitable care of their bodies. To the extent that a person has knowledge of the effects of various things on his health, then to that extent his body's welfare is his own responsibility. Just as one can relate to a child in ways that have implications for his health, so can one relate to one's body in ways that have health-implications. In order to promote and maintain the child's health, the parents are obliged to formulate accurate concepts with respect to bodies in general, and their child's body in particular. In order to promote and maintain one's own health, one must have an accurate body-concept. It may be said that rational body-care becomes possible only when an accurate body-concept has been achieved.

Let us illustrate what we mean by an inaccurate body-concept. In societies where medical knowledge is not available, there may be only imperfect concepts of the causes of health and of illness.[9] Consequently, one may observe that entire sectors of a population suffer from some chronic ailment which they all accept as "natural," as part of the scheme of living, for instance, rickets, or TB. It is only from the standpoint of the contemporary scientific concept of the body that it becomes possible to make judgments about how healthy (or sick) an entire society might be.

An inaccurate body-concept, and an inaccurate concept of bodies in general is displayed in many ways. Thus, many middle-class people in our society may grow up in ignorance of the process of reproduction; a nineteen-year-old student of the author's once indicated she had no accurate knowledge of menstrual functions and their role in female anatomy and physiology. This ignorance probably derives indirectly from social taboos on discussion of sexual matters.

An aging person with false pride may fail to acquire an accurate concept of the decrease in his powers of muscular strength and endurance. Because he misjudges his strength and endurance, he may endanger his heart through overindulgence in exercise. But just as a person may overestimate his body's capacity, so may he underestimate it. In times of war and other major stress, increasing knowledge is gained of the human's incredible capacity to endure extreme physical conditions.

The attainment of an accurate body-concept is aided by parents who dispense reliable knowledge to their children, by formal education which includes education for physical health, and by rational efforts on the part of the person to acquire reliable knowledge about his own body.

THE BODY AND HEALTH

Personality, the Body, and Health

Personality refers to the stable and characteristic ways in which an individual behaves in life situations. Behavior produces consequences, not only to the external environment, but also to the body itself. One can evaluate personality with respect to its *physical-*health consequences; thus, it is meaningful to speak of a physical-health-promoting personality and a physical-disease-producing personality.

A PHYSICAL-HEALTH-PROMOTING PERSONALITY. An individual with a personality of this sort is one who has acquired fairly stable habits for the rational care of his health. He has adequate concern for his body's needs, and he has efficient means of meeting these needs. When he observes himself becoming excessively fatigued, he rests. He makes sure his diet will be suitably balanced to maintain his weight and his health. Since health is a value for him, he strives to gain it and maintain it.

A PHYSICAL-ILLNESS-PRODUCING PERSONALITY. This term describes the individual of whom it can reliably be said that weakness and susceptibility to illness are the regular and inevitable consequence of his modes of relating to the world.[10] His habits, value-hierarchy, and general behavior patterns are such as to produce chronic stress to his body, thus lowering its resistance to intercurrent illness and infection, and imposing strain on various organ-systems.

The ambitious professional man may be so absorbed in the enhancement of his career, that he neglects his health. A person might be obliged to repress various needs and emotions, because of an unhealthy self-structure, thus keeping his autonomic nervous system in chronic upheaval, with psychosomatic consequences.

Certain cultural groups and social classes, with their accompanying modal personalities, are more prone to various illnesses than others.[11] The American male has a higher incidence of peptic ulcers than, say, the Chinese male. Diabetes is more frequent, or typical, in some American subcultures than in others. The sociologist is able actually to construct a "sociology" of illness, showing correlations between modal personality for a given class or group, and proneness to the development of various illnesses. Thus, the man who is

acculturated to the values, practices, and style of life of the advertising profession, will probably become afflicted with stomach ulcers.
If he attains executive status in some corporation, he increases his
chances of developing heart disease.

Various socially-defined patterns of indulgence, such as smoking,
or overeating, may have the consequence of shortening life, or of
promoting physical disease. A compulsive smoker, who smokes so
heavily as compensation for various unconscious need-frustrations
may prove to be a person who is actually cutting years from his life.
A compulsive overeater almost definitely is increasing his likelihood
of heart trouble in later years.

Thus, we see that personality has health-implications and health-
consequences. If a person values physical health, it is obvious that
his personality—his stable behavior patterns—must be of such a kind
as will be compatible with physical health.

Handicap and Healthy Personality

It is naturally a very desirable thing for a person to possess an
intact body which functions well, is energetic, and which will last
a long time. But it may happen that a limb is amputated or otherwise crippled. A sense modality may be lost, e.g., loss of sight,
hearing. Or some chronic illness may be contracted, an illness which
drastically limits the scope of an individual's potential activities. Or
the person may be grossly disfigured by scar tissue.

If we ignore such psychological factors as pride, values, and goals
in the handicapped person, and view him strictly as a kind of machine, certain facts become immediately apparent. Although his overall capacity to come to terms with his environment has been reduced
by his handicap, it has not been eliminated completely. Most of the
basic functions which an organism is supposed to perform can still
be performed, though it may be necessary that these functions be
carried out either in different ways, or with reduced overall competence. Thus, a blind person can still be sensitive to all the properties of his physical environment save those which were mediated
by vision. The single amputee can still locomote in his environment,
though he may have to hop on one leg, or limp with a prosthesis.
The double amputee could, if necessary, drag his body along by
means of movements with his arms and hands. Conceivably, a per-

son with legs and arms amputated might be able to roll his torso in ways which would move him across a room.

Now, let us view a handicapped individual as a whole person again. As a modal member of society, he will undoubtedly share the values of his society. His goals will be similar to those of most members of his society. Like the nonhandicapped person, he will want affection, recognition for achievement, some degree of autonomy, or self-sufficiency, etc. But unlike other members of society, his ability to achieve these ends may be reduced somewhat by his handicaps. In fact, the word handicap is meaningless except when used in connection with assorted valued ends. Thus, loss of hearing will only be a handicap in those pursuits where hearing is the sole means to a given end. Loss of sight is a handicap in those activities which are most efficiently directed by the visual sense.

Let us explore some of the possible reactions to handicap, and then try to specify which of these reactions are in accord with the principles of personality hygiene and those which are unhealthy.

HEALTHY REACTIONS TO HANDICAP. When a person suffers some affliction which results in a handicap, there may be, quite naturally, some rather devastating emotional reactions. These include a sense of hopelessness, anxiety about the future, and losses in self-esteem.

Once the fact of handicap has been accepted by the individual, however, the healthy thing to do is to make an assessment of (a) the residual capacities of the body, and (b) the goals and values of the person. When this assessment has been accomplished, it becomes purely a mechanical problem, readily solved (at least in principle), of bringing these two sets of factors into satisfying relationship with one another. If the person's values and goals must remain fixed, then the individual must experiment with his body until he can find ways of accomplishing those ends with new means. Thus, a professional dancer following the amputation of a leg, may wish to continue his profession. He will be obliged to acquire an artificial leg, and practice until he can attain some measure of proficiency that will approximate his previous level.

It is probably easier for a person to leave his goals and values intact, and strive to find new ways of achieving them with his now-altered body, than it is for the person to change his values and goals. It is common for the handicapped person to feel hopeless, and sorry for himself; but with resolve, courage, and encouragement, he can be guided back to the problem of finding new ways of pursuing his former goals. The task which is far more difficult to accomplish is to change the handicapped person's value-system, in order to bring his goals within the realm of possible achievement. Thus, an artist, who derives his livelihood and important personal satisfactions from painting, will be obliged to change some of his goals if he is blinded. He has to learn new goals in some way, in order to obtain satisfactions in living. This is no small task. It can probably be best accomplished through a close interpersonal relationship with individuals who derive their major satisfactions from activities which will be *possible* for the handicapped person to perform. By means of identification with the value-system of these persons, the handicapped one will come to share those values, and thus find new satisfactions.

The blinded artist might establish a very close relationship with a person—blind or seeing—who derives much satisfaction out of teaching, or some form of handicraft that a blind man could accomplish. In time, provided the right conditions are met for identification to occur, the blind artist will come to value teaching just as his friend or therapist does, and will derive satisfaction from those activities.

It is by means of identification that we acquire our most important values, and it is through identification that we change our values from time to time throughout life. By implication, then, since identification appears to be one of the means by which values are acquired, it follows that people who treat with handicapped persons must learn as much as they can about *the means of promoting new identifications*. If the process of identification could be perfectly controlled, much of the task in rehabilitating handicapped persons would be rendered lighter.

UNHEALTHY REACTIONS TO HANDICAP. In general, a reaction to handicap must be adjudged unhealthy when it interferes with the person's capacity to find meaningful satisfactions in ways that are personally and socially acceptable.

When once blindness, crippling, or debilitating disease have afflicted a person, it is natural that his life will be thrown into some sort of chaos. Plans for the future will have been disrupted. It becomes a physical impossibility for the person to exploit former sources of satisfaction. If his security, and self-esteem have been dependent upon certain kinds of activity which are now precluded, then his life will seem empty and futile indeed, following the handicap. Thus, an athlete who earns his living, and who derives his self-esteem from athletic prowess will be overwhelmed with depression when a heart-ailment necessitates giving up this form of activity. A woman whose self-esteem is predicated primarily on her physical beauty will see little point in living following accidental burning which mars her face with unsightly scars.

The reactions of depression, self-pity, or anxiety about the future are natural, even inevitable when handicap occurs. What we are interested in here is the person's reactions to these emotional responses. The healthy reactions already have been described. The most common unhealthy reaction is *resignation.*

Resignation to handicap refers to the response of giving up, of digging in for a life which is devoid of satisfactions. The resigner assumes that there can be found no meaningful gratifications in life, that post-handicap life will consist in helplessness, frustration, emptiness—in short, that it will be an endurance test to be passively submitted to until death occurs.

When resignation occurs, and lasts for more than some period of time, say six months to a year, it becomes necessary to assume that the resigner is deriving some kind of masochistic enjoyment out of his affliction and the limitations it imposes on him. In addition, the affliction may give the resigner the "right" to make all manner of unreasonable claims on other people, in accordance with the slogan, "Since the world has handed me such a dirty deal, I am entitled to a lot of support and consideration from other people." Horney [12] has documented this mechanism thoroughly in her discussion of neurotic claims.

Perhaps the best means of rooting a resigner out of his masochistic orgy is to "blast" him out—with scolding, anger, even contempt. Naturally, this blasting should be viewed as a last resort, when other means, such as inspiration, encouragement, and the like have failed. The best person to accomplish this blasting is a person who has himself accomplished a healthy reaction to a similar, or worse handicap. Such a person is better equipped through personal experience with intimate knowledge of all the advantages accruing to resignation, and all the devious defenses that can be developed against healthy mastery.

Another unhealthy reaction to handicap which may be observed is the attempt to *deny the existence of the handicap*. A "denier" insists that he can do everything which he could do prior to the onset of the handicap, and proceeds to attempt this. Objective appraisal may reveal that it just is not so, yet the denier persists in his attempts to live just as he did before the affliction. This adjustment must be called unhealthy because it violates the precept concerning accurate knowledge concerning the self, and also because it will probably be impossible for the person to carry out his life as he did earlier. If he can, it will be at the expense of other values which are quite important to happiness.

GROWTH PROBLEMS AND HEALTHY PERSONALITY

As a person grows from infancy, through childhood to adulthood, and then to senescence, a number of personality problems arise in consequence of the changes in the body and its performance-potentials. The young child has to learn the limits to the things his body will enable him to do, no less than the aged man or woman has to come to terms with restricted physical powers.

Most of the problems a person has with his body are related to *problems in interpersonal relationships*.

The young infant, for example, may express through bodily malfunctioning, the fact that his relationship with his mother is one that is failing to gratify psychological needs—needs for affection, understanding, and love.

The child's ability or inability to gain voluntary control over bowel and bladder sphincters may reflect inadequacies in the mother-child interaction. Feeding, sleeping, and eliminative disturbances, the stock-in-trade of the pediatrician, all may derive from the psychological climate in which the child is reared.

By the time a person has attained puberty, a whole host of new problems arise. There is the problem of physical awkwardness, stemming from rapid and uneven growth, at a time of life when muscular agility is highly valued by one's peers. Adolescent acne poses appearance-problems, at a time when the young person is becoming acutely aware of the importance of being attractive to the opposite sex. Pubescent young women have the problem of coming to terms with their newly developed capacity to menstruate. Many young girls are ill-prepared for this event, and experience their first menstruation as a frightening shock. Further, the presence of strong sexual urges, attendant upon maturation of the sexual apparatus, poses problems of morality to most adolescents in our culture.

Aging has its own problems, growing out of the gradual waning of physical vigor, and youthful beauty, both highly prized in our society. Perhaps we could say that vigor and beauty are *overly* prized in our society, so that the older person finds it difficult to accept his decreased powers and changed appearance and to find a useful and satisfying role and status in society.

All of these problems attendant upon physical growth and change are made easier to resolve in a healthy way only if a person has a healthy self-structure. The self-structure has got to be sufficiently flexible and elastic, not only to accommodate changes in behavior and personality structure, but also to accommodate changes in the body itself.

HEALTHY ACCEPTANCE OF THE BODY

Another way of stating the optimum personality-hygiene values with respect to the body is as follows: The healthy personality will do all that he can to make his body attractive in appearance, and healthy in its functions. Beyond that point, he more or less accepts his body as *one accepts nature*. Up to a point, one can control and master nature; beyond that point, one comes to terms with it. So with the body. To the extent that one can control one's body, it is healthy to strive to make it a thing of health and beauty. Beyond that point, one can best relax and enjoy it. And in truth, if one's attitudes are right, one's body can indeed be a very rich source of pleasure and satisfaction for the self.[13]

SUMMARY

The body plays an important role in personality health which has been insufficiently studied. In order to promote such study, some technical terms may prove helpful in organizing the various aspects to be studied. The *actual body* refers to the body as it is. The *body-*

concept (body-image) refers to the totality of beliefs and perceptions which a person formulates with his body as their object. The *public body-concept* describes the perceptions and beliefs which a person wants others to hold with respect to his body. The *body-ideal* is the way a person wants his body to be. The *ideal body* is the culturally defined set of values and ideals pertaining to the body.

The body is intimately involved in what psychoanalysts describe as ego-development. The first signs of a developing ego are provided by the appearance in a child of voluntary control over various aspects of his body's functions.

The appearance and health of the body are important determiners of a person's sense of security and of self-esteem. Overconcern with the body's health and appearance are described as *hypochondriasis* and *narcissistic overconcern*. These patterns are unhealthy because they impel the person to ignore many other important values during the process of attending obsessively to health and appearance. The cultural concept of an *ideal body*, insofar as it is internalized as a body-ideal, makes many persons become concerned about being overweight, being underweight, the size and shape of their nose, the smoothness of facial complexion, the size of their genitalia, their muscles, their breasts. A *healthy body-ideal* is fairly flexible, self-affirmed, and yet not too discrepant from the cultural concept of an ideal body.

A *healthy body-concept* is accurate. Without an accurate body-concept, it is difficult to devote rational care to the body.

An individual's personality structure has implications for physical health. Some personality structures actually predispose an individual toward various diseases. A healthy personality includes traits and habits which have the consequence of achieving and maintaining physical health.

There are healthy and unhealthy reactions to *physical handicap.* Healthy reactions include appraisal of the residual capacities of the body, and modification of values and goals in the light of the remaining capacities. Unhealthy reactions include resignation to an unrealistically curtailed life, and a denial of, or repression of awareness of handicap.

Bodily changes attendant upon physical growth and decline induce the development of problems which call for healthy solution.

Such solution is facilitated in the individual who has a healthy self-structure.

The healthy personality does all he can to make his body attractive and healthy, and then he relaxes and enjoys his body.

NOTES AND REFERENCES

RECOMMENDED READINGS ARE MARKED WITH AN ASTERISK (°)

1. Cf. Hoffer, W., "The development of the body ego," *Psychoanalyt. Stud. Child,* V, New York, International University Press, 1950, pp. 18–23.
2. This term was employed by Schilder in his now classic monograph. See Schilder, P. F., *The image and appearance of the human body,* London, Kegan Paul, 1935.
3. Secord, P. F. and Jourard, S. M., "The appraisal of body-cathexis: Body-cathexis and the self," *J. consult. Psychol.,* 1953, **17,** 343–347. These findings were confirmed and extended in a study by Johnson, who demonstrated that attitudes of acceptance toward the body were related to the number of somatic complaints. See Johnson, L. C., "Body-cathexis as a factor in somatic complaints," *J. consult. Psychol.,* 1956, **20,** 145–149. A related series of studies has been reported by Fisher on the implications of the unconscious "body-image" (which he approaches by means of the Rorschach test) for psychosomatic illness and for other traits of personality. Cf. Fisher, S. and Cleveland, S. E., "The role of body image in psychosomatic symptom-choice," *Psychol. Monogr.,* 1955, **69,** No. 17 (Whole No. 402). Also, by the same authors, "Body-image boundaries and style of life," *J. abn. soc. Psychol.,* 1956, **52,** 373–379.
4. Cf. Secord, P. F. and Jourard, S. M., *op. cit.* Also Jourard, S. M. and Remy, R. M., "Perceived parental attitudes, the self, and security, *J. consult. Psychol.,* 1955, **19,** 364–366."
5. Jourard, S. M. and Secord, P. F., "Body-cathexis and the ideal female figure," *J. abn. soc. Psychol.,* 1955, **50,** 243–246.
6. Jourard, S. M. and Secord, P. F., "Body-size and body-cathexis," *J. consult. Psychol.,* 1954, **18,** 184.
°7. See Mead, M., *Male and female,* New York, Morrow, 1949, pp. 138–142, for a discussion of this point.

*8. See, for example, Bruch, H., "Psychological aspects of obesity," *Psychiatry,* 1947, **10**, 373–381.

*9. See Whiting, J. W. M. and Child, I. I., *Child training and personality,* New Haven, Yale University Press, 1953, pp. 119–128, for a discussion of different concepts of illness in various cultures.

10. Any textbook which is devoted to the field of psychosomatic illness will give elaborations and documentation of this point. See, for example, Alexander, F. and French, T. M., *Studies in psychosomatic medicine,* New York, Ronald, 1948.

11. Cf. Ruesch, J., "Social technique, social status, and social change in illness," in Kluckhohn, C. and Murray, H. A. (eds.), *Personality in nature, society, and culture,* New York, Knopf, 1953.

12. Horney, K., *Neurosis and human growth,* New York, Norton, 1950, Ch. 2.

13. Cf. Maslow, A. H., *Motivation and personality,* New York, Harper, 1954, pp. 206–207.

QUESTIONS FOR REVIEW AND EXAMINATION

1. Define body-concept, body-ideal, ideal body, public body-concept, and body ego.

2. Comment from a personality-health point of view on hypochondriasis and narcissistic overconcern with the body.

3. Comment on the cultural concepts of an ideal body in relation to personality health.

4. Why are obesity, skinniness, etc., causes for concern for many people in our society?

5. What is a healthy body-ideal? A healthy body-concept?

6. Explain how personality can have implications for physical health.

7. What are healthy and unhealthy reactions to handicap?

8. Use this chapter as a guide in describing and evaluating the relationship that someone has established with his own body.

CHAPTER 13

Therapy and the Promotion of Healthy Personality

TREATMENT OF SYMPTOMS

When an individual has an unhealthy personality, he usually suffers. The name which psychologists give to the suffering he experiences varies. Some unhealthy personalities suffer from chronic anxiety and fear. Others from guilt, feelings of inferiority and worthlessness. Still others complain that their life feels empty, joyless, and devoid of any meaningful satisfactions. Some manifest the clinical symptoms of neurosis and psychosis: phobias, obsessions, and hallucinations. As in the field of physical medicine, where pain is the signal that all is not well with the body, so with personality; the above-mentioned experiences signify to the individual that all is not well with his personality.

When a person suffers from physical pain associated with wounds or infections, he generally strives to alleviate the pain with palliatives, viz.: aspirin, and other drugs, or else he seeks rational treatment that will combat the causes of his suffering.

When a person suffers from "psychological pain," [1] he can seek temporary relief by means of assorted palliative measures, or else seek to alter the basic conditions which have been responsible for his suffering. Naturally, the personality hygienist values most highly those attempts at treatment which will remove the causes of the psychological suffering. In general, this rational sort of treatment calls for either some kind of alteration of personality structure, some alteration of the environment, or both. The temporary kind of treatment may be designated "symptom-treatment," or psychological first aid, since its aim is to relieve the patient from the immediate experience of suffering.

EXAMPLES OF SYMPTOM-TREATMENT IN THE SELF. Let us suppose a person is suffering from chronic anxiety. His anxiety takes the form of specific worries, worries about health, money, and career. If the person attempts to treat himself for these symptoms, he may *drink* each time his worries become too intense. While intoxicated, he may think about ill-health and the lack of money, but the unpleasant emotional tensions will likely be mitigated. Unfortunately, the cure of the symptoms in this case lasts only as long as the effects of the alcohol. Upon sobering up, the person will again find himself plagued with the chronically recurrent worries.

Another type of symptom-treatment which a person resorts to commonly is *repression,* the refusal to think about the objects of his worry. Each time the themes of health, money, and career present themselves to his thoughts, or arise in conversation, he changes the subject and thinks about or talks about something more pleasant. Unfortunately, the unwanted thoughts, with their concomitant feelings will tend to sneak into his mind when he least expects them, viz.: when he is at the point of falling asleep, or when his attention wanders from some task at which he is engaged. In fact, the repressed thoughts make his attention wander; the represser may find it difficult to concentrate on his job. Furthermore, though the person attempts to repress his own thinking about the unwanted subjects, he cannot very well control the conversation of other people in his life. They may, from time to time, introduce the unwanted themes into discussion, thus forcing the person to think about, and feel the emotion associated with the undesirable themes.

A method for the alleviation of symptoms which is quite common is the *quest for reassurance* from other people. The anxious individual may induce others, subtly or openly, to persuade and reassure him there is no reasonable ground for worry. They tell him his body is in A-1 shape, his funds are adequate for most usual needs, and his employer really thinks highly of his abilities and his contributions to the firm. If the reassurer is eloquent, he may succeed in alleviating the experience of anxiety as long as he is with the anxious person. Yet when the unhealthy one is alone, or away from the uplifting influence of his reassuring friend, he will again find himself faced with his recurring worries.

The unhealthy personality may avail himself of *assorted defense mechanisms* in addition to repression, in his quest to relieve himself of psychological pain. He may think about health, money, and work, but in a highly intellectualized way, thus relieving his anxiety through verbal reformulation. Or, he may resort to disowning projection, "It is not I who am worried, but others." He would then display a perhaps compulsive concern for the health, finances, and career of all of his friends, while showing no apparent concern over these aspects of his own life. All of the mechanisms of defense which were mentioned in Chapter 10 may be viewed in one sense as automatic attempts on the part of an individual to relieve himself of the symptoms of his unhealthy personality.

One way a person might adopt for the avoidance or reduction of psychological suffering is a *specialized arrangement of his social environment.* This arrangement might involve keeping people at a distance, or keeping oneself surrounded by admirers or helpers. So long as this arrangement is maintained, the person may be able to work and avoid personality disorganization. But if any alteration is introduced into this environmental arrangement, the person becomes disorganized and suffers acute anxiety. In fact, one way in which unhealthy personality manifests itself is the relatively narrow range of environmental variation within which the person can get satisfactions, perform responsibilities, and avoid anxiety. The healthier the personality, and the stronger the ego, the broader will be the range of environmental variation within which satisfactions can be gained and responsibilities performed.

MEDICAL AND PSYCHOLOGICAL SYMPTOM-TREATMENT. Physicians, psychiatrists, and clinical psychologists may be obliged to treat symptoms in cases where a full understanding of the causes of the suffering is not available, or when causal treatment is inadvisable because of expense, or the possibility of precipitating severe psychosis.

Some examples of *medical and psychiatric* symptom-treatment include the various forms of shock therapies—electroshock, insulin shock, etc.; the prescription of tranquilizing drugs such as reserpine, thorazine, milltown, and similar medicines.

Psychological symptom-treatment includes such procedures as reassurance, inspiration, and striving to strengthen the sufferer's defenses rather than trying to help him do without them.

COMMENTS ABOUT SYMPTOM-TREATMENT. We can make some general summary statements about the limited value of symptom-treatment for unhealthy personality, whether this treatment is attempted by the individual himself, or by well-intentioned other persons.

The symptoms which produce suffering, or which are the suffering, arise as a by-product of the patient's way of life. His way of life, his stable and recurring modes of relating to the world and people, is mediated by his very personality structure. This structure includes his modes of perceiving and interpreting the world, and his self-structure. *So long as the personality structure remains unaltered, then the conditions responsible for the symptoms remain continually present.* The devices mentioned above for the relief of symptoms then serve somewhat the same function aspirin does for physical pain. A headache may be caused actually by some circulatory defect; while the aspirin relieves the pain for awhile, it does nothing to remedy the circulatory defect. The headaches will recur as long as the cause is operative. So with psychological suffering. It will recur so long as its causal conditions remain in existence. The attempts at symptom-treatment can at best provide only temporary and conditional relief from suffering.

It should not be assumed from what has been written above that there is no place for symptom-treatment in medicine or in psychiatry. When it is impossible or impracticable to discern the root causes of suffering, or to remove these causes, then symptom-treatment becomes a must. Furthermore, in personality problems, anxiety may be so intense as to prevent the person from communicating with the very therapist who is trying to help him. In instances such as these, the use of sedation and tranquilizing drugs may be strongly indicated. They reduce anxiety to the point where the patient can begin to cooperate with his therapist, and they may permit the patient to carry out his daily round of responsibilities without being hospitalized.

One danger may be noted, however, about the use of such symp-
tom-treatments as tranquilizing drugs. In eliminating emotional
stress, they may produce such a sense of well-being that the patient
loses all incentive for the more basic, rational treatment of his difficulties. He may become overly dependent on his drugs, since the
basic causes of his difficulties persist. A prospective patient for personality therapy has to feel his suffering acutely in order to have the
motivation to go through the often lengthy and distressing period
that therapy entails.

THE RATIONAL SOLUTION OF
PSYCHOLOGICAL SUFFERING

The suffering of anxiety, deprivations, and guilt, all signify some
lack of adjustment to the world, especially to other people. Adjustment implies changes in the person, or changes in the world, which
must occur before the suffering disappears and is replaced by happiness or satisfaction.

Now, both healthy and unhealthy personalities fall heir to psychological suffering. They differ, however, in the adjustments which they
undertake in order to remove the suffering. The unhealthy personality generally adjusts in ways which are at best stopgaps: he treats
symptoms. The healthy personality strives for rational cure, for
alteration of the basic conditions responsible for the suffering. Often-
times it would appear to the onlooker that the efforts of the healthy
personality at rational cure are indirect, or roundabout. Yet this is
only appearance. For often the causes of suffering are not readily
observed; the symptoms only are detectable. The causes have to be
discovered by means of directed inquiry.

Suppose a person is suffering from the following symptom of unhealthy personality: He is a salesman, and each time he approaches
a customer, he becomes so overwhelmed with anxiety his mind goes
blank, he cannot speak coherently, and he stands in danger of losing
his job because of falling sales. The anxiety-reaction in the presence
of customers is his symptom. If he attempts to eliminate the symptom only, he might do such things as take a few drinks prior to
meeting each customer; or he might perform certain rituals which
serve the function of reassuring him of his adequacy as a salesman,

etc. The only thing wrong with these attempts to reduce the intensity of the symptom is that they do nothing to eliminate the causes, which may lie in some area of his life quite remote from his occupation.

A rational attempt to get rid of the symptom would entail an assessment of most aspects of his personality, aspects which to him or to an observer might seem unrelated to his problem. It might be found, for example, that he has many recurring problems in his relationships with his spouse, with his friends, and his family. Study of his self-structure might disclose he is striving to defend and maintain a self-concept which is quite alienated from his real self. It might even be found that basically, his interests do not lie in selling, but in some other area of endeavor. A cure of his symptom might best be accomplished by efforts directed at overcoming his self-alienation, and at improving the nature of his relationships with his spouse, friends, and family. His symptom is not just a fear of customers; rather, it is a disguised expression of these other problem-areas, problems which, for one reason or another, the person does not feel so acutely as he feels his panic with customers.

We can use the term *healthy adjustment* to refer to those efforts on the part of a person to effect a rational cure of psychological suffering. In principle, there are two broad modes of adjustment possible to the individual: changing the structure of the self and changing the structure of the environment. The former is referred to as *autoplastic* adjustment, while the latter is *alloplastic* adjustment. We can speak now of healthy and unhealthy autoplastic and alloplastic adjustment.

AUTOPLASTIC ADJUSTMENT

Autoplastic adjustment is healthy when the individual alters his personality structure in the direction of healthy personality. It is unhealthy when the personality changes move the individual further away from personality health.

HEALTHY AUTOPLASTIC ADJUSTMENT. Let us suppose that suffering occurs as a consequence of an inaccurate self-concept. The individual believes that he is inferior to others, that he is a sinner, unlovable, etc. If he is able to examine, in a broad perspective, all of his past feelings and actions, as well as all of his present feelings and actions, he might emerge from the study with a more empirically based concept of his personality, with a self-concept which is more in accord with evidence. As we have seen, an accurate self-concept is one of the defining characteristics of healthy personality. Autoplastic adjustment of this sort—which removes the suffering and at the same time changes the personality in the direction of health— is healthy autoplastic adjustment.

UNHEALTHY AUTOPLASTIC ADJUSTMENT. Let us suppose a person is suffering because he does not receive the love and affection of his mother. As a consequence, he feels anxious, and worthless. His mother may herself possess an unhealthy personality. Before she will bestow her affection on her son, he must conform with certain of her demands. These demands include a renunciation of self-assertion, repression of hostility, and pursuit of a vocation of her choice. The son then complies with these demands. The very act of compliance changes personality in an unhealthy direction. Furthermore, the consequences of compliance actually produce a number of new symptoms of unhealthy personality. We should be obliged to regard the foregoing as a case of unhealthy autoplastic adjustment.

ALLOPLASTIC ADJUSTMENT

In alloplastic adjustment, the personality structure remains unchanged; instead, the suffering person strives to modify his environment, including the behavior and personality structure of other persons, so that his needs will be satisfied and his suffering relieved. In order to make judgments about the health or lack of health in alloplastic adjustment, we must have knowledge of the present personality health of the individual, and we must also be able to observe the consequences to his personality of his attempts at alloplastic adjustment.

HEALTHY ALLOPLASTIC ADJUSTMENT. An individual may already possess most of the traits of a healthy personality, namely, reality-contact, accuracy of the self-concept, healthy emotionality, etc. He encounters a situation where he suffers: a person is condemning him for certain kinds of behavior, and he experiences a sharp loss of self-esteem and of security in consequence. He may strive to convince and persuade the other person of the injustice of his condemnation, by arguments, and by debate. If he is successful, then the suffering is relieved. If he has done everything at his disposal to achieve this and still fails, then he might assert with some validity that his suffering is unwarranted. It is not he who is sick or wrong, but rather his condemner. And so he may cut that person out of his life.

Or, a person may find himself suffering because of the way in which his work environment is set up. He does not like the physical or the social arrangements in his work situation. He may devote his skills and efforts to altering these arrangements; if these fail, then he might seek another position where work can be accomplished at a lesser sacrifice of ease, productivity, and comfort, and where an unhealthy change in the self is not required.

UNHEALTHY ALLOPLASTIC ADJUSTMENT. The mode of adjustment attempted by the individual with an unhealthy personality is to strive to modify the entire world so it will accommodate his peculiar set of needs. Thus, if he can feel safe only so long as people report that they love him, he will engage in a continual campaign to solicit people's affection. If he can experience self-esteem only when people praise him, he will tropistically seek out a praising environment, or else attempt to beguile or force people to praise him. The neurotic mother who strives to keep her children dependent upon her—she dreads being abandoned by them, and can find satisfactions in life only in the performance of the role of mother—illustrates unhealthy alloplastic adjustment.

WHEN TO SEEK HELP IN ACHIEVING PERSONALITY HEALTH?

The answer to this question should be perfectly obvious. When one suffers from physical pain, and one's own attempts at treatment and cure fail, then one consults a professional person, the physician. When one suffers from psychological pain, and one's attempts at self-treatment fail, either at a symptomatic or a causal level, then one should consult a professional personality therapist.

The professional personality therapist may be a psychiatrist, a clinical psychologist, or a social caseworker. He has been schooled in the science of personality, and knows in general the varieties of unhealthy personality, the causes of personality illness, and the basic principles for effecting personality changes in the direction of health. He is trained to apply these principles to individual cases.

PERSONALITY THERAPY

WHAT DOES THE PERSONALITY THERAPIST DO? In this section, we shall speak at the level of general principles rather than in specific terms, for there are wide individual differences among personality therapists in rationales for their therapeutic behavior, and in the ways in which they perform their professional tasks. But explicitly or implicitly, their procedure is as follows:

1. They *describe* the present personality structure of their suffering patient, in order to answer the question, "How is he now?"

2. They *evaluate* his personality against some concept of personality health, in order to formulate a picture of the extent to which the patient deviates from a healthy personality. The specific patterns of deviation from personality health have traditionally been assigned names, after the fashion of disease names in physical medicine. In fact, in psychiatry, a symptom is regarded as a symptom of mental disease. In other words, each deviation from personality health might be called a symptom. We can distinguish between *ego-syntonic* and *ego-dystonic* symptoms, and between *manifest* and *latent* symptoms. Ego-syntonic symptoms are deviations from personality health which the patient likes, or does not experience as unwanted. Ego-dystonic symptoms are deviations from personality health which the patient wishes he were rid of. Manifest symptoms may be ego-dystonic or not. The term manifest means they are obvious and readily perceived by the person and/or the therapist; the patient feels them and wishes he were rid of them. Latent symptoms refer to deviations from personality health which are discovered by the therapist only after investigation.

3. The therapist seeks next to *formulate a plan of action* designed to alter the conditions responsible for the symptoms. This stage involves the problem of formulating the supposed causes of unhealthy personality, so they can be subjected to attempts to modify them.

4. Then, finally, the therapist *undertakes his therapeutic activities,* he behaves in ways designed to stimulate growth toward health in his patient.

HOW DOES THE THERAPIST INTERPRET PSYCHOLOGICAL SUFFERING? While it may seem academic and unimportant, yet *the point of view from which a person regards psychological suffering will strongly influence his attempts to treat it.* If one interprets suffering as a by-product of "sin," then efforts at cure will be directed toward eliminating the evil, and perhaps directing the sinner in the paths of "righteousness."

If suffering is thought to derive from "weak will-power," then treatment will consist in efforts designed to inspire the patient to "strengthen his will."

If suffering is regarded as evidence of "mental disease," then one will seek to find the "cause," remove it, and thus restore the patient to "normal"—the way he was before he became "sick."

Another way of interpreting suffering and symptoms is to regard them as a by-product of a *weak ego.* It will be recalled that the ego is a hypothetical component of personality which is held to be the *agent* of *adaptation and adjustment.* If the ego is weak, the person is unable to tolerate suffering long enough to determine the most healthy means of reacting to threat, anxiety, and deprivation. Consequently, behavior is undertaken which reduces suffering in the short-run, but does not get at root causes. When unhealthy personality is viewed as evidence of a weak ego, then one way of interpreting rational personality therapy is to regard it as efforts aimed at *increasing ego strength.* When we have been able to formulate a more complete understanding of the ego, its functions, and its strength, then of course therapy will be a more effective tool than it is at the present time.[2]

In more recent years, psychological suffering has come to be regarded by many psychiatrists and psychologists as evidence of an *impasse in personality growth.* In other words, they conceive of man as an organism with a fundamental tendency to grow toward health and full functioning—self-actualization.[3] Obstacles in the path of growth make themselves known by producing suffering. Suffering may signify the person has been striving to preserve his present growth-status and to avoid further growth, or that some factors are blocking growth. When suffering is so interpreted, the efforts of the therapist are then aimed at identifying the aspects of personality and environment which impede growth and striving to alter these so that growth can resume.

SOME AIMS OF PERSONALITY THERAPY. When a patient voluntarily seeks the assistance of a therapist, he does so because some aspects of his personality or his milieu are preventing him from achieving satisfactions in living. It should be apparent that the therapeutic aim will be strongly determined by the nature of the patient's deviations from personality health.

Detailed analysis of the patient's total life situation may disclose that the factor which is most responsible for all of the difficulties in living, and all of the unhealthy traits, is some one "root cause," viz.: impaired reality-contact, or alienation from the real self, or more specifically, repressed emotion.

If such a root cause can be diagnosed, then it follows that the therapist's chief aim will be to alter this particular trait in healthy directions. If it is indeed the root cause, then when it has been effectively altered, the other unhealthy traits which are dependent upon it should alter in healthy directions by themselves.

However, it is not always easy to formulate the dynamics of the patient's difficulties with such clarity, in advance of the therapeutic work. More frequently, the therapist simply begins work with the patient, and diagnosis goes on concomitant with therapy.

A distinction is often drawn between *personality counseling,* and *intensive personality therapy.* In counseling, some one specific life-problem is the chief focus of the therapist's and patient's attention. The aim is to so release the patient's problem-solving powers that he will be able to resolve the problem by himself, without giving up any of his autonomy as a person.[4] With therapy, the aim is to achieve more basic changes in the patient's modes of relating to his social environment and to his real self. Thus, we might speak of vocational counseling, marital counseling, counseling of parent-child problems, etc. Personality therapy is a more intensive procedure, with more radical aims, namely, the quest for changes in basic personality structure.

A psychiatrist may select a broader range of aims for the treatment of patients than problem-counseling or intensive personality therapy. Because he is a physician, he is qualified to administer treatment procedures which the psychologist is not trained to employ. And so, with a given patient, the psychiatrist might seek to relieve symptoms by means of various drugs, without effecting any changes in basic personality structure. Or, he might strive to eliminate certain psychotic symptoms by means of electric shock therapy, with the aim of getting the patient out of a state hospital. But it should not be assumed that such procedures constitute a "cure" of the patient; he probably still retains the modes of relating to the world which were contributing to the development of his psychosis in the first place. It is only in special cases that the therapist will select as a practicable aim the alteration of the total personality in the direction of health.

A good question to ask in connection with a therapist's aims is, "Should the therapist aim at restoring the patient to normal, that is, to the way he was before he began to suffer? Or should he strive to help the patient attain a condition closer to optimum personality health than prior to the development of the symptoms?" If we regard the patient's pre-symptomatic personality structure as a *symptom-producing structure*, it becomes apparent that simply removing symptoms will not be a rational treatment. The optimum aim should be to so change the personality structure that the individual will no longer react to life situations in ways which encourage the development of symptoms.

How Does the Therapist Promote Personality Growth?

During the process of an individual's life, his personality structure often goes through radical changes. Personality growth may be viewed as change in directions valued by the personality hygienist, i.e., in the direction of health. When the patient arrives at the therapist's office, he can be regarded as a person whose personality structure has been frozen, as it were (it prevents him from effecting healthy adjustments), at some stage on the long journey toward health and self-actualization. The "normal" personality (see Chapter 1) can be regarded likewise as a person whose growth toward health has been frozen, but perhaps he does not suffer sufficiently to motivate him to seek help in overcoming the barriers to growth. The task of the therapist is to engage in those activities which will serve to thaw out the patient's adaptive capacities and remove the barriers to further autonomous growth toward health.

The therapist may achieve these ends (a) by manipulating the environment of his patient directly, or behaving toward the patient so the latter will either alter his present environment or move to a newer, more health-provocative milieu; and (b) by so behaving toward the patient that the latter's personality structure will be altered in the direction of health as a direct consequence of the therapist-patient relationship.

ENVIRONMENT-MANIPULATION. It may often happen that a patient's symptoms represent reactions to a social environment which produces the symptoms in an almost direct causal relationship. That is, the persons with whom the patient is required to interact daily place demands and restrictions on him which produce the symptoms. This is often the case with young children. Their parents relate to them in ways which are directly inductive of unhealthy personality. The therapist, in order to promote the personality health of his patient may not be required to work directly with his patient. Instead, he may find it necessary to undertake counseling or therapy with the patient's intimate associates, with the end in view of altering their impact on the patient. Frequently, simple advice is all that is necessary to change the ways in which others relate to the patient, with the consequence that the latter is able to move further in the direction of personality health than he had been able hitherto.

In other instances, the therapist may urge the patient to move to a different milieu, to surround himself with persons who have personalities different from those which he finds in his present, pathology-producing environment. Thus, he may be advised to divorce his spouse, change jobs, move to a different part of the country, etc. Or, it may be necessary to place the patient in a special hospital which constitutes a growth-promoting milieu.[5] There are many times when a therapist can observe clearly that growth toward health is obstructed by a marriage, a certain friendship, or a certain relationship with an employer. Of course, the question arises, why does not the patient himself take the initiative and dissolve the pathology-producing relationship? The answer to this question is not always simple. It can generally be shown that the pathology-producing relationship is satisfying important needs in the patient, and he is reluctant to forego these satisfactions for the risk of starting anew.

When the patient strongly resists attempts to get him to change his milieu, the efforts of the therapist are generally directed toward an analysis of the needs which are being gratified in the present environment and toward an analysis of the anxieties concerning the projected changes in life-setting. It happens quite frequently that the patient is able to gain an insight into the reasons for his remaining in tho unhealthy milieu, and thus becomes able to effect the moves at his own initiative.

Therapist-Behavior Which Provokes Growth

We are concerned here with those activities of the personality therapist [6] which are believed to overcome impasses in the patient's quest for growth and health, and which actually produce healthy changes in the patient. In what follows, the reader must understand that no single therapist actually follows any set pattern in his behavior with his patient; yet, despite individual differences, probably all successful personality therapists do some or all of the things which will be mentioned.

THE THERAPIST OBSERVES THE PATIENT. The patient, usually under the incentive of psychological suffering, talks about his life, his feelings, and his thoughts, to the therapist. He does so because he has been led to expect that such behavior on his part is necessary in order to enable the therapist to help him. The therapist listens carefully to what the patient *says* and studies carefully what the patient *does* while in his presence. As time proceeds, the therapist gradually formulates an "other-concept" concerning the patient, a set of beliefs concerning the motives, values, emotional responses, and the self-structure of the patient. He continually formulates, revises, and reformulates this other-concept as more information is made available to him. By the time the therapy has been completed, it may be assumed that the therapist has acquired a fairly accurate concept of his patient's personality. He does not hesitate to make inferences about the patient's needs and motives on the basis of dreams, gestures, omissions, facial expressions, and other subtle cues; but these inferences are always tentative, and are continually checked against subsequent information.

THE THERAPIST IS HONEST WITH HIS PATIENT. The therapist, from time to time, conveys to the patient his opinions and judgments concerning the patient's motives, needs, etc. These communications are honest. Often, what the therapist has to say comes as a shock, a surprise, to the patient. He had not thought about his behavior in just that way; or he believed his motives and feelings were something different from what the therapist said. When the patient asks the therapist what he is thinking or feeling about him, the therapist will either give an honest answer, or else strive to understand the motives behind the inquiry. It may be seen that the relationship between a therapist and his patient has many of the characteristics of healthy interpersonal relationships as these were described in Chapter 7.

THE THERAPIST DIRECTLY OR SYMBOLICALLY SATISFIES MANY OF THE PATIENT'S NEEDS. The patient, when he comes in for therapy, has many needs unfulfilled. The therapist attempts to discern precisely what the patient needs in order to feel secure, trusting, accepted, and he may either provide these need-objects through his own behavior in the relationship,[7] or attempt to aid the patient in his attempts to find satisfactions outside the relationship. Psychoanalysts strive to curtail any real satisfactions which the patient finds in the relationship. It most often happens that many of the patient's needs are gratified in the relationship without any deliberate effort on the part of the therapist. This accidental gratification occurs through what the psychoanalysts call the *transference*.[8] The therapist in many ways represents an ambiguous stimulus, and as such, his personality may be autistically perceived by the patient, according to the latter's needs, emotions, and expectancies. Thus, the transference situation serves a number of therapeutic functions; it offers the patient an opportunity to satisfy his need for a father-figure or a mother-figure, and at the same time it provides for the therapist an invaluable source of hypotheses concerning the nature of persons who influenced the life history of the patient.

THE THERAPIST RESPECTS HIS PATIENT. For the patient, the relationship with the therapist is often the first time in his life that he experiences respect on the part of another for his uniqueness and individuality. The therapist manifests this respect by not pressuring his patient and by not putting conditions on his attention, affection, and interest in what the patient is saying. Simply being attentively listened to is often an invaluable means by which the patient's self-esteem is lifted from a low point to a more tolerable level.

THE THERAPIST DOES NOT "USE" THE PATIENT. In everyday life, the intimates of the patient may have been using him for ends of their own. Thus, they may have profited in their own quest for valued ends by his ineffectuality, or by his passivity, or other unhealthy traits. The therapist, as a consequence of his training, and presumably higher degree of personality health, is able to resist using the patient's traits as a means for reaching personal and private ends. It was pointed out earlier (Chapters 6, 7) that certain interpersonal relationships can continue only so long as one or the other partners remains thwarted in his growth. In the therapy-relationship, the therapist strives to act in ways which will provoke growth. If the patient expresses affection for him, or shows dependency, the therapist does not feed his own self-esteem with this helplessly loving behavior. Instead, he strives to understand and interpret the meaning of this behavior to the patient.

THE THERAPIST ENCOURAGES AND PERMITS FREE EMOTIONAL EXPRESSION. The freedom of the therapeutic situation is such that gradually the patient is able to vent fully all his feelings about all of the significant persons in his life, including the therapist. The therapist actually encourages this emotional catharsis by refraining from counter-reactions of an emotional sort. Instead, he usually will accept the expression of feeling, and perhaps try to help the patient understand why such intense feelings were repressed originally, and why they were not acknowledged earlier in life. In fact, if a therapist observes that his patient avoids expressing any feelings about anything, he will call it to his attention, and explore with him some of the reasons for such an avoidance of emotional expression.

The release of suppressed and repressed emotional tensions is believed to be one of the most important contributors in the therapeutic process to the attainment of personality health in general, as well as healthy emotionality in particular.

THE THERAPIST TRIES TO UNDERSTAND THE PATIENT, AND TO PROMOTE SELF-UNDERSTANDING IN THE PATIENT. The trained personality therapist may be expected to be something of an expert in the general field of personality. When he has learned enough about his patient, he has become an expert about his patient. One of his aims is to enable his patient to become an expert about himself—to understand how he came to be as he now is, and to know how he now is. The therapist accomplishes these ends by means of well-timed interpretations [9] which he communicates to the patient at selected stages of treatment.

How Therapy Promotes Personality Growth

PROMOTING INCREASED NEED-SATISFACTION. Part of the patient's suffering stems from the fact that he is failing to find satisfactions in living. This deprivation-suffering may derive either from the fact that the need-objects are not available in the patient's present milieu, or else inner obstacles prevent the patient from availing himself of satisfactions which surround him on all sides. He is "starving in the midst of plenty."

Working from the premise that need-gratification is an important means toward personality health, as well as a sign that it has been achieved, the therapist strives to make it possible for his patient to satisfy more of his needs. He tries to identify just what it is his patient needs in order to experience satisfactions in living, and then tries to ascertain precisely why these satisfactions have not been obtained. If it is a case of an impoverished environment, the therapist might help the patient make a move to one where gratifications are more readily obtained, without the requisite of radical changes in personality structure. Frequently all that is required is a little urging or encouragement on the part of the therapist, in order to overcome the patient's inertia, or his fears at leaving a familiar environment.

The situation is different when the deprivations occur in a potentially gratification-rich environment. In this case, the barriers to gratification lie in the structure of the patient's personality. Thus, the patient may be starved for affection, or for simple acceptance from other people. The question arises, what is preventing him from acting in ways that will secure these need-objects from the people with whom he lives? Investigation may disclose that the precise ways of acting which could be almost guaranteed in our culture to achieve the valued responses from other people are not available to the patient for some of the following reasons:

1. Past conditioning experiences have led him to expect rejection, scorn, ridicule, or punishment for any attempts on his part to elicit the wanted responses from other persons. He believes in advance that other people are basically cruel, rejecting, and malicious.

2. His conscience includes very stringent taboos which condemn as sinful the very satisfactions he so badly needs for happiness.

3. His self-concept includes the unwarranted belief that he does not have the capacity to learn effective ways of behaving in order to achieve satisfactions.

4. He has acquired other-concepts with respect to people which lead him to believe they should give him what he needs without any request or effort on his part. These other-concepts, however, are no longer accurate.

The therapist, after identifying these barriers to satisfaction, may direct his efforts toward their removal. Thus, he may urge the patient to test his predictions that efforts to get satisfaction will evoke rejection or punishment from others. Or he may explore with his patient the nature of the ideals which comprise his conscience, so the patient may be able to reformulate some of the ideals which are not rational or appropriate to his present age and status. Or he may strive to help the patient experience successes of varied sorts so that his self-concept can now include the assertion, "I am a competent and capable person." Or he may help the patient learn the art of testing the validity of his other-concepts. The results of these efforts quite likely will enable the patient to avail himself of satisfactions which are available in his environment, thus increasing his happiness in living.

PROMOTING REALITY-CONTACT. It can be assumed that the patient suffers from impaired reality-contact in various realms of life. His self-concept may be inaccurate; his other-concepts may be autistic; his expectancies fail to be in accord with objective or scientifically grounded estimates of probability. Yet, his behavior is regulated by his perceptions, inaccurate though they be. While accurate cognition is not the sufficient condition for healthy behavior, it is a necessary condition. Thus, anything which the therapist can do that will increase the accuracy of the patient's perceptions and beliefs, and which strengthens the reality-testing habit, will move the patient closer to the ideal of personality health.

The patient, in talking to the therapist, will often give a statement of his reasons, or motives, for acting in certain ways. If the therapist points out other possible or plausible interpretations, but of a less pride-enhancing nature, it may encourage the patient to be more honest in formulating his motives to himself and others. By verbalizing evaluations of the patient which differ from the patient's self-descriptions (by being more accurate) he may assist the patient in the task of formulating an accurate self-concept. By questioning the patient's other-concepts, he may guide the patient toward self-questioning when he makes statements and judgments about the motives and traits of other persons in his life. By correcting mis-information about matters for which reliable knowledge exists, physiology, psychology, embryology, anthropology, etc., the thera-pist may promote in his patient the acquisition of accurate knowl-edge about the world. By correcting the patient's misinterpretations of his (the therapist's) thoughts, opinions, and judgments about the patient, the therapist will promote reality-contact in the immediate therapeutic situation.

All of these activities will tend to promote reality-contact, and the acquisition of a fairly stable reality-testing habit in the patient—both of which are healthy traits.

PROMOTING HEALTHY EMOTIONALITY. The patient will generally display some or all of the varieties of unhealthy emotionality which were described in Chapter 4. Most commonly, patients seeking per-sonality therapy on a voluntary basis will be emotional repressers, or chronic emotional suppressers. If they are repressers, then they typically will be uncognizant of their own emotional tensions when in fact these tensions have been provoked by life situations. The therapist will be skilled in identifying subtle signs of emotional tension when these exist, and he will suggest tactfully to the patient that perhaps he has these feelings, when the evidence for them is obvious in the therapeutic situation. Generally, the patient will deny that he feels the things which the therapist is suggesting; but he denies it for a number of reasons which gradually will evaporate as therapy proceeds. One reason for repressing is the dread that other persons will condemn or punish the individual when he has these feelings. The therapist fails to be punitive or rejecting of the patient, even when he knows what the patient is feeling. This may encourage the patient to avoid repressing, at least while in the therapy-session. Another reason for repression is the nature of the self-structure; the person may think of himself, with some pride, as a nonemotional person; hence, he would experience emotional responses as threats to his sense of identity and to his self-esteem. As his self-structure gradually changes in the therapeutic relationship, he no longer needs to repress his feelings, but is instead able to feel them and acknowledge to himself that they exist

The patient who chronically suppresses his emotions does so because he fears the probable consequences of open expression. Through time, the patient will gradually acquire courage to test the reactions of the therapist to increasingly less-controlled emotional expressions. As he finds that the therapist does not reject or condemn him as he had anticipated, he will allow himself to express what he feels in more open ways.

As the patient's reality-contact improves, the frequency with which irrational affects occurs will diminish. It will be recalled that irrational affects are emotional responses occasioned by autistic interpretations of reality. The more the patient is able to achieve veridical cognition, about himself and the outside world, the more rational and appropriate to the situation will become his emotional responses. This too is healthy.

In all likelihood, the more the patient moves in the direction of healthy emotionality, the more physically healthy will he become, since it has been shown that many physical disabilities derive from chronically suppressed emotional tension.

Finally, as the patient comes to be less and less alienated from his self, he will become increasingly autonomous and self-reliant. This implies that he will be less dependent upon others for important satisfactions in living. The upshot is that another powerful reason for emotional suppression and repression will have been removed, and the patient will be increasingly able to display selective suppression and release as his characteristic mode for controlling emotions.

PROMOTING HEALTHY SEXUALITY. It is perhaps a universal truth that the patient seeking personality therapy suffers from some form of unhealthy sexuality. Most patients have been unable to talk frankly and openly to another person about their sexual activities, anxieties, guilts, etc. For many patients, the therapy-relationship is the first time in their life they have exposed their thinking and feelings and experiences apropos sexuality to the view of another human being.

Where there have been unrealistic anxieties concerning sexual practices, and where there have been false beliefs with respect to the "facts of life," simply talking about sex to a trained therapist is itself conducive to achieving a healthier sexual adjustment. Misinformation can readily be corrected, and the anxieties attendant upon misinformation can be relieved, with almost immediate benefit to the patient. The author counseled a university student who had grave inferiority feelings as his presenting complaint. Further discussion revealed he felt inferior because of the size of his penis. He had never seen another male naked, even though he lived in a dormitory, and so he had no basis in experience for making comparisons. The author took a book of anatomy from his shelf, and had the student read a few lines concerned with average sizes. The patient was hugely relieved, and never concerned himself about this further.

As the patient talks about his life, it will become apparent to the therapist what functions (in addition to pleasure and the expression of love and esteem) sexuality is serving for the patient. As the patient comes to be aware of some of the irrelevant needs which sexuality is gratifying, it may become possible for him to experiment with other means of satisfying these needs in a more direct manner, thus releasing sexuality from some of the functions for which it is psychologically ill-suited. Thus, if he is using sex as an "opiate" for an unsatisfying interpersonal life, he may make direct efforts to improve his relationships with people. If he is using sexuality as a means of bolstering self-esteem and reassuring himself of his masculine prowess, he may be enabled after the insight to base his self-esteem on other kinds of valued achievement.

If he has been repressing sexual thoughts, it may be possible for the patient to alter his conscience to the extent where thinking sexy things is not deemed a sin or grounds for guilt.

PROMOTING HEALTHY INTERPERSONAL RELATIONSHIPS. It may be assumed without doubt, that the patient's relationships with other people fall far short of the criteria of a healthy interpersonal relationship. The therapy-relationship itself can be regarded as *an actual living experience in relating to another person, and to the self, on a healthy basis.* The therapist tries to promote self-knowledge, self-like, self-concern, activity which promotes growth and happiness for the self, honest communication with the self, reasonable demands upon the self, and self-respect in the patient. In relating to the patient, the therapist displays these attitudes toward himself and toward the patient. The latter will acquire some of these attitudes on a trial and error basis, and others through identification with the therapist.

DECREASING DEFENSIVE REACTIONS TO THREAT; PROMOTING A HEALTHY SELF-STRUCTURE. The patient may be regarded as a person struggling to defend an inaccurate or unhealthy self-structure against threat. To that extent, the patient is actively resisting pressures for him to grow; i.e., to keep modifying his self-structure so it keeps pace with the changing facts of his real self.

Prior to seeking therapy, it can be assumed the patient was ashamed or afraid of his real self and strove to repress it insofar as possible, in order to keep intact an inaccurate self-concept.

The therapist strives continually to ferret out the patient's real self whenever he can discern it through the web and network of defenses, evasions, and distortions. By continually being alert to unconscious or disguised expressions of the patient's real self, and by continually communicating the observations about the real self to the patient, the latter gradually becomes more alerted to it. If the therapist is continually accepting of these real-self manifestations, it can be expected the patient will identify with this accepting attitude of the therapist, and come to recognize and accept his real self. Thus, the cancerous process of self-alienation which Horney described so vividly will be stopped, and genuine growth of the self-structure will become possible.

As the patient's self-concept becomes increasingly congruent with his real self, the occasions for threat will be reduced, and hence the necessity for defensive reactions to threat will be curtailed. Further, the patient may actually learn, or be taught the methods for making threat an opportunity for growth of the self-structure, rather than an occasion for a frightened escape from facing the real self.

In many ways, the therapist will indeed function as a teacher, during the process of therapy. As he becomes alerted to the assorted defense mechanisms the patient is addicted to, he may point them out to the patient, thus making him aware, often for the first time, of the fact of self-deception and self-alienation. When once the patient has learned how defense mechanisms work in himself, it may become possible for him to choose between growth and defense each time a threat to the self-structure is experienced, instead of defending his self-structure automatically and compulsively.

PROMOTING A HEALTHY CONSCIENCE. During the process of personality therapy, the patient's conscience will very likely become a subject of joint scrutiny for the patient and the therapist. Possibly for the first time, the patient will become aware of the make-up of his conscience, its origins in his earlier life history and the role it has played in the production of his misery. He may acquire the ability to reformulate some of his values and to conform with this revised conscience.

PROMOTING A HEALTHY RELATIONSHIP WITH THE BODY. Inevitably in therapy the patient's attitudes, beliefs, ideals, and practices with respect to his body will come to be examined and evaluated for their impact on overall personality health. If therapy is effective, the patient should learn to live more comfortably with his body, to take rational care of it, and to respect its needs.

PERSONALITY THERAPY: THE PROMOTION OF EGO-STRENGTH

One overall way of regarding personality therapy, is to interpret it as a deliberate attempt on the part of the therapist to increase the patient's ego-strength. We can interpret all forms of personality illness, with the psychoanalysts, as evidence of a weak ego. Ego-weakness manifests itself in all of the assorted unhealthy patterns which we have described throughout the text. A strong ego, presumably, is betokened by a healthy personality—an individual who displays: (a) effective instrumental behavior, (b) efficient reality-contact, (c) the ability to suppress and express emotional tensions selectively, (d) healthy sexuality, (e) healthy interpersonal relationships, (f) a healthy self-structure, (g) healthy reactions to threat, (h) a healthy conscience, and (i) a healthy relationship with his own body.

Thus, any and all efforts of a therapist to promote changes in personality-structure in the healthy directions cited above may be viewed as efforts which contribute to an increase of ego-strength in the patient.

LIFE EXPERIENCES WHICH PROMOTE
PERSONALITY GROWTH TOWARD HEALTH

Personality health is a goal of growth and change; it is the ideal which is visualized by the special class of professional Utopians called personality hygienists. In Chapter 1, some of the tentative pictures of personality health were sketched, and these were given assorted names by their respective authors. Thus, the healthy personality has been called the genital character, the productive character, the self-actualizing person, the creative artist, the autonomous character, the integrated personality, etc. Our more detailed concept, as it has been spelled out in various chapters, has borrowed richly from these overlapping portraits. It must again be asserted that these concepts are heuristic, or fictional in nature; they are concepts of the possible. They embody the values and ideals for man of their respective authors.

Yet these ideals can be approached and approximated in actuality. We have suggested in this chapter some of the means by which the individual himself, and the professional personality therapist strive to move the individual closer to the goal of growth.

Let us now consider some of the life experiences which are encountered by almost everyone, *which can have growth-provocative consequences*. Perhaps from the samples given below, the reader might be able to deduce certain clues which will enable him to recognize opportunities for growth when they stare him in the face.

THREAT TO THE SELF-CONCEPT: ANXIETY AND GUILT. Anxiety and guilt are experienced by most persons every day. As with pain, there is a short-range manner of treating these unpleasant affects, and there is, in principle, a growth-productive way of handling them. The short-run manner consists in assorted devices aimed at reducing the unpleasant affects immediately. The growth-provocative methods may compel the person to experience his pain for longer intervals, but this toleration of pain will pay dividends in the long run. If the person reacts to his anxiety and guilt by engaging in reality-testing, by attempting to discern why he is experiencing these affects, he will be able to make at least a serious attempt at effecting the alterations in the situation, or in his self-structure and modal behavior repertoire, which move him closer toward health. Thus, he may learn some new skills, or he may alter his conscience, or his self-concept, or alter some of his modes of relating to other people, after he has investigated the sources of his threat. In short, the healthy personality will view threat, not as something to be avoided like the plague, but rather as a welcome sign that growth is incipient.

NEW CHALLENGES AND RESPONSIBILITIES. The explorer of unknown lands is truly an intrepid character. When he goes to some uncharted place, there is a limit to the preparations he can make in anticipation of unforeseen exigencies. He must have considerable faith in his own resourcefulness, in his ability to improvise means for the solution of problems he could not have expected in advance. So it is with the research scientist who is undertaking an investigation of some completely new area. He does not know in advance what kinds of technical problems in measurement he will encounter. He has faith that as these come up, he will do the best he can. As he meets and masters these problems, he grows. He grows because he has extended his skill-repertoire.

Seen from a phylogenetic viewpoint, man has incredible adaptive and learning potential (potential ego-strength). In the healthy personality, this adaptive capacity and growth-potential is not curbed or hampered by fear, an unhealthy self-structure, or other barriers. In point of fact, the extent to which adaptive capacity is unimpaired in an individual is one of the useful indices of personality health which is available to the diagnostician. Challenges and new responsibilities often require radical alterations in the present personality structure of the individual, if he is to meet and master them. It is because challenges and responsibilities evoke a person's adaptive capacity that the personality hygienist regards them as opportunities for growth. The unhealthy personality avoids challenges and novelty as being too threatening.

BROAD AND DEEP INTERPERSONAL RELATIONSHIPS. Every person with whom one relates represents something unique. Although there are broad similarities among persons in a given culture, yet each single personality also represents a unique variation on the cultural theme. The more persons with whom an individual establishes meaningful friendships, with whom he communicates at other than a superficial level, the more opportunity he will have to grow. For with each person he is obliged to learn new modes of relating, new modes of interpersonal behavior; he is obliged to modify many of his generalized other-concepts; in the process of relating, he becomes acquainted with new values and ideals, with some of which he might identify. He becomes acquainted with a broader range of possible modes of solving life problems, some of which he may adopt when the need arises. Perhaps most important, he "uses" a broader range of his real self. Thus, personalized interactions with many people provide an opportunity for growth. The unhealthy personality is likely to be less able to relate to others on an individualized basis. Rather, he practices long-rehearsed modes of interpersonal behavior with each person who is viewed, not as an individual, but rather as a member of some crude *class* of persons, e.g., men, women, children, foreigners, etc. For each class, he has his interpersonal modes of relating, and he acts in those ways, despite the broad individual differences which may exist among members of these classes. He does not learn or grow in his interpersonal relationships.

ACUTE PSYCHOTIC AND NEUROTIC EPISODES (NERVOUS BREAKDOWNS). The psychiatrist is familiar with these phenomena, since it is part of his professional task to treat patients so afflicted. Nervous breakdowns can be viewed as growth crises. They signify, among other things, that the patient's personality structure is no longer an effective tool for solving life problems, or for achieving valued ends in his present milieu. The acute and painful symptoms indicate that either the environment must be prevented from changing (which is usually impossible), or else the patient must extinguish his old habitual modes for handling the world and learn new ones. It is of crucial importance that the patient suffering a nervous breakdown seek a professional therapist who will attempt to do more than cure symptoms through rest, sedation, electroshock, change of scene, prescription of a holiday, etc. None of these prescriptions will alter the basic personality of the patient unless they have been carefully chosen toward that end. If the nervous breakdown is to be a growth opportunity, then the patient or his therapist must take those steps necessary to promote the development of healthy traits. If this goal is effected, the likelihood of recurrence of the breakdown is reduced, and the patient's adaptive capacities will have been restored.

Life experiences can be viewed from the standpoint of whether or not they will sap an individual's ego-strength, or whether they will actually promote ego-strength. Thus, a chronically stressful situation might, in time, deplete an individual's ego-strength resources; if he is obliged to continue meeting the situation, it could be predicted the quality of his performance will deteriorate. In order to be able to continue his role in that situation, he may find it necessary to have a holiday, or a change of scene, where there is no pressure whatsoever on him to meet high standards of performance. Under the less stressful conditions, he may well regain his previous level of ego-strength.

Life experiences which promote or increase ego strength would be those which result in an increased skill-repertoire, or which increase the person's level of performance of his present skills. In addition, any experiences which reinforce an individual's self-esteem and his sense of self-confidence would promote ego strength. Nothing breeds future success like past and present successes.

Other people's confidence in one's own capacity to solve problems appears to lend a person increases in self-confidence, and hence in ego-strength. If one is the recipient of love and faith from others, self-love and self-confidence will be promoted, and both of these seem to increase ego-strength.

A healthy personality would learn to gauge his present ability-level against the challenges presented by the environment, and seek out (or not avoid) situations which he could master, or which he could learn to master, without too much sacrifice of other values.

PERSONALITY HEALTH AND UTOPIA

Man is a biological being of incredible plasticity. As he is found in nature and in society, his personality structure varies enormously, and yet is compatible with relative longevity, energy and productivity, and even happiness. The science of personality, that branch of psychology which is concerned with the description, explanation and control of individual behavior, is still in its infancy, but it carries with it a weighty responsibility. When we understand with greater clarity how personality is formed, then we can apply this knowledge to the task of *forming* the kinds of personality which are deemed healthy. Naturally, this raises the question, "Who will do the forming?" Aldous Huxley, in his *Brave New World* presents one answer to this question. In this novel, written in the 1920's, the leaders of the world had absolute control over the growth and development of the members of society. They decided how many people of what kinds were needed to keep the society running. They actively produced so many idiots to perform menial tasks, so many persons trained to sheer love of other kinds of hard work, etc. Everyone's physical needs were taken care of, and all people were conditioned so they would *love doing* what the leaders decided *they had to do* in order to keep the society functioning.

In a personality-hygiene Utopia, the picture as the present writer visualizes it would be different from the monstrous Brave New World. In the first place, a *flexible concept* of personality health would have been formulated as the goal of growth. Second, tested knowledge would have been gathered by personality scientists with respect to the optimum means of achieving this goal. All the persons who had anything to do with personality molding, parents, teachers, employers, etc., would be instructed, or at least have available effective advice, as to how to mold in the direction of health. Further, each individual person would come to place a positive value on growth toward health, and he would implement this value by the kinds of decisions he made. Stated another way, the individual would regard growth of the self toward self-actualization, or toward health, as among his most important values, to be sacrificed to nothing. With such a value so strongly affirmed, he would always strive to act in ways which were instrumental toward its attainment, or at the very least, did not detract from its attainment.

But here, we must raise a very practical question: "How can an individual know what will promote his growth and health, and what will impede growth and health?" The person might indeed come to affirm in words the value of growth, but without action toward that end the affirmation is no more than sound and fury. Personality hygienists would have to find some way of building in to the person the skill which I will call *value-analysis*. Value-analysis refers to the ability, in each concrete situation, to discern what values are at stake. Thus, an individual might be strongly tempted to divorce his wife. Here are some of the values involved: (a) freedom from his wife, (b) prospects of loneliness, (c) chances to make a better marriage, (d) the possible consequences for his children, (e) the growth-implications of divorce, and (f) the growth-implications of remaining married, trying to work through the impasses in the marriage. If the person values growth more than anything else, he will be obliged to ascertain which of the alternatives, divorce or remaining married, is more compatible with maintaining his present degree of personality health or with moving further in the direction of health. He must then act on the basis of the decision most conducive to growth.

We can only wonder what the world would be like if the personality-hygiene Utopia were achieved. The present writer believes that it would be a happier world, and it has been with this faith that he has written this book as an attempt to move us closer to that end.[10]

SUMMARY

Suffering of some sort is the inevitable consequence of an unhealthy personality. Psychologists describe this suffering in different ways, depending on its specific causes and quality, viz.: anxiety, guilt, inferiority-feelings, deprivation, etc.

Just as a person seeks relief from physical pain, so does he seek respite from psychological suffering.

Attempts to relieve suffering fall into two major categories; these are called *symptom-treatment* and *rational treatment.*

Examples of symptom-treatment for psychological suffering include drinking, repression, seeking reassurance, the use of defense mechanisms in addition to repression. Other persons may seek to relieve the sufferer by means of advice, or medical treatment.

The main flaw in symptom-treatment lies in the fact that while in the short run it may be effective in relieving the suffering, it does not remove the causes of the suffering; hence, when the effects of the treatment wear off, the symptoms will recur.

Rational treatment of psychological suffering consists in the attempt to ascertain the nature of the conditions responsible for the suffering, followed by direct efforts to alter or remove these conditions and causes.

We use the term *healthy adjustment* to describe those efforts on the part of the person to effect a rational cure for his own psychological suffering. There are two modes of adjustment available to the individual subjected to psychological suffering: *autoplastic* adjustment, or changing the self, and *alloplastic* adjustment, or changing the environment. Healthy and unhealthy patterns can be identified for both of these modes of adjustment.

When a person's efforts at adjustment fail to effect a rational cure of his psychological suffering, he should seek the assistance of a trained personality therapist: a psychiatrist or qualified clinical psychologist.

The therapist seeks to describe and evaluate the individual's personality structure, and to ascertain the causal conditions responsible for the symptoms. Then, he evolves a plan of action, or a strategy designed to alter or remove these conditions, and proceeds to carry out his therapeutic activities.

As a general rule, the modern personality therapist regards the patient, not as a "sick," or mentally ill person, but rather as an individual whose growth has been obstructed by barriers of assorted kinds. His therapeutic activity is aimed at removing these obstructions to growth and at promoting the patient's *ego-strength.*

The therapist removes obstacles to growth toward health, or promotes health, by means of environment-manipulation and by means of his direct relationship with his patient. The kinds of therapist-behavior which promote growth in the patient include: accurate observation of the patient; honesty; striving to find ways of increasing the satisfactions in the patient's life; respect for the patient; avoidance of using the patient's lack of health for private ends of the therapist; the encouragement of full emotional expression; and attempts to promote self-understanding in the patient.

The therapist may help a patient suffering from important need-deprivations achieve a richer supply of gratifications by helping him to change environments or by striving to remove some of the personality-structure factors which prevent the person from achieving satisfactions presently available in his milieu. Reality-contact, and the reality-testing habit, may be promoted in the patient by careful examination of the patient's beliefs and perceptions and by encouraging him to adopt an attitude of doubt toward many of his first impressions and conclusions about himself, other people, etc.

Healthy emotionality may be promoted by failing to punish open expressions of emotionality, and of course through the improvement of reality-contact. Healthy sexuality may be promoted through open discussion of sexual problems, and through aiding the patient to satisfy in more direct ways some of the needs which sexuality had been charged by the patient with the task of alleviating.

Healthier interpersonal relationships may be promoted simply through the experience of having a healthy relationship with the therapist. Healthy reactions to threat may be promoted by aiding the patient toward a reformulation of his self-structure, so that the frequency of threat is reduced and the way is shown for the use of experiences of threat as an opportunity for growth. Healthy conscience may be promoted, as well as a healthy relationship with the body, by analysis of the role these factors play in promoting suffering. All of these consequences may be interpreted as contributing to, and resulting from, an increase in ego strength.

A number of life experiences encountered by every one which provide opportunities for growth toward personality health (if handled correctly) are described. These include anxiety and guilt, new challenges and responsibilities, broad and deep interpersonal relationships, nervous breakdowns, etc.

Finally, a personality-hygiene Utopia was described, wherein reliable knowledge would be available for the guidance of parents, teachers, and others in their efforts to promote personality health in children; where each person would strongly affirm the value of personality growth toward health, and have knowledge of the kinds of decisions which he must make and act upon in order to reach and maintain personality health.

NOTES AND REFERENCES

RECOMMENDED READINGS ARE MARKED WITH AN ASTERISK ($^\circ$)

1. Szasz has written two excellent analyses of the psychology of pain. See Szasz, T. S., "The nature of pain," *Arch. Neurol. & Psychiat.*, 1955, **74**, 174–181. Also, "The ego, the body, and pain," *J. Amer. Psychoanalyt. Assoc.*, 1955, **3**, 177–200.

2. The psychoanalysts have been working toward a deeper understanding of the ego. See Hartmann, H., "Comments on the psychoanalytic theory of the ego," in *The psychoanalytic study of the child*, Vol. V, pp. 24–96, New York, International University Press, 1950.

3. The assumption that man has an innate tendency to growth toward health is widely held to-day, and may be found in the writings of Rogers, Horney, Goldstein, Maslow, Whitaker and Malone, and many others.

*4. See, for example, Rogers, C. R., *Counseling and psychotherapy*, Boston, Houghton Mifflin, 1942, for an excellent discussion of the rationale for counseling. The term "intensive therapy" is usually used with reference to efforts, as in psychoanalysis, to produce radical changes in the total personality structure.

5. Redl and Bettelheim have vividly described environments which promote growth. See Redl, F. and Wineman, D., *Controls from within*, Glencoe, Illinois, The Free Press, 1952, Ch. 1. Also, Bettelheim, B., *Love is not enough*, Glencoe, Illinois, 1950.

6. A good overview of goals and techniques of personality therapy is to be found in Wolberg, L. R., *The technique of psychotherapy*, New York, Grune & Stratton, 1954.

7. See Maslow, A. H., *Motivation and personality*, New York, Harper, 1954, Ch. 16, for a discussion of need-gratification in therapy.

*8. See Thompson, Clara (ed.), *An outline of psychoanalysis*, New York, Modern Library, 1955, pp. 471–561, for extended discussions of transference.

*9. See Colby, K., *A primer for psychotherapists*, New York, Ronald, 1951, pp. 82–95, for an excellent discussion of interpretation in personality therapy.

10. See Fromm, E., *The sane society*, New York, Rinehart, 1955, for a superb analysis of the relations among men, society, and personality health.

QUESTIONS FOR REVIEW AND EXAMINATION

1. List the common methods by which a person "treats" psychological symptoms by himself; also methods by which the psychologist and psychiatrist often undertake symptom treatment.

2. When is symptom treatment advisable, and when is it inadvisable?

3. Describe, giving examples, healthy and unhealthy autoplastic and alloplastic adjustment.

4. What does a personality therapist do?

5. How does a personality therapist promote growth in his patient? Illustrate with examples from various aspects of personality.

6. Describe and evaluate someone's personality using all the chapters of the book as a guide. Indicate which aspects of personality seem to be "normal," i.e., common, which aspects seem healthy, and which aspects seem to call for further growth.

Index